Micros...
Solutions

Erik Thomsen
George Spofford
Dick Chase

Wiley Computer Publishing

John Wiley & Sons, Inc.

NEW YORK · CHICHESTER · WEINHEIM · BRISBANE · SINGAPORE · TORONTO

Publisher: Robert Ipsen

Editor: Robert M. Elliott

Managing Editor: Brian Snapp

Text Design & Composition: Pronto Design & Production, Inc.

Designations used by companies to distinguish their products are often claimed as trademarks. In all instances where John Wiley & Sons, Inc., is aware of a claim, the product names appear in initial capital or all capital letters. Readers, however, should contact the appropriate companies for more complete information regarding trademarks and registration.

This book is printed on acid-free paper. ∞

This publication is designed to provide accurate and authoritative information in regard to the subject matter covered. It is sold with the understanding that the publisher is not engaged in professional services. If professional advice or other expert assistance is required, the services of a competent professional person should be sought.

Library of Congress Cataloging-in-Publication Data:

Thomsen, Erik, 1959-

Microsoft OLAP solutions / Erik Thomsen, George Spofford, Dick Chase.

p. cm.

ISBN 0-471-33258-5

1. OLAP technology. 2. Microsoft software. I. Spofford, George, 1965- .
II. Chase, Dick. III. Title.

QA76.9.D343T47 1999   99-2692
006.3–dc21   CIP

Printed in the United States of America.

10 9 8 7 6 5 4 3 2

For Mor. Tak
—Dick Chase

To Lisa, with love and appreciation, and to as-yet-unnamed, who I look forward to meeting
—George Spofford

To Marjorie, for her patience during this time
—Erik Thomsen

CONTENTS

ACKNOWLEDGMENTS

This book was possible through the efforts of a number of individuals and organizations. First and foremost, Lisa, Francie, Samantha, and Marjorie provided dozens of late nights, early mornings, and entire weekends of their spouses' and dads' quality time with faultless grace. Joshua Sutherland and Bethany Rawcliffe helped render the images and text into a manuscript. Bill Baker, Amir Netz, Corey Salka, and others at Microsoft provided invaluable support for our work with multiple versions of OLAP Services. (We can't forget Mosha or Irina, either!) The support of Barbara Gaskin, Alan Levin, and Decision Support Technology, Inc. was crucial for making this book possible. Jeff Koss contributed to early understanding of how to work with OLAP Services. The DSS Lab provided the use of its facilities and databases for developing applications. A special acknowledgment goes to Josie Kaufmann and Clariion, for providing the high-end Fibre Channel storage systems required to develop and work with large-scale OLAP Services databases. Bob Elliott, Emilie Herman, and Brian Snapp of John Wiley & Sons helped turn the manuscript into the actual book you hold in your hands.

When we started the "Plato" project at Microsoft in 1996, our goal was to bring OLAP to the masses. From an initial budget of three full-time employees, to the acquisition of technology and people from Panorama, to the delivery of Microsoft SQL Server OLAP Services in late 1998, this single idea drove our project.

We started with a small band of OLAP believers. Corey Salka and I had worked previously for IRI Software, makers of Express, now part of the Oracle product line. We had seen firsthand in corporation after corporation how OLAP delivered value. Corey worked in the Excel group at the time, focusing on the Pivot-Table feature. Gunnar Mein and Goetz Graefe were two other true believers. This tiny group started discussing OLAP as early as fall 1995.

Convincing Microsoft to pursue OLAP was a different story. We submitted the first budget for Plato in April 1996. At that time, SQL Server 6.5 was just going into beta release. That version featured the cube and rollup operators, and many at Microsoft felt they were sufficient for data analysis. Corey and Gunnar wrote an excellent justification for OLAP, which we submitted as part of our overall middleware FY97 budget request. In the end, we received just enough budget to form a team to explore OLAP. Corey became the first member of the Plato team.

As Corey and Gunnar were laying plans to build an OLAP product, they looked at a variety of companies and technologies that might jump-start the effort. During a visit to one particular company, they met two people who later impacted Plato in significant ways: Tom Conlon and George Spofford, whose contributions I'll discuss shortly. Tom Conlon later joined Microsoft and took Corey's place as the Program Manager for PivotTables in the Excel group. Tom's crucial role in Plato was to be the sponsor for OLAP in Excel. Excel's early acceptance of Plato added instant credibility to our efforts. Their high standards for quality and process helped us mature as a team.

The seminal event in the early days of Plato was the discovery of Panorama Software and the acquisition of key people and technology. Sadly, I missed this entire period of Plato's history. During the first year and a half of Plato's life, I was either under a non-compete from a previous company (Oracle) or totally involved in shipping the Windows NT 4 Option Pack. To make a long story short, Rony Ross and Amir Netz from Panorama were trying to make contact with Microsoft. They met with the team at Microsoft Israel who referred them to Corey. At about the same time, Nigel Pendse of the OLAP Report was telling Tom Conlon about a small Israeli company with an innovative OLAP product. Corey and Tom put two and two together and arranged to meet Rony and Amir when they came to the United States.

When Corey and Gunnar finally saw the Panorama product, they knew this was the jump-start they had been searching for. In less than three months, they performed due diligence and structured and closed a deal. In January of 1997, six employees of Panorama moved to Redmond, Washington and became Microsoft employees. They were Amir, his brother Ariel, his wife Merav, Mosha Pasumansky, Sasha Berger, and Edward Melomed. Merav joined the Office team. The others, along with Stephen Bremmer and Corey, became the core of the Plato team. All are still part of the Plato team.

In 1997, the team settled in and started designing and building Plato. I paid little attention to the team in those days being under non-compete for most of the year and otherwise involved. Some readers of this book might remember the alpha release that the team shipped in September of that year. In 1998, the team delivered the so-called Beta 2 release. We called it Beta 2 because it shipped with the second beta release of SQL Server 7.0. This was the first real beta release of the product. Beta 3 followed in July and the final version went to manufacturing in December of 1998. January of 1998 was also the start of my day-to-day involvement with the team and the product.

Shipping Plato was an enormous effort. Eighty and one-hundred-hour work-weeks were the norm through most of 1997 and all of 1998. Our twenty-plus person team exceeded its food budget many times over. Our motto became, "No food, no OLAP!" Despite the hours, it was a joyous effort. A young, energetic team with a clear mission (OLAP for the masses), good leadership, and plenty of food can accomplish anything. As a bit of an industry veteran, I delighted in seeing the team grow in both confidence and capability.

At the time of this writing, it's fair to ask, how well did we do? Did we truly bring OLAP to the masses? The answer is surely mixed. I do believe we have done the most of any OLAP product to bring the power of sophisticated data analysis to a wider audience. The Wizards in the OLAP Manager and the tight integration with Microsoft Office enable more people than ever before to build and use OLAP databases and applications. Plato has changed the face of OLAP.

That said, we have more work to do. We have specific plans in coming versions to further improve the ease-of-learning, ease-of-use, and ease-of-integration of OLAP. But that is only half of the story. An important component of bringing OLAP to the masses is the legion of authors, consultants, and trainers that help the whole of the market adopt the technology in general and our product in particular. And that leads me to the importance of this book and the role of one of its authors in the development of SQL Server OLAP Services.

Corey and Gunnar met George Spofford in 1996. They realized instantly that George was one of those people who really knew OLAP at every level. They made sure to invite him to the earliest, and subsequently all, Plato design previews and reviews. He was vocal at every turn suggesting features but also helping us sort through myriad options and make the right feature adds and cuts. George received, and tested, every version of Plato produced. Before most people in the industry knew much at all about Plato, George was posting bug reports!

His critiques of the software have pushed the team to improve the product in many ways. Lest you think of George as a Plato shill, we've found to our occasional dismay that he tells-it-like-it is, good or bad. Fortunately for you, the reader, he tells you where the warts are *and* how to work around them.

Erik Thomsen is well known to us in the OLAP and broader database business. His book, *OLAP Solutions* (Wiley, 1997), is the first widely accessible treatment of the subject. Through articles, presentations and speeches, and consulting efforts, Erik has done much to drive the adoption of OLAP in industry.

Every key technology that goes on to mass adoption can trace some part of its success to a seminal book. Charles Petzold's book on Windows Programming comes to mind. This book, Microsoft OLAP Solutions, may very well be that book for OLAP Services. We did our best with the product and its documentation. George, Erik, and Dick take you beyond what we could put in the box and help you discover ways to make OLAP Services work for you, in your business. Unlike books that regurgitate the product documentation, George and his fellow authors explain what's going on behind the scene. See, for example, the discussion of member key and member name when building dimensions.

I sincerely hope that you enjoy this book and profit from its advice and insight. We had a blast building OLAP Services. George, Erik, and Dick certainly seem to have enjoyed their experiences with the product and in writing the book. We all hope you feel the same way when you deploy your OLAP solutions.

—Bill Baker, Product Unit Manager
Microsoft SQL Server Decision Support Product Unit

This book teaches the database administrator (DBA) or power analyst how to build effective analytical application systems in Microsoft SQL Server 7 OLAP Services (which we will refer to simply as *Microsoft OLAP Services* or *OLAP Services*). Our goal is to present the features and capabilities of OLAP Services to you in a practical and complete way, provide you with an approach to and guidelines for understanding how to apply OLAP Services to your own applications, and give you practical examples to jump-start your own implementations. Because the world of multidimensional modeling and analysis is different from the world of transactional databases and applications, throughout the book we will give you guidelines for thinking about modeling and analysis. This book is not meant to be a comprehensive guide to OLAP technology, however. If you are interested in a such a book, we recommend *OLAP Solutions* by Erik Thomsen (Wiley, 1997). Since we assume that many readers will be developing their first OLAP applications with this Microsoft product, we do introduce some basic OLAP concepts where appropriate.

OLAP Services is both a product and a toolkit. Many interesting applications will be built that really leverage the toolkit side of it by creating custom code in other environments like Java, C++, Delphi, and Visual Basic (perhaps even Perl!). Some basic OLAP Services tasks require manipulation of programmer-level interfaces, and we describe these manipulations in this book. However, we leave to other books the task of describing to programmers the ins and outs of OLAP Services server and client programming.

There are a number of topics that, as useful as they may be, we were unable to include in this book. We stay within the realm of OLAP data structure and processing, focusing on logical design, physical design, and implementation. We do not really address topics that require software development. The primary administrative interface for OLAP Services is actually defined in terms of ActiveX Automation objects, only some of whose useful functionality is exposed by the GUI administrative tool provided with the product. Sophisticated systems based on OLAP Services may have a significant custom software aspect to them, and even simple systems are likely to involve software provided by other parties. For that reason, we do address programming for some of the most basic needs that most applications will have.

Caveats

Providing a detailed guide to such a new product carries with it certain risks, which we hope will not affect you. Like all software, Microsoft OLAP Services has some bugs. As we prepare this, the first release has been made and a service pack is already in the works. Thus, some of the information that we provide on how to perform tasks and phrase queries may have changed by the time you read this. We may provide information on how to compose a query, for example, when the version you are working with provides a more direct route. Or the way we tell you to do something may not work because we anticipated a glitch would be worked out in a certain way and it wasn't.

Organization

This book is divided into four major sections. The first section (Chapters 1 through 4) introduces the logical OLAP structures that Microsoft OLAP Services provides, the product's physical and computational architecture, and the basics of designing and implementing a database. The second section (Chapters 5 through 9) describes the MDX language that is used for querying and calculations, which includes a detailed, illustrated reference to all of the MDX functions and operators that are available. The third section (Chapters 10 through 14) describes more advanced topics such as maintenance, database optimization, and advanced database design. The last section of the book (Chapters 15 through 16) presents two mildly sophisticated tutorials. Finally, the book's three appendixes provide references to the key properties available through queries (Appendix A), a glossary (Appendix B), and a reference on using the CD-ROM that accompanies the book (Appendix C).

The Accompanying CD-ROM

The book's CD-ROM contains the source databases for the tutorials, two pieces of additional software for working with OLAP Services, and the Visual Basic source code for that software. These programs fill in functional areas not addressed by the first release of administrative GUI for OLAP Services, enabling you to examine and manipulate important components of a database. You can also use the programs as code examples for the areas of programming that we don't discuss in the book!

Stylistic Conventions

Throughout the book, text that represents code, such as a query or a programming language construct, will be in a monospace font like this:

```
This is some code
```

Getting Started

This exploration of Microsoft OLAP Services should be interesting, even fun. One of the key benefits of OLAP technologies is the ability to simplify complex analyses. What seemed difficult or infeasible before may now seem quite possible, even straightforward.

OLAP Structures and OLAP Services

Microsoft OLAP Services is based on and tightly linked to relational databases. However, Microsoft OLAP Services is a *real* multidimensional information system, where all information is modeled in terms of OLAP structures, not relational structures. The OLAP structures are a valuable feature because many important analyses are difficult or impossible to phrase in SQL using tabular structures. Even when information is presented in relational terms, an understanding of OLAP structures will help you with multidimensional analysis and querying. Accordingly, in Chapter 1 we will examine the OLAP structures provided by OLAP Services and provide a set of techniques for depicting them. Any familiarity that you have with tables, keys, joins, and star schemas will help you understand the capabilities and operations of OLAP Services. If you are familiar with other OLAP products and are new to the capabilities of OLAP Services, this chapter will help you relate the structures of OLAP Services to tools you have already mastered.

General OLAP Structures

While it is possible to build some OLAP cubes quickly with limited knowledge of basic OLAP structures, reading this section now may save you considerable time later when you are setting up some part of the database. If you have prior OLAP experience, you may wish to skip most of this chapter, but you will probably want to read the description of the structure diagramming technique we give here because we will use it throughout the book.

The basic OLAP structures that we will describe here are *dimensions*, *measures*, *hierarchies*, *levels*, *cubes*, *cells*, *formulas*, and *links* to source databases. These, taken together, define the logical structure of an OLAP database and the calculations it can support. The set of structures we have just listed are for the core logic of a system. Microsoft OLAP Services employs other structures, both for additional computation ability and for a number of implementation details. We will discuss these additional structures in subsequent chapters. First, we will describe the basic structures from 35,000 feet, and then explore in more depth how OLAP Services implements them.

Dimensions and measures are really defined in terms of each other and are simply the names for two complementary uses of data. *Measures* are the data that we wish to analyze, while *dimensions* define the organization of those measures. Our data warehouse may contain a sales transaction table that has fields for store, time, customer, product, number of units, and dollar value sold. If so, we will generally analyze unit and dollar sales by store, time, product and customer. In this case, Units and Dollar Value will be our measures, and Store, Time, Product, and Customer will each be a dimension. If we ship goods, we may track orders and shipments by day, product, customer, order, units on hand, units delivered, units received, and price for each. In this case, our analyses will likely use Units and Dollar Value as measures and Time, Product, Customer, and Warehouse as organizing dimensions. If we manufacture goods, then Rates of Production, Defect Rates, Operating Costs, and so on may be measures, which are organized by Time, Assembly Line Configuration, Product Created, and Plant.

The elements of a dimension are called *members*, and they are generally organized to support analyses. Almost all but the simplest dimensions organize their members into one or more *hierarchies*, which correspond to paths of aggregation and allocation between lower-level members like business units and days and higher-level units like corporations and years. When a group of related members shares a common meaning, it is useful to refer to that common meaning as a *level*. For example, a level construct named month may contain all of the month-level members in a time dimension.

A *cube* is an association between a set of dimensions and a set of measures. The combinations of members from each dimension of the cube define the logical space in which the values for the measures can appear. Each unique intersection composed of one member from every dimension in the cube is called a *cell*. Additionally, within a cube, it can be useful to talk about the set of cells defined by specifying a member from one or more than one dimension. For Microsoft OLAP Services, these are called *slices*. We have found it extremely useful to think of the non-measures dimensions as forming a set of *locations* that our measures are the *contents* of, and we will use those terms as well. To relate all these terms, consider the following. Suppose we have a cube with Time, Geography, and Product dimensions and whose measures are Units Received and

Units Shipped. In this case, specifying "(Jan. 1994, Montana, Sheet Metal, Units Shipped)" identifies a cell; specifying "(Jan. 1994)" identifies a slice that is one member wide through the Geography, Product, and measures dimensions; and specifying "(Jan. 1994, Montana)" identifies a slice that is one member wide in two dimensions, through the Product and Measures dimensions. The specification "(Jan. 1994, Montana, Sheet Metal)" identifies a location, which can also be considered a slice.

All of these relationships can be difficult to understand purely by using words. However, a simple notation can communicate them much more easily.

Introduction to Multidimensional Domain Structure Diagrams

In this section, we will describe a Multidimensional Domain Structure (MDS) notation for diagramming the key structures of Microsoft OLAP Services. The usual table-join notations are perfectly adequate for communicating table relationships, such as with a star or snowflake schema. However, we need something else when we are diagramming the hierarchical overlap of data in two partitions (a structural concept explained later) or the measure and dimension relationships between related cubes. MDS techniques were first introduced in *OLAP Solutions* (Erik Thomsen, Wiley, 1998). In this section, we will use forms that assist in communicating the features that are specific to OLAP Services in addition to the logical-structure diagramming techniques described in *OLAP Solutions*.

As with the syntax of a natural language, there are many "right ways" to diagram some aspect of an OLAP system. For example, there is no single, prescribed way to render constructs like a dimension. Rather, there is a set of forms in which each form emphasizes certain aspects and diminishes others and is generally more useful in one context and less useful in others. For example, dimensions may be represented as stick figures or as boxes. A stick figure would generally be more useful for emphasizing the use of a collection of dimensions, while the box would generally be more useful for emphasizing the detailed aspects of that dimension. Figure 1.1 shows a representative example of the two forms. Diagrams that show great detail for many objects will require much more ink and will be more frequently used on wall-sized whiteboards than on printed pages. Groups of related objects (like dimensions or cubes) may be oriented horizontally or vertically, depending on how we wish to position them in relation to other visual elements. In short, while the visual syntax is a technique that can be used for formal depictions, it is also very flexible.

OLAP Services Dimensions

The first OLAP Services structure we will take a look at is dimensions because they form the backbone for most of the other structures.

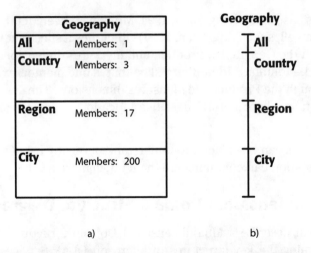

a)   b)

Figure 1.1 Alternative representations of a dimension.

Overview: The Structure of a Dimension

Each Microsoft OLAP Services dimension is composed of one or more named levels, each of which holds one or more of the members of the dimension. If a dimension has more than one level, then the members within each dimension can be arranged in one or more hierarchies. A dimension that has only one level will not be hierarchical. Each hierarchy is fully connected through its levels, which means that when a dimension has two or more levels, every member at the leaf level has one parent, each member at the top level has one or more children, and on each level in between (if there are any) every member has a parent and one or more children. There are no orphans at any level, and every leaf-level member has ancestors going all the way to the root member(s). Composing a hierarchy strictly of named levels means that all leaf members are at the same distance from the root.

Figure 1.2 diagrams some permutations of dimension structures. Figures 1.2a and 1.2b show an irregular hierarchy in two different ways, and Figures 1.2c and 1.2d show two different balanced hierarchies in which the members are arranged into clear levels. Notice that the hierarchy shown in Figure 1.2d does not have a single top member. Although the members at the top level do not have any parent-child relationship between them, OLAP Services will treat them as if they were siblings anyway.

In an MDS diagram, dimensions are shown in one of two basic ways: as a box or as a line segment. The usual reason in showing a dimension as a box is to enclose a set of descriptive attributes about the dimension and possibly levels within the dimension. The usual purpose in showing a dimension as a line segment is to

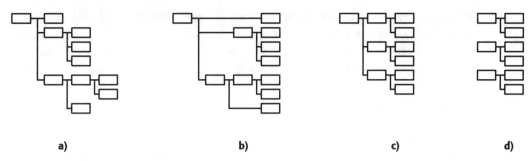

a)   **b)**   **c)**   **d)**

Figure 1.2   Various hierarchies of members.

either indicate the simple fact of usage of that dimension or to also provide a simplified depiction of the levels and/or member ranges within the dimension.

Figure 1.3 shows each of these two forms for a time dimension. Figure 1.3a shows a box form of a time dimension with four levels: All, Year, Quarter, and Month. There is a small amount of descriptive information for the dimension as well as for each level, such as number of members in the level. Figure 1.3b shows a line-segment form of the same time dimension. We simply use separator lines within the line segment to delimit the separate levels. We can annotate each level's segment in a number of ways, for example, by highlighting members or ranges of members. We have given the All level much less vertical space than the other levels because it only has one member. Figure 1.3c shows the same line figure with the vertical space for each level roughly proportional to its relative size, which makes the relative aggregation of each level more apparent. Figure 1.3c also includes representations for two months and quarters.

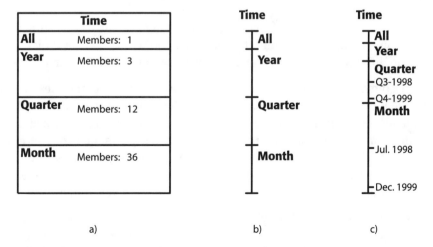

a)   **b)**   **c)**

Figure 1.3   Various MDS depictions of a time dimension.

Using named-level hierarchies is straightforward when all of the members within a dimension neatly fit into one conceptual level or another. For example, time members at the level of hour, day, month, quarter, and so on will cleanly fit into this structure. Frequently, the members of a geography dimension will more or less fit into neat levels, like Store, City, State, Region. Geography may not be thoroughly neat, however. If you are building a dimension for the locations of multiple countries, one country may naturally have provinces and cities while another may have regions, provinces or states, and cities. In this case, each country has a different set of neat, named levels, but different countries have different sets of them. The members of other types of dimensions and hierarchies may not fit cleanly into named conceptual levels at all, for example, the various line items in a chart of accounts or the branches in an organizational chart.

Regardless of the conceptual domain that is being modeled by the hierarchy or dimension, Microsoft OLAP Services requires the members to be organized into an even set of named levels. We will discuss some principles for leveling in Chapter 3. For now, just note that in OLAP Services you need to approach dimensions in terms of an even set of named levels. If you already have tables in which each level's members are already organized in columns, then you have a close match with the requirements of OLAP Services. We discuss the linkage between the dimensions of OLAP Services and the columns of tables in the last section of this chapter and in Chapter 2.

Multiple Dimensional Hierarchies in OLAP Services

Many applications require that multiple hierarchies be used for the members in a dimension. For example, you may wish to aggregate your stores by geographical region or by the chain they belong to or aggregate financial data by a fiscal calendar as well as by the standard calendar. Microsoft OLAP Services provides a mechanism whereby multiple hierarchies may appear to be defined for the same named dimension. Generally speaking, you would use these hierarchies to provide different paths of aggregation for lower-level members in a dimension.

When a dimension is logically organized into two or more hierarchies, we can diagram that fact and the relationship between the hierarchies in either the box form or the line-segment form. Figure 1.4 shows a box form and a line-segment form for the same three time hierarchies: one of fiscal years, quarters, months, and days; one of 12-month calendar years, 3-month quarters, months, and days; and one of 52-week years, 13-week quarters, weeks, and days. Notice that each form clearly indicates the levels that are common and the levels that are divergent.

We say Microsoft OLAP Services "provides a mechanism" for multiple hierarchies because in an OLAP Services database, the different hierarchies of a dimension are defined as if they were different dimensions with similar names.

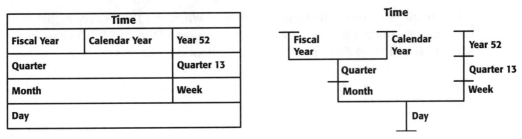

Figure 1.4 Various MDS depictions of multiple hierarchies.

Thus, the dimensions are identified as hierarchies of a common dimension purely in terms of syntax. As far as the overall database and applications are concerned, they exist as a hybrid between separate dimensions and different hierarchies. To the DBA, OLAP Services identifies multiple hierarchies in a dimension slightly differently than it does to a client. We will look at them from both the DBA's and the client's point of view here. To convey the nature of hierarchies as independent dimensions, we will frequently refer to *hierarchy-dimensions* when referring to dimensions that are used as particular hierarchies.

While hierarchy-dimensions will appear to a client as different hierarchies of one dimension, in fact, Microsoft OLAP Services treats them semantically as separate dimensions in every way. For example, they need not have any members in common! You can define one hierarchy of a dimension as consisting of Store, City, State, and Country levels and another hierarchy of the same dimension as consisting of Months, Quarters, and Years (not that you would want to!). Even when hierarchy-dimensions are formed using the same members at one or more levels, their levels and members are considered to be from completely different dimensions. Since they are treated as different dimensions, a member that is part of each can have two different names on two different hierarchies. A typical example of this would be a quarter being named "Q4 1997" on a calendar time hierarchy-dimension and "Q1 1998" on a fiscal period hierarchy-dimension. There is no feature anywhere in Microsoft OLAP Services for the semantic checking of common features between different hierarchies of a dimension. It is up to you to ensure meaningful semantic relationships between them. In any context where multiple dimensions can be used, any or all of the independent hierarchy-dimensions can be used in combination. For example, a cube may use only one hierarchy-dimension for a given semantic dimension, two hierarchy-dimensions, or any other combination of them.

The syntactic division is independent of the other characteristics of dimensions. A private dimension and a public dimension (the distinction is described in the section "Dimension Types" later in this chapter) may each be named as separate hierarchies of the same dimension. When the DBA views aggregated data through the cube data browser, which is part of the OLAP Manager, he or she will see the two dimensions as independent dimensions of the result data. Note that considering multiple hierarchies as multiple dimensions also has implications for aggregations (an important consideration that is treated in Chapters 3 and 11).

Multiple hierarchies being implemented by multiple dimensions may seem confusing at first to a DBA, especially one who has worked with other OLAP tools. It is important to remember, however, that the presentation OLAP Services shows to the DBA and to the end user are quite different. Thus, the DBA who is setting up a database or the application developer who is implementing a series of analytical reports can each do things with the data that logically should not be possible. That is, the client can compose queries that intersect the members of a dimension along one hierarchy with other members of that same dimension along another hierarchy, which is not logically possible if you assume that the members really are coming from the same dimension. (Coming from backgrounds in which we used other OLAP tools, the authors had to work to make full sense of hierarchies-as-dimensions as well as their pitfalls and capabilities.)

To an application that is accessing the database through OLE DB for OLAP or ADO, the hierarchy-dimensions appear as separate hierarchies in a single dimension. Many applications that use individual hierarchies would simply traverse one hierarchy or the other and not even consider traversing both at once. In such a case, logically speaking, the application won't trip over the multiple-dimension nature of the hierarchies since the application isn't trying to treat the two hierarchies as being potentially active at the same time. In other words, the application sees the structure represented by the MDS of Figure 1.5a, while the DBA sees the structure represented by the MDS of Figure 1.5b.

More advanced applications may try to mix members from different hierarchies. Consider a store dimension of two hierarchies, one by Geography and

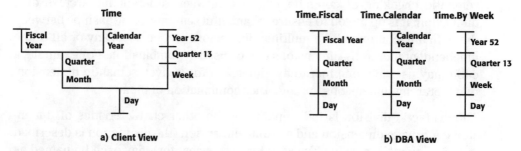

a) Client View   b) DBA View

Figure 1.5   Client versus DBA view of multiple hierarchies.

one by Chain Affiliation. In a state regional regulatory analysis model or a regional economic analysis model, both hierarchies could be multiple levels deep. An example of the simultaneous use of both hierarchies would a query for the percentage contribution of the stores in a chain to the city that contains them or another query that just drills down on stores in a city that are members of a type of chain. Another example, in a corporate budgeting model that aggregates business units by business purpose and by geography, a simultaneous allocation of costs down from multiple parents.

In cases where the user is performing set operations between the hierarchies—such as drilling down on parents from two different hierarchies to get the children that they have in common—it is straightforward enough to treat the parent information of one of the hierarchies as pieces of member property information. Member properties will be explained in the section "Member Properties (Attributes)" later in this chapter. For now, it will be sufficient to say that they are additional pieces of information associated with members. Member properties can be used in the query we posed earlier regarding members that are children of parents on two hierarchies. Using member properties, the query can be phrased as requesting children of a parent on one hierarchy whose member property information corresponds with ancestor member property values from the other hierarchy. (Get the city's children whose ancestors' member property information matches the name of the chain.)

Although members from two dimensions may even have the same basic names, queries cannot reference the members in common as though they were from the same dimension. This makes the cases where parents on multiple hierarchies are referenced in one calculation the most complicated of all to deal with. An example of this type of case would be where costs are being allocated down multiple hierarchies or contribution-to-parent in one hierarchy is calculated from children along another hierarchy.

The All Level and All Member

Each hierarchy on each dimension (except a cube's measures dimension) may be configured to have an "All" level or to not have one. Usually, you will want to define an All level for a dimension, and when a dimension is defined through the OLAP Manager interface an All level defined by Microsoft OLAP Services is enabled by default. Although an OLAP Services-defined All level is created and managed by OLAP Services, you can also provide your own All level when you create the dimension, which may have certain advantages. An All level will contain a single member that, for our purposes, can be referred to as the "All member," though you can give the member a more descriptive name like "All Products" or "Company Everyone" in either an OLAP Services-defined All member or in your own All member. The All member has three special properties:

- **It is the default member for queries on the cube.** If a client's query doesn't specify any members from which to reference data for a dimension, then the All member of that dimension is the default member. (OLAP Services doesn't give you a way to override this default, but read Chapter 14 on using your own external functions for ideas on useful defaults that you can specify.) Note that this kind of default behavior is required to make the multiple-hierarchies-as-multiple-dimensions behavior work when you are treating each hierarchy-dimension as a hierarchy. (This is true of both All members defined by OLAP Services and DBA-defined All members.)

- **It is the reference member on which a virtual cube will join a cube to another cube.** Although we have not discussed cubes yet, this point bears stating here. The section titled "Virtual Cubes" later in this chapter will describe this role in more detail. This property is true of both All members defined by OLAP Services and All members defined by the DBA.

- **An All member defined by OLAP Services will not correspond to anything in the underlying database.** For example, it cannot have any associated member properties. This is because it is not created from anything in the underlying database. A DBA-defined All level will be defined from the underlying database, and its All member will be treated as any other member.

Members in a Dimension

A member is simply a uniquely identifiable unit within a dimension. All members have textual names, though the names may be derived from non-textual table columns in the underlying database (such as numbers, dates, and so on). All members also have member keys, which are the actual units of identification. The key and the name for each member may be the same, or they may be different. Microsoft OLAP Services allows member keys and member names to be duplicated within any level and between levels. Whether they are duplicated or not, a member is uniquely identified by the concatenation of a member's key value with the key value for each of its ancestors up to the top level of the dimension.

For each dimension, OLAP Services gives the members a single global ordering. This ordering follows a hierarchical sorting of the dimension: at each level, all children of each parent are ordered relative to each other. (For the members in each level, you have two choices regarding how the children are to be ordered under their parent.) Thus, at every level there is some order that is consistent from each query to each other query, and parents and children can be ordered together. Figure 1.6 shows a numbering of the members of a small dimension according to this ordering. We will refer to this ordering as the "database" ordering of members. (Microsoft documentation refers to the "natural" ordering in

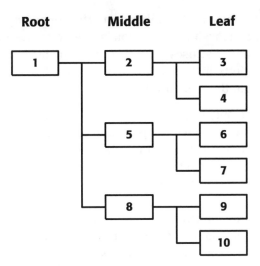

Figure 1.6 Database ordering of members shown in ordinal numbers.

dimensions, but as there is no one natural ordering for employees, products, companies, and so on, we will use *database* instead.) Within each level, members can be ordered under their parents either lexicographically by name value or by the values of an associated key column in an underlying dimension table.

Member Properties (Attributes)

Member properties are additional pieces of information about each member. They are conceptually similar to measures in a cube in that they are data organized dimensionally, but organized only by one dimension. Each defined member property applies to all of the members of one level of the dimension. Member properties are treated by Microsoft OLAP Services as strings, even though they can be based on a variety of types. A member property can be defined in terms of OLE DB data type definitions, though these map to the (fairly) standard set of underlying database number and string data types.

Since member properties are associated with members of a dimension level, they are available from every cube that uses that dimension level. (Some cubes may not use the dimension level, in which case the properties will not be available there. See the discussion of cubes in the section "Cubes and Measures" later in this chapter.) OLAP Services does not document a limit to the number of properties that can be defined for any level or dimension.

Member properties may be used as the basis for virtual dimensions (described in the section "Dimension Types" later in this chapter), which can also be used as dimensions of a cube. If a virtual dimension is used by some cube, the property is still accessible within that cube as a member property. For example, suppose a Product Color property of a Product dimension is used to create a virtual Product Color dimension. A cube that uses both of these dimensions will be able to access the member property as a property and have its data organized by both the virtual dimension and the regular dimension.

Although member properties are only organized in the database by one dimension, in practice almost all properties have the potential to change over time, and most do. Customers change addresses and marital status, manufacturers buy each other's product lines, packaging sizes change, Social Security numbers will eventually be recycled, and so on. Expedience is the reason these are considered time-invariant relationships between a member and another data type rather than true time-varying values like those of any other measure. If time were made an explicit dimension of every datum, the database would get far more difficult to manage physically, and analysis steps would become more cumbersome. Handling changes to dimension structures over time is treated in Chapter 10 on maintaining applications.

Member properties and cube measures have some similarities and some differences. We will examine these in the section "Cubes and Measures" later in this chapter. We can represent member properties in an MDS diagram by listing their names along with the level they are defined in. For example, Figure 1.7 shows a product dimension with four levels and weight and packaging properties for the SKU level.

Dimension Types

Dimensions come in different flavors. They may be either shared or private, and they may also be either regular or virtual. Regardless of the dimension type,

Product	
All	Members: 1
Family	Members: 8
Brand	Members: 160
SKU	Members: 2,000
	Properties: Weight Packaging

Figure 1.7 MDS including member properties for a level.

they are treated identically in all queries and can be used to dimension regular or virtual cubes. These dimensions may also be treated identically for applications that communicate with Microsoft OLAP Services through OLE DB for OLAP or ADO for MD. The four flavors—shared, private, regular, and virtual—are described in the following paragraphs.

Shared dimensions may be used by more than one cube. For example, a time dimension may be shared between a cube holding production data, a cube holding sales data, and a cube holding inventory data. They may also be used by only one cube or by no cubes at all. Operationally, a shared dimension may have its structural information updated independently of update operations on the cubes that use it. (Chapter 10 discusses the update dependencies between cubes and dimensions in detail.)

A *private dimension* is defined within a particular cube and that cube alone. Although "private," it is visible to the rest of the database, a client can query along it, and it can be a dimension of a virtual cube that incorporates the cube that owns the private dimension. (Since it is completely visible, perhaps a better name for it would have been "personal" rather than "private"!) Operationally, a private dimension has its structural information completely rebuilt whenever the cube that contains it is rebuilt.

Regular dimensions may have one to 64 levels altogether and are based on table columns or column expressions. Any cube that uses a regular dimension may use all of its levels, or only a subset of them (we describe this in more detail in the section titled "Cubes and Measures" later in this chapter). The members of regular dimensions may have associated attributes or member properties. From an operational standpoint, Microsoft OLAP Services may store precalculated aggregates at various levels of regular dimensions (trading space for time in queries). There is no documented limit on the number of members in a dimension or level in a regular dimension, though there is a limit of 64,000 children under any parent member.

A *virtual dimension* is defined from a member property for a level of a single regular dimension. For example, if a Product dimension's SKU level has a Color property, then a virtual dimension can be created from the color property, and the leaf-level members of the dimension will be the distinct values of the color property. A virtual dimension has exactly two levels: leaf and All. Since each virtual member is a property value from another dimension, that virtual member may correspond to a set of members from the underlying level. Although logically each virtual member could drill to a set of underlying real members, there is no metadata mechanism to do that. Operationally, all the aggregation that is required to reduce that set to the single virtual member is performed at query time. There is a limit of 760 members in a virtual dimension.

The two types of distinctions—shared/private and regular/virtual—are almost independent of each other: a dimension may be shared and regular, private and regular, or shared and virtual. Virtual dimensions cannot be private, however. You cannot simply declare a public dimension's property as a private virtual dimension. (However, if you really wanted that property to function as a member of a private dimension, you could always create it as a private dimension from the underlying table structures.) The major difference between a regular dimension and a virtual one, apart from the structural restrictions on the latter, is operational. We noted some of the operational differences earlier in this chapter; we will explore the processing of dimensions and cubes in Chapters 2 and 10.

With a few exceptions, shared dimensions, private dimensions, and virtual dimensions may each have the same name. You cannot have two shared dimensions in a database with the same name, and a cube's private dimension cannot have the same name as a shared dimension used by the cube. Each cube can have a private dimension that has the same name as another shared dimension. Virtual dimensions, being shared, cannot have the same name as a regular dimension. You can, however, denominate a virtual dimension as being a hierarchy-dimension and make several virtual dimensions appear to be multiple hierarchies of the same dimension.

Although virtual dimensions are called dimensions, they are logically speaking simply alternate hierarchies for a dimension (in contrast to "multiple hierarchies," which are logically separate dimensions!). While you can organize a cube by multiple virtual dimensions derived from a single dimension, the members of each virtual dimension are logically 1-N with the members of that dimension. The members of any regular dimension are logically uncorrelated (M-N) with the members of any other regular dimension. For any two virtual dimensions based on even a single regular dimension, their virtual members will be in an M-N relationship. However, any two records that correspond to one member of the regular dimension will correspond to exactly the same member in each of the two virtual dimensions, so they are not independent dimensions with respect to the data.

Virtual dimensions are very useful for allowing the ability to provide additional breakouts and aggregations of data without exploding the dimensional volume that the aggregated data is stored in.

Time versus Regular Dimensions and Levels

Microsoft OLAP Services reserves a special internal property for marking dimensions and levels as having time-related types. The only real purpose of this property in the first release of OLAP Services is to allow certain functions in MDX (the query and calculation language used by OLAP Services) that are usually used for time-related operations to identify the Time dimension in a cube as being a default dimension. Other than that, the type of a dimension or level makes no difference to any logical or operational aspect of OLAP Services. A dimension whose members reflect time periods may be marked as a Standard dimension, and a dimension representing customers could (perversely) be marked as a Time dimension with no loss of functionality.

There are certain MDX functions that default to using the Time dimension. When a cube contains only one dimension that is marked with the time type, then this default may be safely employed. (When a cube contains multiple time-typed dimensions—for example, multiple time hierarchy-dimensions—the default is problematic.)

When a dimension is marked as being time-typed, then levels within it may be usefully marked as being of the following types: Years, HalfYears, Quarters, Months, Weeks, Days, Hours, Minutes, and Seconds. There are various MDX functions that will use levels marked with these properties. OLAP Services will not prevent you from marking more than one level in a dimension as being of the same type (for example, marking two levels as being of the type Month), but any function that is looking for the month level of the time dimension may well get confused.

Cubes and Measures

A cube in Microsoft OLAP Services is a collection of measures that are organized by a set of dimensions. Just as the measures define the primary data used in calculations, cubes define the data that our client tools can access. (This ignores member properties, but the primary focus of our OLAP Services databases will be on analyzing measures, not properties.) The collection of measures in an OLAP Services cube is represented by a measures dimension, where each member represents a separate measure. Cubes are the context for all calculations in OLAP Services. Since all measures are defined as part of a cube, all aggregation of data takes place within cubes. All calculations, whether defined on measures or defined on members of other dimensions, take place within the context of a cube. All MDX queries are directed against cubes.

Base measures in OLAP Services are only of numeric types, though you can choose from a set of numerical representations (integer, single-precision float, etc.) Because dates are internally represented as numbers, you can use them as measures too, though the types of calculations that you can meaningfully perform with them are very limited. You can also use counts of text-typed values (or counts of any other row type, for that matter) in database tables as numerical measures; see Chapter 3 for more details. Calculated measures can be string-typed as well as numerical.

Though each cube must have a different name than every other cube, all cubes may share private dimension names, measure names, and as many dimensions as desired with other cubes.

The measures dimension is treated by MDX queries and OLE DB for OLAP metadata interfaces in the same way as other dimensions. However, there are a few differences between the measures dimension and the other dimensions you may define for a cube that are worth pointing out. First, the measures dimension of a cube has only one level and no "All" level/member, so it is completely non-hierarchical. Second, each member in the measures dimension represents a separate measure, so there are some additional properties associated uniquely with them, such as data type and aggregation function. In OLE DB for OLAP these additional properties are provided through a special measures metadata rowset. The measures dimension is analogous to a private dimension because each cube has its own measures dimension, and the dimension has the same name in each cube. A virtual cube will use a base cube's measures dimension a little differently than it will a private dimension, however.

In MDS diagrams, cubes may use a variety of diagram components. A key part of each cube diagram is the set of dimensions and the measures used. We will generally employ the line-segment form of a dimension in a cube diagram because it is more compact. Cube aspects that are organized by the dimensions, such as measures and partitions (described in Chapter 2), are shown next to the

Measure and Member Terminology

Before going further, let us inject a little terminology into the discussion. Going further than the terminology used in the first release of Microsoft's documentation for OLAP Services, we will refer to "base measures," "calculated measures," "base members," and "calculated members". So-called measures end up being both "measured" and "derived." That is, the phrase *calculated measure* is really an oxymoron (though we understand it in context!). However, we would like to reserve the term *measure* in general for references to both the measures directly obtained from tables and those calculated through formulas. Similarly, when we want to specifically talk about non-calculated members of a dimension, we will call them *base members*. *Calculated Members* will be those members defined only in terms of a calculation. When we want to talk about members in the abstract, we will simply use *members*. End of terminology discussion.

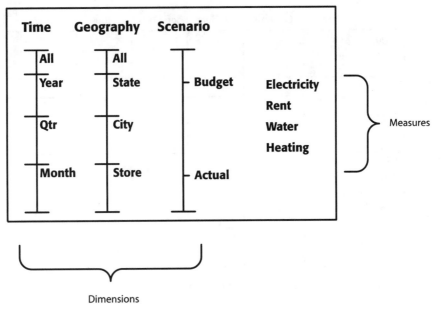

Figure 1.8 Basic MDS template for cube diagrams.

dimensions' line segments. Although a measure functions like a dimension in that it forms a domain of values, it is treated syntactically in MDX like a member of a measures dimension. We conserve space as well as highlight that treatment by lining up the names of measures vertically in one column. Figure 1.8 shows a basic MDS template for a very simple cube for analyzing stores' fixed costs by time, geography, and scenario (showing Actual and Budget members in the Scenario dimension).

Sometimes, we just need a high-level view of what the database's dimensions and cubes are and which dimensions or measures are used in which cubes. To do this, we lay out the cubes and dimensions in a grid and simply highlight the intersections that correspond to a use of the dimension in the cube. We can omit the measures for each cube, or we can include them. Figure 1.9 shows an example of this view, including the measure for each cube. We have shaded in the intersections just to show the presence or absence of a usage relationship between the dimension and the cube. We can also fill in the cells with additional information about the association as needed.

Regular Cubes

Regular cubes define a framework for aggregating input data. All base measure data that is input to a cube is automatically available as aggregates at each level

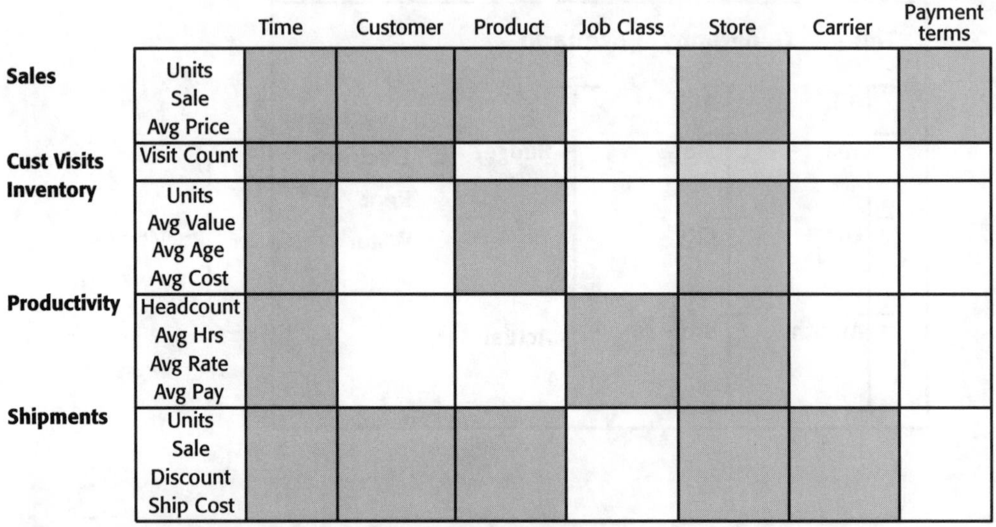

		Time	Customer	Product	Job Class	Store	Carrier	Payment terms
Sales	Units Sale Avg Price	■	■	■		■		■
Cust Visits	Visit Count	■	■			■		
Inventory	Units Avg Value Avg Age Avg Cost	■	■	■		■		
Productivity	Headcount Avg Hrs Avg Rate Avg Pay	■			■	■		
Shipments	Units Sale Discount Ship Cost	■	■	■		■	■	■

Figure 1.9 MDS of dimension-cube-measure relationships.

above the level at which it came into the cube. Each base measure of a cube comes from a column in a fact table. All the data for a regular cube must enter the cube at a single level-combination from the cube's dimensions. Although all data for a cube must enter that cube at one level-combination only, the combination may be formed from any level in each of the cube's dimensions except the All level defined by OLAP Services (if any). (You can enter data into a cube at a dimension's DBA-defined All level, but that cube might as well not even use that dimension if that is where the data is actually supposed to enter.) For example, consider a cube that is formed out of a shared Store dimension that has levels of City, Store, and Cash Register; a shared Product dimension that has levels of Department, Category, and SKU; and a Time dimension. This cube could bring data in by SKU, Day and Store or by Category, Day, and Cash Register —but not both. Figure 1.10 shows an MDS depiction of data entering at each of these level combinations and aggregating up through the other levels.

To successfully map input data to these non-leaf levels, Microsoft OLAP Services requires you to mark as "disabled" all the levels below the level at which the data enters. A disabled level is completely invisible to the user of a regular cube. He or she cannot reference it or its members in queries nor obtain metadata about its members through a client query API. When a cube dimension level is disabled, all levels below it in the hierarchy become disabled as well. For example, if the category level of our product hierarchy were disabled, then the SKU level would be disabled as well. In an MDS diagram for a cube, that dimension might simply show only the enabled levels.

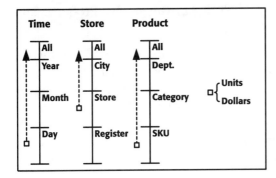 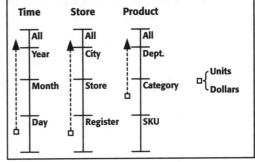

Figure 1.10 MDS depiction of data entering at different combinations of dimension levels.

In Chapter 2 we will go into much more depth on the operational architecture of cubes.

Virtual Cubes

Virtual cubes are essentially join views of one or more regular cubes. Although a client can examine metadata information in DSO or OLE DB for OLAP to determine whether a cube is virtual or not, there is no difference between the two in terms of how the cube is calculated or queried. Virtual cubes do not hold any measure data themselves; a query for data in a virtual cube retrieves stored data from the underlying regular cube(s).

A virtual cube is created from one or more regular cubes. (Since the term *regular* doesn't quite connote the relationship of any cube to a virtual cube, we will also use the term *base cube* to refer to one of the cubes on which a virtual cube is based.) In the first release of Microsoft OLAP Services, there is a limit of 32 base cubes per virtual cube. Like a regular cube, each virtual cube has one measures dimension, whose measures will be taken from the measures dimensions of each other cube. (A virtual cube can have any subset of measures from each regular cube it is based on, as long as it has at least one from each cube.) Like a regular cube, a virtual cube must use at least one dimension, which can come from any of its base cubes. Each virtual cube may use for its dimensions any subset of the non-measures dimensions from each of its input cubes. For example, a sales cube consisting of Geography, Time, Products, and measures could have a virtual cube created on it that exposes just the Geography and Time dimensions in addition to some measures. Given a human resources (HR) cube that uses the same Geography and Time dimensions as well as a Job Category dimension and measures, one or more virtual cubes could be constructed that combine these two cubes. Each virtual cube could use as its dimensions any combination of the Geography, Time, Product, and Job Category dimensions—

for example, all four; just Geography and Time; or Geography, Products, and Time; and so on.

A virtual dimension can be used as a dimension of a virtual cube even when none of the regular cubes that comprise the virtual cube use that virtual dimension, so long as the virtual cube uses the dimension that contains the member property that defines the virtual dimension. Suppose that the city level of the Geography dimension has a member property based on it called "Size Classification," which contained a category for the land area of the city (tiny, small, medium, large, huge). A virtual dimension has thus been created from Size Classification that is called "City Size." Even if neither the sales cube nor the HR cube uses the City Size dimension, a virtual cube that uses the Geography dimension can also use the City Size virtual dimension.

When virtual cubes join two or more cubes, they need to relate the measures and their values in some way. A virtual cube automatically joins its measures along the dimensions shared by input cubes. For example, in a virtual cube that uses Geography and Time to organize its sales and HR information, a given Geography and Time intersection will identify values of the sales cube's measures that are related to that Geography and Time. It will also identify values of the HR cube's measures that are related to that Geography and Time. For the dimensions that are not shared, the measures values are taken from the All member, if there is one. If there isn't one, then the virtual cube takes the measures values from an arbitrary member of the dimension (the first member of the top level). For example, an Employee Hours Worked measure would be available at any Geography by any Time member, but only at the Product All member.

Figure 1.11 shows an MDS depiction of a virtual cube derived from the sales and HR cubes that exposes all dimensions of its two base cubes. Note how the measures from the HR cube apply only to the Product dimension's All member. Note as well that measures from the sales cube only apply to the Job Category dimension's All member.

You may also build a virtual cube from just one base cube and expose a subset of its dimensions and/or measures. For example, a virtual cube could be built off of the HR cube just described that slices away the Job Category dimension and exposes only the Geography and Time dimensions. One reason you might do this is as a technique for limiting away sensitive details since OLAP Services's data security is based on cubes (more on this in Chapter 12). However, note that any dimensions of the underlying cube that are not exposed will have their related data taken from the All member (or its synthetic equivalent). You could not, for example, define a virtual cube to slice the Time dimension at the "1995" member or the Employee dimension at the "Pay Grade 3" member.

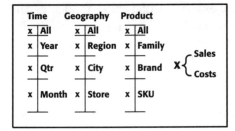 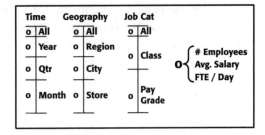

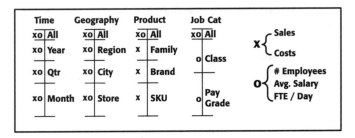

Figure 1.11 MDS of a virtual cube and measure applicability.

Virtual cubes, like regular cubes, may have some of their dimensions' levels disabled. By default, dimension levels disabled in a regular cube are enabled in a virtual cube that is using it, even if the virtual cube uses only one base cube. Although Microsoft's OLAP Manager provides an interface for disabling a regular cube's dimension levels, you can use DSO with other software to perform this function on virtual cubes. Of course, no data will exist in the re-enabled levels for the measures coming from that base cube, but calculated members can calculate new data within those levels. Member properties for the re-enabled levels become visible as well.

Although a virtual cube combines dimensions and measures from one or more cubes, it does not automatically take on any of the calculated members that may have been defined for any of the cubes. A virtual cube can have calculated members defined for it just as any other cube does, however; you just need to redefine them. By the time you read this, utilities will exist that ease the burden of copying calculated member definitions from a base cube to its dependent virtual cubes.

When you diagram a virtual cube, an important relationship to capture is the joining of the base cubes into the virtual cube. A virtual cube can use all or only one of the dimensions from each of the input cubes. So, unlike the diagram that shows the dimensional commonality between cubes, the virtual cube replicates the dimensions between base cubes and the virtual cube. We can also selectively disable or enable levels in the virtual cube differently than we do in the base cubes, which is easily captured in the diagram. A virtual cube's measures may have different names than they do in their base cubes, and the virtual cube diagram helps capture that. Diagrams like that shown in Figure 1.11 indicate the virtual cube's dependency on its base cubes, while Figure 1.12 shows the detail of dimension and measure connections between the virtual cube and the base cubes.

Similarities and Differences between Cube Measures and Level Properties

In a relational database management system (RDBMS), there is no functional difference between a member attribute and a measure. In Microsoft OLAP Services,

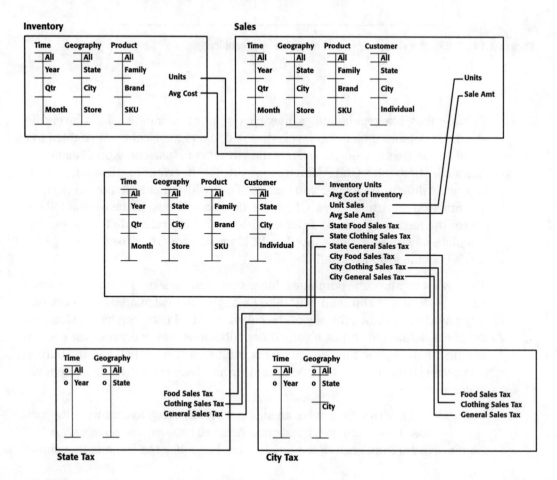

Figure 1.12   MDS detailing dimension and measure connections.

however, there are similarities and differences between measures and a level's member properties that are worth mentioning. The main similarity is that both are data organized by dimensions. There are some notable differences as well:

- Properties cannot be the target of calculations (described in the next section, "Formulas"). Only values associated with measures can be the target of calculations. Properties can be used as inputs to calculations, just as measures are (albeit with different syntax).

- Properties are stored and retrieved only as character strings, while base measures are stored and retrieved only as numbers.

- Properties are not automatically aggregated. For example, if your store dimension has a store-level property named "[Square Footage]," your dimension will not automatically have a city- or state-level aggregate [Square Footage] that is the sum of the individual stores' values. Although the MDX language specification indicates that properties and measures are referenced in queries by identical syntax, OLAP Services requires that you use different syntax to reference them. You cannot define property formulas on a dimension in the same way that you can define calculated members in a cube.

However, if you wish to treat the data values of properties as though they were measures of a cube, you may easily create a cube that is dimensioned by the one dimension with measures created from the property columns. You can then join this cube to any other cube in a virtual cube.

Formulas

Microsoft OLAP Services allows new calculations to be specified in a straightforward way. All calculations within OLAP Services (apart from the implicit aggregations of base measures) are specified by creating new *calculated members*. Calculated members are always created within the context of a single cube, and each one is specific to its cube. Each calculated member appears to be a member of some dimension of its cube and has one associated formula. For example, a calculated measure named "Average Production Cost" would be a member of the cube's measures dimension, while a calculated member on the Scenario dimension might calculate the difference between Budget and Actual scenarios.

Calculated members and base members of dimensions have some important similarities and differences. Like base members of any dimension, calculated members intersect with all members of all other dimensions. On hierarchical dimensions, they can be treated as children of other base members (except members of the leaf level). In addition, calculated members may not be defined to be children of other calculated members. If they are not explicitly made to be children of a member in the dimension, they will be siblings of the root-level member(s). If they are made to be a child of a member, they will be siblings of the other children of that member as well. Calculated members also appear in the OLE DB metadata that lists the members of dimensions for a given cube.

However, since calculated members exist only within the context of a cube, it is not possible to share calculated members between a base cube and a virtual cube that uses that cube. This is true for both calculated measures and calculated members on the non-measures dimensions. For example, if a base sales cube has a calculated measure named "Margin Percentage," a virtual cube will not be able to access this Margin Percentage calculated measure (and will have to have its own Margin Percentage measure defined in order to provide that calculation). If there exists a calculated member on the Geography dimension of the HR cube (from our earlier cubes discussion), that member will not be available in the virtual cube derived from it. Even if the same calculated member exists in both base cubes, it will still not be available in the virtual cube.

In MDX statements, by default OLAP Services does not consider calculated members to be part of sets of members associated with dimensions, hierarchies, and levels. A special MDX function (AddCalculatedMembers()) must be used to include them. In OLE DB for OLAP, OLAP Services augments the Measures and Members rowsets with an Expression property to provide the formula used for each member, if there is any. Calculated members will have a non-null value for this property, while base members will have a null value.

Chapters 5 through 9 on MDX will discuss formulas and calculations in detail.

Linkage of Structures to RDBMS Schemata

Microsoft OLAP Services is strongly based on relational databases. All dimension levels and cube measures need to correspond to columns of tables, views, or queries. They can be in many different tables or all in one table, so long as dimension tables and fact tables can be joined in a single query. OLAP Services uses a highly declarative linkage between dimension and cube structures and RDBMS tables. Once the links are created, OLAP Services will form all queries on the linked tables and manipulate all query results. The only procedural work on your part as far as OLAP Services is concerned is triggering OLAP Services to build its internal dimension and cube representations from the linked tables, as necessary. (These internal representations are discussed in Chapter 2.) *OLAP Solutions* (Erik Thomsen, Wiley, 1998) describes the possible types of links that can exist to relate data in table form to dimension and cube structures. In the remainder of this section, we describe the subset that OLAP Services implements.

For dimensions, *level-column* links are the only type of link supported by OLAP Services. Each dimension level is linked to a column of a table such that the parent-child relationships for each member in each level of the hierarchy are determined on a row-by-row basis. *Parent-child* links, where two table columns describe the parent-child relationships one relation at time, are not supported. Figure 1.13 diagrams the linkage between a product dimension and a set of product dimension tables.

For cubes, *column-dimension* links are supported for the dimensions, and *column-member* links are supported for the measures. A column-dimension link connects a table column to a dimension; each value in a row for that column identifies a member in that dimension. A column-member link connects a table column to a particular member of a dimension. When the two types of links are combined between a cube and a table, for each row processed OLAP Services identifies each cell value with its appropriate measure and dimensional location.

Microsoft OLAP Services supports neither *table-member* links nor *value* links. A table-member link associates an entire table with a member from a dimension. For example, suppose a cube that you wish to use your transaction data in has a Scenario dimension with actual and forecast members, and while the table that holds your transaction data is entirely "actual," it has no column that states this. Ideally, you could link this table to the cube as is, but you would need a table-member link. You can simulate a table-member link by creating a column in the fact table that has only one member value (preferably by using a view, with a constant value in the appropriate column). Value links are required

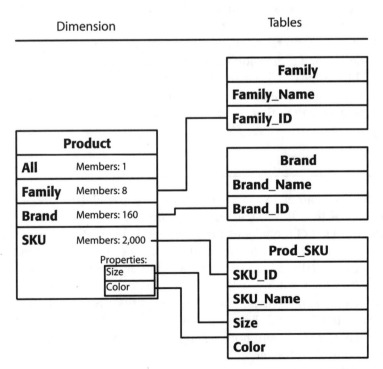

Figure 1.13   MDS of the links between a dimension and its tables.

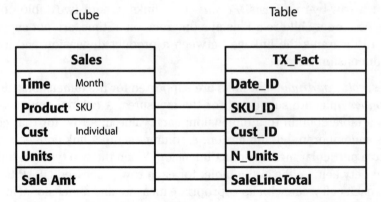

Figure 1.14 MDS of the links between a cube and its tables.

when each of the dimensions of a cube, including the measures, have their members identified in a column, and there is one column left over containing the value for that cell. (This is sometimes called a "type 0 table.") You cannot really simulate column-value links because OLAP Services cannot construct a measures dimension from the values found in one of the measures dimension. Instead, you would have a measure called "value" (or something similar) with a column-member link on it.

It includes Size and Color member properties for the SKU level of the dimension. Figure 1.14 diagrams the linkage of a cube to its fact table. This figure omits much of the detailed information that we might include for a linkage. The tutorial chapters (Chapters 15, 16, and 17) include linkage diagrams that carry all relevant detail for a dimension's and cube's connection to tables. Notice that in Figure 1.14 we have shifted the layout from the other cube template for dimension and measure elements so as to make the layout more graceful; we could also have used the other template and routed the link lines accordingly.

Summary

Throughout this chapter, we have explored two parallel topics: gaining an understanding of the OLAP structures provided by Microsoft OLAP Services and developing a set of techniques for depicting them. Both of these topics are important for understanding the rest of the product's features and fundamental for applying them to the design and implementation of databases and analyses. Beginning with Chapter 3, we will go into more depth about these structures, how OLAP Services implements them, and what their relation to actual database design is. In Chapter 2, however, we will turn our attention to the architecture of OLAP Services and how it supports the structures and features we have described in this chapter.

Microsoft OLAP Services Architecture

T his chapter covers the physical and logical architecture of Microsoft OLAP Services. As a product, OLAP Services is much more a system of related pieces than a single entity. A number of its important architectural features are in place to support the logical model introduced in Chapter 1. The three major areas of architecture we discuss in this chapter are as follows:

- Core component architecture
- Storage and query processing architecture
- Client/server processing

Although security is also a legitimate architectural issue, we will not treat it here. Instead, we devote Chapter 13 to discussing the security architecture and implementation issues.

In this chapter, we will not go into exhaustive depth on each architectural area, nor will we explore all of the application implications of each area. Chapters 3, 4, 10, and 12 will cover these in detail. Instead, we will lay out the groundwork so none of the architectural areas will be unfamiliar to you later on. We will first take a look at the core component architecture. Next, we will explore the storage and calculation architecture that drives much of OLAP Services's internal functionality and shapes an application's implementation. Finally, we will look at the way OLAP Services stores and maintains its internal information.

Core Component Architecture and Platforms

The two core components of Microsoft OLAP Services are the database server process and the Microsoft PivotTable Service. (Although the PivotTable Service and Microsoft Excel's PivotTable feature have similar names, they are separate entities.) OLAP Services's two other important components are the Decision Support Objects (DSO) library and the OLAP Manager administration interface. Although the OLAP Services metadata repository is not an active software component like the others, it is also a core part of the OLAP Services system. A diagram of these five components and their relationships is shown in Figure 2.1.

The Microsoft OLAP Services database server runs as a Windows NT service (named "MSSQLServerOLAPServer"), and is started and stopped through the standard services interfaces of Windows NT. For example, it can be started and stopped through the NT Control Panel's Services applet. While MSSQLServerO-LAPServer is running it will consume some of the server machine's memory space and other resources. We will discuss how to adjust these in Chapter 11.

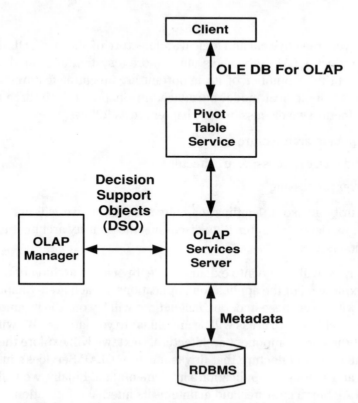

Figure 2.1   Diagram of the components in the overall system.

The PivotTable Service component is the client query interface for OLAP Services. It is an in-process COM server, which means that it is a dynamic-link library that COM loads into a client program as necessary. To a client, the PivotTable Service exposes an OLE DB for OLAP interface that the client will use to obtain metadata and issue queries. The PivotTable Service will execute queries in either MDX or SQL, though it supports only a limited subset of SQL syntax. Client query programs only talk to the OLAP Services server through the PivotTable Service, which communicates with the OLAP Services server through its own specialized protocol. A complete discussion of OLE DB for OLAP and ADO for MD for client development is beyond the scope of this book, but we will discuss some of the relationships between these interfaces and OLAP Services query processing as the need arises.

Although the PivotTable Service and the server are separate entities, the PivotTable Service can perform some of the functions of the server. In terms of storage and calculation, it can be thought of as a client-side OLAP Services that in most respects has a subset of the server's features, with a few extra capabilities of its own. For example, the PivotTable Service has basically the same calculation and data-modeling ability as the server (without the advanced storage management abilities that we discuss later in this chapter). Moreover, although calculations can be performed at the server as well as at the client, there are some aspects of answering a query that can only take place in the PivotTable Service. There are also many other similarities and differences between the PivotTable Service and the server. While the PivotTable Service can be used on its own to create applications that have significant utility, we will not discuss its abilities as a stand-alone OLAP database in depth in this book. (The second edition of this book will very likely give it a detailed coverage, however.)

Although we are speaking of PivotTable Service client and database server components, "client" and "server" are roles as opposed to computer machine distinctions. The MSSQLServerOLAPServer service requires Windows NT (Server or Workstation) to run, and only one instance of it will run on any computer. The PivotTable Service can run on a separate computer running Windows NT, Windows 95, or Windows 98, or it can run on the same NT machine as the MSSQLServerOLAPServer service.

When the OLAP Services server is installed, an ActiveX Automation library called Decision Support Objects (DSO) is also installed on the server machine. This ActiveX library provides the API by which metadata is created and managed at the server and the various processing operations are controlled. Management and administration tools can be developed for it in a variety of Win32 programming environments, including C/C++, Visual Basic, Java, and Delphi. Although a full discussion of DSO is outside the scope of this book, some aspects of building applications and the robust management of a server and its data will require additional DSO programming. We will cover some DSO basics in Chapter 14 to demonstrate how to address those areas. The tools provided on the accompanying CD-ROM include source code samples that illustrate DSO programming as well.

The GUI tool Microsoft provides to manage OLAP Services servers and their databases is the OLAP Manager. This is implemented as a Microsoft Management Console (MMC) snap-in and uses the DSO interface. The OLAP Manager that ships with the first release of OLAP Services provides a reasonably complete interface to some of the important functions of administering a database, but there are a good number of other important functional areas that you will need to address through your own DSO programming. Throughout the book, we will attempt to clarify what operations you can perform through the OLAP Manager and what operations must be performed through other DSO programs.

OLAP Services maintains internal metadata regarding the databases, dimensions, cubes, and their components in a repository database. When OLAP Services is installed, that repository resides in an Jet/Access .MDB-format database file in the directory that holds the server executable files. The repository can be placed into another relational database; the OLAP Services installation also includes a utility that will migrate the repository into an SQL Server database.

Storage and Query Processing Architecture

Microsoft OLAP Services is a product that is designed to support data analysis, and as such it functions primarily (like other DBMSs) as a storage and calculation engine. The way a large number of the structures and features link together is influenced by the way OLAP Services addresses storage and calculation logic issues. Although the product is built to support analysis along the data model described in Chapter 1, these engine-related issues will dominate any discussion of its storage and processing architecture. We will therefore start with a discussion of the fundamentals of the OLAP Services storage architecture.

Fundamentals of Stored Aggregates in OLAP Services

Microsoft OLAP Services is relatively optimized for data warehouse-based OLAP systems, which have as their basis large tables of data that are frequently requested at various levels of aggregation. The aggregation steps can consume large quantities of RAM and CPU resources. Because of the quantities of data involved and the bandwidth available on today's networks and computer busses, performing this aggregation on the database servers where the input data resides is far and away the most cost-effective approach. Most client queries will involve these aggregates, so the processing performed at the server will be leveraged among the clients.

One characteristic of most OLAP applications is the need to provide fast access to aggregated source data. Precalculating all possible aggregates can lead to a tremendous increase in the storage requirements for the database, while calculating all aggregates every time there is a query makes for slow query response times. In addition to aggregates, other calculations (differences, ratios, etc.) also require you to accept some trade-off on storage and processing time. The approach taken by OLAP Services is to precalculate some of the possible aggregate data values, and leave any remaining aggregation and all other calculations to be calculated on the fly at query time. The stored, precalculated aggregate data values will be frequently referred to as "aggregates" or "aggregations." In OLAP Services's calculation architecture, only base measures (those directly read from fact tables) can be pre-aggregated and stored.

In OLAP Services terminology, an *aggregation* represents some amount of input data aggregated to some combination of levels from each dimension in the cube. (We refer to "some combination of levels from each dimension" rather than "some level of the cube" because one aggregation may consist of data that is at the customer-city-by-product-category-by-quarter combination, while another may be at the individual-customer-by-product-category-by-month combination, and so on. These are combinations of levels, not individual levels.) A fact table containing data by day, store, and product SKU and a set of three stored aggregations for it is represented in Figure 2.2.

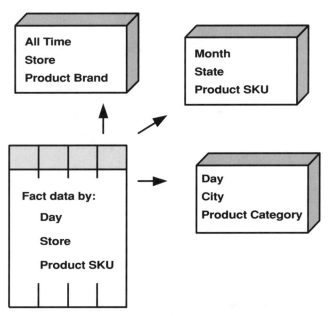

Figure 2.2   Fact table and aggregate level-combinations.

When a query uses measures from some combination of levels for which aggregates are not stored, OLAP Services will derive it from some other stored aggregation. To facilitate OLAP Services's particular calculation architecture, the only aggregation functions that can be applied to base measures are SUM (the default), COUNT, MIN, and MAX. These aggregation functions make it easy to derive other levels of aggregation from them. SUMs and COUNTs are added together, and the minimum or maximum of existing minimum or maximum aggregate values is taken. Figure 2.3 depicts the possible derivation of month-by-state-by-product category-level aggregates from either the stored aggregates for day, city, and product category levels or the month, state, and product SKU-level aggregates.

The fact that these four are the only implicit aggregation functions influences application design. For example, a measure that you really want to aggregate as an average must instead be created as two measures, namely, one that aggregates by SUM and another by COUNT. The average is then calculated from the SUM and the COUNT.

Calculation Architecture

To satisfy complex OLAP queries and calculations, you need to perform a variety of different calculations. These include aggregations, differences, allocations, moving and cumulative averages and sums, and more. OLAP Services is optimized for instances where additional processing stages (those not involving simple aggregation of fact table columns) are secondary, both in terms of

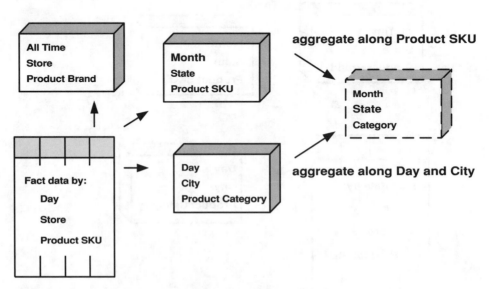

Figure 2.3　Deriving aggregations from other aggregations.

resources required and in terms of calculation dependencies. All calculations that are specified in MDX are carried out at the time the query is executed. (Calculations specified in MDX include not only things like query filter conditions but also all calculated members.) So, OLAP Services has a clear two-tier basic calculation architecture. This is diagrammed in Figure 2.4, which depicts the flow of calculations from input into tables through end-user queries.

This calculation architecture must be kept in mind when you are designing some type of cubes. There are cases when you want to perform calculations at leaf-level cells and aggregate the results. Primarily, this occurs when you are multiplying a rate by some number of units. Examples of this include multiplying average salary by number of employees to get dollars per year, multiplying dollars per watt by watts consumed to get dollars, multiplying gallons per minute by minutes to get gallons used, and so on. MDX also provides the SUM, COUNT, MIN, and MAX operators, so in theory you might not need to use the aggregations provided by the lower tier of calculations. However, actual practice dictates that you will want them as much as you can get them. Aggregating at the server is much faster per cell, on average, than performing the same aggregations on the fly using MDX. When multiple users are querying for the same aggregations of calculated results or one user makes the same request multiple times, the inefficiency is multiplied. Microsoft OLAP Services does support calculation of query results at both the client and at the server. Optimization of client and server calculation resources is covered in Chapter 11.

Accessing Functions in External Libraries

One aspect of the Microsoft OLAP Services calculation mechanism that is worth mentioning here is its support for libraries of external functions (usually referred to in Microsoft's documentation as "user-defined functions," or "UDFs"). OLAP Services can use global functions that are defined in an ActiveX library and are accessible through ActiveX Automation. You can refer to them

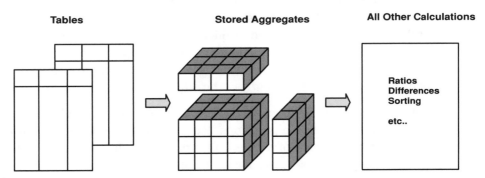

Tables   **Stored Aggregates**   **All Other Calculations**

Ratios
Differences
Sorting

etc..

Figure 2.4   Depiction of calculation architecture.

in MDX expressions using a syntax that is similar to the syntax of intrinsic MDX functions, and OLAP Services will pass values to them and retrieve their results using normal Automation interfaces. There are a number of applications for this, and we devote Chapter 14 to the development and use of external functions. When OLAP Services is installed, the function library for Visual Basic for Applications is also installed and registered for use, and most of the functions it contains may be used in MDX expressions. If Microsoft Excel is installed, its function library is available as well.

Partition Architecture, Storage, and Querying

Data storage for a regular cube is divided into partitions. Every cube has at least one partition, and particular situations will benefit from multiple partitions. A partition is a physically separate region of storage for some subset of the cube's data. Within this storage, each partition stores various aggregations of the cube's base measures. Generally, the reasons to create multiple partitions for a cube stem from a need to optimize physical access patterns related to the data. This may include patterns of data updating (which may lead to partitioning by time, by source of update, or both), patterns of data querying (which may lead to partitioning by regions that different queries focus on), or patterns of data storage (which may lead to partitioning by the physical servers that hold subsets of the data).

While OLAP Services partitions are available so the DBA can manage the physical storage of the database, they are invisible to client queries. OLAP Services will transparently draw aggregates from each partition as necessary to satisfy a user query. This is in addition to transparently selecting the right aggregates to use within and across partitions.

The set of definitions for the aggregations that are held in a partition is called that partition's *aggregation design*. For example, a partition's design may consist of a (product category, month, city)-level aggregation and a (product brand, quarter, store)-level aggregation of the cube's base measures. Each partition has its own design. Partitions may share an aggregation design with other partitions, or they may have their own independent designs. The actual design is held independently for each partition. Although you may copy a partition's design from another partition of the same cube, you may later modify the aggregation design of either partition independently of the other's aggregation design.

Each partition is based on a single fact table; however, a single fact table may be the basis for multiple partitions. Partitions may be defined to correspond with a particular region of a cube, with a particular condition of data in the fact table, or both. In the initial packaging of Microsoft SQL Server 7, only the Enterprise Edition allows you to define multiple partitions for a cube (which itself requires Windows NT Server Enterprise Edition). If you are working with the

Standard Edition, everything we discuss about individual partitions will apply; however, nothing we discuss about multiple partitions in a cube will apply.

Partitions Based on Cube Regions

You can associate a partition with a particular region of a cube by specifying a slice in one or more dimensions to which the partition corresponds. Note that partitions can only be associated with a slice in a non-measures dimension. In RDBMS terms, you can partition your cubes horizontally but not vertically. (Virtual cubes provide a form of horizontal partitioning.)

When a partition is associated with a cube slice, it is actually associated with a hierarchical region that corresponds to the members chosen for the slice. If the slice chosen is a leaf member in its dimension, then the partition will be associated with that member only. If the slice chosen is a non-leaf member in that dimension, then the partition will be associated with that member and all of its descendants. A slice will always be associated with all ancestors of the slice member as well, since it contributes to the ancestors' aggregate values. Figure 2.5 shows an MDS of a cube being divided into three partitions along the time dimension. Each partition is defined so as to contribute data from a different

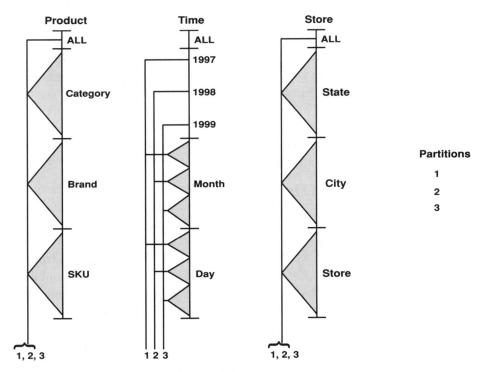

Figure 2.5 Cube divided into three partitions.

year. This means that partition 1, for example, will hold all data for 1997 at the year, quarter, month, and day levels across all product dimension members and across all store dimension members, while partitions 2 and 3 will contribute data for 1998 and 1999, respectively, across all of the other dimensions' members.

Note that you may define more than one partition as corresponding to a slice. Microsoft OLAP Services does not track this condition, and you should be careful when creating partition slice assignments in the OLAP Manager. Chapter 3 covers this in more detail. For example, you may have fact tables that each correspond with a different sales region and year and yet only partition the cube on year slices. In this case, although multiple partitions refer to each time slice, the data does not overlap. When OLAP Services receives a query for data in one of those years, it will use data from each of these partitions to satisfy the query. Since 1997, 1998, and 1999 all contribute to the cube's All-time aggregation, a query to the All-time level will reference data for each of these partitions.

In some cases, you may have fact tables and partitions whose corresponding slice definitions overlap in the hierarchy. For example, consider two partitions that are specified to hold data for two different fact tables. One fact table will be for the state of Rhode Island and the year 1998, while another fact table will be for the city of Cranston, Rhode Island, and the month of March 1998. Figure 2.6 shows an MDS of this partition arrangement. In this case, a query for data about Cranston in April or February will only be directed to the (Rhode Island, 1998) partition, since the (Cranston, March) partition has no data to contribute to it. Similarly, a query for any other city in Rhode Island for any time period at all will also not involve data from that partition. However, a query for data for Rhode Island at the year level would involve data from both of these partitions because data for Cranston in March will contribute to these aggregate values along with the data in the partition that is specifically for (Rhode Island, 1998). When executing queries, Microsoft OLAP Services only involves those partitions that may contribute to the query result and does not access partitions that will not contribute any data to it.

When a partition has been defined as representing only a slice of data, OLAP Services does not assume that the associated fact table contains only rows for that partition's slice. When OLAP Services generates SQL to retrieve rows from the fact table, it uses member information that defines the slice so as to restrict the rows retrieved. As a result, you can populate the partition from tables that have more than just data for that slice. If that fact table only contains data that corresponds to that subset of the cube, then nothing is lost, but the execution of the SQL will contain extra, unnecessary overhead. On the other hand, there is some documentation value in defining the partition to correspond to that slice (in addition to the fact that the server only accesses it to solve queries that correspond to that slice).

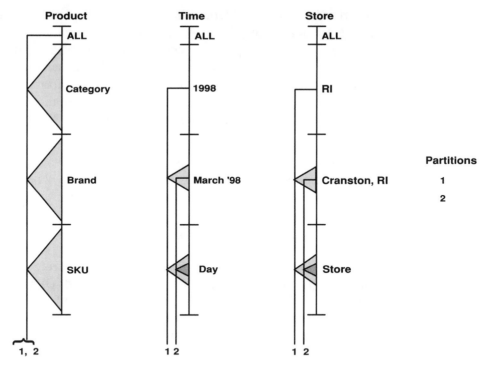

Figure 2.6 MDS of hierarchically overlapping partitions.

Partitions Based on Data Conditions in the Table

Each partition may also have an associated WHERE clause (in the SQL dialect of the RDBMS that holds the fact table) that can be used to restrict the rows from the table. This is functionally equivalent to basing the partition on a view in that RDBMS that uses the WHERE clause to restrict the rows. However, you do not need to have DBA privileges in the source database to use the WHERE clause, and it documents the conditions for populating the partition very clearly.

The WHERE clause can restrict the table in an arbitrary fashion so long as it does not rely on any particular tables being joined to the fact table. For example, it may simply restrict the rows of the table based on some column values from that table. It can also include additional nested select statements. For example, a WHERE clause of

```
fact_table.store_id IN ( SELECT store_id FROM top_sellers WHERE month =
'June 1999')
```

would restrict the rows that are retrieved to those for a special subset of stores.

Although dimension tables are sometimes joined to the fact tables when the server accesses the fact table, you cannot rely on any dimension table being joined as a part of the access. All tables that are being joined need to be listed in the FROM clause of the query. You have only limited control over the FROM clause that OLAP Services uses, and the control that you do have more easily specifies that tables can be excluded from the FROM clause than that they can be included in it. If you need a WHERE clause to refer to information in the dimension tables (or to any other tables), go back and create the view on the fact table that joins to the dimension table and then use that view as the source for the partition's data.

Also, you must keep in mind that if multiple partitions use the same fact table and their WHERE clauses overlap, Microsoft OLAP Services will not be aware of it, and the partitions will double-count the overlapping rows.

Partition Storage: ROLAP/HOLAP/MOLAP

As used in this book, the terms *MOLAP*, *ROLAP*, and *HOLAP* refer to the way the data for a partition is physically stored and accessed. OLAP Services allows each partition to have one of three storage forms, and Microsoft uses the terms MOLAP, ROLAP, and HOLAP to label them. These terms do not have crisp definitions across the industry, but OLAP Services defines them as follows:

MOLAP (Multidimensional OLAP). All data in the partition is stored in a specialized, proprietary file structure that is relatively optimized for the access patterns of the OLAP Services server. This includes both the lowest-level cell data held in the fact table (which is copied into the partition) and all precalculated aggregations.

ROLAP (Relational OLAP). All data in the partition is stored in RDBMS tables. In addition to using the fact table as is, OLAP Services will create and use an aggregate table for each aggregate level-combination specified in the aggregation design.

HOLAP (Hybrid OLAP). When a partition is defined as HOLAP in the OLAP Manager, the fact table for the partition is used as is, just as in a ROLAP partition. All precalculated aggregates are stored in the specialized MOLAP storage form.

Each partition of a cube can have its own storage form. OLAP Services transparently handles the pre-aggregation and query processing across partitions, so each partition appears the same to queries as any other.

In a MOLAP partition, leaf-level cells are copied from the fact table into the MOLAP partition. After partition processing, no additional SQL is used to access data within the fact table. All MOLAP partitions are stored in the OLAP Services data directory that corresponds to the database. This means that all data needs to be brought into the file system of the OLAP Services server. We will explore some of the implications of this in Chapter 11. Despite the fact that atomic fact rows are being transported out of the RDBMS and into the OLAP Services server process, OLAP Services can generate a set of stored MOLAP aggregations very swiftly. This is because it can generate multiple level-combinations of aggregations in a single operation. This contrasts with a GROUP BY in SQL, which is essentially limited to one level-combination of aggregations for each SELECT … GROUP BY that is executed.

In a ROLAP partition, however, the aggregate tables are all computed within the RDBMS schema in which the fact table resides. No cell data needs to be brought into the OLAP Services server. All aggregations will be performed by SQL statements of the form

```
INSERT INTO CUBExxx( … ) SELECT ...
```

which moves no data between the RDBMS and OLAP Services. However, the creation of aggregate tables by SQL is likely to be a good deal slower than the equivalent aggregation in a MOLAP partition. When OLAP Services accesses a ROLAP partition, it generates SQL to access the data, and it will use the OLE DB driver specified in the data source definition to access the aggregates as well as the leaf data.

The structure of each aggregate table is clean and consistent, though their naming will not be useful to applications. The name of each dimension-level column in the table is derived from the name of the level in that dimension and a level-identifier number suffix and is given the type given in the member key property for that dimension's level. Each measure column in the table is defined with the type given for the measure in the cube definition and has a name that is derived from the aggregation function given for it in the cube as well as the name of the measure in the cube. While it is possible to imagine using these summary tables for SQL reporting applications, we must point out that this requires taking control of the aggregations created (so as to ensure the existence of the table) and giving up the use of OLAP Services's aggregation-optimizing features. If the cube's aggregation storage is ever adjusted, you may well find that a summary table you are interested in will disappear. We would suggest that you treat these summary tables as black boxes whose covers were left unlocked. Besides, you can query the same information by posing SQL queries to OLAP Services!

A HOLAP partition combines some of the qualities of the other two partition types. The leaf-level data remains in the fact table as atomic-level facts, and whenever OLAP Services needs to access leaf cells it will generate SQL to access them. Stored aggregates are created in the specialized MOLAP storage form and placed in the file system of the OLAP Services server. Whenever OLAP Services needs to access the stored aggregates in query processing, it will do so with the same speed as with a MOLAP partition. However, the file system issues are similar to those that come up with MOLAP partitions.

The basic difference between HOLAP and MOLAP partitions is the duplication of leaf-level cells into the server's file system. The specifics of an application will determine whether or not it is preferable to perform this duplication. The duplication affects the storage required, query response time, query load on the underlying RDBMS, and data consistency between stored aggregations and underlying fact tables.

Multiple partitions may be merged together into one partition if they are of the same form (ROLAP/HOLAP/MOLAP) and have the same aggregation design. Merging partitions may be useful to improve query performance. Deciding which partitions to use when answering a query imposes overhead on OLAP Services, and using fewer partitions simplifies the decision. If the reasons for having multiple partitions involved the patterns of updating data in the fact tables and the patterns have changed (perhaps because the year has ended, so no new transactions will be going into that year's tables anymore), then it may make sense to merge the partitions. This topic is treated in Chapter 11.

Write-Back Partitions

OLAP Services allows you to mark a cube as being able to accept cell data written to it by a client through the PivotTable Service (in addition to being able to have data enter through a fact table). Data may only be input at the leaf level of cells for that cube. Data so input from the client is stored in a *write-back partition*, which is not exactly the same as the partitions that we have been discussing so far but is very similar.

In a write-back partition, data entered at the client is physically stored in an RDBMS table that OLAP Services creates for that purpose. As values are entered at the client, the difference between that value and the most recently recorded cell value is stored as a row in the write-back table, thus forming a trail of changes. These changes will be aggregated just as the rows of any other partition would be aggregated when a query involving that cell is answered. You can convert this partition to a normal partition of cell data at a later time. While we do not discuss write-back partitions in the text of this book, a code sample for creating and using them appears on the accompanying CD-ROM.

Definitions, Storage, and Processing

There are three forms of storage for information within a Microsoft OLAP Services system: metadata in the OLAP Services repository, database structures held within the server file system, and database structures held in external RDBMS systems like Microsoft SQL Server or Oracle8.

Each OLAP Services server stores all databases in a single directory tree. The root directory for this tree is specified during the installation process, and it may also be changed after installation. Each database has its own subdirectory under the root directory, along with a small related file in the root directory. Within a database's directory, OLAP Services maintains a separate file for each dimension that contains its detail information, with the same base name as the dimension and a suffix of .DIM. Each cube in that database has both a file of internal information with the same base name as the cube and a suffix of .MDL as well as its own subdirectory within the database's directory whose name is the name of the cube. The cube's subdirectory contains files holding all MOLAP-format data for the cube and information on all partitions of the cube. Note that you do not have the option of placing database files (cube data, etc.) on specific devices; the only level of management you are given through OLAP Services is to specify the root directory for the databases. A representation of this directory and file structure is shown in Figure 2.7. You can also specify a

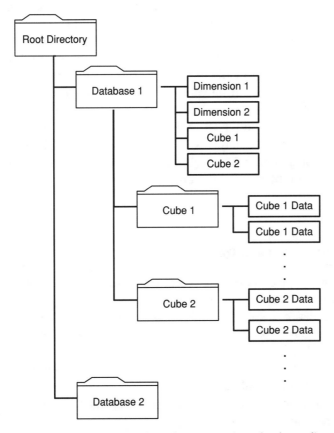

Figure 2.7   Representation of OLAP Services database directory structure.

directory that OLAP Services will use to place temporary working files. By default, this is the same directory as the database directory.

Although the files that hold dimension information and all MOLAP-format data are based on RDBMS tables, OLAP Services does not employ any means for tracking changes to these tables made by other software. Incorporating dimension and cube information from the tables requires OLAP Services to perform processing operations. Different kinds of processing are required depending on the structure that is being processed (dimension, cube, or partition) and on what has changed between the definitions and the tables since the last processing. Processing cubes and dimensions at the right times is critical if you want to ensure that clients are accessing accurate and complete information. All processing is transactional, from updating definitions to re-creating all stored aggregates. If any error is encountered during a processing operation, the transaction is unwound, and the database's data is left at the state it was in when the processing began.

All of the detailed information about a dimension (the names and keys of members, the values for member properties, and the parent-child relationships) is held within that dimension's file. When Microsoft OLAP Services processes the dimension, it creates or updates the dimension file's representation of the dimension based on the results of its SQL queries against the dimension's table(s). This includes incorporating values for all member properties within the dimension as well as structural information like the relationships between members in the hierarchy. Although OLAP Services requires this internal representation, the original tables may also be required when OLAP Services processes cubes. For example, the SQL that is generated to populate cubes with data may join fact tables to the dimension tables.

File System Placement of Database Files

Under Windows NT 4.0, the device and directory used for OLAP Services's root database directory should have sufficient storage and performance characteristics for data warehouse-like applications (a smaller number of large writes, and a larger number of read operations than write operations). Since all databases are in one directory tree, they will all be on one logical device. Windows 2000, which was not available when this book was written, is supposed to give you the ability to mount logical disk devices within a directory tree. Through this technique, you should be able to place the storage of different databases and different cubes within a database on separate devices.

OLAP Services also maintains its own internal representation of a cube, even when the cube's aggregations are fully stored as ROLAP partitions (which are entirely represented as RDBMS tables). In general, many of the modifications you can make to a cube's definition will cause it to be marked as "not up to date." The processing of a cube may involve more or less work by the server, depending on the type of change. (Chapter 10 goes into detail on the types of changes and their impacts.) In any event, OLAP Services does not track changes to the fact tables that form the raw data for the cubes. This creates the possibility that HOLAP and ROLAP cubes may be out of synch with their aggregations; see Chapter 10 for a discussion of this issue.

When cubes are divided into storage partitions, the partitions of the cube may be processed individually to incorporate new data without having to reprocess the entire cube. This is an important feature of partitions because it means that partitions that hold unchanged information do not need to be recalculated as new data comes in; only the partitions that hold new data need to be reprocessed.

We have included only a brief description of the implications of processing here. Chapter 10, which covers the maintenance of dimensions and cubes, provides a comprehensive road map to the impact that changes to and the processing of dimensions, cubes, and partitions have on any dependent cubes and partitions.

Dimensions and Processing

Dimensions can be processed in two ways, which are called "rebuild" and "incremental update." A *rebuild* process discards existing dimensional information and re-creates it all from the underlying tables. When a dimension is created for the first time, when levels have been added or removed, or when base members have been deleted, the dimension will need to be (re)built. If a dimension is rebuilt, its dependent cubes will need to be reprocessed as well.

Incremental update processing preserves the existing member key and name information. If a dimension has been incrementally updated, a dependent cube may still be used as it is by clients. Though it will not show data for any new members until it is reprocessed itself, a dependent cube will reveal these members in its metadata and in queries. When a dimension is changed only by the addition of members in one or more levels or when the DBA-defined member property values for members have changed, then the dimension may be processed by incremental update to pick up these changes.

Cubes and Processing

There are three types of processing for cubes and their partitions. They are called "full," "refresh," and "incremental update."

A *full* processing of a cube will re-create all partitions from scratch. All precalculated aggregates in all partitions are replaced by new ones. In addition, any dimensions that need reprocessing will be reprocessed, and any new dimension information from incrementally processed dimensions will be incorporated. It is possible for a full processing of a cube to trigger full processing of one or more of its dimensions, which will then impact other cubes. (This is discussed in Chapter 10.)

When a cube undergoes *refresh* processing, all aggregations in each partition of the cube are cleared and completely recalculated, but the dimension state remains unchanged. Refresh processing of a cube is equivalent to processing each partition of the cube. Processing an individual partition discards and recalculates all the stored aggregations in the one partition but leaves the other partitions of the cube untouched. The transactional nature of processing is such that when multiple partitions of a cube are being processed in a single operation, a failure or cancellation of processing in one partition will undo all of the partition processing already performed in that operation, and the original aggregates will be retained.

In *incremental update* processing, Microsoft OLAP Services uses a WHERE clause supplied by the DBA at the time of processing to select data from a fact table, create aggregations from it, and update the existing stored aggregations using the new aggregated values. This is suitable for instances when there is new fact data available, but the structure is otherwise unchanged. Incremental processing affects only one partition rather than the cube as a whole. If the partition was defined using a WHERE clause (described earlier in the "Partitions Based on Data Conditions" section), then the WHERE clause supplied for the incremental processing is combined with the WHERE clause in the partition definition, modifying its definition.

When incremental processing adds new data to ROLAP partitions, their existing summary tables are updated. OLAP Services first directs the underlying database to create new tables for aggregates of the new data, then performs an update step to incorporate new aggregates for existing rows, and finally performs an insert step to add in new aggregates where aggregate rows didn't exist before.

In this first release, the OLAP Services server does not remove the RDBMS tables created for an incremental process once the processing has been completed. This will hopefully have been corrected by a service pack by the time you read this.

When OLAP Services processes multiple partitions of a cube, its default behavior is to process all of them sequentially, though they might be on multiple machines or otherwise capable of being fruitfully parallelized. Through DSO, it is possible to specify that multiple partitions are built in parallel, which can provide a significant boost in total cube pre-aggregation speed (especially since ROLAP partitions are somewhat slow to create). While a detailed explanation of how to do this is outside the scope of this book, it is worth noting that taking good advantage of this functionality will require you to consider the number of distinct processes that can usefully happen in parallel. Too many concurrent processing operations on one machine will cause the process to be slower than it would if they were performed sequentially.

Client/Server Processing

When the PivotTable Service is connected to a Microsoft OLAP Services server, MDX is first parsed by the PivotTable Service, and the range of cell data required to satisfy the query is determined. If the necessary data exists in the PivotTable cache, then any required calculations are performed in the PivotTable service and delivered to the client. If the necessary data is not in the PivotTable cache, the PivotTable Service issues a query to the server for the required input data and stores it in its cache.

All calculated members and named sets defined for a cube are stored in the server as database objects that contain MDX commands that will create the corresponding members and sets. When the PivotTable Service first accesses metadata for a cube from the server, it downloads the definitions of all calculated members and named sets that are stored at the server to the client. The communication of calculated members is a two-way street; during a session, a client can create new calculated members, and the PivotTable Service will transmit the definition as needed to the server for server-side calculations. (Because they affect the design and optimization of applications, these features are discussed in Chapter 11.)

OLAP Services will attempt to distribute the processing between client and server based on the resources that are required to satisfy a query. For cubes stored at the server, if too much data will be passed across the network, then the calculations will be performed at the server and the results passed to the client. For example, querying for the top ten products in a small product dimension level could be easily handled at the client, while querying for the top ten products in a very large product dimension level would be handled at the server. (The definition of "large" is established in the server's performance options, which are accessible through DSO or through the OLAP Manager. The default is 1,000 members in the level.) The performance implications of server-side versus client-side calculation are discussed in Chapter 11.

When a client is connected to a database on the OLAP Services server, there are at least two and perhaps even more layers of cache that may be holding the data the layers of cache are using. PivotTable Service will first seek to satisfy the query out of its own cache. If it needs additional cells, it will go to the server, which will attempt to answer it out of its cache. If the required data is not in the server cache and an RDBMS level of a partition (either a ROLAP partition or the leaf level of a HOLAP partition) is involved, the server will generate SQL to retrieve it, and the RDBMS will also attempt to satisfy the query out of its own cache. (Note that the requested data may well not be in the RDBMS cache if it is not in the OLAP Services cache, because, presumably, the RDBMS is serving more clients than just the OLAP Services server.)

Given that the PivotTable Service has the ability to transform data held in its cache (take subsets, aggregate further, add calculations to, etc.), it will usually make sense from a resource point of view for a client to use the PivotTable Service as its cache manager rather than add yet another layer of caching on top. This, of course, is not an absolute because there may be performance reasons to use an application-level cache in some kinds of clients, but for typical end-user browsing of formatted numbers and text the investment in software layers will not likely pay off.

Summary

In this chapter we have examined the code components, data structures, and processing flows that comprise the Microsoft OLAP Services system and an OLAP Services database. We have explained these elements in enough detail so we can discuss them in greater depth as they become relevant to the particular application concerns covered in the remainder of the book. In Chapter 3, we will begin to bring these elements together by describing the basics of designing and implementing an OLAP Services database.

Database Design Basics

The last two chapters looked at the features involved in the logical and physical design and implementation of a Microsoft OLAP Services database. This chapter presents the practical steps required to put this accumulated knowledge to work and build an OLAP Services database. Each section covers various elements of this process, in the general order in which you would approach them in an actual project. Our coverage includes detailed explanations of what you need to do and why you need to do it. In Chapter 4 we then demonstrate specific step-by-step examples for building an OLAP Services database.

Designing and building useful OLAP Services databases encompasses many tasks. At the most basic level lie the more mundane mechanical chores of creating and editing databases and their various objects. As you'll see, Microsoft OLAP Services makes the physical implementation quite simple. This simplicity tempts us to dive right in and start creating our databases and cubes. With little thought, it's very possible to create a working multidimensional cube in a matter of minutes. Though it may prove an enjoyable exercise, however, it's doubtful that such a cube would provide much long-standing benefit.

The simplicity of Microsoft OLAP Services does not remove the complexity entailed in OLAP. It merely shifts the burden of some of OLAP's technical detail from human to machine. Building a successful implementation requires delving into the more creative process of analysis and design. Logical OLAP design methodologies lay outside the scope of this book. We limit our focus here to specific examples of the fundamental tasks that lead to a successful Microsoft OLAP Services project. We leave open the manner, order, and depth in which you choose to execute these tasks. For a detailed exploration of logical OLAP design, we recommend *OLAP Solutions* (Wiley, 1998) by Erik Thomsen.

As we discussed in Chapter 1, OLAP Services expects the data used to create OLAP databases to be organized in a star or snowflake warehouse schema. For many OLAP projects the structure of an existing warehouse will suffice. In some situations, however, reality will require new tables or views in the source database. Although this book is not intended as a primer for data warehousing, we will provide some guidance in how to adapt existing relational data for use with OLAP Services.

Steps for Creating an OLAP Services Database

There are seven basic steps to creating an OLAP Service database:

1. Know your data and what you're trying to understand.
2. Design the Microsoft OLAP Services dimension and cube schema.
3. Create an OLAP Services database in the OLAP Manager Console and create a connection to the source data.
4. Create dimensions that are based on tables in the data source.
5. Create one or more cubes that connect fact tables in the source data to dimensions created in OLAP Manager.
6. Define the initial partition(s) and their storage properties and aggregations for the cube(s) and process the partition(s) so as to populate the aggregations with data from the data source.
7. Define any necessary calculations on the aggregate data.

In this chapter we focus on the first two steps in the process: knowing the data and designing a database. In the next chapter we go through the last five steps—physically creating a database in OLAP Services.

Know Your Data and What You're Trying to Understand

Carpenters live by the maxim "measure twice, cut once." Correcting a measurement is much simpler than correcting an errant cut in a piece of wood. A bad measurement merely needs re-marking; a bad cut requires, at the least, more effort and time and, at the worst, throwing out a perfectly good piece of wood. With decision support, an OLAP solution is our "cut" and defined problems are our measurements. It behooves us to pay close attention to the words of the carpenter. Nothing leads to never ending or even failed projects faster than a solution created for a poorly defined problem. And because our solutions are always evolving to cover new problems, we will usually have to live with our cuts, both good and bad, for quite a while.

In Chapter 1 we first discussed the data schema required to feed OLAP Services. To recap that discussion for those diving in right here, OLAP Services requires an OLE DB data source that contains at least one fact table from which cubes can be built. Columns in the fact table define numeric measures (such as amount sold or sale price), broken out by each dimension to be used for analysis (such as time period, department, and customer). Data sources may also (and, as we'll explain later in the chapter, should) contain a collection of dimension tables that extend the dimensional information provided in the fact table. Dimension tables contain at least a key column and generally one or more description columns. Dimension tables may also contain columns for the attributes of individual dimension elements (such as product color or size) and keys to one or more other dimension tables. Dimension tables relate to a fact table through a key column. The relationship to the fact table can be direct (star schema) or indirect (snowflake schema) through one or more intermediate dimension tables. Though there are other variations, these are the schemata OLAP Services works with and the schemata that cover the majority of situations you'll run into.

To begin to understand the existing data for the purpose of analyzing it, you must start at the end, with what the analyst (maybe you) wishes to learn from the data. Knowing the types of questions an analyst may ask allows you to determine if the appropriate data exists, or if not how it can be obtained. It is not necessary (and not possible) to know all the specific questions the analyst will ask of the data. It is necessary (and possible) to know the nature and limits of the questions the analyst will ask. For example, if a financial analyst wishes to study expenses for various departments over time, the data source must contain a fact table that contains one or more expense measures by date and department. You also need to know as much as you can about the levels over which the analysis will take place. What granularities of time provide the greatest value? Of customer groups? Of product characteristics? Of geography? If one level satisfies a primary interest of the analyst, at what other levels would they look to put something they see into context? As the designer, you do not need to know at the outset which specific departments or dates must be included. At the minimum, you only need to make sure that you have data organized by department and date. Ideally, you should also confirm that you have data within the range of departments and time periods that the analyst wishes to study.

When starting a project with Microsoft OLAP Services, you should ensure that all of the following conditions are met in your logical and physical design:

- The required data must exist and aggregate through SUM, COUNT, MIN, or MAX functions.

- Dimension data must exist in appropriate table form.

- Desired dimension data must exist.

- Dimensions must have members at all aggregate levels.

- All facts in a table must relate to the same level of members in a dimension.

These five conditions are discussed in detail in the following sections.

The Required Data Must Exist and Aggregate with SUM, COUNT, MIN, or MAX Functions

As we mentioned in Chapter 1, OLAP Services only aggregates data within dimensions that are using summation (the default), count, minimum, and maximum functions. Some data, such as ratios, do not aggregate properly with any of these functions. To accurately report ratio measures, values must be calculated after the aggregation of a ratio's composite values. Consider Percent Profit, which is calculated as the ratio of Profit to Revenue. The total Percent Profit for all products does not equal the SUM (or MAX, MIN, or COUNT) of Percent Profit values for various products. To get the correct value for all products we must calculate the ratio after summing Revenue and Profit.

If the values required for a given ratio do not exist, it may be possible to back them out from the existing data. Continuing with our Percent Profit example, if Revenue and Percent Profit exist in the fact table but Profit does not, Profit can be determined for each row in the table by multiplying Revenue by Percent Profit. To provide Percent Profit for analysis, you can create a new fact table or view for use as the basis for your cube, or you can create a measure in a cube that is defined by an SQL function to derive a value for Profit prior to aggregation. Look for columns in your tables that represent rates or other ratios. Measures that are ratios are frequently multiplied with other facts that have related units, and aggregates of those products may be desired.

In some dimension hierarchies, data that may aggregate by summation does not simply roll up through addition. For example, in a dimension that represents a hierarchy of financial accounts, data values for most children roll up into their parents. Some parent values, however, are not necessarily the sum of all child values. All forms of revenue may roll up and all manner of expenses too. Profit, however, equals Revenue less Expenses. To obtain accurate Profit values in a financial account hierarchy we must either reverse the sign for expense items before they enter a cube or add calculated members that perform the subtraction. Note that calculated members can be more problematic. They do not fully participate in a hierarchy. Members may not roll up to a calculated member, and calculated members may not roll up values into other members, though they may be created as children of a base member.

Chapter 12, on advanced database and application design, and Chapter 15, a tutorial on healthcare benefits analysis, also discuss how to use account dimensions.

Dimension Data Must Exist in Appropriate Table Form

Microsoft OLAP Services requires that dimension information be laid out such that each aspect of each level forms its own column in the tables: all member identity keys, names, property values. Although this is one way to represent hierarchies in a relational database, it is not the only way. Figure 3.1 shows a situation in which dimension data may exist in a dimension table but be unusable by OLAP Services.

The dimension table form shown in Figure 3.1 contains every member within a hierarchy in a single column. The `parent_id` column determines the hierarchical relationship among members by relating each row back to the `member_id` column in another row. In this form of the table, hierarchical depth (distance from the root) and height (distance from the leaf) are also stored in separate columns. Tables in this form are very useful for two reasons. First, no special accommodations need to be made to represent an unbalanced hierarchy, where leaf members may be at different hierarchical distances from the root. Second, it is also very easy to move subtrees within the hierarchy (for example, to move a product from one category to another); only the parent key for the top node that is being moved needs to be changed.

Member_Id	Parent_Id	Member_Name	Generation	Level
0	0	Products	1	2
1	0	Widgets	2	1
2	0	Thingies	2	1
3	1	Super Widgets	3	0
4	1	Deluxe Widgets	3	0
5	2	Auto Thingies	3	0
6	2	Manual Thingies	3	0

Figure 3.1 A parent-child hierarchy table.

With OLAP Services, the easiest way to use the kind of table shown in Figure 3.1 is to use SQL to create a snowflake schema, with a new table for each level and a balanced hierarchy (Chapter 15 provides a detailed example that does just this). In a sense, this sort of parent-child hierarchy table is a union of a set of fully snowflaked dimension tables where all member information from all levels has been unioned together into just one table. If you anticipate that the dimension's hierarchical relationships may change over the lifetime of the dimension, or that the hierarchical relationships are far from balanced, you can help to simplify the maintenance task by deriving the snowflake tables from a tree table like that shown in Figure 3.1.

Advantages of Distinct Dimension Tables

OLAP Services can only create a dimension from columns in a table or tables. Dimensions may be created using one or more columns in a fact table or from one or more separate dimension tables. We strongly recommend that you utilize dimension tables that are distinct from any fact table although this is not a requirement for OLAP Services. This approach offers multiple advantages:

- It enhances usability while optimizing storage.
- It optimizes dimension maintenance.
- Members exist regardless of fact data, strengthening the concept of domain.

Enhances Usability while Optimizing Storage

With distinct dimension tables we can optimize storage for facts by using small dimension keys yet still provide our users with clear dimension information through the dimension tables. Separate dimension tables that join to the fact tables provide you with significant flexibility in dimensional structures and can save you large quantities of storage. In addition, because of the way Microsoft OLAP Services internally uses dimension and join key information when processing cubes and responding to queries, separate dimension tables can help these operations be more efficient as well.

Member names, of course, should always be descriptive. For the user, "Super Duper Widgets" makes more sense than "12987." Yet a fact table that contains twenty-five-character descriptions in dimension columns requires much more disk space than one that uses four-byte integers. Consider a 250,000-record fact table that contains three such dimensions along with some measures. A rough calculation of 250,000 rows * 3 columns * 25 bytes is 31,250,000 bytes in the fact table for keys alone (not to mention the requisite indexes). Using the integer key, however, would require 250,000 * 3 * 4 bytes, or 3,000,000 bytes. Moreover, all related indexes would be correspondingly smaller and much faster to build and search. This storage efficiency also gets carried through to OLAP Services storage because OLAP Services creates aggregations based upon the dimension key columns (regardless of partition type).

Optimizes Dimension Maintenance

Creating a separate dimension table saves processing time. When OLAP Services processes a dimension in any way, it performs a SELECT DISTINCT on the columns and expressions that describe the levels. When the dimension information is embedded within the fact table, this will be a much larger operation. There will be a much greater degree of redundancy in the dimension data held in the fact table, and the data involved in processing the dimension may be several orders of magnitude larger.

Members Exist Regardless of Fact Data

Defining dimensions on dimension tables that are separate from fact tables allows us to display dimension members even if the fact table contains no data for those members. We often gain significant insight when we discover that data related to a particular member doesn't exist for a given variable. Consider an analysis of sales data for a group of products, for example. A chart of sales by product from a cube that is using the fact table to define the product dimension might look like the chart shown in Figure 3.2. Basing products on a separate dimension table, however, would result in a chart similar to that shown in Figure 3.3.

Just a quick glance at the chart in Figure 3.3 readily reveals something that requires our attention. Either we have been selling no Wonder Widgets, the particular store in question does not carry Wonder Widgets, or our fact table lacks the needed data. For analysis, our dimensions form domain definitions that are separate from the facts they organize. If we separate out that domain information to a separate table, it becomes easier to validate the facts. Note that there are mechanical subtleties in the way OLAP Services queries dimension tables and fact tables such that discrepancies between the two will get resolved in different ways. When a cube is being processed based on that fact table, the fact data identified by dimension members that do not exist in the dimension structure (depending on the specific way in which the dimension and fact table are joined in the schema) would be ignored or result in errors. We explore this specific problem in greater detail in the section "All Facts Must Relate to the Same Level of Members in a Dimension" (though it's worthwhile to note here that this specific problem can be most easily prevented by enforcing referential integrity in the data source).

Fact tables do not need to contain separate columns for every dimension you wish to use to analyze the data the fact tables contain. Dimensions can also be

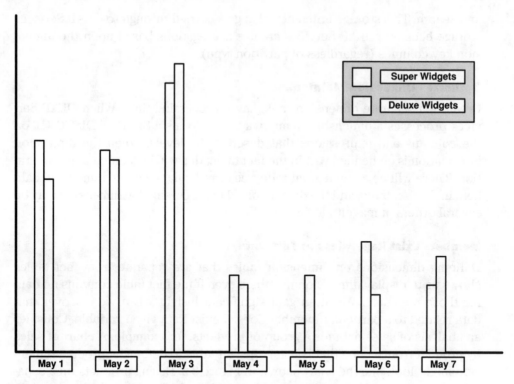

Figure 3.2 Sales by day based on products in fact table.

joined to a fact table indirectly through columns that are common with other dimension tables in a cube schema (at some point, at least one dimension table must join the fact table). For example, in a schema that involved "mini-dimensions" whose members were each clusters or tuples of members from other dimensions, the fact table can join to the dimension tables via the mini-dimension table. Figure 3.4 shows an example of a schema of patient visit information that is related to a minidimension composed of physician/ailment combinations.

TIP

The OLAP Manager will allow you to include any arbitrary table in your cube schema and create a join between it and any dimension table or the fact table. Through DSO, you can also perform the equivalent specification of joins between dimension and fact tables and other tables. While this capability appears at first glance to be a convenient way to limit the rows returned from a fact table or dimension table, it actually makes no difference. The first release of OLAP Services ignores any tables that are not actually dimension or fact tables or that do not somehow connect a fact table and dimension tables together.

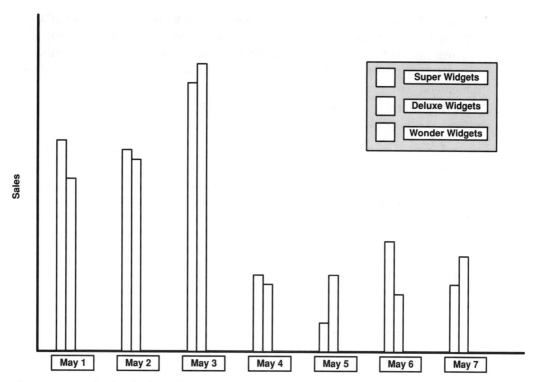

Figure 3.3 Sales by day based on products in dimension table.

Snowflake Dimensions and OLAP Services

It is much easier to manage dimension metadata by snowflaking dimension source tables than by using denormalized dimension tables. We strongly recommend that you use snowflaked dimension tables with Microsoft OLAP Services as much as possible. OLAP Services only uses inner joins to relate the tables of a dimension when it is processing that dimension. This ensures that all

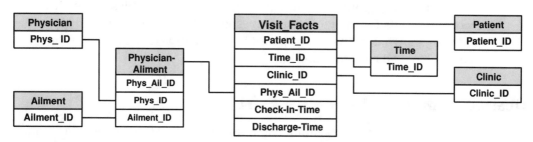

Figure 3.4 Star schema representation of fact table/minidimension/dimension join.

members in upper levels have at least one child in a lower level. Though this is a problem for dimensions with irregular hierarchies, it is a good thing for most dimensions. With snowflaked dimension tables, we are able to store additional properties for members at higher levels without increasing the size of our dimension tables. We also eliminate referential integrity problems between levels—for example, the possibility of inconsistent data values for member properties at non-leaf data.

Snowflaking dimension metadata is generally discouraged in traditional data warehousing, however. In comparison to a star schema, a snowflake schema introduces inefficiency into SQL queries through additional joins while saving only limited space. For example, say we want to view facts for states where states are the top level in a customer dimension that contains levels for state, city, and customer. With a snowflaked customer dimension the SQL would look something like this:

```
SELECT state.description, sum(fact.amount) as Amount
FROM fact INNER JOIN customer ON
  fact.customer_id = customer.customer_id INNER JOIN city ON
  customer.city_id = city.city_id INNER JOIN state ON
  city.state_id = state.state_id
GROUP BY state.description
```

However, with a geography dimension that follows a star schema, our query would look something like this:

```
SELECT state.description, sum(fact.amount) as Amount
FROM fact INNER JOIN customer ON
  fact.customer_id = customer.customer_id
GROUP BY state.description
```

In Microsoft OLAP Services we can use snowflaked dimension data without any such penalties. Because OLAP Services pre-joins and stores all dimension information in its own denormalized internal structures, it only needs to refer to dimension metadata in the data source when it is processing dimensions and cubes. Regardless of the form of storage, OLAP Services will use only the internal dimension information when it is processing queries made against a cube.

Moreover, if you are going to combine cubes whose facts enter at different levels of granularity, you must snowflake the dimension tables or you will get incorrect results for the facts that correspond to non-leaf levels. Adopting the policy of snowflaking wherever possible increases your flexibility in creating and combining dimensions and cubes.

Desired Dimension Data Must Exist

The simplest way to create dimension information is to use the value from a single column. For example, in a well-maintained data warehouse, the member identity keys for a dimension may be found as the values of a dimension key column in a dimension table, and a single descriptive name attribute column in that table may be exactly what you want to use as a member name column.

You may also derive dimension data (member names, member keys, and properties) from existing data using SQL column expressions. For example, in a customer dimension source table that has customer last name and first name as separate columns, a customer's full name could appear as the member name in a customer dimension level using an SQL function like

```
"customer"."lastname" + ", " + "customer"."firstname"
```

for the Member Name Column property. A powerful implication of the fact that you can use SQL functions to define levels is that you have the ability to create multiple levels based on condensed information in a single column. Consider an account column that contains a ten-character code. The first two characters identify a company, the next three a department, and the last five an account. To create an account dimension, you may define the member key for the top level as `SUBSTRING([column],1,2)`, the next level as `SUBSTRING ([column],3,3)`, and the bottom level as `SUBSTRING([column],6,5)`.

(These examples are based on a Microsoft SQL Server data source. The extent to which you can use SQL functions and specific syntax will depend on the SQL variant of your RDBMS source.) Having the ability to manipulate source columns like this in a Microsoft OLAP Services dimension definition allows us to use source tables with less massaging required ahead of time.

Using SQL Expressions to Define Dimension Members and Measures

You can define dimension members and cube measures with SQL expressions even if you do not have the ability to define views in the source. The power to be able to use any SQL expressions you want comes with a caveat, however: the SQL functions that you use depend on the SQL variant used by the source RDBMS. On the plus side, this allows you to leverage the power of the SQL native to the RDBMS. On the negative side, it can limit portability. For example, expressions that work against SQL Server may not work against Oracle8 or DB2, and code developed on Microsoft Access may not work against SQL Server. The databases that will need to deal with this most are those divided into multiple partitions or migrated from one server to another. OLAP databases created specifically for a single RDBMS source need not be concerned by it. We ourselves will use the Access variant, if any, because it offers readability and makes it easy to follow along with the examples that are provided.

Keys and OLAP Services

We will refer to key columns frequently throughout this book. The precise meaning of *key* depends on whether the word is used within the context of the relational data source, an OLAP Services dimension structure, or an OLAP Services dimension structure within a cube. It is important to understand the differences in meaning since the terminology increases the opportunity for confusion.

Within the context of a relational database, key columns refer to primary and foreign key columns. For example, in a properly designed relational warehouse, a dimension table will have a primary key column that relates to a foreign key column in the fact table. Figure 3.5 shows a typical relationship between a dimension table and a fact table.[1]

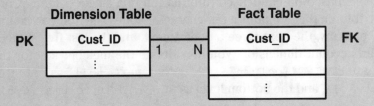

Figure 3.5 Diagram of typical fact table/dimension table relationship.

Within the context of a dimension, however, the key column refers to the column that contains identifiers for a level's members. A key column may or may not be used to join the dimension table to other dimension tables in the dimension schema or the fact table in a cube schema. A dimension level's key column also may or may not be the same as the column that defines the member name. Figure 3.6 shows a fact table/dimension table relationship in which the primary key for the dimension table is not a part of the dimension definition.

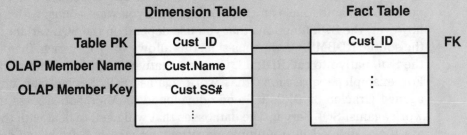

Figure 3.6 Diagram of fact table/dimension table relationship where dimension table key is not part of dimension definition.

[1] Primary key and foreign key here are functional relationships. Many properly designed warehouses will not declare them as such in their data definition language (DDL), however.

TIP

To alleviate confusion, we will use the terms *table keys* or *join keys* when referring to traditional keys in the relational data source and *member key columns* when referring to the key columns that define members in dimension levels.

Member Names

Although member names do not need to be unique within a level, each member within a level should be uniquely identified by concatenating its name with the names of all of its ancestors. For example, while there may be a single member key that corresponds to the state named Oregon and the city named Portland as well as a single member key that corresponds to the state named Maine and the city named Portland, there must not be two member keys corresponding to the state named Oregon and the city named Portland. If two member keys whose names and ancestors' names were the same, there would be no way to uniquely reference them in queries.

When a non-textual type is used for member names, you may want to explicitly convert the name to a string to take control of the numbers created. Otherwise, the default function used by OLAP Services that converts the value in a record to a string may give you a result other than what you want. For example, if the days of the month are represented as standard strings of digits ("1" through "31"), when they are ordered by name they will end up in the order "1", "10", "11", …, "2", "20", … etc. If they were represented instead as "01", "02", … "31", then they would be sorted into the order "01", "02", …, "10", "11", …, "20", …

Dimensions Must Have Members at All Aggregate Levels

As we discussed in Chapter 1, dimension hierarchies in OLAP Services are fully connected: members in non-leaf levels must have children in the next lower level.

Duplicate Member Names: A Caution

Be aware that the first release of Microsoft OLAP Services does not enforce uniqueness for names as reliably as it does for keys. For a sufficiently large number of duplicate member name values in a level, OLAP Services will return a "Dimension Member Is Not Unique" error when processing the dimension. Unfortunately, the value of "large" is random. Sometimes OLAP Services will return an error for only a single duplicate member name value; sometimes it won't return an error until there are 1,000 duplicate values. Hopefully, a service pack that fixes this bug will be available by the time you read this.

Figure 3.7 illustrates a simple geography dimension hierarchy that has levels for state and city as well as its source table. Every state has at least one child city.

We may often find, however, that our dimension data does not fit the schema shown in Figure 3.7. Finance and budgeting databases often present these types of problems. Figure 3.8 shows a simple financial account hierarchy where not all members have children at lower levels.

In the simple hierarchy shown in Figure 3.8, "Cost of Goods" and "Misc. Costs" have no children while "Taxes" has two children. We call such dimension hierarchies *irregular hierarchies*. Figure 3.9 shows snowflaked dimension tables that define these hierarchies in a data source. Using SQL, we can get a fair representation of the dimension hierarchy by querying the tables using an outer join. For example,

```
SELECT acct_category.category_id, account.account_id FROM acct_category
LEFT OUTER JOIN account ON acct_category.category_id = account.category_id
```

would include all account categories whether or not they are represented in data in the account table. However, Microsoft OLAP Services only uses straight joins when it is processing a dimension that is based on snowflaked dimension tables. The data set that results from a straight join between the two dimension tables based on the `category_id` column would not include records for categories that have no related records in the account table. Consequently, the resulting OLAP Services dimension would also not include those members.

State	City
Massachusetts	Boston
Massachusetts	Cambridge
California	Los Angeles
California	San Francisco

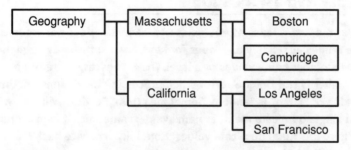

Figure 3.7 A simple geography dimension and its data source.

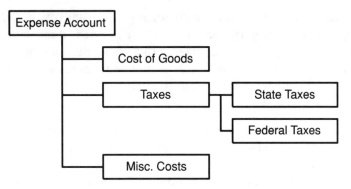

Figure 3.8　Simple irregular hierarchy.

One solution to this problem would be to create a view in the data source that joins the snowflaked tables with an outer join so as to create a data set that includes all members of the dimension and then base our dimension on this view. Note that in the data set returned by this view the accounts for the categories with no children appear as NULL or empty. "Cost of Goods" and "Misc.

Category_Id	Category_Description
01	Cost of Goods
02	Taxes
03	Misc Costs

Category_Id	Account_Id	Account_Description
01	00001	State Taxes
02	00002	Federal Taxes

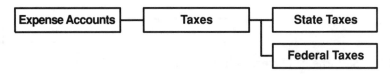

Figure 3.9　Snowflake schema of irregular hierarchy and OLAP Services dimension.

Costs" would have children, though with member key and name values of NULL. Although it may seem surprising, in an OLAP Services dimension, NULL (or an empty string) is a perfectly valid member key or name value. When OLAP Services creates the dimension it will include all members present in the data set, including NULL members in lower levels. Figure 3.10 shows a view and the dimension based on this view.

OLAP Services allows members to have NULL key and name values as a practical way to accommodate the fact that it requires all members to be in named levels. The real world does not always fit within a structure of fixed levels, and we frequently use irregular hierarchies to handle and capture the complexity we find in it. While OLAP Services allows NULL member names and NULL member keys, from a conceptual point of view we really want to have some other value for the name of a member at any given level. Blank names appearing as the result of a query may cause more than one user a good deal of confusion.

If the SQL dialect of your RDBMS data source supports conditional operators in column expressions, you could create a name for a blank member that is equal to the value of its parent. Using our account example with a Microsoft SQL Server database, the column definition for account_description would be:

```
ISNULL(accounts.account_description, accounts.category_description)
```

Category_Id	Category_Description	Account_Id	Account_Description
01	Cost of Goods		
02	Taxes	00001	State Taxes
03	Taxes	00002	Federal Taxes
04	Misc Costs		

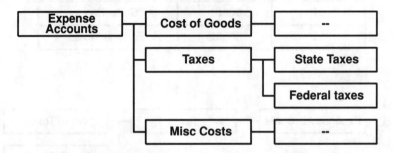

Figure 3.10 Star schema of irregular hierarchy and OLAP Services dimension.

You can include such a column expression in an SQL view to be used as the source table for the dimension or in the Member Name property of the level in the definition of the OLAP Services dimension. Using the name of the nearest ancestor that has a name in place of NULL is more useful than using some arbitrary fixed name (such as "input" or "dummy").

Although later in this chapter we fully describe the steps for creating a dimension in OLAP Services, we will briefly suspend our discussion of dimension source data here to explore how OLAP Services handles duplicate member keys in dimensions' source data. We noted in Chapter 2 that Microsoft OLAP Services stores all dimension data in internal dimension structures. Processing a dimension creates these structures by retrieving data from the data source according to the dimension design. By default, when we add a level to a dimension while designing our dimensions in OLAP Manager or through DSO, OLAP Services assumes that all member keys in the level are unique within the dimension. If they are not, OLAP Services will complain with a "Duplicate Member Key" error when the dimension is processed. Setting a level's "Unique Members" property ("isUnique" in DSO) to "False" tells OLAP Services to qualify members at the tagged level with member keys at upper levels when building the internal dimension structures. In our earlier example, the member keys for the children of "Cost of Goods" and "Misc. Costs" are both NULL. To uniquely identify them we need to include references to the parent by setting the "Unique Members" (or "isUnique") property of the account level to False.

Non-Leaf Data Entry

Of course, in analysis we may not always care about data below a certain dimension level. Consider an expense budgeting cube for a department store chain that has a Store dimension containing levels for Store and Store Department. Many expenses, such as heating, taxes, or rent, may apply only to the entire store and not to specific departments. A fact table that contains these expenses mixed with departmental expenses may contain empty values in the Store Department dimension column. While the company may enter budget amounts at various levels, we can satisfactorily analyze all of our data at the store level. To accurately view budgets in a Microsoft OLAP Services cube and to hold these store-wide-only amounts, we have two choices. We can choose to add an additional member to the department level of the Store dimension that represents the "All-store input." This is analogous to what we did for our earlier chart of account example. We can also choose to design our cube so that data enters at the Store level instead of at the Store Department level. In this case, through virtual cubes we will still be able to use this cube's data with data that enters at other levels in other cubes.

Although you may utilize a shared dimension that has multiple levels in any cube, fact data does not need to enter the cube at the leaf level defined for the dimension. Within a cube you may redefine a non-leaf level as the leaf level by disabling all levels below the data level contained in the fact table. You need to disable these levels for the data to enter the cube correctly. When OLAP Services reads records from the fact table, it will create a join to the lowest enabled level of a cube. If you don't disable the lower levels, the fact table will be processed as though the data actually entered the cube at the leaf level (and then aggregated). In the event that the fact table corresponds with a level that is higher than the lowest in the cube, that join will duplicate each fact record for as many times as it has descendants from the level of input. Figure 3.11 diagrams this situation.

Note that when you are disabling levels, for all intents and purposes these levels and their members do not exist in the cube. The cube's metadata that is exposed to clients through OLE DB for OLAP will not contain these levels or members. When an MDX expression refers to these disabled levels or their members and error will result at the client. Likewise, MDX set operators will not reveal these members: requesting the child of a lowest-non-hidden-level member will result in an empty set of children. In applications some facts enter the cube at a non-leaf level, you will need to have the ability to allocate this data or otherwise work with it at lower levels. In these applications you will need to use virtual cubes. We discuss this further in the section titled "Virtual Cubes."

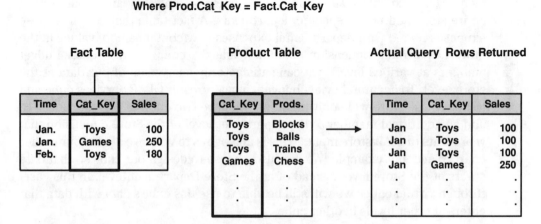

Figure 3.11 Table schema, join, and duplicated records as a result.

All Facts in a Table Must Relate to the Same Level of Members in a Dimension

As we described in Chapter 1, each fact must relate to a single member in the lowest level used by each dimension in a cube. Consider a simple cube with sales dimensioned by time, products, and geography. Time contains levels for year, month, and day; products contains levels for product category and product; and geography contains levels for state and city. Figure 3.12 shows sample data from a fact table for this cube.

In the fact table shown in Figure 3.12 sales are generated from days in different months, products in different product categories, and cities in different states. Dimension columns contain only member keys for a single level in their respective dimensions. This is a very ordinary case. Our products are identified by individual name or SKU, our cities or stores are identified by name, our time is identified by date, and we can summarize our data. If one of the dimension columns contained a member key value for a higher level in the dimension (say the last record contained a geography member key value for Rhode Island instead of Providence) then that fact would be ignored or would generate an error when the cube is processed. Whether the data is ignored or there is an error depends on the member key column that is defined in the cube for the level used.

Let's return to the case of the irregular hierarchy described earlier. To relate specific facts to specific members in our accounts dimension the fact table would need to include columns for both category and account because the values in the leaf level alone do not clearly identify a single member in the dimension. If the fact table included only the account column, the relationship between facts for "Cost of Goods" and "Misc. Costs" would be ambiguous because there are identical member key values for accounts below both the "Cost of Goods" and "Misc. Costs" categories.

NULL values for some of our member's keys will also cause problems in our cubes. These problems stem from the mechanics of Microsoft OLAP Services and the SQL it generates. As we discussed in Chapter 2, OLAP Services generates SQL to retrieve data from the data source so it can populate aggregations

Day	Product	Geography	Sales
12/3/1998	Flutie Flakes	Buffalo	$500
12/3/1998	Pot Roast	Philadelphia	$600
1/6/1999	Coffee Milk	Providence	$50

Figure 3.12 Fact table for simple sales cube.

with that data. The SQL generated is based upon the measures and dimensions that are defined in the cube schema. By default, the dimension member key columns in the SQL statement are based upon the member key column assigned in the dimension. To populate a simple cube using only our earlier example of an expense accounts dimension, OLAP Services would use the following SQL:

```
SELECT "dim_acct_star_nochild"."category_id",
"dim_acct_star_nochild"."account_id",
"fact_star_nochild"."amount"
FROM "fact_star_nochild", "dim_acct_star_nochild"
WHERE ("dim_acct_star_nochild"."category_id"="fact_star_nochild"."cate-
gory_id") AND
("dim_acct_star_nochild"."account_id"="fact_star_nochild"."account_id")
```

If account values are NULL, this SQL would not return values for "Cost of Goods" and "Misc. Costs" since inner joins discard rows that join on a NULL value. Within the context of the cube, however, we can modify the member key column used by any dimension level in the cube to point to any other column in any other table (this can be done either through DSO or the OLAP Manager). The following SQL results when the member key value for the category and account levels in the cube is changed so as to pull the values from the fact table instead of the dimension table:

```
SELECT "fact_star_nochild"."category_id",
"fact_star_nochild"."account_id", "fact_star_nochild"."amount" FROM
"fact_star_nochild"
```

You may notice that this second statement is also much more efficient than the first. When we build our cube in Chapter 4 and later in Chapter 11 on optimizing databases and queries, we discuss in more detail how specifying the member key column can improve processing performance.

TIP

You'll be able to optimize your cube for better processing performance if the member key values in the leaf level of a dimension are unique and the dimension table joins to the fact table by this key.

There is an alternative to including both dimension columns for this single dimension in the fact table. Instead, we could create a single table instead of a view for our dimension and add a primary key column with unique values for each dimension member at the leaf level (see Figure 3.13). We can reduce the two columns that contain member keys in our fact table to a single column that contains key values that are related to our new dimension table. Doing this identifies the unique member, which avoids any possible problems created by NULL member keys. This approach also affords us the usual benefits of com-

Pk_Id	Category_Id	Category_Description	Account_Id	Account_Description
1	01	Cost of Goods		
2	02	Taxes	00001	State Taxes
3	02	Taxes	00002	Federal Taxes
4	03	Misc Costs		

Figure 3.13   Star schema of irregular hierarchy and OLAP Services dimension.

pact opaque dimension join keys. The SQL that Microsoft OLAP Services would use to populate a cube based on these tables would be the following:

```
SELECT "dim_acct_star_nochild"."category_id",
"dim_acct_star_nochild"."account_id", "fact_star_nochild"."amount"
FROM "fact_star_nochild", "dim_acct_star_nochild"
WHERE
("dim_acct_star_nochild"."pk_id"="fact_star_nochild"."expense_pk_id")
```

We can get even better mileage out of this table by following the optimization tip we just offered. To do this, we set the member key column for the accounts level in our dimension definition to the pk_id column in the dimension source table and the "Unique Members" property for the level to "True." In the cube we set the member key column for the accounts level to the related column in the fact table. When processing the cube, OLAP Services would use the following SQL:

```
SELECT "fact_star_nochild"."account_pk_id", "fact_star_nochild"."amount"
FROM "fact_star_nochild"
```

Unique Member Key Values

In the member key column of the source table levels in a dimension can be tagged as having unique values. For example, think of a geography dimension that uses the levels of state and city. If state is the top level in a geography dimension, states will logically be unique. In this dimension, Cities (if keyed by city name) may not be unique within the city level because the level would contain duplicate values for cities that are common to multiple states (such as Portland in both Maine and Oregon). However, if the identity keys defined by the member key column for the city level are unique, then OLAP Services can consider the members as unique even if two or more share the same name. OLAP Services utilizes the Unique Members property to optimize SQL queries that are generated internally. If members at a level are unique, OLAP Services only has to specify member key values from that column to access the correct records through SQL. Otherwise, to distinguish them it needs to include the member key columns from higher levels as well.

If a fact table uses non-unique member keys to hold data at a level, then OLAP Services will not be able to avoid joining the dimension table to the fact table when it processes a cube. Note that if you tag a level as having unique members and the members are not truly unique, OLAP Services will generate an error when it attempts to process the dimension.

Section Summary

Microsoft OLAP Services is flexible in how it attaches to dimension and fact table structures. Depending on the requirements of your application, you may need to devote more or less attention to putting your data into a particular form so as to take advantage of features of OLAP Services. In this section, we have focused on how to understand your database and ready it for use by OLAP Services. In the next section, we will begin to explore how to approach the design of a database in OLAP Services.

Design OLAP Services Dimensions and Cubes

Just as relational database design requires that you make decisions about table structure and contents and the relationships among tables, OLAP database design requires that you make decisions about cube and dimension structures and contents and their relationships with each other. OLAP Services presents you with myriad options for organizing your databases. As we have seen, dimensions come in such flavors as shared, private, and virtual. Dimensions may contain multiple levels, and levels may have member properties that are associated with level members. A database may contain one or many cubes that are either of the stored or virtual flavors. The number of dimensions and cubes you may create depends upon the data you have to work with. The various flavors and options you select will depends upon the presentation you wish to offer and the performance characteristics you wish to enable.

This section covers the broad design decisions you need to make before building your OLAP database. We cover in detail those options and features that can have a dramatic effect on your upfront design. There are significant interrelationships between features as well as between features and table structures. Those features and options that do not alter design decisions are described step-by-step in Chapter 4. We will cover the settings that may be safely modified later but that have important ramifications for maintenance and/or optimization in detail in Chapter 10.

Dimension and Cube Names

Determine the names you really want for your dimensions and cubes before creating anything! Once a dimension or cube is created and saved, its name *cannot* be changed. This is particularly important if you should ever need to use multiple hierarchies (which we will get to later in this chapter) because multiple hierarchies are designated only through dimension names.

Dimension and cube names (and indeed all Microsoft OLAP Services object names except for non-measure members) may consist of only letters, digits, spaces, underscores, and the characters @ and #. Dimension and cube names must also start with a letter, and OLAP Services strips leading or trailing spaces when the dimension or cube is saved. An exception to this are dimensions, which can also contain a single period in their names. This is used to denote multiple hierarchies for a dimension.

Shared versus Private Dimensions

When building dimensions, one decision you need to make is whether to create them as shared or private. Private dimensions can be defined from separate dimension tables just like shared dimensions. Private dimensions will always be processed with the cube, so there is no chance that a private dimension will be either incrementally or fully processed separately from the cube. However, private dimensions and shared dimensions have the same characteristics regarding the existence of members and the requirement that join keys be

Some Things You Just Can't Change

Although you can change your mind about almost any property for anything you create in OLAP Services, there are a few things that cannot be modified:
—Database names
—Dimension (virtual and shared) names
—Cube (real and virtual) names
—A cube's data source
—A dimension's data source

To change any of these, you must discard the original database cube or dimension and rebuild it from scratch. Note that this can have a domino effect on other objects. For example, if you delete a dimension, OLAP Services will remove it from any cubes that use it and delete any virtual dimensions that are based on member properties in the dimension's levels. Full documentation of the effects of changes made in OLAP Services can be found in Chapter 10.

present for rows in the fact table. Although OLAP Services does not provide any interface in the OLAP Manager for doing this, member properties can be defined upon private dimensions just as on shared dimensions through DSO. The only major limitation of private dimensions, apart from the fact that you cannot join to another cube via that dimension, is that virtual dimensions cannot be defined from the properties of private dimensions. By using the appropriate naming, private dimensions can participate in multiple hierarchies with other private dimensions or shared dimensions in the cube.

In general, a dimension should be shared unless there is a compelling reason to keep it private to a cube (such as a prohibiting it from being used in another regular cube). Private dimensions offer no significant advantages over shared dimensions, but they do require that the cube be fully processed if there are any changes to the dimension or its data.

Multiple Hierarchies

In the first release of Microsoft OLAP Services, multiple hierarchies are defined through a naming convention that uses dot notation within a dimension's name. For example, to create two hierarchies within a product dimension—one containing products organized by product category and one organized by manufacturer—you create two dimensions with the appropriate levels, naming them "Product.ByCategory" and "Product.ByManufacturer", respectively. It is up to the client whether they are treated as distinct dimensions or two hierarchies within a single dimension. The current OLAP Manager interface always treats multiple hierarchies as distinct dimensions. Note that the OLAP Manager does not require these dimensions to have any characteristics in common outside of their name. You will therefore need to ensure that common levels and common members have appropriate names and settings and are defined on the correct table or set of tables. Because multiple hierarchies are just defined by names, you can also define multiple virtual dimensions as being hierarchies of a dimension.

As we mentioned earlier in this chapter, one side effect of each logical hierarchy being a separate physical dimension is that OLAP Services will create aggregations between the two dimensions. For example, as illustrated in Figure 3.14, if you create fiscal-year and calendar-year hierarchies for time and use them both in a cube, OLAP Services may create aggregations that intersect meaningless combinations of levels (like an aggregation that stores data at the fiscal-quarter, calendar-month level). The larger the database in terms of level-combinations from each dimension and the larger the total cell space of the cube, the larger the number of aggregations created to support meaningless space will be. For some dimensions and cubes, such aggregations may always be meaningless, and for other dimensions and cubes there might be a justification for clients to create

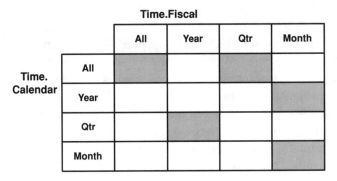 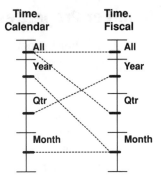

Figure 3.14 A multiple hierarchy and meaningless aggregations.

queries as though they were independent dimensions. (However, if that really were the intent of the database, you should just declare the two as separate dimensions so as to make the metadata description of the cube clear.)

The ideal pattern of meaningful aggregations would look like the aggregations shown in Figure 3.15. From Chapter 1, you may recall that this ideal pattern of aggregations has the same pattern as the applicability range of measures in virtual cubes. There are significant design and implementation trade-offs between creating a regular cube that uses multiple hierarchy-dimensions and composing a virtual cube that uses multiple hierarchies out of regular cubes, which each use a single hierarchy-dimension. This is an advanced cube construction topic that we will treat thoroughly in Chapter 12, on advanced database and application design.

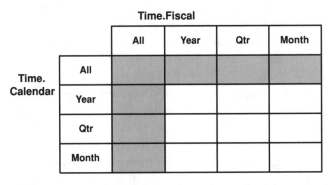 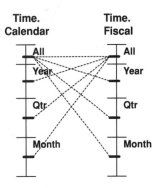

Figure 3.15 A multiple hierarchy and meaningful aggregations.

Member Properties

Member Properties allow you to economically store properties for members in a given level in the dimension structure. Microsoft OLAP Services permits you to base the property on almost any columns in any table that is included in the dimension schema. These properties can be used in MDX queries to filter result sets or to create virtual dimensions (discussed in the next section) so that cube data can be viewed accordingly. You may wish to use member properties to create alternative labels for members (such as product number and product name) or values that apply to a member regardless of any other dimension (such as a product's color or weight).

Member property values must be unique for each member within the level it is assigned. That is, each member in a level can have only one corresponding value in the data source column that is selected for a member property for that level. For example, "Week Number" can be a property of a specific date because any date belongs to only one week. "Date," however, cannot be a property of months because months may have more than one date.

Unlike measures, member properties are not automatically aggregated. When OLAP Services queries for a dimension's property values, it issues a SELECT DISTINCT for all members of a level and their properties. No GROUP BY clause is created, so any aggregations that would be part of the process of creating a member property would need to be performed behind a view. However, as we mentioned earlier in the chapter, member properties can be defined with SQL expressions that are based on columns in the dimension source table.

As we described in Chapter 1, OLAP Services treats and stores member properties as text regardless of their actual data type. If the member properties are not textual, you may want to take explicit control over how they are represented as a string. To do this you can convert the member properties to the desired formatted string by using an SQL expression for either a column in a view that is used as the source of the dimension or the property's source column in the dimension definition. For example, you may wish a price to be displayed with two or three decimal places, or you may wish to format a commission as a percentage. A client will not need to devote any logic to converting the property to a string for display. However, a client will have to perform its own processing of the returned property value if it wishes to display it in a different format. This is especially true of date/time values. Clients that wish to do additional calculations using the properties, or that otherwise wish to use the property value as a number, will need to interpret the strings as numbers (and, in the case of percentages, scale the quantity down by a factor of one hundred).

Virtual Dimensions

Member properties may be used to create virtual dimensions. As we discussed in Chapter 1, virtual dimensions can be used to provide added dimensional analysis in a cube, which decreases cube storage size but increases query processing time. Virtual dimensions contain only a base level and an All level. To the degree that data must aggregate from real members to a virtual member or to the virtual All, OLAP Services will perform the aggregations at query time. Because aggregations of a virtual dimension will not be stored on the server, several small virtual dimensions can noticeably decrease the storage that is required for aggregates in comparison with equivalent real dimensions. There is no free lunch, however—those same dimensions will noticeably increase the time it takes to satisfy queries. For example, consider a dimension that contains 50,000 products with about 50 different values for a member property of color. Assuming for the sake of clarity that colors are evenly distributed among products, we would have 1,000 products per color. This means that OLAP Services must aggregate about 1,000 product values per virtual member returned with each query against the cube! There is no or little additional calculation required to return a base measure value for a virtual dimension's All member, as it will be the same as the value for the underlying regular dimension's All member.

Virtual dimensions give you the flexibility to use multiple properties of a real dimension to break the dimension out on multiple display axes. For example, given a single time dimension in a cube, you can use a virtual dimension of month name/number to display months for a year on rows of a query and the years across the columns. Figure 3.16 diagrams this schema and shows a sample query grid.

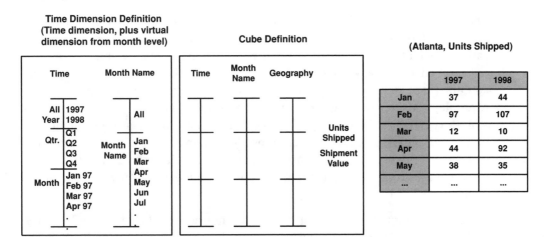

Figure 3.16   Virtual dimension from a regular dimension providing a breakout dimension.

Virtual dimensions also provide useful alternate hierarchies for the underlying base dimension, and they can be named so they appear as an additional hierarchy in the base dimension. Notice that in order to use them as alternate hierarchies of the underlying dimension, you must name the regular dimension with a hierarchy-dimension name (like `Time.ByCalendar`). If you don't, Microsoft OLAP Services will not let any virtual dimension share its dimension name prefix.

Virtual Cubes

Virtual cubes allow you to provide a single view on multiple cubes. With virtual cubes you may view multiple cubes' measures along both common and distinct dimensions. They store no aggregations of their own, though they may contain calculated members and other definitions. A virtual cube can contain any dimension of any cube upon which it is based. Common dimensions are shared as single dimensions while measures dimensions are not to be shared.

With virtual cubes you can provide a common framework for multiple cubes of related dimensionality that contain data that enters at different levels. The enabling or disabling of levels for a virtual cube is completely separate from the enabling or disabling of levels for its input cubes. As a result, when you browse the virtual cube you will be able to query and create calculations with members in the lowest level defined by the dimension itself, regardless of level enabling/disabling in any of the base cubes. For the budgeting cube that has data entering at both department and store levels, you would be able to see actual data down to department, along with budget data at the store level, and you would be able to calculate new department-level measures based on actual and budget measures. Figure 3.17 shows an MDS of the three cubes and the regions of the virtual cube where the different measures will be applicable.

The ability for dimension levels that are disabled in a regular cube to be enabled in a dependent virtual cube helps with data browsing and analysis because cells can be calculated and viewed for the lowest level used in any cube. However, it does not change how write-back functions: only at their lowest level in a regular cube (in all dimensions) can measures be written to from a virtual cube. For example, consider our earlier budget analysis virtual cube, which combines store-level actuals input, department-level actuals input, store-level budget input, and department-level budget input. In this example, measures from the store-level budget cube could only be updated from the cube at the store level, and measures from the department-level budget cube could only be input at the department level.

There is one important implication for the interaction of a virtual cube and a write-back-enabled regular cube from which it is built: if a virtual cube does not include all dimensions of the source cube down to the levels at which data is

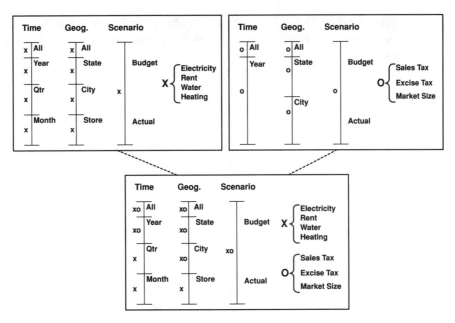

Figure 3.17   Two base cubes of the same dimensions but different levels, a virtual cube, and measure applicability ranges.

input, users will not be able to write data back to the underlying cube through the virtual cube.

When you encounter difficulties designing a cube, pause to consider whether a virtual cube offers a solution. As our earlier department store chain budget example showed, our warehouse contained budgeted expense information by store and actual expense information by store and department. One option for including both pieces of information in the same cube was to modify the fact and dimension tables to include a member for budget data in the department level. However, corporate policy may not allow us to make such modifications in the warehouse. We could write a memo to the warehouse people and wait for them to make the change for us, or we can create a virtual cube that contains measures for the actual and budget cubes, sharing the store dimension between them. We can then add calculated members to the cube so as to provide information such as variances between budget and actual.

You can also use virtual cubes to solve certain security scenarios. Consider a cube for analyzing labor expenses that includes dimensions for business unit, time, activity, and employee. While we want all of our users to be able to view all labor costs by business unit, time, and activity, we don't want everyone to be able to see sensitive data broken out by employee. To accomplish this without creating a whole new cube, you can create a virtual cube that is based on the labor expense cube but omits the employee dimension. You can then give read permission for the virtual cube to all users but restrict access to the real cube to only those users allowed to view labor costs by employee. For more detailed information about using virtual cubes to solve security issues, see Chapter 13.

The first release of the OLAP Manager for Microsoft OLAP Services offers only a wizard for creating and modifying virtual cubes. The wizard allows you only to select dimensions and measures and name the cube. When selecting like-named measures, the wizard creates new names for the duplicate measures by appending a number to the original measure name, incremented by the order in which they are added. For example, if you create a virtual cube using two cubes that contain an "amount" measure, adding both measures to the virtual cube will result in an "amount" and an "amount 1" measure. Unfortunately, the OLAP Manager offers no way to determine which cube these amount measures actually originate from. If you didn't write the source of the cube's measures down, you won't be able to find the source later unless you do some programming with DSO. OLAP Manager currently offers no interface for adding calculated members or modifying member names. These tasks must be accomplished with DSO using an application development language such as Visual Basic or Delphi. By the time you read this, however, utilities should be available from Microsoft and third-party developers that enable more granular manipulation of virtual cubes without forcing you to do your own DSO programming.

Partitions

As we explained in the previous chapter, the Enterprise version of Microsoft OLAP Services allows you to create multiple partitions for each cube. Because of partitions' ability to physically implement logical segments of data, they offer a powerful tool for both maintaining and optimizing a system. You should give careful thought in the initial design of the system because partitions can add duplicate data or eliminate vital data if you are not careful with them.

Every cube has at least one partition. The primary or default partition gets created automatically when you create the cube. This default partition may be modified in the same way as any other partition. Although you cannot define a slice or filter when you first create a cube, you can define a slice or WHERE clause filter for the primary partition after the cube has been created. This should be done before you process the cube, however, so cube data will reflect the slice definition when it is processed.

Take a look at your data and consider the applications you will build upon it. How often will the data source be updated? Will updates include distinct chunks of data? Will queries access certain slices of data more heavily than others? Will your data be drawn from different databases on different servers, or will it all come from one database?

Use slices to define data in the partition and filters only to filter out unnecessary or overlapping data. Although slices and filters do the same thing when you are loading data, Microsoft OLAP Services will use slices when it resolves queries submitted to a given cube. If a query requires no data from a partition defined by a given slice, OLAP Services will not attempt to retrieve data from that partition when it processes the query. Consider a cube with two partitions sliced by year. To answer a query for data in 1998, OLAP Services will only access the partition defined as containing 1998 data. As you may guess, this can have a tremendous effect on response time for large cubes, particularly for queries that must reach into the underlying fact table in HOLAP or ROLAP partitions.

Things to Watch Out For: Overlapping Partitions

We briefly mentioned in Chapter 1 that OLAP Services does not track overlapping partitions and that overlapping partitions can cause double-counting if they share any fact rows. Because it is important to understand why this is, let's examine it further.

Figure 3.18 diagrams five partitions that have been defined for a cube. Each of the current year's quarters has its own partition, as does the prior year. This is

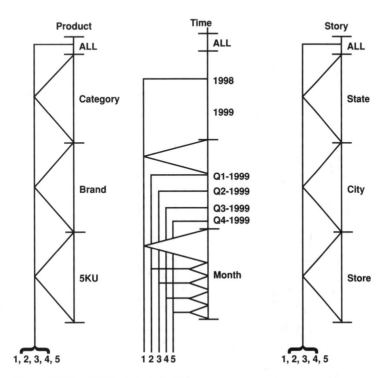

Figure 3.18   MDS of five partitions.

a sensible partition structure to have when partitions are being used to manage updates of data. Set up this way, the current year will be just fine.

Now, let's fast-forward in time. The year changes, and the DBA adds a new year, new quarters, and new months to the time dimension. He or she also adds a partition for the first quarter of the new year. Since the prior year is now stable, the DBA adds a partition for the 1999 slice. An MDS of this is shown in Figure 3.19. Do you see the problem that's brewing?

The MDS clearly shows the difficulty. In addition to the partitions for each of the four quarters for 1999, there is also a partition for the year 1999, which includes all of 1999's quarters as well. If these partitions share a fact table, then the values will double-count. Although OLAP Services will not attempt to populate any partition with data that does not belong in it, the fact that applications can find it useful to store data for the same cells in multiple partitions means that OLAP Services will not try to prevent this case from occurring. Whenever you query data within 1999, you will now get COUNTs and SUMs that are precisely twice what they should be. The "All-time" level will also get a double contribution from 1999. To resolve this, the four partitions for the quarters of 1999

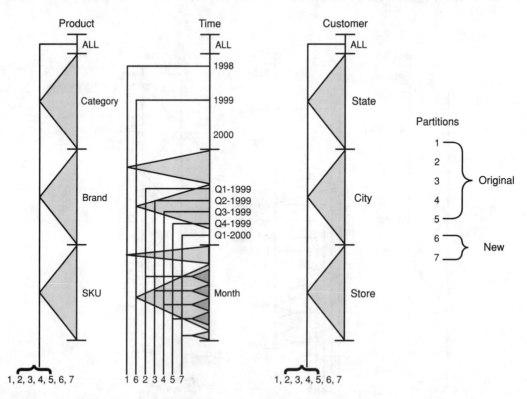

Figure 3.19   MDS showing redundant four quarters and years.

can be merged into a single partition (in Chapter 10, on maintaining applications, we discuss merging partitions in detail).

Notice how clearly a technique like MDS shows the relative positioning of partitions. The OLAP Manager does not provide an interface for detecting overlap of partitions. Perhaps third-party tools will appear that provide feedback on the coverage of a cube by its partitions. The more subtle your scheme of partitions, the more difficult it may be to uncover overlaps, unless you are careful about documenting them. For example, partitioning by slices in two or more dimensions (geography and time being prime examples with scenario as a good third possibility) brings with it a larger number of possible combinations.

Things to Watch out For: Incomplete ("Underlapping") Partitions

When you are defining multiple partitions and assigning them regions of a cube, there is an error related to overlapping partitions that will be less difficult to find: the incomplete coverage of a cube by its partitions. Overlap announces itself in the data because the numbers are all larger than they should be; however, this can be subtle. Incomplete coverage announces itself because there are empty spaces in the cube, even though you are confident that there is data in the fact tables to support the cells. However, you still need to determine whether an existing partition was misdefined (for example, accidentally defined as using a member from a level that was too low on the dimension for a slice) or whether a partition is simply not defined at all. If the partition was misdefined and you add a new partition, you will introduce an overlap!

Summary

In this chapter we discussed all of the basic—and some not so basic—guiding principles for designing a database in Microsoft OLAP Services. With this information you will be able to create a well-designed and productive OLAP Services database. We covered actions that must be taken in RDBMS data source as well as in OLAP Services. We will focus on database design issues again in Chapter 11, on optimizing databases and queries, and in Chapter 12, on advanced database and application design. With design issues in mind, in Chapter 4 we will look at using the OLAP Manager to actually implement a database.

The Basics of Building a Database with the OLAP Manager

O nce we have a design for our dimensions and cubes, we begin the actual process of building them by creating a database on our Microsoft OLAP Services server. A database serves as the logical storage space for the objects that define the OLAP system we want to create. Creating an OLAP Services database is a purely mechanical process. The most difficult decisions to make are which server to create the database on and what to name it. In this chapter, we will actually go through the steps of creating OLAP Services objects through the OLAP Manager interface.

The step-by-step examples throughout this chapter use the data found in the sample Solutions.mdb Microsoft Access database, which can be found in the "data\" directory on the CD-ROM that accompanies this book. To use this sample data source, you need to either set up an ODBC data source for the Access database on the server that is running OLAP Services, or import Solutions.mdb database into an SQL Server database. For directions on how to do either of these, read the document titled setuprdb.doc, found in the root directory of the CD-ROM.

Creating an OLAP Services Database

To create a database, start by selecting the server for the database in the OLAP Manager Console. Select "Action|New Database" from the console menu or right click on the server and select "New Database." Enter a database name and description as

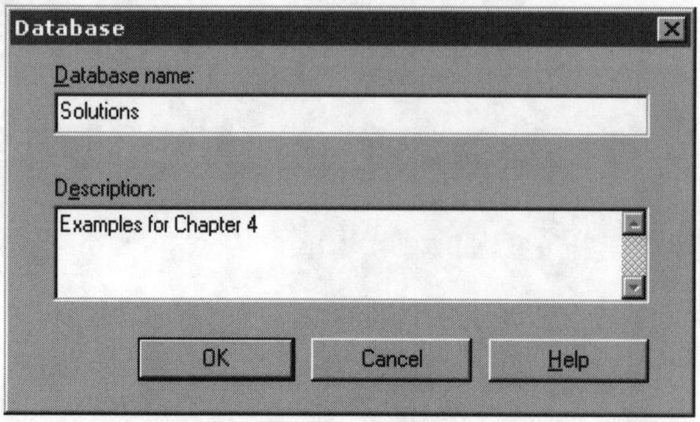

Database

Database name:

Solutions

Description:

Examples for Chapter 4

[OK] [Cancel] [Help]

Figure 4.1 Database creation wizard.

shown in Figure 4.1 and click OK. That's it. Honest. You now have a Microsoft OLAP Services database. Of course, we need to tell the database where our fact and dimension tables are by setting up a data source. You can add new data sources at any time during the life of a database. To make it easier to follow the examples in this chapter (and throughout this book) we recommend that you use the Solutions.mdb Microsoft Access database included in the CD-ROM that came with this book.

To add a data source, expand the branches under the database in the tree pane of the OLAP Manager console to select the Data Source folder, as shown in Figure 4.2. Right click on the folder and select "New Data Source," or select "Action|New Data Source" from the console menu. You will then be presented with the data source wizard as shown in Figure 4.3. Select the appropriate OLE DB provider for

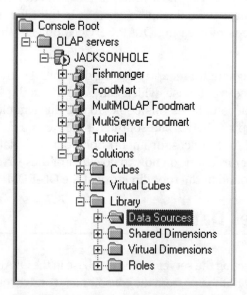

Figure 4.2 Data Source folder in the OLAP Manager console.

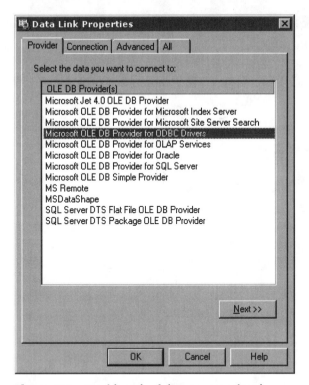

Figure 4.3   Provider tab of data source wizard.

the data source from the list as shown in Figure 4.4 ("OLE DB Provider for ODBC Drivers" if using the sample database set up as an ODBC data source) and click "next>>" The next screen can vary dramatically depending on the provider you select. Enter the information shown in Figure 4.4 and click "OK" if you are using our sample database and you've set up an ODBC data source for it according to the instructions in the setuprdb.doc file in the CD-ROM that accompanies this book.

Creating Dimensions: Levels, Members, and Hierarchies

This section describes the detailed steps that are required to create shared dimensions in Microsoft OLAP Services. We will cover the creation of private dimensions later in the section entitled "Creating a Cube: Bringing It All Together."

Four primary steps are required to create a dimension:

■ Select one or more dimension tables in a data source.

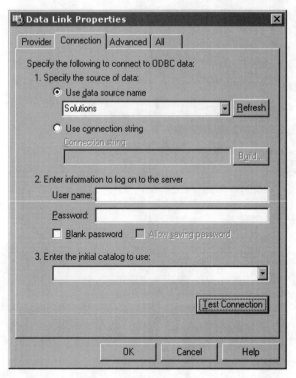

Figure 4.4 Properties page of data source wizard.

- Identify the type of dimension.
- Select columns from the table(s) for levels.
- Provide a name for the dimension.

The OLAP Manager enables you to create dimensions directly in the Dimension Editor or by using the dimension wizard. It is a matter of personal preference whether you choose to use the wizard or editor to tackle these tasks. The wizard offers the advantage that it guides you through the four basic tasks. It also offers the new user clear explanations of the initial steps in creating dimensions. Even so, once the wizard has finished you will still most likely have to perform at least some editing of the dimension, such as adding descriptions or selecting member name columns that are different from member key columns. We'll start by creating standard dimensions for customers and products and finish by creating a time dimension.

Creating a Standard Dimension

Because this is our first journey through the dimension-building process, we'll start with the wizard. To begin, right click on the Shared Dimensions folder in

Manually Creating a Dimension with the Editor

The steps for initializing a new dimension are as follows:

- From the OLAP Manager console, right-click on the Shared Dimensions folder and select "New Dimension|Editor." You can also do this from an existing dimension editor session by selecting "File|New Dimension|Editor" from the dimension Editor menu or by right-clicking on the dimension in the tree pane and selecting "New Dimension."
- A dimension table selector will appear. Expand a data source, select a table, and click "OK." You can only select one table when creating a dimension. If the dimension is based on multiple tables, you will be able to add new tables later.
- On the Basic tab of the properties pane, enter a name and description for the dimension.

To add levels, do the following:

- Select "Insert|Level" from the Editor menu or right-click on the dimension or a level in the tree pane. From the column selection dialog select a column and click "OK."
- Drag a column from a table in the schema pane and drop it on the dimension or on one of the levels in the tree pane. When the column is dropped on the dimension, it is added as the bottom level of the dimension. If it is dropped on an existing level, it is added immediately above that level.
- Select a column from a table in the schema pane. Right-click and select "Insert as Level." The column will be added as the bottom level of the dimension.

To add a new table, do the following:

- Select "Insert|Tables" from the Editor menu or Right-click anywhere in the schema pane and select "Insert New Tables."
- From the table selection dialog select a table and click "Add" to add it to the schema. This step can be repeated as needed.
- The editor automatically creates joins for you based on columns with the same name.

To join tables, do the following:

- Drag a column from one table in the schema and drop it on the join column in another table.
- Select a column in a table in the schema panel. Select "Insert|Join" from the Editor menu or right-click and select "Insert Join." From the column selection dialog, select a column to join to.

To remove table joins, do the following:

- Select a join line in the schema pane. Right-click and choose "Remove" or press "Delete" on the keyboard.
- Select a column in a table in the schema panel. Select "Edit|Remove Join" from the Editor menu or right-click and select "Remove Join."

the Library folder of your database. Select "New Dimension," followed by "Wizard." As shown in Figure 4.5, your first task is to indicate the relational schema that defines the dimension. Select the "Single Table/Star Schema" option to create a dimension that is based upon a single table. To create a dimension that uses multiple related tables, select the "Multiple Table/Snowflake Schema" option.

If you chose to work with a star schema, you will next choose a single table on which to base the dimension (see Figure 4.6). For a snowflake schema, you will be given the opportunity to choose multiple tables (see Figure 4.7). In either case, if you do not see the data source that contains the table(s) you wish to use, you may create a new data source for the database by clicking on "New Data Source." Be sure to select your data source carefully. Once a dimension has been created, you cannot change its data source.

When you are creating a dimension that is based upon a snowflake schema, the wizard next asks you to verify the joins between the dimension tables. By default, the dimension wizard preselects joins based upon column names and joins identically named columns. It is vital that you take the time to investigate the table joins that the wizard picked. Because the wizard does not pay attention to indexes and relationships set up in the data source, in many cases they may be incorrect.

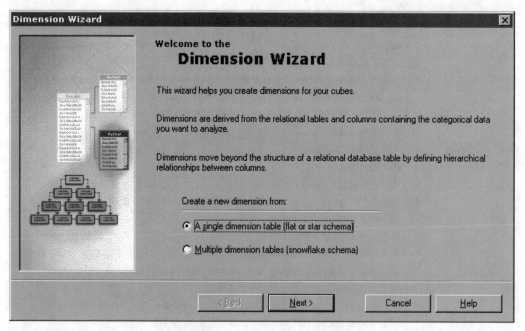

Figure 4.5 Dimension wizard start page.

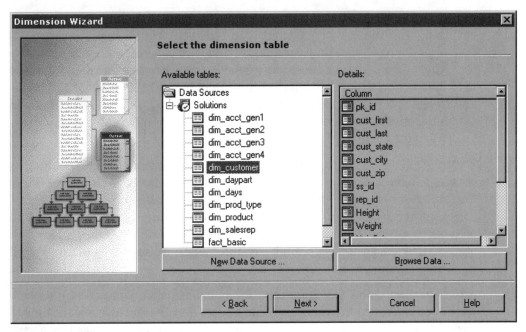

Figure 4.6   Table selection for a single table dimension.

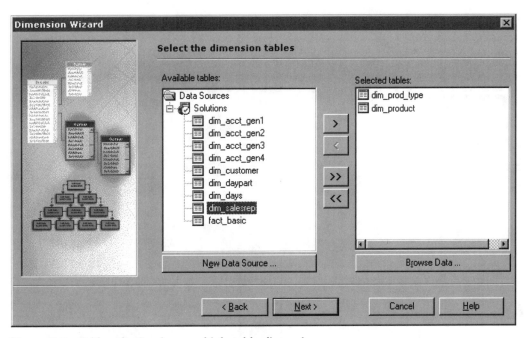

Figure 4.7   Table selection for a multiple table dimension.

In Figure 4.8, the wizard guesses that table dim_prod_type joins the dim_product table on the pk_id column. The correct relationship, however, is dim_prod_type.pk_id to dim_product.type_id. You can correct relationships by removing unwanted joins and adding desired ones. Remove unwanted joins by right clicking on a join line and selecting "Remove" (or left clicking and pressing "Delete" on your keyboard). To create a join, simply select a key column in one table, drag it, and drop it on the related field in another table. The correct table joins for the preceding example are shown in Figure 4.9.

Your next step is to tell the wizard what type of dimension you are building, as shown in Figure 4.10. You can choose between a standard or a time dimension. The dimension wizard will create a time dimension using one of several standard time hierarchies based on a single date/time column. We'll explain how to use the dimension wizard to create time dimensions in the section titled "Creating a Time Dimension" later in this chapter. For now, select Standard to build the customer and product dimensions.

After selecting the tables to be used in your dimension, you need to indicate which columns contain members that belong to the different levels of the dimension. To identify a column as a dimension level you may either drag it from the Available Columns box and drop it on the Dimension Levels box, double-click on

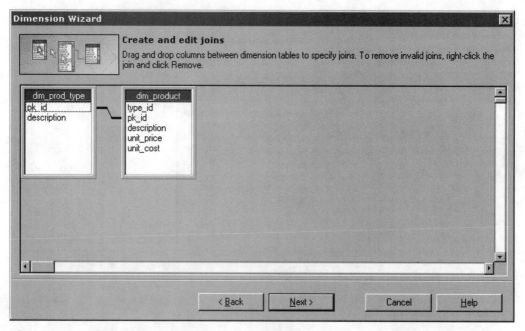

Figure 4.8   Default table joins based on column names.

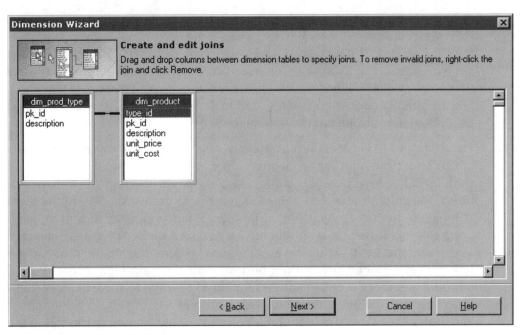

Figure 4.9   Corrected table joins.

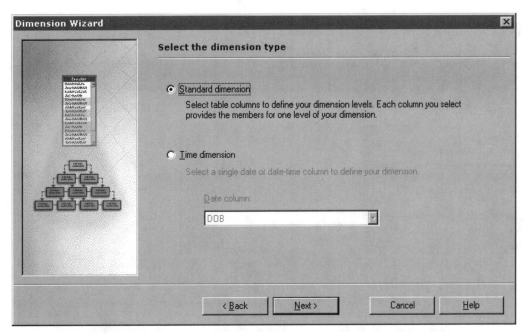

Figure 4.10   Selecting a dimension type in the wizard.

a column to move it to the Levels box, or select one or more columns and use the right-arrow button (>) to assign the levels. Pressing the double-right-arrow button (>>) assigns all columns as levels. Note that assigning a column to a level removes it from the "Available Columns" list. To remove a level, simply reverse the process. Select columns for the customer dimension as shown in Figure 4.11. For the product dimension, use pk_id from dim_prod_type as the first level and pk_id from dim_product as the bottom level.

Leave "Count Level Members Automatically" checked if you want the wizard to count the number of members in each level as you select them. As each level is added in, Microsoft OLAP Services will count the unique values of the column you have selected in order to determine where the level belongs in the hierarchy. Unless you have a fairly unusual situation, each progressively lower level should have a greater number of unique member keys than the next-higher level. One case where the number of unique lower-level member keys would be less than the next-higher level would be if the members are themselves numbered relative to their parents. Suppose you were basing a time dimension with levels of year, week-number, and day-of-week on a table that has rows like those shown in the following table:

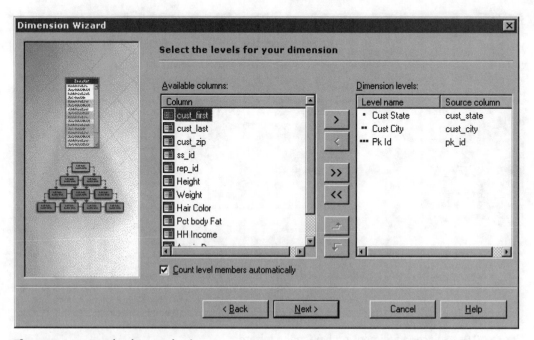

Figure 4.11 Level column selection.

YEAR	WEEK	DAY
1998	W1	1
1998	W1	2
...	...	...
1998	W51	6
1998	W52	7

In this case, you would end up with fifty-two or fifty-three unique values at the week level, but only seven at the day level.

Suppose you are prototyping the database with a subset of dimension information, and many cousin members have the same name (because they rely on parent members to provide their full identity). In this case, you may have picked just the right subset of dimension data to make it appear that you have fewer members at a child level than at a parent level. In some situations, it may be perfectly valid to have child levels that have fewer members than their parents. The data source may not yet be completely populated with data, in which case the level order may be correct even though at design time the data does not support it (it will, hopefully, by the time you are ready to process your cube!).

If the levels are not organized in ascending order, OLAP Manager will warn you. In large dimensions, however, counting distinct members can take a good deal of time. If you are working with large dimensions and feel confident about the correct level order, you should uncheck the "Count Level Members Automatically" option to speed up the creation of the dimension.

Note that in Figure 4.11 we selected the cust_id column for the bottom level of this customer dimension. Columns selected in the dimension wizard are assigned to both the member key and member name column properties of their respective levels. As we discussed in Chapter 3, given a choice you should generally select a column that has the smallest possible data type for the member key column in order to optimize dimension storage. In our example's customer table we could also use the ss_id column to uniquely identify customers, but it is a nine-byte character column versus the four-byte integer of cust_id. In the wizard, we select the member key column rather than the name column. We do this because changing the key column in the editor later will also change the name column for the level while changing the name column does not alter the key column. We'll look at how to edit member properties as soon as we finish our discussion of the wizard.

TIP

When selecting columns for levels in the dimension wizard, select member key columns rather than member name columns.

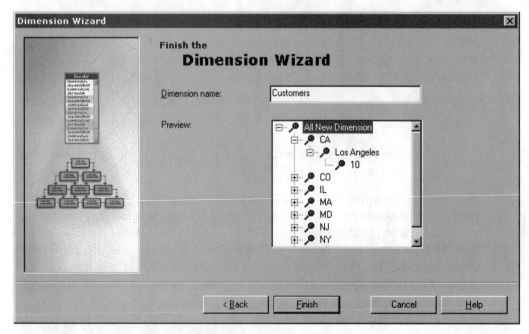

Figure 4.12 Naming a dimension in the wizard.

The final step is simply to provide the new dimension with a name, as shown in Figure 4.12. Choose the name carefully; you will not be able to change it later.

Editing Dimension Properties

When the wizard finishes, OLAP Manager presents you with the dimension editor (Figure 4.13). Here you can make any refinements or modifications to the dimension. If the dimension object properties are not visible, simply click the button labeled "Properties" or choose "View|Properties" from the Editor menu to expand the pane. The properties pane displays all applicable properties for the dimension object currently selected. You may edit any property except the dimension's data source and name. In the next section, we'll go through the dimension and level properties in order of importance as opposed to the order in which they appear in the dimension editor.

Descriptions and Names (Dimension Levels and Member Properties)

As you've probably noticed, the wizard does not allow you to enter dimension or level descriptions. To make things easier on everyone, it is a good idea to add some type of description to a dimension and its levels. It's frustrating to return

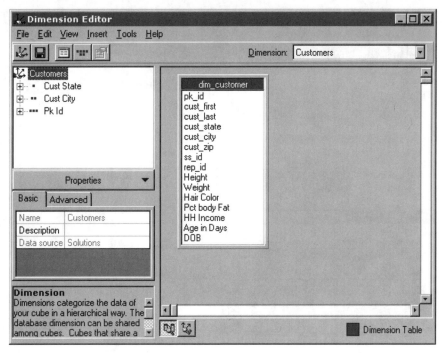

Figure 4.13   The dimension editor.

to a database after six months only to discover you have no idea what the dimension "Company" is about (our company? other companies?).

The wizard also offers you no opportunity to modify the default level names. It does a fairly good job at guessing desired level names (removing hyphens, capitalizing first letters, and so forth). For most of us, however, the columns chosen probably have names only a DBA could love, like "cust_id" or "cust_state," resulting in level names like "Cust_Id" and "Cust State." To make things easier for end users and front-end developers, you want to make level names as intuitive as possible, like "Customer" and "State."

Remember, the purpose of OLAP is to make data more accessible and analysis simpler. The more you can do at the start to make a database easy for others to understand, the less explaining you'll have to do later. Our dimension with descriptive level names can be seen in Figure 4.14.

"All Level" and "All Caption"

"All Level" and "All Caption" can be found on the Advanced Properties tab for the dimension. All Level may be set to Yes or No, and you may enter any name for "All Caption", following the same naming rules for dimensions and cubes

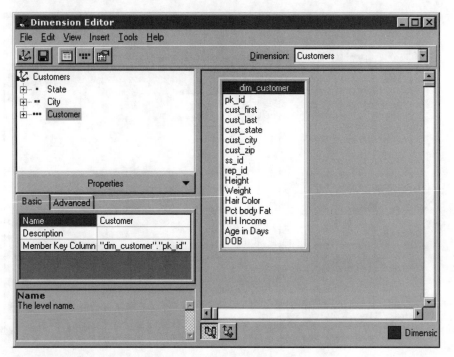

Figure 4.14   Dimension with descriptive level names.

described in Chapter 3. By default, dimensions contain an All level with a caption of All [dimension name]. The All level serves as the ultimate level in the dimension, representing the aggregate over all members of each level in the dimension. If there were no All level, default aggregation would stop at each member in the highest level. Non-hierarchical dimensions usually do not need an All level. For example, consider a scenario dimension that contains one level comprised of members like "Actual" and "Budget". An aggregated value consisting of actual and budget amounts would do little but waste space or processing time. By not declaring an All level, we save ourselves the trouble of ensuring, on a cube-by-cube basis, that we have prevented All-level aggregates.

"Type"

Type can be found on the Advanced Properties tab for the dimension. A dimension can be specified as either "regular" or "time." Type serves as a useful tag, but it has no effect on dimension or cube processing or on query performance. It is used by several time-specific MDX functions (see Chapter 8 for details on MDX time functions) and by front-end developers to identify time dimensions easily. Levels also have a Type property (described in a later section) that let you tag levels for specific time types such as Year, Month, Day, and the like.

When you use the wizard to create a time dimension, it automatically sets the dimension type value to time.

"Member Key Column" and "Member Name Column"

Member Key Column and *Member Name Column* are properties of dimension levels. The member key column is located on the Basic tab, and the member name column is located on the Advanced Properties tab.

As we noted in Chapter 2, Microsoft OLAP Services stores dimension information and cube aggregations internally according to the key column. In a dimension, however, OLAP Services allows us to display and use member names that are based upon a different column or a valid SQL function. By default, when you create a level the dimension editor uses the same column for both member key and member name. To make your cube easier to use (by making member names easier to understand), you always want to set the Member Name Column property to a column or SQL function that, where possible, provides a descriptive member name (again, "Super Duper Widgets" will make much more sense to those browsing your cube than "1234"). To optimize both dimension and cube storage, you want to use a key column that contains a smaller data type (the four-byte integer requires less space than a twenty-character string).

You may edit these properties by simply typing in a new column name definition. When entering column names, you must enter them in the format "tablename"."columnname" (including dot and quotation marks). Microsoft OLAP Services also allows key and name columns to be defined with any SQL functions that work against the data source. For example, a typical customer table stores first and last names in separate columns. You may have noticed earlier that we gave the level that was based on cust_id the label Customer Name. To have a customer's full name appear as the member, we can use a SQL function like

```
"customer"."cust_last" + ', ' + "customer"."cust_first"
```

for the member name column, as shown in Figure 4.15. One of the more important uses of this feature is that is gives you the ability to build dimensions with multiple levels that are based on a single column. Date columns serve as the most informative example. In the section titled "Creating Time Dimensions," we discuss how the wizard can easily create time dimensions using most of the common time hierarchies (by eliminating much of the typing you'll be doing here!). However, it's worthwhile here to see how to do this manually:

- Using the editor, create a dimension based on a table that contains a date/time column (you can use the dim_days table in the Solutions.mdb database).

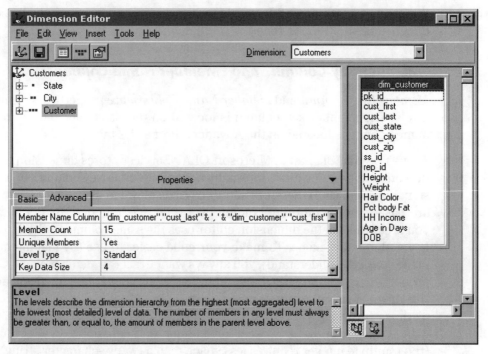

Figure 4.15 Editing the member name column.

- Add three levels by dragging the date/time column onto the dimension three times.

- Name the first level "Year" and enter
  `DatePart('yyyy',"dim_days"."date_id")` for the member key column
  and `Format("dim_days"."date_id", 'yyyy')` for the member name column.

- Name the second level "Month" and enter
  `DatePart('m',"dim_days"."date_id")` for the member key column
  and `Format("dim_days"."date_id", 'mmmm')` for the member name column.

- Name the third level "Day" and enter
  `DatePart('d',"dim_days"."date_id")` for the member key column
  and `Format("dim_days"."date_id", 'mmm. dd')` for the member name column.

- View the dimension by selecting "View|Data" from the Editor menu and browse through the dimension members.

You can also select a column for either the key or name column properties from assigned dimension tables by clicking on the ellipses (. . .) next to the property.

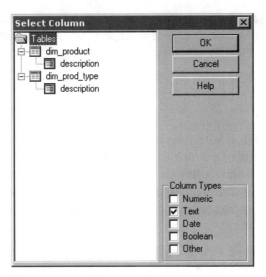

Figure 4.16 Column selection dialog.

This opens a column selection dialog, as shown in Figure 4.16. You can use this dialog to change the member name columns for the type and product levels in our product dimension, selecting the description columns from the appropriate table.

The column selection dialog allows you to select a single column from a dimension table. It includes check boxes that show or hide columns, which can be selected according to their data type. By default, when you are selecting a member name column only Text is checked. When you are selecting the member key column, Numeric, Text, and Date are checked.

A level's member key column for a dimension does not have to be the column that relates the dimension table to a fact table. A level's member key column is used in a regular (non-virtual) dimension to create the internal dimension structure and as the key OLAP Services aggregations (again, regardless of data storage type). Dimension columns may be joined to the fact table based upon any column. The join is used to build the query to get the appropriate data. An example would be when a product and product type relate to a fact table based on an opaque identifier column.

If you did not create your data source, or have little or no control over it, you may find that descriptive columns are not indexed in the data source. You can dramatically improve performance by using an indexed column instead of a descriptive column as the key column when you are processing dimensions that have a large number of members. The use of HOLAP storage extends the impact of using non-indexed columns as member keys to run-time query performance because aggregations are linked back to relational data based on the member keys. We go into this in greater detail in Chapter 11, on optimizing databases and queries, but it's important that your data source be well optimized with indexes.

"Order by Key"

Using the key column rather than the name column enables you to alter the display order of member names in addition to offering potential processing and storage benefits. Continuing with the time dimension we created earlier, select the month level and change order by key on the Advanced Properties tab to "False." Press Enter to commit the change and take a look at the dimension members. Notice that the months are now ordered alphabetically, or by the value of the member name column.

Because these levels were created with a date/time column, the editor set order by key to "True" by default. For other data types, the dimension editor sets order by key to "False" by default. For some dimensions, such as time, members have meaningful ordering apart from their names, and it would make more sense to order them by dimension key. Dimensions whose members represent products, customers, and geographies, however, would probably benefit from being ordered by name because alphabetical ordering will make it easier to locate child members under a parent.

Consider for a moment the dim_daypart table in the Solutions.mdb database containing the parts of a day, as shown in Figure 4.17. Create a dimension based on this table in the dimension editor using the description column as the source for the level. As you would expect, the dimension editor uses this column as both the member key and the member name columns. Browse the dimension data, however, and notice that the members sort in the order Afternoon, Evening, Midday, and so on. To order the members correctly, change the member key column to the id column and set order by key to "True." Now browse the dimension and notice that the members sort in the desired order.

ID	Description
1	Morning
2	Mid Day
3	Afternoon
4	Evening
5	Night

Figure 4.17 Table containing parts of a day.

"Key Data Size" and "Key Data Type"

Key Data Size and *Key Data Type* indicate the size and type of data, respectively, for the level key column of the aggregation tables for a cube. In most cases, the editor accurately sets these according to the data type and size of the key column in the data source. Microsoft OLAP Services uses these values to create internal dimension structures and cube aggregations (though data type appears to be ignored in MOLAP cube data storage). As we mentioned in our discussion on OLAP database design in Chapter 3 because key column size can adversely impact data storage requirements, you should always double-check these values, especially if you use SQL functions to define the member key column. Continuing with our time dimension example, look at the key data size and key data type values for the year level. When we added a date/time column from a Microsoft Access table, the editor set the member key column to

```
Format("dim_days"."date_id", 'medium date'),
```

with a data type of char and a size of 20. Though we edited the member key column for year to

```
DatePart('yyyy',"dim_days"."date_id"),
```

the key data size and key data type remain unchanged. Obviously, we do not need to use twenty bytes to store a four-byte character or integer value. Change the key data size by typing in the correct size and change the type by selecting the appropriate type from the drop-down list.

"Member Count"

Microsoft OLAP Services uses the *Member Count* when it is designing aggregations for a cube. We cover this fully in Chapter 11, on optimizing databases and queries. OLAP Services updates these values only when a level is added to a dimension and OLAP Services's "Count Dimension Members" property is enabled.

"Unique Members"

We discussed *Unique Members* in Chapter 3 on database design basics. This property indicates whether all the member key column values in a level are unique and can be set to "Yes" or "No" on the Advanced Properties tab. When you have "Count Level Members Automatically" checked, the dimension wizard attempts to determine uniqueness for you automatically. It is not always accurate, however, so you should verify this value in the editor after you create a dimension with the wizard.

"Level Type"

Level Type is related to dimension type. A dimension can be specified as either "standard" or "time." The levels of a time dimension can be meaningfully tagged as being of the corresponding time level (Year, Quarter, Month, etc.). Level type serves as a useful tag, but it has no effect on dimension or cube processing nor on query performance. It is used by several time-specific MDX functions (see Chapter 8 for details on MDX time functions) as well as by front-end developers to easily identify time dimensions and members. Microsoft OLAP Services makes no attempt to verify the cardinality of relationships between different time levels, so you could have exactly thirty days in every month, for example. When you are creating a time dimension with the wizard, it automatically sets the level type to the appropriate value for the time levels selected in the wizard.

Creating a Time Dimension

Creating time dimensions is one of the most powerful ease-of-use features OLAP Manager and the dimension wizard offers. It's perfectly acceptable to create a time dimension that is based on a table containing separate columns for years, quarter, months, and the like. However, we demonstrated earlier that by using SQL functions you can also create time levels that are based upon a common date/time column. To save time, the wizard will build these formulas for you for numerous common time hierarchies. The resulting hierarchy will be limited to relationships provided by SQL functions supported by the underlying database. But, if those are acceptable, these features can save you some effort. Let's go through the steps of using the wizard now.

After you select dimension tables containing date columns, the wizard prompts you to choose between a standard dimension or a time dimension, as shown in Figure 4.18. When you select a time dimension you also select which column in your dimension table contains time values. The wizard next asks for the dimension levels for the time dimension. You may select from the following standard time hierarchies:

- Year, Quarter, Month, Day
- Year, Quarter, Month, Day, Hour, Minute
- Year, Quarter, Month
- Year, Month, Day
- Year, Month, Day, Hour, Minute
- Year, Month
- Year, Week, Day
- Year, Week, Day, Hour, Minute
- Year, Week

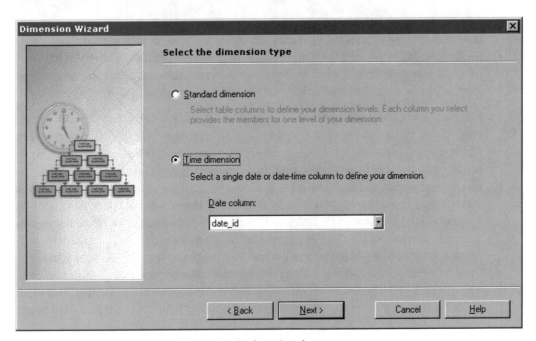

Figure 4.18 Selecting a time dimension in the wizard.

If none of these satisfies your desired time hierarchy, select the closest match. You can add other time levels through the OLAP Manager's dimension editor or additional DSO programs later.

Along with selecting the levels, you must also indicate the starting point for a year. If your data works by fiscal year, the wizard orders the key columns accordingly and provides accurate labels. To get an idea of how much typing you can save by using the wizard, here's the member key formula (in Microsoft Access parlance) for a year level in a time dimension that has a fiscal year starting October 1:

```
DatePart('yyyy',iif (Month("dim_days"."date_id") < 10 or
(Month("dim_days"."date_id") = 10 and Day("dim_days"."date_id") <
1),DateAdd('yyyy', -1, "dim_days"."date_id"),"dim_days"."date_id"))
```

And here's the member name column formula:

```
DatePart('yyyy',iif (Month("dim_days"."date_id") < 10 or
(Month("dim_days"."date_id") = 10 and Day("dim_days"."date_id") <
1),DateAdd('yyyy', -1, "dim_days"."date_id"),"dim_days"."date_id"))
```

Note that the wizard uses the SQL syntax of the data source. With Microsoft Access, the month member name column is defined as `format(datecolumn, "mmm")`. With an SQL Server data source, the member name formula would be defined as `datename("m",datecolumn)`. Though you can use the full power of the data source's native query language to manipulate member values in numerous ways, you should try to be conservative if there is a chance your data source may change down the road. You may, for example, prototype your database using an Access database, and then move up to SQL Server for the production environment. If you do this, however, you will need to redefine the time dimensions created with the wizard because SQL Server does not recognize format.

For clarity, you may also want to change the SQL expressions that the wizard creates for member names at some time levels. For example, the default member name column for a day level will simply be the number of the day in that month. In reports where the higher-level member (month) appears in the hierarchy, the month name (like January) will be available to provide context. However, when you are only looking at days, you may not readily know what day it is. Additionally, Microsoft OLAP Services defaults to Unique Members set to No. If your analyses and reports may use the days of months without reporting the months back in addition to using the hierarchy, you will want to change the default member name column. For SQL Server in the United States, the column function `convert(CHAR, "dim_time"."DateVal", 107)` will provide day names in the format "Mon, DD, YYYY" (three-letter month abbreviation, day number in month, and four-digit year).

Member Properties

We covered member properties in detail in our discussion on design in Chapter 3. To quickly summarize here, member properties allow you to easily store more member attributes than just name. Remember that Microsoft OLAP Services does not validate that an assigned property is unique for members in the level—so be careful when assigning member properties.

To add a member property, do the following:

- Select a level in the tree pane of the dimension editor.
- Select "Insert|Member Property" from the menu or right click and select "New Member Property."
- From the column selection dialog, select the column in the dimension table that contains the property values and click OK.

Once the property has been added you can modify its name, source column, and description properties, as shown in Figure 4.19. As with member key and member name columns, you can also use any valid SQL column expression for the source column property.

Processing Dimensions

When you process a dimension the dimension information is stored in internal OLAP Services data structures. Dimensions (and any cubes that are dependent

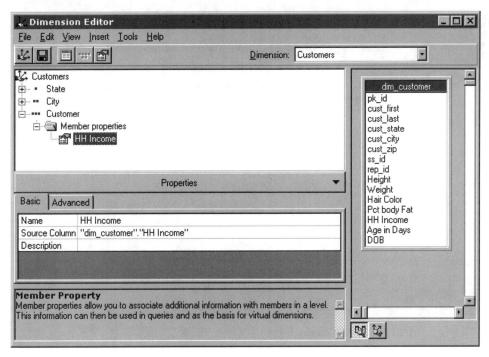

Figure 4.19 Editing a member property.

on them) need to be processed to incorporate changes to dimension metadata in the source data table(s) or if the structure of a dimension changes. Dimensions must be processed before cubes that use them can be populated with data, though OLAP Services will automatically process any new or structurally modified dimension when it processes a dependent cube.

To process a dimension, simply select "Tools|Process Dimension . . ." from the Editor menu. This will perform a full process of the dimension. You can also process a dimension by right clicking on a dimension in the console tree pane and choosing "Process." If you use the latter method and the dimension has been processed before, OLAP Manager will ask you if you wish to perform an incremental update or rebuild the dimension structure. Incremental update is used to refresh a dimension with any new members in the data source. We discuss the incremental updating of dimensions in more detail in Chapter 10.

When you process a dimension, OLAP Manager will inform you of the status of the process with the dialog shown in Figure 4.20.

Microsoft OLAP Services performs three steps when processing a dimension. First, it initializes the internal data structures that are needed to store dimen-

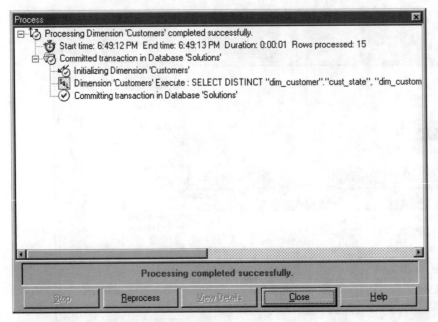

Figure 4.20 Dimension processing dialog.

sion data. Then it queries the data source for the dimension data itself. Finally, OLAP Services commits the changes.

Virtual Dimensions

As we mentioned earlier, you create virtual dimensions from the member properties of levels in an existing dimension. Virtual dimensions only have a single leaf level, plus an "All" level. Microsoft OLAP Services calculates aggregations across the members of a virtual dimension at run time. In a large dimension, this can have serious performance implications, so you should use virtual dimensions judiciously. Moreover, through the OLAP Manager interface, virtual dimensions can only be created with a wizard, and they cannot be edited except to change the member property that is used for the virtual dimension.

To create a virtual dimension, do the following:

■ From the OLAP Manager console, select "Action|New Virtual Dimension" from the menu or right click on an existing virtual dimension or on the Virtual Dimension folder and select "New Virtual Dimension."

■ Select the member property from the desired dimension (only dimensions that contain levels that have member properties are displayed, as is shown in Figure 4.21)

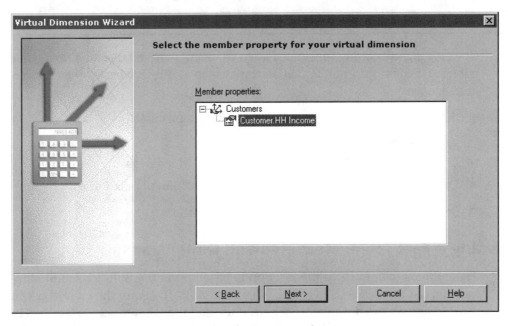

Figure 4.21   Virtual dimension wizard: Selecting a member property.

■ Enter a name for the virtual dimension (see Figure 4.22). As usual, when you are creating a database object use all due caution when taking this step; you will not be able to change the name later.

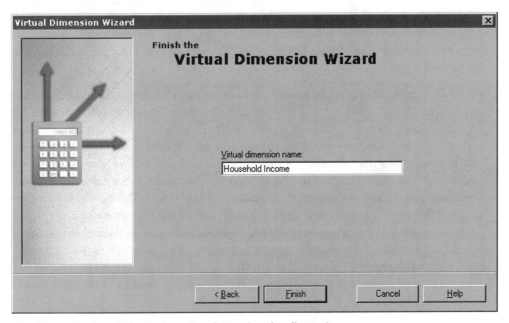

Figure 4.22   Virtual dimension wizard: Naming the dimension.

Creating a Cube: Bringing It All Together

Cubes bring everything together. Everyone using your database will use your cubes to analyze the data. In this section, we cover the five basic steps for creating a cube:

- Selecting a fact table, measure columns and dimensions.
- Refining the cube definition.
- Creating calculated members and/or private dimensions.
- Designing aggregations and processing the cube to populate it with data.
- Adding partitions.

Selecting a Fact Table, Measures and Dimensions

The cube we will build in this section is based upon the Solutions.mdb database on the CD-ROM that accompanies this book. To create the cube you will need to have created the customer, product, and time dimensions described in the preceding section. As in our discussion of dimensions, we'll begin with the wizard, though you can also create cubes by using the editor alone. Start by selecting "Action|New Cube|Wizard . . ." from the OLAP Manager console menu (or right click on the Cube folder or on an existing cube in the tree pane of the console and select "New Cube|Wizard . . ."). OLAP Manager begins by welcoming us to the cube wizard and gives a short description of the wizard. So we don't have to be bothered by this screen each time we start the wizard, Microsoft OLAP Services thankfully allows us to turn this part of the wizard off by checking the "Skip This Screen in the Future" box in the bottom left of the welcome screen.

Your first task, shown in Figure 4.23, is to select a fact table that contains all the measures and dimensions you wish to use in your cube. As with the dimension wizard, simply select a table from any of the displayed data sources and click "Next>". If you don't see the data source you wish to use, you may create a new data source for the OLAP Services database by pressing the "New Data Source . . ." button. Be sure to select the data source that contains the dimension metadata for the dimensions that the cube will use. The primary partition for a cube can have only one data source, and OLAP Services does not allow cubes to use dimensions whose underlying tables reside in data sources other than the one used for a cube's primary partition. Once a cube has been created, you cannot change its data source. (In the rest of this chapter, all examples use the fact_basic table in the Solutions.mdb database on the CD-ROM that accompanies this book.)

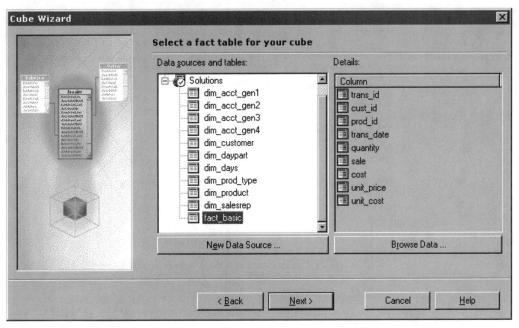

Figure 4.23 Selecting the fact table in the cube wizard.

WARNING
Once a cube definition is saved in OLAP Services, you cannot change its name or data source.

With a fact table selected, you must now identify the columns in the fact table that contain your measures, as shown in Figure 4.24. The penultimate step in this example is to select the dimensions used in the fact table (see Figure 4.25). You may also create one or more new shared dimensions with the dimension wizard by clicking on the "New Dimension . . ." button. The wizard will now create default joins between the tables used by the dimensions and the fact table. The joins are determined strictly by matching column names, irrespective of any indexes or relationships defined in the data source. If the wizard cannot find common column names between a dimension table and the fact table, you will receive a warning like the one shown in Figure 4.26.

Finally, provide a name for your cube as shown in Figure 4.27. As with dimensions, take care when entering a name because you will not be able to change it later.

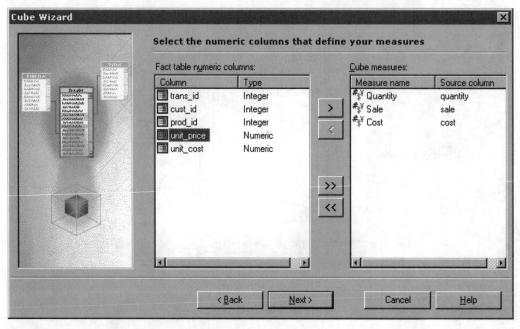

Figure 4.24 Selecting measures in the cube wizard.

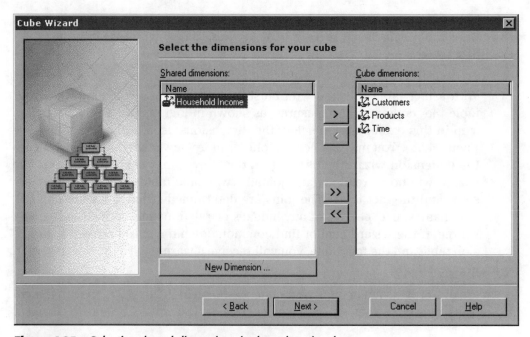

Figure 4.25 Selecting shared dimensions in the cube wizard.

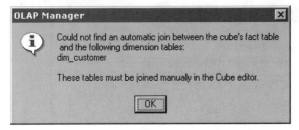

Figure 4.26 Warning dialog for indeterminate table joins.

Refining the Cube Definition

When the wizard completes, OLAP Manager opens the cube editor. Here, you can make any necessary refinements or modifications to the cube. Remember that the wizard warned us that it could not identify a join between pk_id and the fact table (see Figure 4.28). To join the tables, simply drag the appropriate column in the dimension table (in this case, pk_id in the customer table), and drop it on the join column in the fact table (in this case, cust_id). You may also notice that the wizard has kindly added joins between the fact table and dim_product on unit_price and unit_cost, but it didn't add the join we want

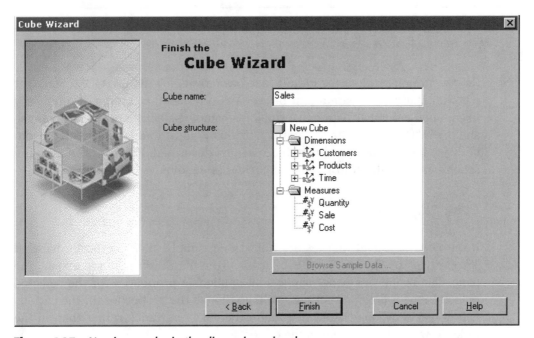

Figure 4.27 Naming a cube in the dimension wizard.

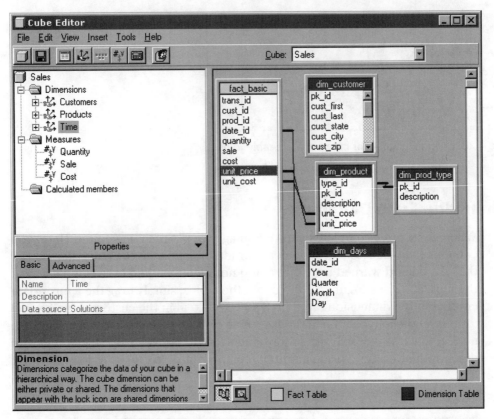

Figure 4.28 OLAP Manager cube editor.

(between dim_product.pk_id and fact_basic.prod_id). Again, OLAP Manager will automatically create a join between two tables that are based upon any like-named columns. To remove the joins, simply select them with the mouse and press "Delete" on the keyboard. Obviously, you should also create the join between dim_product and fact_basic as just described. Figure 4.29 shows the schema in the cube editor with the correct table joins.

Cube Properties

If the cube object properties are not visible, simply click the button labeled "Properties," or choose "View|Properties" from the Editor menu to expand the pane. The properties pane displays all applicable properties for the selected object. In the following sections, we'll go though the properties for the various cube objects by object, but in rough order of importance rather than in the order in which they appear in the editor.

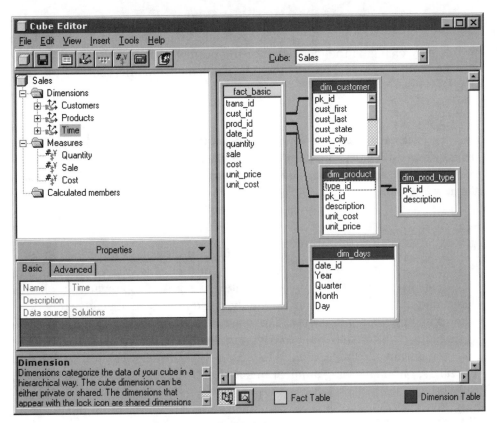

Figure 4.29 Sales cube with corrected table joins.

Description and Name

Just as the dimension wizard does not allow you to enter dimension descriptions, the cube wizard does not allow you to enter cube or measure descriptions. Again, the more descriptions you include, the better. Remember that the cube name cannot be changed after it is saved for the first time (as it is when you finish creating a cube with the wizard).

"Fact Table"

The "Fact Table" property resides on the Basic property tab for the cube. The fact table identified in this property is the one assigned to the cube's primary partition. In the Enterprise version of Microsoft OLAP Services, you can create additional partitions for a cube that can use different fact tables. Although you can't change a cube's name or data source, you can change its fact table within the data source. In the initial release of OLAP Services, changing the fact table in the cube editor does *not* change the fact table for the primary partition. When OLAP Services processes cubes whose fact table has been changed it actually uses the original fact table that was identified in the primary partition. If you are using the Enterprise version of OLAP Services, you can manually correct the problem by changing the fact table for the primary partition. Hopefully, a service pack that fixes this problem will be available from Microsoft by the time you read this.

WARNING

Until a service pack is released you should never change the fact table for a cube unless you are using the Enterprise version of OLAP Services. Note that when you change the fact table for a cube you will lose any measures that are not included in the new fact table.

"Fact Table Size"

The "Fact Table Size" property, which resides on the cube's Advanced Properties tab, represents the number of records in the fact table. Microsoft OLAP Services uses the fact table size to estimate the sizes of aggregations when it determines an aggregation plan. Generally, you do not need to change this value when building your initial cube. However, if you are trying to influence the aggregation plan you may want to edit the value. For more information on when you would want to change a cube's Fact Table Size property value, see Chapters 10 and 11, on maintaining applications and optimizing databases and queries, respectively.

"Aggregation Prefix"

When using ROLAP storage, OLAP Services prefixes the names of tables that contain aggregations with the "Aggregation Prefix" value in the format "prefix_cubename_aggregationid". By default, the first few characters of the cube name are used as the prefix. Note that in the initial release of OLAP Services this value is ignored. Microsoft has stated that this error will be fixed in the first service pack, which will, hopefully, be available by the time you read this.

Cube Dimension Properties

The cube editor displays all the properties for dimensions that you could see in the dimension editor, but you cannot edit them. It also presents a few new properties that relate to the cube. These new properties play a strong role in cube optimization, which will be covered in greater detail in Chapter 11.

"Aggregation Usage" and "Enable Aggregation"

You can tell Microsoft OLAP Services to limit the creation of potential aggregations for any dimension. By default, all aggregations are allowed. Other options include allowing only bottom- or top-level aggregations or limiting aggregations by specific level (Custom). When Custom is selected, you permit aggregations for a given level by setting its "Enable Aggregation" property to "Yes." The "Enable Aggregation" property is only enabled in the editor if the dimension's "Aggregation Usage" is set to "Custom." We cover these settings in greater detail in Chapter 11, on optimization.

"Member Key Column"

As we discussed in Chapter 3, you can modify the *member key columns* for levels in shared dimensions within the cube. This setting does not affect the member key column for the shared dimension itself. Rather, it determines the SQL statement that OLAP Services uses when it processes the cube data. Changing the member key column allows you to optimize this SQL for performance. Consider a cube that has a customer dimension that is joined to a fact table by a `customer_id` column. By default, OLAP Manager sets the member key column to `customer_id` in the customer table when you add the dimension to the cube. When OLAP Services processes this cube with the default setting, it will use the following query:

```
SELECT "Customer"."customer_id" FROM "fact_table", "customer" WHERE
("fact_table"."customer_id" = "customer"."customer_id").
```

Changing the key column to `fact_table.customer_id`, however, will result in the query

```
SELECT "fact_table"."customer_id" FROM "fact_table".
```

Note, however, that for such optimization to work, you must ensure relational integrity within the RDBMS source. If the fact table contains a member that is not present in the dimension table, the processing of the cube will fail with an "Unknown Dimension Member" error.

"Disabled"

Setting a dimension level's "Disabled" property to "Yes" prevents the level and any levels below it from being available for use. As in our discussion on design in Chapter 3, disabling lower levels in a dimension is the only way to allow data in a fact table to enter a cube above the leaf level. At the same time, as we noted earlier in this chapter, disabling levels prevents members in lower levels from being used in MDX calculations or queries and from appearing as dimension metadata in clients through OLE DB for OLAP. Essentially, the leaf level of the dimension in that cube is the lowest enabled level.

Measure Properties

Measures have their own distinct properties, which can be manipulated in the cube editor. We describe them in the following sections.

Description and Name

As with dimension levels, you'll want to double-check measure names. Default names that are based on table columns like "Txn Quant" or "Tx Amt" may not be well understood by your cube's users. Although we know they mean "transaction quantity" and "tax amount," most of the business analysts using your cube may feel more comfortable with explicit labels like "Transaction Quantity" and "Tax Amount." Measure names can contain up to fifty characters—use them!

Measure descriptions can be important sources of information for analysts, particularly if you plan to use the database for a broad series of analyses. One very important piece of information that you can provide for the measure is its units. For example, a head count measure might have units like "Qty (people)" and a pay rate measure such as "dollars per hour." An analyst or downstream report builder will find this information important when he or she tries to understand what measures mean in order to understand existing calculations or create new ones. In any case, clarifying the units is an important exercise when you are building the right aggregations. The maximum length for the comment field is not documented, but it should be long enough for you to be usefully descriptive.

"Source Column"

The "Source Column" measure property identifies the source of the data the cube should use for the measure. You can modify a measure's source column by clicking on the ellipses next to the property and selecting a column from the cube's fact table. As with member key and name columns in dimensions, SQL expressions can be used to create new values. This comes in handy in situations where you want to create a measure by using a formula based on one or more columns in a fact table. Microsoft OLAP Services resolves such formulas, in the form of an SQL expression, prior to aggregation. Consider a fact table that contains sales transactions by product and customer and that includes measures for the quantity sold and the unit price for the product. A calculated member "Total Sales" that multiplies quantity by unit price would be accurate at leaf levels but not at aggregate levels—we would never want the sum of units times the sum of price values. To get a total sales amount at all aggregations we can create a new measure with the following SQL expression:

```
"facttable"."quantity" * "facttable"."unit_price".
```

With this expression in the source column, the result is calculated before aggregations are performed.

"Aggregate Function"

Microsoft OLAP Services limits you to four methods for creating stored aggregations of measures data. By default, all aggregations are additive (SUM). You may also select from COUNT, MIN, and MAX as aggregation functions. Consider a cube for analyzing temperature patterns in the United States. COUNT will aggregate the SQL `count(*)` of rows grouped by the dimension keys from the fact table. The fact table contains temperature by location, elevation, and time, and you want to see High, Low, and Average temperatures. With the column that contains temperature, create a measure for high temperature by using the MAX aggregation and low temperature using MIN. To get an average temperature, you would create a measure based on temperature using the SUM aggregation function and another using COUNT. Then you would create a calculated measure for "Average Temperature" that divides the SUM aggregate measure by the COUNT measure.

"Data Type"

The "Data Type" can affect the size of the data stored in aggregations. The default value is based upon the data type of the source column in the fact table. Microsoft OLAP Services will suggest "Double" for measure columns of any floating-point type (including currency), "Big Integer" for measure columns of any integer type, and "Date" for measure columns of any date type. You should always double-check this value if you create measures that use SQL functions as the source column. For example, suppose you create a new measure that is based upon an integer measure column in the fact table and edit the source column to be an expression that returns a floating-point value (say,

```
"facttable"."unit_price" * "facttable"."units_purchased"
```

so as to get a value for the total sale amount). In this case, you must change the data type for the measure to a floating-point type. If you don't, OLAP Services will convert the value to an integer when the cube is processed. For some type conversions, processing could result in an error if you are using ROLAP storage and if the RDBMS doesn't handle that type conversion automatically.

For ROLAP storage, OLAP Services uses the value of the Data Type property for the data types of measure columns in aggregation tables. The exact data type it uses will be the closest match available in the RDBMS. For example, since SQL Server does not have a "Big Integer" data type, columns in aggregation tables for measures that are defined as "Big Integer" in OLAP Services will also be defined as "int" in SQL Server.

For MOLAP and HOLAP storage forms, the value of the Data Type property determines how OLAP Services itself stores and manipulates aggregations. For example, single floats are manipulated as 32-bit floating-point numbers with a range of $+/- 3.4 \times 10^{38}$, and double floats are manipulated as 64-bit floating-point numbers with a range of $+/-1.79 \times 10^{308}$. Both "Small Integer" and "Integer" are manipulated as 32-bit integers (with a range of $-2,147,483,648$ to $2,147,483,647$), while "Big Integer" measures are manipulated as 64-bit integers.

"Is Internal"

The "Is Internal" property tags measures indicate that they are used for internal calculations. Like disabled levels, users querying a cube cannot see measures that have this property set to "Yes". Unlike disabled levels, measures with Is Internal set to "Yes" are included in aggregations and can be used in MDX calculations. The measures will not appear in OLE DB for OLAP metadata for the cube, but they can be referred to by name. (This makes it unsuitable for providing security on data values.) For example, in our aggregate function count example we may want to make the temperature measure internal to hide it from users who are browsing our cube. You must use DSO to set the Is Internal property of a virtual cube's measure.

"Display Format"

"Display Format" contains a format string that may be used by a front-end application to format values for display. This can be any Microsoft Office/VBA format string or a custom string that your front end can utilize. If it is an MS Office/VBA format string, the PivotTable Service will make both a value that is formatted according to the format string and a numeric value of a result available for use by the client. If it is a custom string, the client will need to interpret the format string and result value on its own.

Creating Calculated Members and/or Private Dimensions

In addition to the basic building blocks of shared dimensions and measures, the OLAP Manager interface allows you to add calculated members and private dimensions to your cube.

Calculated Members

The ability to create new measures that are based upon simple or complex calculations is one of the most important features of any OLAP tool. While looking at summarized data across multiple dimensions can be informative, true enlightenment often arrives only after we have manipulated the data in meaningful ways. For now, however, we will just focus on the basic mechanics of creating calculated members. More exhaustive coverage of MDX calculation features and how they can be used to derive meaning from data can be found in Chapters 5 through 9.

Keep in mind, however, that Microsoft OLAP Services does not store calculated member values in the database. Instead, calculated members are always calculated as they are requested. Obviously, complex calculations can have a serious effect on the end user's experience as a result of decreased query response time. In the OLAP Manager you create a calculated member by selecting

"Insert|Calculated Member" or by right clicking on an existing calculated member or on the Calculated Member folder and selecting "New Calculated Member." This brings up the calculated member builder shown in Figure 4.30.

By default, calculated members appear in the measures dimension of the cube. You can place a calculated member in any other dimension, however, by selecting a different parent dimension and, optionally, a parent member in that dimension. Editing a calculated member is as simple as typing in an MDX expression in the value expression window. As our earlier sales example showed, to obtain profit in our sales cube we simply subtract cost from the sale amount. For those with strong "mousal" dexterity, expressions can be built by dragging and dropping objects from the dimension tree in the data pane to the expression box and then clicking on the various numeric and operator buttons. To save the calculated member, just click OK.

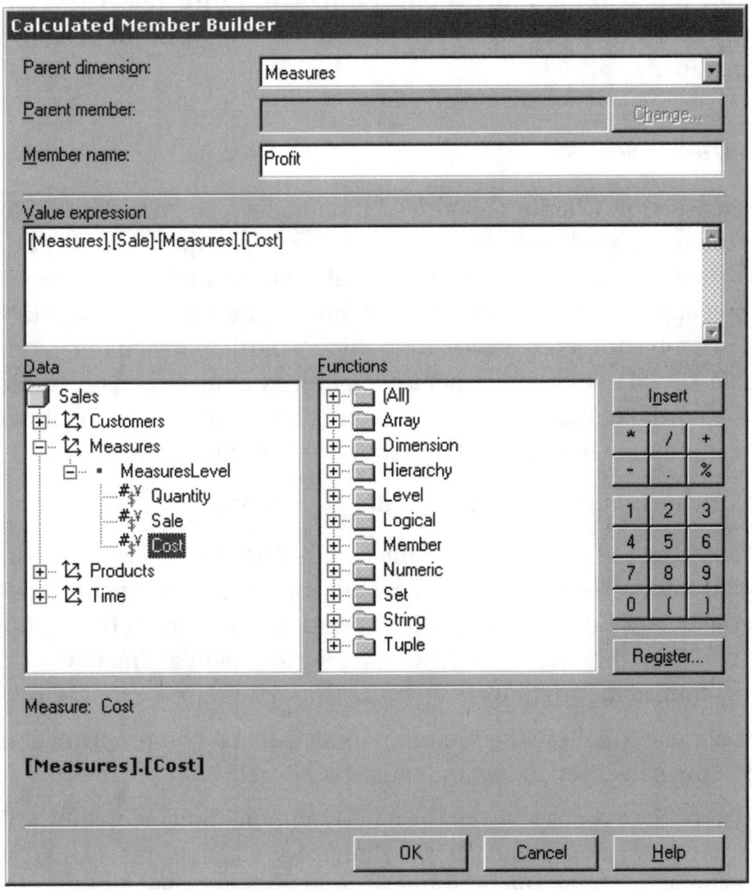

Figure 4.30 Calculated member builder.

Calculated members also have the following additional properties, which can be modified on the Basic and Advanced Properties tabs in the cube editor or through DSO:

Name. The name for the calculated member.

Parent dimension. The dimension that contains the calculated member.

Parent member. The member in the dimension hierarchy that the calculated member should be placed under (if any).

Value. The MDX expression for the calculated member.

Solve order. The order in which the calculated member should be evaluated in relation to other calculated members. As you may imagine, this can be very important when you are using several calculated members. See Chapter 5 for a full discussion of solve orders for calculated members.

Format string. Identical to "Display Format" for measures.

ForeColor, BackColor, FontName, FontSize, FontFlag. Other properties that may be used by client tools to format the display of the results of calculated members.

Private Dimensions

As we discussed in Chapter 3, on OLAP database design, private dimensions function the same as shared dimensions, except that they can only be used by the cube they are created in or by virtual cubes that use that cube. Private dimensions can be created from one or more columns in the fact table, from columns in a table for a dimension that already participates in the cube, or from a new table joined to either the fact table or an existing dimension table. Figure 4.31 shows a private dimension in our sales cube example that is based on the "Hair Color" column in our customer dimension table.

To add a private dimension to a cube, do the following:

- Right click on the cube, on the Dimensions folder, or on an existing dimension and select "New Private Dimension" or "Insert|Dimension|Private" from the cube's Editor menu. You can also drag a column from a dimension table and drop it on the Dimensions folder to create a dimension that has that column as the first level.

- If you choose to follow the menu method, select a column from a table in the column selection dialog and click OK.

- The rest of the process works the same as in the dimension editor. You can add or move levels and modify the dimension's properties. Unlike shared dimensions, however, the member properties for the levels may only be specified through DSO.

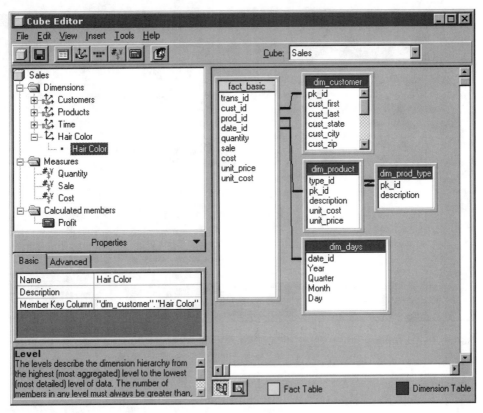

Figure 4.31   A private dimension in the cube editor.

Designing Aggregations and Processing the Cube

Now that you know how to create a cube, populating it with actual data is a simple three-step process. We defined the various storage types in Chapter 2. Here, we'll simply step through the process of defining aggregations and processing cubes so they can be queried. To begin, open the storage wizard by selecting "Tools|Design Storage."

Your first task is to select the data storage method for the cube, as shown in Figure 4.32. You must choose between MOLAP, ROLAP, or HOLAP. We provided definitions and the advantages and disadvantages of each in Chapter 2, so we won't repeat them here. Next, choose a performance or storage target as shown in Figure 4.33. At this point, you inform OLAP Services of your priorities for storage or performance and let it select aggregations for the cube. As we discussed in Chapter 2, there's a direct relationship between storage and query performance in OLAP. Increasing query speed requires more pre-aggregation, which in turn increase storage. The animation in the performance-versus-size

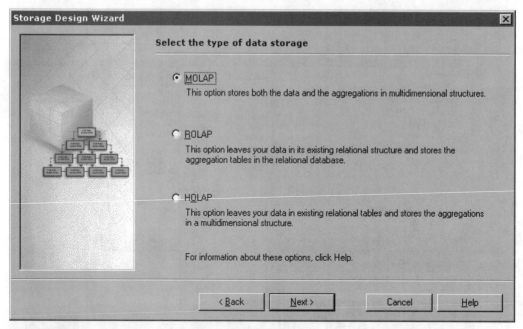

Figure 4.32   Aggregation wizard: Selecting a storage type.

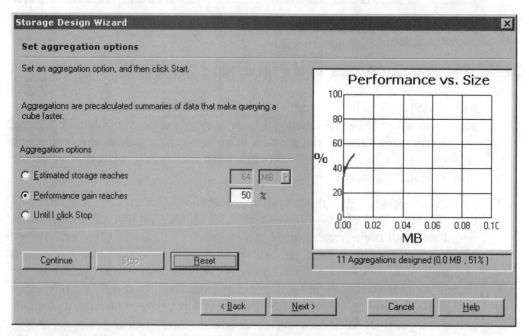

Figure 4.33   Aggregation wizard: Selecting performance targets.

pane illustrates the exponential growth in storage that is required for decreasing increments of performance as OLAP Services designs aggregations. OLAP Services does not enable you to influence aggregation design except through such broad criteria as limiting the estimated data storage size or limiting the estimated performance or through a random threshold that you determine yourself by pausing aggregation design.

Finally, the wizard asks whether you wish to process the cube or simply save the aggregations for processing later. When processing a cube, Microsoft OLAP Services first processes any new or modified dimensions. With all required dimensions processed, OLAP Services processes the cube itself. As with dimension processing, OLAP Services populates cubes with data by selecting all relevant data from the fact table through SQL queries and then writing that data to the designed aggregations. The dialog showing the processing of our sales cube is illustrated in Figure 4.34.

Double-clicking on the SQL icon in the processing dialog displays the SQL OLAP Services uses to process the cube, as shown in Figure 4.35.

Adding Partitions

The `fact_basic` table we used to build our cube contains only data for 1999. We also have data for 1998 in the `fact_basic_1998` table. Occasionally, the

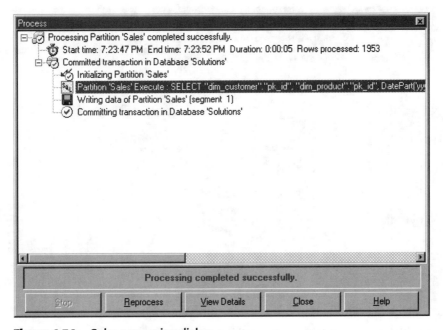

Figure 4.34   Cube processing dialog.

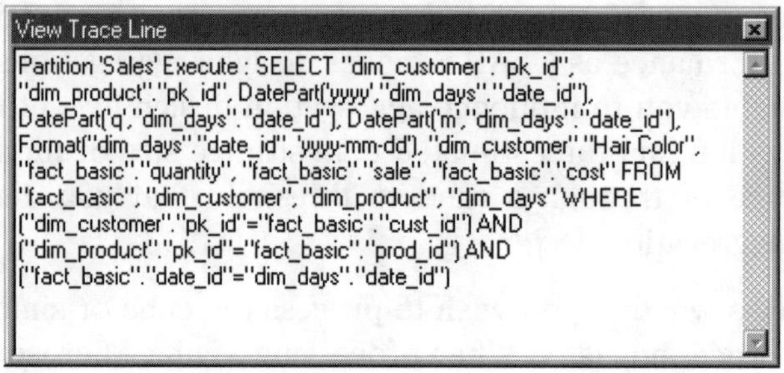

View Trace Line
Partition 'Sales' Execute : SELECT "dim_customer"."pk_id", "dim_product"."pk_id", DatePart('yyyy',"dim_days"."date_id"), DatePart('q',"dim_days"."date_id"), DatePart('m',"dim_days"."date_id"), Format("dim_days"."date_id", 'yyyy-mm-dd'), "dim_customer"."Hair Color", "fact_basic"."quantity", "fact_basic"."sale", "fact_basic"."cost" FROM "fact_basic", "dim_customer", "dim_product", "dim_days" WHERE ("dim_customer"."pk_id"="fact_basic"."cust_id") AND ("dim_product"."pk_id"="fact_basic"."prod_id") AND ("fact_basic"."date_id"="dim_days"."date_id")

Figure 4.35 SQL generated for processing sample cube.

users of our cube will need to see data for 1998, but since most of our users' queries will only be against current year data, it makes sense to put the data for last year into its own partition. As we mentioned in Chapters 2 and 3, if we define the partition as containing only 1998 data, OLAP Services will ignore this larger partition for queries that do not request 1998 data, which will make the bulk of our users' queries perform faster.

To create a partition, right-click on the Partitions folder under the cube in the tree pane of the OLAP Manager console and select "New Partition" to start the

Partition Wizard
Specify the data source and the fact table
If you want to select a different data source or fact table for your new partition, click Change.
Data source:
Solutions
Fact table:
fact_basic_1998
Change...
The new data source must contain the identical schema used by your cube. That is, the fact and dimension tables for this partition must contain the same columns that exist in your cube.
The required dimension tables are:
"dim_prod_type", "dim_product", "dim_days", "dim_customer"
< Back
Next >
Cancel
Help

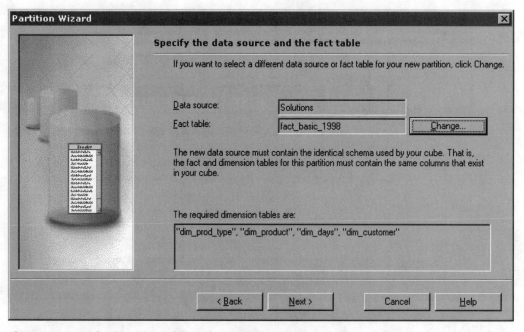

Figure 4.36 Selecting a fact table in the partition wizard.

partitions wizard, as shown in Figure 4.36. Select the fact table that contains the data you wish to include in the partition (in this case, fact_basic_1998). By default, the partitions wizard selects fact table used for the primary partition. To change this, click on the "Change . . ." button and select a different table from the data source. If you are selecting a different table, remember that it must contain the same columns as the fact table that is used in the primary partition.

In the next step (see Figure 4.37), you identify the slice of data that the partition will contain. Again, this is the only way that OLAP Services knows that the partition contains a particular subset of data. You may define the slice according to any single member within a dimension. You can use members from multiple dimensions but only one within any given dimension. For example, we could define the slice for the time dimension as 1998 and slice the customer dimension on Boston, Massachusetts. We cannot, however, define the customer slice as including both Boston, Massachusetts and Cranston, Rhode Island. To slice on 1998, select the time dimension with the mouse and select "1998" from the dimension hierarchy that is displayed on the right side of the dialog. The dialog should now resemble the one shown in Figure 4.38.

In the final step (see Figure 4.39), you provide a name for the partition and set the aggregations. Optionally, you may also define a filter and aggrega-

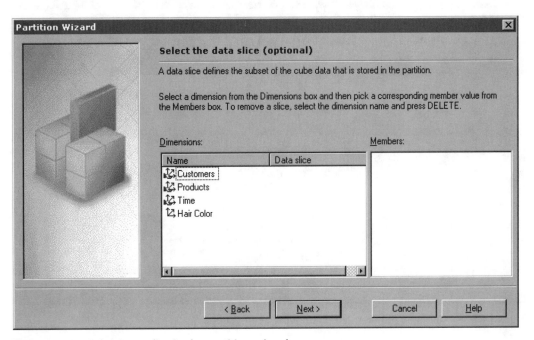

Figure 4.37   Selecting a slice in the partition wizard.

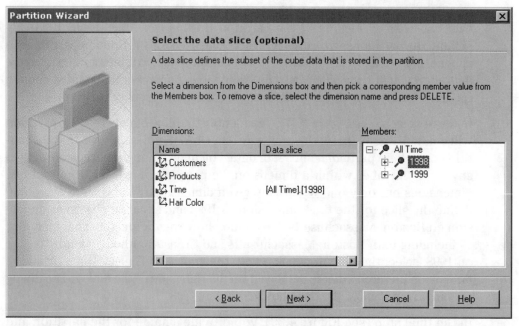

Figure 4.38 Partition wizard with a slice defined for 1998.

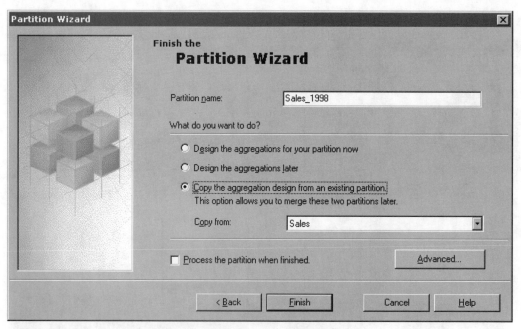

Figure 4.39 Naming a partition and identifying aggregations.

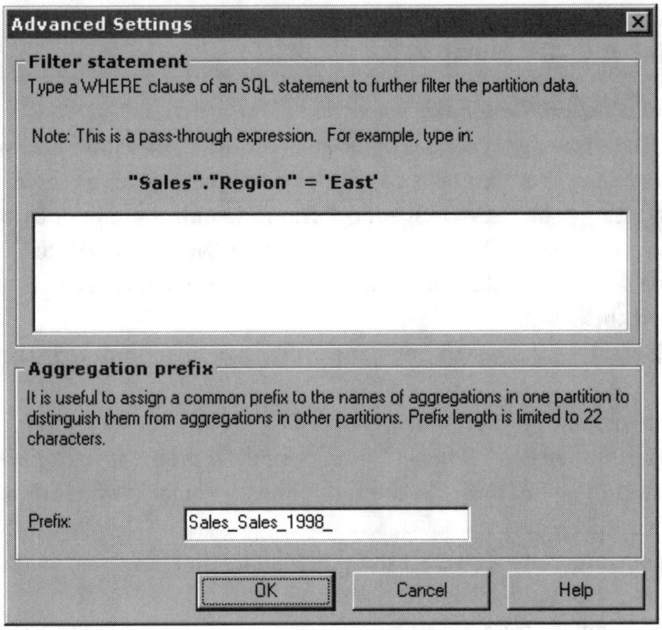

Figure 4.40 Partition wizard WHERE clause.

tion prefix. You can use aggregations that are already designed for any other partition in the cube, or you can design new aggregations that are specific to this partition. Since the data in this partition will be queried much less frequently than the data in other partitions, you might want to use fewer aggregations to save storage space. Designing aggregations for partitions is done in exactly the same manner as we described earlier in this chapter. If "Design Aggregations for Your Partition Now" is checked on the last screen of the aggregation wizard, the aggregation wizard will start when you press the "Finish" button. Since we've already walked through the process of designing aggregations, we'll simply copy the aggregations from our primary partition.

Clicking the Advanced Properties button opens a dialog where you can enter a WHERE clause that OLAP Services will use to filter the fact table data it will use to populate the partition. You may also define an aggregation prefix for the partition (see Figure 4.39). The aggregation prefix is optional and only relevant for ROLAP storage. Microsoft OLAP Services uses the aggregation prefix to name ROLAP aggregations in the same manner as described earlier for cubes.

Manually Creating a Cube with the Editor

To initialize a new cube, do the following:

- From the OLAP Manager console, right-click on the Cube folder and select "New Cube|Editor." You can also do this from an existing cube editor session by selecting "File|New Cube|Editor" from the Editor menu or by right-clicking on a cube in the tree pane and selecting "New Cube|Editor."
- A fact table selection dialog will then appear. Expand a data source, select a table, and click OK.
- On the Basic tab of the properties pane, enter a name and description for the cube.

To add shared dimensions, do the following:

- Select "Insert|Dimension|Manager" from the Editor menu or right-click on the Cube or Dimension folder in the tree pane and select "Dimension Manager."
- In the dimension manager, select the dimensions that you want to use with your fact table and click OK.

To create table joins, do the following:

- Drag a column from one table in the schema and drop it on the join column in another table.
- Select a column in a table in the schema panel. Select "Insert|Join" from the Editor menu or right-click and select "Insert Join." From the column selection dialog, select a column to join to.

To remove table joins, do the following:

- Select a join line in the schema pane. Right-click and choose "Remove" or press "Delete" on the keyboard.
- Select a column in a table in the schema panel. Select "Edit|Remove Join" from the Editor menu or right-click and select "Remove Join."

The editor offers you three methods for adding measures to a cube:

- Select "Insert|Measure" from the Editor menu or right-click on the Measure folder or an existing measure in the tree pane. From the column selection dialog select a column from the fact table and click OK.
- Drag a column from a table in the schema pane and drop it on the Measure folder.
- Select a column from the fact table in the schema pane, then right-click and select "Insert as Measure."

Summary

In this chapter, we walked through the mechanics of building dimensions, cubes, and other Microsoft OLAP Services objects using the OLAP Manager console. In Chapters 10 (Maintaining Applications) and 11 (Optimization), we will delve into many of the topics covered here in greater detail. In Chapters 15 and 16 we will work through tutorials that apply the features we have introduced here in sample applications. In Chapter 5 we'll adjust course a bit and discuss how you can get data out of your OLAP Services cubes with MDX queries.

Introduction to MDX

This chapter introduces the syntax and semantics of the MDX language implemented by Microsoft OLAP Services. In OLAP Services, all analysis beyond simple aggregation is performed using MDX queries and expressions. When you are developing and using an analytical application in Microsoft OLAP Services, you will need to use MDX both for full queries and for calculations. These two uses are intertwined, so we will introduce them both in this chapter. The person who is implementing an OLAP Services solution will create calculations before users execute any queries, so the order of usage might be "design calculations, then design queries." However, we will look at queries first because MDX calculations will be easier to understand within the context of queries.

The specification for OLE DB for OLAP describes the full relationship between MDX queries and the structure of rows and columns that convey the queried information back to the client program. In this chapter, we mention a few of the relevant aspects of this relationship, but we primarily focus on the more logic-related side of what queries are asking for rather than the programming-oriented aspect of how queries come out.

We explained in Chapter 2 that queries against OLAP Services cubes are always requested through the PivotTable Service on the client and that the PivotTable Service will usually perform run-time calculations needed to provide results for a query. While OLAP Services will sometimes perform run-time calculations on the server, it is the PivotTable Service that determines whether calculations will

A Note on Our MDX Style

Within MDX, some functions and operators are optional in certain circumstances. Our examples in this chapter will frequently include some of these optional functions and operators for the sake of creating a consistent style. However, we may leave optional operators out if an expression is short and sweet and including the operators would generate a relatively high amount of syntactic noise. We will also frequently break up queries and statements onto multiple lines so the components of each will be a little clearer. This style will also allow us to easily reuse snippets of text from one query to the next. Although many users and applications will only use MDX that is generated by a program, at the time this book was written we had not seen any tools that could substantially help you create the more sophisticated expressions and queries that MDX enables.

MDX function syntax is fairly irregular. Some functions use the standard function format—*Function* (*Arguments*); other functions use an object method format—*Object.Function* (*Arguments*). There is no intuitive way to determine which functions are expressed in which format, and functions that are conceptually quite related will nonetheless use different formats. Furthermore, those object-style functions that take no arguments use no parentheses (in the style of Pascal and current versions of Visual Basic, unlike C++, Java, and SQL functions which do use parentheses even when a function takes no arguments). Even after you have used MDX for some time, it is easy to trip up on which functions use which format. In this text we will therefore use the following convention for referring to MDX functions by name: If a function *ThisFunction* is written in standard function format, we will refer to it as "*ThisFunction*()." An example of this usage might be the sentence "The Order() function sorts information based on data values." If a function *ThatFunction* is written in object method format and it takes arguments, we will refer to it as ".*ThatFunction*()", as in "The .Lag() function lets you reference data elements some number of members away." If a function *OtherFunction* is written in object method format but it takes no arguments, we will refer to it as ".OtherFunction", as in "The .Children function returns all children members of a parent member." In using this style, we hope the text will not only describe functions and their semantics but also help reinforce their actual syntax.

be handled locally or instruct OLAP Services to perform them remotely. To make our explanation of MDX easier to follow, however, we will generally refer to Microsoft OLAP Services as a whole rather than distinguish between OLAP Services and the PivotTable Service. Our primary goal in this chapter is to provide guidance on how to construct and use MDX queries and statements, so we hope to avoid unnecessary confusion by referring to the product as a whole instead of specific subsets of the product. See Chapter 11 for an in-depth discussion on the relationship between the PivotTable Service and OLAP Services in processing queries.

The Very Basics

We will start off by looking at MDX queries that don't involve what appear to be calculations. Even if an application only uses aggregations of base measures, the end user will still only access the data through MDX queries. Throughout this chapter we will mix descriptions of the abstract properties of a query in with concrete examples to build up a comprehensive picture of MDX.

To prepare you for the concrete examples used in this chapter, imagine the following very simple sample database. There is a time dimension that has two base members: June-1998 and July-1998. There is a store dimension that has two base members: Downtown and Uptown. The cube is called TrivialCube, and it has two base measures: Sales and Costs. This means that we can have eight cells (two times for two stores for two measures); some initial values for this example are shown in Figure 5.1 in a tabular format. We will expand the example as we go, but these initial values we will give us some explanatory mileage.

Let's say we want to look at a grid of numbers that has our downtown store's sales and costs for both months, June and July. MDX queries result in grids of cells. The grid can have two dimensions, like a spreadsheet or table, but it can also have one, three, or more. (It can also have zero; we'll talk about that in the section "Data Model: Queries"). The grid we want to see is shown in Figure 5.2.

Like SQL, an MDX query includes SELECT, FROM, and WHERE. (Although MDX and SQL share these keywords in form, don't look for too many similarities in their meaning.) Whereas SQL only lets you put columns of tables into columns of a query, the result of an MDX query is itself another cube, and you

Stores	Time	Sales	Costs
Downtown	June-1998	1200	1000
Downtown	July-1998	1300	1050
Uptown	June-1998	1000	800
Uptown	July-1998	1000	900

Figure 5.1   A trivial data set in `TrivialCube`.

Measures

	Sales	Costs
June-1998	1200	1000
July-1998	1300	1050

Time

Figure 5.2 Simple result grid.

can put any dimension (or combinations of dimensions) on any axis of that result. In MDX terminology, the term "axis" applies to an edge or dimension of the query result. Referring to "Axis" rather than dimension makes it simpler to distinguish the dimensions of the cells in the cube being queried from the dimensions of the cells in the cells of the results (each of which can be a combination of multiple cube dimensions.) The MDX query in the following example would specify the cells we want to see:

```
SELECT
    { [Measures].[Sales], [Measures].[Costs] } on columns,
    { [Time].[June-1998], [Time].[July-1998] } on rows
FROM TrivialCube
WHERE ( [Stores].[Downtown] )
```

You may be able to make a number of generalizations immediately from this example. Let's break this simple query down into pieces:

1. MDX uses curly braces, { and }, to enclose a set of elements from a particular dimension or set of dimensions. In our simple query there is only one dimension on each of the two axes of the query (the measures dimension and the time dimension).

2. In an MDX query, you specify how dimensions from your database map onto axes of your result cube. Each query may have a different number of result axes. The first three axes have the names "columns", "rows", and "pages" so as to conceptually match a typical printed report. (You can refer to them in another way, as we will see in "Axis Numbering and Ordering".) Though our simple query does not show more than one dimension on a result axis, when more than one dimension maps to a result axis each cell slot on the axis is related to a combination of one member from each of the mapped dimensions.

3. "Columns" always comes before "rows" (and "rows" always comes before "pages"). We'll see why in "Axis Numbering and Ordering".

4. The FROM clause in an MDX query names the cube from which the data is being queried. This is similar to the FROM clause of SQL which specifies the tables from which data is being queried. The initial release of Microsoft

OLAP Services only supports a single cube in the FROM clause.

5. Any other dimensions that don't appear in the columns or rows (or other axes) will nevertheless still have some member involved in the query. The WHERE clause provides a place to specify any such member or members. If you don't specify any such members, then OLAP Services assumes some reasonable defaults. The use of parentheses in our simple query will be explained in the section "Data Model: Tuples and Sets."

Once OLAP Services has determined the cells of the query result, OLAP Services fills them with data from the cube being queried. So, every query has at least a SELECT . . . FROM . . . WHERE framework. In addition, MDX has some other components that we will devote the remainder of this chapter to describing:

- How metadata entities are named in MDX
- The MDX data model
- Simple MDX construction
- Dimensional calculations as calculated members
- Named sets
- Detailed parts of MDX queries

How Metadata Entities Are Named in MDX

We need to look now at how Microsoft OLAP Services's metadata entities are named in MDX because we will need to refer to OLAP metadata wherever we use MDX. Dimensions, cubes, levels, members, and member properties all have names that need to be expressed in MDX queries. Two key aspects of MDX identifiers as they are used in OLAP Services are as follows: the delimiting of names within surrounding text, and the multi-part nature of many names.

Delimited and Multi-part Names

When you write a name in MDX, it can be delimited or undelimited. Undelimited names, as in SQL and many other languages, start with a letter, and one or more letters, numbers, or underscores may follow them. For example, `Production` is a legal name. Names in OLAP Services can also be delimited by square brackets—*[*, and *]*—in which case spaces, periods, commas, and other characters can be used. For example, `[Production of Widgets]` and `[1997]` are also both legal names. OLAP Services does not have any published limitations on valid member names; however, cube, dimension, and level names have some restrictions, which we enumerated in Chapter 3.

When the name of a member at any level is enclosed within brackets, any characters may be used in that name. In OLAP Services's way of handling names, the leading bracket starts the name, and every character until the closing bracket is acceptable. Names can even contain the open and closing bracket characters. If a closing bracket symbol is to be part of the name, then in MDX you have to use double closing brackets ("]]") when the name contains a closing bracket. For example, the literal name "Table [with chairs]" would be written as `[Table [with chairs]]]`. Leading and trailing spaces are part of the name. Moreover, the member can have an empty name too, which you would reference with `[]`.

MDX makes use of identifiers that have more than one name part, and in these identifiers the names are separated by a period. Cubes and dimensions form the primary part of these names. For example, `[Time].[1998]` would identify the `[1998]` member of the time dimension, and `[SalesCube].[Measures]` `.[Profit]` identifies the Profit member of the Measures dimension of the SalesCube cube. Notice that `[1998]` is listed in brackets. If it weren't, it would be interpreted as a number. Also, notice that the periods are placed between the bracketed sections: `[Time].[1998.Quarter1]` is a different reference than `[Time].[1998].[Quarter1]`.

Names versus Unique Names

When you reference metadata entities like levels and members in a query, you need to understand the importance of the distinction between a name and a unique name. Microsoft OLAP Services can use names that don't clearly spell out what the entity is, but it will usually be to your advantage to use unique names where possible. For example, if there is only one member anywhere in your cube whose name is "Profit" or "[1998]", then referring simply to `Profit` or `[1998]` in a query or expression will be adequate. However, for any member, its name in that level may not be unique. (Recall from Chapter 3 that even if the member key is unique, the name might not be. For example, "Springfield" is a city name shared by 31 U.S. states.) If you were simply to refer to `[Springfield]` in MDX, OLAP Services will pick one of the Springfields and use it, but you won't have much control over which one. The solution to this problem is to use the unique name of the appropriate member.

Software tools that help you construct MDX queries will relieve you of most of the burden of constructing unique names. These tools may not always be available for the MDX you write, however, so you should understand how unique names are constructed. We devote the remainder of this section to a description of the unique names for the various OLAP Services structures.

Dimensions

The unique name for a dimension is simply the name of that dimension (like [Time] or [Measures]).

Hierarchies

The unique name for a hierarchy is the name of the dimension, followed by a period, followed by the name of the hierarchy (e.g., [Time].[Fiscal] or [Product].[ByManufacturer]. If the dimension has only one implicit hierarchy, then the name of the dimension is the name of the hierarchy, so no *.Hierarchy* needs to be added to the dimension's name. That is, you would write [Time] instead of [Time].[Time].

Levels

The unique name for a level is the unique name for its hierarchy, followed by a period, followed by the name of the level. For example, the sole level of the measures dimension of a cube is named [Measures].[Measures Level]. Levels of other dimensions might be named [Geography].[State] or (in the case of a multiple hierarchy) [Time].[Fiscal].[Quarter].

Members

Use the following algorithm when forming the unique name for a member:

1. Start with the name of the dimension.
2. Starting at the top level (the All level if there is one), append a dot (.) followed by the (non-unique) name of the desired member's ancestor at that level (or the name of the member if you've reached its level).
3. Moving down levels, repeat the last step until you've reached the level of the member.

For example, depending on your choice of names for the All member caption, the root member in a time dimension that has an All level would be named [Time].[All Time]. If this dimension has levels of Years, Quarters, and Months, then the unique names for some members at lower levels may be [Time].[All Time].[1998], [Time].[All Time].[1998].[Quarter 1], and [Time].[All Time].[1998].[Quarter 1].[January].

Member Properties

The unique name for a member property is the unique name for its level, followed by a dot, followed by the name of the property. For example, the unique name for the store square-footage property in a geography dimension might be `[Geography].[Store].[SquareFootage]`.

Other Considerations

If you are constructing a unique name outside the context of a cube, then you need to put the cube's name and a dot at the very beginning, followed by the name of the dimension and all the other parts as we detailed earlier. This situation arises when you create or drop named sets or calculated members. For example, the unique name of "January 1998" in a cube named Production History would be `[Produc-tion History].[Time].[All Time].[1998].[Quarter 1].[January]`.

Throughout our discussions of MDX, we will tend toward using simpler names for the sake of brevity. For example, we will place an unambiguous member name immediately after the dimension's name, as in `[Time].[January 1998]`. If we actually have an unambiguous member named [January 1998] in the time dimension, then this is a perfectly adequate way to reference it in Microsoft OLAP Services. We will, however, generally enclose names in the square-bracket delimiters even when special characters like spaces aren't part of the name. You can see an example of this in the trivial query with which we started this chapter.

There is another reason to put all names in square brackets and to qualify member names with at least the name of the dimension: if the name is not delimited by square brackets, it may be interpreted as the name of an external function or an MDX operator (perhaps an operator that is only added to the language in a subsequent version of the language). When you are constructing calculated members, named sets, saved MDX queries, or external functions, you cannot really anticipate all the other names that may come into play when they are used in new ways later on.

The MDX Data Model

MDX uses a data model that is based on OLAP Services's dimensions and cubes but is even richer (and somewhat more complex, though not terribly so). Understanding it is the key to unlocking powerful analyses and even to understanding why some basic operations and syntax work the way they do. In this section we will explore what this data model is.

Data Model: Tuples and Sets

The terminology of MDX includes tuples and sets in addition to all the other terms we have used with Microsoft OLAP Services so far. Tuples and sets are very similar to members and dimensions, but a little more generalized. Because they are the basic elements of many MDX operations, we need to explain them before exploring how they are used.

Tuples are essentially multidimensional members. MDX works by identifying cells based on tuples. Recall that an MDX query can put more than one dimension on a result axis. Each result slot may correspond to a member from more than one dimension, such as `[Store].[NYC Fifth Avenue Store]`, `[Time].[1998]`, `[Product].[Leather Jackets]`, `[Scenario].[Actual]`, `[Measure].[Sales]`. An example of a tuple is the combination of members from each dimension. Seen another way, each cell value in OLAP Services is identified by a tuple comprised of one member from each dimension in the cube. The tuple [Product].[Leather Jackets], [Time].[1998], [Store].[Fifth Avenue NYC], [Measures].[Sales] may completely define a cell with a value of $13,000. A single member is a simple tuple. The "dimensionality" of a tuple refers to the set of dimensions whose members compose it. In OLAP Services, the order in which dimensions appear in a tuple is also an important part of a tuple's dimensionality. Any and all dimensions can be part of a tuple, including members of the measures dimension. Note, however, that a tuple refers to a slice of the cube (with an individual cell being the ultimate slice). Depending on the context that it is used in, a tuple either refers to that combination of members or to the value(s) in the cell(s) that the tuple specifies.

Syntactically, a tuple can be specified in the following ways. If it is comprised of a member from only one dimension, that dimension can be listed by itself (as with `[Product].[Leather Jackets]`). If it is comprised of members from more than one dimension, the members must be surrounded by parentheses (as with `([Time].[1998], [Product].[Leather Jackets])`). You can always put a single member within parentheses. However, it's not required if the tuple is defined by just that member—with the exception of the WHERE clause of a query. Some MDX operators return tuples. These tuples can be within parentheses or not. The WHERE clause of the trivial query we presented earlier contains a tuple, which is why the member in it was placed in parentheses. Syntactically, OLAP Services requires that the tuple of the WHERE clause be within parentheses, even if it consists of only one member.

Sets are simply ordered collections of tuples. A set may have more than one tuple, only one tuple, or it may be empty. Unlike a set in mathematical terms, an MDX set may contain the same tuple more than once. Although sets might be better called "collections," we are stuck with the term *set* for now. Depending on the context in which a set is used, it either refers to that set of member combinations or to the value(s) in the cell(s) that its tuples specify.

Syntactically, a set may be specified in a number of ways. Generally, a set can be specified by enclosing its members in curly braces ("{and }"). One such example is the expression { [Time].[June-98], [Time].[July-98] } from our earlier trivial query. An example of a set involving multiple dimensions would be

```
{ ([Time].[1998], [Product].[Leather Jackets]),
([Time].[1997], [Product].[Silk Scarves]) }.
```

Whenever one or more tuples are explicitly listed, you will need to enclose them within braces. Some MDX operators and functions also return sets. The expressions that use them do not need to be enclosed in braces if the set is not being combined with more tuples, but we will tend to enclose set expressions with braces for the sake of style.

Although a single member is by default a tuple of one dimension, a set that has only one tuple is not equivalent to a tuple. As far as MDX and OLAP Services are concerned, the tuple

```
([Time].[1998 Week 1], [Product].[HyperGizmos])
```

is not the same as the set

```
{ ([Time].[1998 Week 1], [Product].[HyperGizmos]) }.
```

You might think it reasonable that wherever a set is called for you can use a single tuple and it would be interpreted as a set of one. However, that is not the case. Instead, you will need to wrap the tuple in curly braces as in the second sample just given. Similarly, a set that happens to contain only one tuple is still considered to be a set. To use it in an expression where a tuple is called for, even if you have guaranteed that it only contains one tuple, you must still employ an MDX function that takes a tuple from a set.

Every tuple in a set must have the same dimensionality (i.e., set of dimensions and order of dimensions within each tuple). This means that we can also refer to the dimensionality of a set, which by implication also refers to the dimensionality of each tuple within it. You could use the following tuples in a single query:

```
([Time].[1998], [Product].[Leather Jackets])
```

and

```
(Product].[Leather Jackets], [Time].[1998])
```

However, combining them into the same set will result in an error.

When tuples end up on the axis of a query, the order in which the dimensions appear affects the nesting order in the axis. The first dimension listed becomes the outermost dimension, the second becomes the next outermost, and so on. The last dimension is the innermost. For example, suppose the following set were placed on the "rows" axis in a query:

```
{ ([Time].[1998], [Product].[Leather Jackets]),
  ([Time].[1998], [Product].[Silk Scarves]),
```

```
([Time].[1997], [Product].[Leather Jackets]),
([Time].[1997], [Product].[Silk Scarves] }
```

In this case, the expected presentation for data brought back to a client through OLE DB for OLAP or ADO would be as shown in Figure 5.3. Note that the layout shown in Figure 5.3 is simply conventional; your applications may do something different with the results.

Data Model: Queries

An MDX query is just a result cube that is a transformation of the cube that it is being queried. The result cube can have one, two, three, four, or more axes (up to 64 in Microsoft OLAP Services). It is also possible for a query to be considered to have zero axes, but it will still return a single-cell value. Two examples of a zero-axis query would be

```
SELECT FROM SalesCube
```

and

```
SELECT FROM SalesCube
WHERE ([Time].[1994], [Geography].[Quebec], [Product].[Snorkels], [Chan-
nel].[Superstores]).
```

Since no members were assigned to any (non-slicer) axis in the query, the result is considered to have zero axes and by convention would be a single unlabeled cell. Of course, whether you consider it to be zero-dimensional depends on whether or not you choose to ignore the dimensional information conveyed in the slicer. A one-dimensional query, which selects only columns, will show tuples on one axis and only one column of numbers and will lack a descriptive header apart from the slicer information.

Note that all MDX queries return cells. Many useful OLAP and decision-support system (DSS) queries are of the form "What members belong in this set?,"

---	---	---
1998	Leather Jackets	*cell values*
1998	Silk Scarves	*cell values*
1997	Leather Jackets	*cell values*
1997	Silk Scarves	*cell values*
---	---	---

Figure 5.3   Typical expected client data layout.

where the result that is of real interest is not cell data but members that are associated with cell data or member property values. A query of this form, such as "Show me the top customers that make up the top 10% of our revenue," will result in at least some cell data being returned. Even if you are querying for just these tuples, Microsoft OLAP Services will prepare for you the moral equivalent of an extra column of numbers. This is in contrast to SQL, which will return only the columns that you request.

Simple MDX Construction

Now that we have explored the basics of tuples and sets, let's look at some additional ways to create them. A few MDX operators and functions are used very commonly to create sets. We will introduce them here and describe how they are frequently used. Learning how they work will let us introduce and explore more sophisticated and complex areas of MDX later in the chapter. (More complete and detailed descriptions can be found in Chapter 7, which is a detailed reference on MDX functions and operators.)

- , (comma) and : (colon)
- .Members
- CrossJoin()
- Filter()
- Order()

, (comma) and : (colon)

We have already seen the comma operator used to construct sets; let's deal with it directly here. The tuples that form a set can be enumerated by separating them with commas, as with

```
{[Time].[January 1998], [Time].[February 1998], [Time].[March 1998]}
```

This expression results in a set that holds the first three months of 1998.

Recall that in every level in every dimension, the members of that level are arranged in a particular order (by member key or by name). When it makes sense, we can specify a set as a range of members in that order by listing two members from the same level as endpoints and putting a colon between them to mean "These members and every member between them." (This is similar to a syntax used to specify ranges of cells in spreadsheets like Excel.) For example, the expression

```
{ [Time].[January 1998] : [Time].[April 1998] }
```

is the set of months January through April 1998, inclusive. Most frequently, expressions using the colon to define sets will be used when the database ordering corresponds to a useful real-world ordering, as with time. The colon takes two members on the same level as its endpoints; you cannot use it with more tuples that have more than one dimension. It is not an error to put the same member on both sides of the colon; you will just get a range of one member.

WARNING

■■■■■ Note that the colon only produces members in one direction. Because of the internal mechanics of OLAP Services, if you wanted to produce the range { [Time].[April-1998], [Time].[March-1998], [Time].[February-1998], [Time].[January-1998] }, you cannot just say { [Time].[April-1998] : [Time].[January-1998] }. OLAP Services will instead create the range { [Time].[April-1998] : *last member on level* }.

The comma operator can be used anywhere within a set specification to add tuples or subsets to an overall set. For example,

```
{ { [Time].[January-1998] : [Time].[March-1998] } ,
{[Time].[October-1998] : [Time].[December-1998]} }
```

creates a set of the first three and last three months of 1998, while

```
{  [Time].[1998], { [Time].[January-1998] : [Time].[March-1998] } }
```

creates a set of 1998 and its first three months. When tuples or subsets are concatenated by commas, the order in which the commas join them is the order in which they are returned.

.Members

Getting the set of members for a dimension, hierarchy, or level is a very common starting point for further operations. The .Members operator takes a dimension, hierarchy, or level on its left-hand side, and it results in a set of all members associated with that metadata scope. For example, [Customer].Members results in the set of all customers, while [Product].[Product Category].Members returns all members of the Product Category level in the Product dimension. For example, the query fragment

```
SELECT
{ [Scenario].Members } on columns, . . .
```

specifies a query in which all members of the scenario dimension are laid across the columns.

The following two points will hopefully illuminate the use of the .Members operator more than obscure:

First, hierarchies are implemented as dimensions, and multiple dimensions have different sets of members. As a result, in a dimension that contains multiple hierarchies you cannot simply express `[Dimension].Members`. Microsoft OLAP Services will complain of an unknown dimension if you do. For example, given a logical [Time] dimension that contains two hierarchies, `[Time].[Fiscal]` and `[Time].[Calendar]`, a client taking metadata from OLE DB for OLAP will see one time dimension. However, the expression `[Time].Members` will result in an error. To obtain a set of members, the client must request either `[Time].[Fiscal].Members` or `[Time].[Calendar].Members`. If the dimension has only one hierarchy and that hierarchy does not have an explicit name, then *Dimension*.`Members` will work. For example, if time has only one hierarchy, then `[Time].Members` will work.

Second, when a client uses .Members (or other metadata functions that return the set of members associated with some metadata element), OLAP Services does not automatically include any calculated members in the returned set. This means that the preceding request for [Scenario].Members, as written, will not return any calculated members in the scenario dimension. We can always ask for them by name, however, and OLAP Services provides an AddCalculatedMembers() function to add them into a set. We'll show an example of using AddCalculatedMembers() in the section "Named Sets."

CrossJoin()

There are many occasions when we will want to take the cross-product of members (or tuples) in two different sets (that is, specify all of their possible combinations). The CrossJoin() function is the most direct way of combining the two sets in this way. For example, we may wish to lay out on one axis of a query all months in 1999 and all product categories. We would generate this set with the expression

```
CrossJoin (
   { [Time].[Jan 1999] : [Time].[Dec 1999] },
   { [Product].[Product Category].members }
)
```

We would use it like this:

```
SELECT
CrossJoin (
   { [Time].[January 1999] : [Time].[December 1999] },
   { [Product].[Product Category].Members }
) on columns
. . .
```

Jan 1999	Jan 1999	Jan 1999	Feb 1999	Feb 1999	Feb 1999
Toys	Games	Clothing	Toys	Games	Clothing

Figure 5.4 CrossJoined Dimensions on Columns.

This would result in a set of columns that look like those shown in Figure 5.4. CrossJoin() only takes two sets as inputs. If you want to take the CrossJoin() of three or more sets, such as times, scenarios, and products, you can do it in one of two ways:

```
CrossJoin (
  [Time].Members,
  CrossJoin ([Scenario].Members, [Product].Members)
)

CrossJoin (
  CrossJoin([Time].Members, [Scenario].Members),
  [Product].Members
)
```

Notice that each of these results in a set whose dimensionality is, in order, time, scenario, product.

CrossJoin() is standard MDX. Microsoft OLAP Services also has a non-standard technique for doing the same thing by using * (asterisk):

```
{ [Time]                          } * { [Product].Members }
```

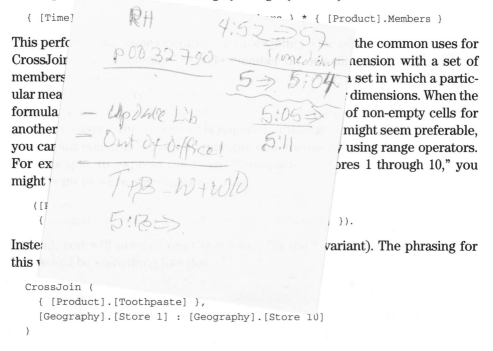

This perfo   the common uses for
CrossJoi   nension with a set of
members   a set in which a particular mea   dimensions. When the
formula   of non-empty cells for
another   might seem preferable,
you car   using range operators.
For ex   ores 1 through 10," you
might

```
([F
{                                     }).
```

Inste   variant). The phrasing for
this

```
CrossJoin (
  { [Product].[Toothpaste] },
  [Geography].[Store 1] : [Geography].[Store 10]
)
```

In the phrasing in the CrossJoin() example we did not use curly braces around the set—they were not needed there. However, since the function requires a set we did use them around the single member [Toothpaste] so we could convert the tuple to a set.

Filter()

Operators like CrossJoin() and : help us construct sets. In contrast, Filter() lets us reduce a set by including in the resulting set only those elements that meet some criteria. Filter() takes one set and one Boolean expression as its arguments and returns that subset where the Boolean expression is true. For example, the expression

```
Filter (
  [Product].[Product Category].Members,
  [Measures].[Sales] >= 500
)
```

will return a set of all product category members in which the associated sales measure value was at least 500. Filter() works on general sets, not just on sets of one dimension's members, so the following expression returns the set of all (product category, city) tuples in which the associated sales value was at least 500:

```
Filter (
  CrossJoin (
    [Product].[Product Category].Members,
    [Store].[City].Members
  ), [Measures].[Sales] >= 500
)
```

This is the first time we have used comparisons. It is worth pointing out that any Boolean expression may be used to filter the set. The following Filter() expression returns those product categories in which the sales in Little Rock, AR were twice as large as the costs and the number of units sold was less than 30 in August 1997:

```
Filter (
  [Product].[Product Category].Members,
  ([Measures].[Sales], [Time].[Aug 1997], [Store].[Little Rock, AR]) > 2
* ([Measures].[Costs], [Time].[Aug 1997], [Store].[Little Rock, AR])
  AND ([Measures].[Units], [Time].[Aug 1997], [Store].[Little Rock, AR]
) < 30
)
```

In determining the value of sales associated with each product category, or each (product category, city) tuple, you must take into account the other dimensions that are associated with sales values. For example, the first two Filter() expressions did not account for the time or times with which the sales values were associated. We can specify any additional dimensions' members that we need to in either the Boolean condition or in the set. For example, if we wanted to specify that we wished to filter 1997's sales in Baton Rouge, we simply say

```
Filter (
  [Product].[Product Category].Members,
  ([Measures].[Sales], [Time].[1997], [Store].[Baton Rouge, LA]) >= 500
)
```

Within the filtering operation, the cell value will be taken from the 1997 Baton Rouge sales at each product category. The result is a set of product category members.

On the more advanced side, we can also specify more members in the set. For example, the preceding operation could be specified as follows:

```
Filter (
  CrossJoin (
    {([Time].[1997], [Store].[Baton Rouge, LA]) },
    [Product].[Product Category].Members
  ),
  [Measures].[Sales] >= 500
)
```

though the set returned would consist of tuples with dimensionality

```
([Time], [Store], [Product]).
```

These Filter() expressions have introduced the concept of query context. Every MDX expression ultimately operates in a context that is set up outside of it. Nested MDX operations are resolved within the context of the operation that invokes the nested operation. Chapter 6 explains query evaluation and context in detail.

Order()

To put the tuples in a set into some ordering based on associated data values, we need to use the Order() function. Order() takes a set, a criterion for ordering the set, and, optionally, a flag that indicates what sorting principle to use (ascending or descending, including or ignoring hierarchical relationships between the tuples). Order() returns a set that consists of the original set's tuples in the new order. The precise operations of the orderings that include hierarchical relationships are fairly complex. Chapter 7 includes a complete description. Here, we will use the examples that don't show this complexity in order to demonstrate Order() in simpler terms.

For example, given the set of product categories in our database, we may wish to sort them in descending order by profit realized in 1997 over all customers. This would be expressed by the following:

```
Order (
  [Product].[Product Category].Members,
  ([Measures].[Profit], [Time].[1997], [Customer].[All Customers]),
  DESC
)
```

Since Order() works on tuples, we can also sort our interesting (product, store) combinations by their profit. For example, the following expression orders each (product, store) tuple according to its profit and returns tuples; Figure 5.5 shows the resulting order.

Note that the BDESC variant breaks—i.e., ignores—the hierarchy. We'd get back a more complex and possibly more interesting ordered set if we instead chose DESC, which respects the hierarchy and the dimensional components of tuples. See the section "Ordering Sets" in Chapter 7 for a full description of ordering sets.

Dimensional Calculations as Calculated Members

The phrases *multidimensional calculations* or *calculations in a hypercube* may be a bit daunting to some users. However, the goal of this chapter is to show that these calculations are actually fairly easy to perform in Microsoft OLAP Services. If you have some experience with SQL, you will find that the numerical calculations that are straightforward in SQL are also straightforward in MDX. However, a great many calculations that are very difficult in SQL are also straightforward in MDX! If you have experience with spreadsheet formulas (with their absolute and relative cell references in two or three dimensions), then you are already familiar with some of the basic concepts of dimensional

```
Order (
Filter(
  CrossJoin(
    [Product].[Product Category].Members
    ,[Store].[City].Members)
  )
  , [Measures].[Sales] >= 500
)
, ([Measures].[Profit], [Time].[1997], [Customer].[All Customers])
, BDESC
)
```

Figure 5.5   Result of ordering tuples.

calculations. MDX provides a much clearer language in which to create calculations, however, and you don't have to put a formula into each cell to calculate the cell. Rather, you can specify a formula and control the range of cells that all share that formula.

It is useful to consider SQL and spreadsheet cell formulas as starting points for understanding how to use MDX. Like SQL, MDX lets you form queries that request a particular set of data to be returned to a client. (And, like SQL, MDX has a SELECT . . . FROM . . . WHERE framework for queries.) In a query, you need to explicitly state from what cube data is to be selected and what ranges of cells should be included on each dimension. However, similar to a spreadsheet, OLAP Services uses equations (MDX expressions) as formulas for defining cell values for calculated members. When defining calculated members, you do not specify a SELECT . . . FROM . . . WHERE framework, nor do you need to define, on any dimension, the sets of members to select from. (There are reasons why you might define sets of members from some dimensions, and we will introduce these in the section "Named Sets"). So, MDX is used in two distinct and important ways in OLAP Services.

Let us use SQL as a baseline for understanding how MDX works. We won't go too far into the SQL side, just enough to make MDX more comprehensible. First, in SQL, if you submit a query like `SELECT store, time, sales - cost AS profit FROM table`, the calculation of `sales - cost AS profit` is carried out once per row. More complex calculations are possible in SQL, but the process of forming them always boils down to trying to line up all of the fields of all of the tables involved onto a single row so a result for the row being returned may be calculated.

Second, in SQL you can also build this profit calculation into the database schema by defining it in a view. For example, the following query

```
CREATE VIEW profits (store, time, profit) AS
SELECT store, time, sales - cost AS profit FROM table
```

creates a new table-like entity with a calculated profit column. In SQL, there is no real way to define calculations in the database without phrasing them as queries. Third, in a spreadsheet, you don't really build calculations into queries as you do in SQL. Instead, you put calculations into cells, and when you wish to see their results you simply bring those cells into view.

Fourth, in MDX queries you put calculations in the axes of a query as new members of dimensions, and the cells get filled in with the results. In this way, the model of an MDX query is a little more like SQL than a spreadsheet. We discuss the basic syntax for this in the next section.

In the previous chapters, we have discussed calculated members as things that are defined for cubes. We have also discussed the OLAP Manager user interface for creating calculated members. Under the hood of OLAP Services, that user interface generates exactly the same MDX statements that create the calculated members we will be discussing in the remainder of this chapter. So, while the calculated members are metadata entities, they are also MDX language constructs. Two of the purposes of this chapter are to give you an understanding of MDX queries and of how to create calculated members for cubes in databases.

Calculated Members and WITH Sections in Queries

The core syntax for defining a calculated member on a dimension is as follows:

```
MEMBER MemberName AS 'member-formula'
```

(There are also other parts of a calculated member that can be specified, but we are focusing on the formula part here.) The member must be associated with a dimension of a cube, so MemberName must contain a dimension name as a component. Earlier in this chapter we talked about the formation of the unique names that an MDX query uses when it references metadata. The rules for constructing the member name are the same as the rules for referencing members in a query.

OLAP Services' MDX provides two variations on this core syntax to define calculated members. One variation defines a calculated member purely within a query. This is like the sales – costs AS profit expression within an SQL query that creates a new column named profit that only exists for the life of the query. The other variation defines a calculated member that will be available to more than one query. We will focus on the first variation here. A calculated member that is defined only for a query is defined in a section of the query that we will call the "WITH section".

The WITH section of a query comes before the SELECT keyword, and forms a section where the definitions private to the query are made. Calculated members and named sets (described in the section titled "Named Sets") are the two things that may be specified in the WITH section. More than one calculated member and named set may be defined in a WITH section. For example, the following query will augment our trivial query at the beginning of this chapter with a profit calculation. We show its result in Figure 5.6 with the profit calculation shaded in.

```
WITH
MEMBER [Measures].[Profit] AS
'[Measures].[Sales] - [Measures].[Costs]'
SELECT
   { [Measures].[Sales], [Measures].[Costs], [Measures].[Profit]} on
columns,
   { [Time].[June-1998], [Time].[July-1998] } on rows
FROM TrivialCube
WHERE ( [Stores].[Downtown] )
```

Measures

Time		Sales	Costs	Profits
	June-1998	1200	1000	200
	July-1998	1300	1050	250

Figure 5.6 Query result with calculated profit measure.

As a member of the measures dimension, the calculated Profit member intersects all members of the other dimensions (of which Time is the only important one in this example). Calculated members can be on any dimension, so we can also query for the growth in sales and costs between June and July with the following query (its results are shown in Figure 5.7 with the growth calculation shaded in):

```
WITH
MEMBER [Time].[June to July] AS
'[Time].[July-1998] - [Time].[June-1998]'
SELECT
  { [Measures].[Sales], [Measures].[Costs] } on columns,
  { [Time].[June-1998], [Time].[July-1998], [Time].[June to July]} on
rows
FROM TrivialCube
WHERE ( [Stores].[Downtown] )
```

Suppose we were trying to perform this same calculation in SQL, and each time period's values were on different rows of the data table. We would have a difficult time accomplishing this with a single query. In MDX, it is quite simple, however. Notice that our syntax for calculating measures and for calculating members on other dimensions is the same.

Formula Precedence

So far, we have only considered formulas for members of one dimension. We will very likely have formulas on members of more than one dimension, which

Measures

Time		Sales	Costs
	June-1998	1200	1000
	July-1998	1300	1050
	June to July	100	50

Figure 5.7 Query result with calculated time growth member.

Measures

	Sales	Costs	Profit
June-1998	1200	1000	200
July-1998	1300	1050	250
June to July Difference	100	50	50

Time (row dimension label)

Figure 5.8 3x3 cells with formulas: A difference and a sum.

raises the issue of what we should do when these formulas intersect. For example, consider the set of base and calculated cells shown in Figure 5.8. They are combined from the queries for Figures 5.6 and 5.7, where each calculated slice is shaded.

In the example in Figure 5.8, we have formulas in two different dimensions; the cell in which they overlap is shaded in. There are two possible formulas for this cell: (July Profit – June Profit) or (June-to-July difference in Sales – June-to-July Difference in Costs). In either case, the answer will be the same, so picking one or the other doesn't make a difference. However, consider Figure 5.9, in which profit is replaced by Margin Pct calculated as (Sales – Costs) / Costs.

The example in Figure 5.9 also has formulas on two different dimensions. The cell in which the formulas overlap, which is shaded in, has two numbers in it. One is the result of (July Margin – June Margin), and the other is the result of ((Difference in Sales – Difference in Costs) / Difference in costs). We are going to be interested in one result or the other, depending on the question we want to answer. The issue that has arisen here is sometimes called dimensional precedence, or formula overlap. How do we control the ordering of calculations among dimensions?

The particular mechanism in Microsoft OLAP Services for dealing with dimensional formula precedence is termed the member's *solve order* and is specified

Measures

	Sales	Costs	Margin Pct.
June-1997	1200	1000	0.20
July-1997	1300	1050	0.24
June to July Difference	100	50	0.04 1.00

Time (row dimension label)

Figure 5.9 3x3 cells with formulas: Ratio and a sum.

when the member is created. Every calculated member has an associated solve order property, which is a non-negative integer that says what the calculation priority of the member is. A higher number indicates that the member is calculated using the values that result from calculations that have a lower number. If you don't specify a number when you specify the formula for the member, it defaults to zero. Fortunately, you can change this number at any point. The numbers are simply relative precedence numbers, so there is no requirement that the smallest number you use be zero (though they cannot be less than zero). Nor is there any requirement that you use 2 or 1 if the highest number in use is 3 and the lowest is 0.

For the example in Figure 5.9, let us say that we are interested in seeing the difference in Margin Pct rather than the Percentage Growth of sales to costs. We would simply give the [Time].[June to July] member a higher solve order number. For example, the following query controls the solve order to give us the growth calculation that is shown in Figure 5.10:

```
WITH
MEMBER [Measures].[Margin Percent] AS
'([Measures].[Sales] - [Measures].[Costs]) / [Measures].[Costs]',
SOLVE_ORDER = 1
MEMBER [Time].[June to July] AS
'[Time].[Jul-98] - [Time].[Jun-98]', SOLVE_ORDER = 2
SELECT
  { [Measures].[Sales], [Measures].[Costs], [Measures].[Margin Percent]
} on columns,
  { [Time].[June-98], [Time].[July-98], [Time].[June to July]} on rows
FROM TrivialCube
WHERE ( [Stores].[Downtown] )
```

A few paragraphs ago we referred to other parts of a calculated member that we can specify in the member definition. The solve order property shown in the preceding query is one of them.

Note the following syntactic point about defining multiple calculated members in the WITH section of the query: Each member definition is simply followed by the next one. A comma is used to separate the formula definition from the solve

Measures

Time		Sales	Costs	Margin Pct.
	June-1997	1200	1000	0.20
	July-1997	1300	1050	0.24
	June to July Difference	100	50	0.04

Figure 5.10   Controlled solve order in a query.

order definition, but *no punctuation*, such as a comma, semicolon, or other device, is used to separate the end of one from the beginning of the next. Instead, they are separated by the MEMBER keyword.

There are two other points regarding solve orders you should keep in mind. First, if members on two different dimensions have the same priority, you should consider the order in which PTS will evaluate them as being random. You should only let formulas on different dimensions have the same solve order number when the formulas are commutative (either when they all involve only addition and subtraction or when they all involve only multiplication and division). Second, the solve order only affects the priority of calculation between dimensions. OLAP Services still uses actual formula dependencies to determine what to calculate first. For example, consider the following four formulas (their overlap regions are depicted in Figure 5.11):

```
[Measures].[Profit]
  AS '[Measures].[Sale Amount] - [Measures].[Total Cost]',
  SOLVE_ORDER = 0
[Scenario].[Amount of Variance]
  AS '[Scenario].[Actual] - [Scenario].[Planned]',
  SOLVE_ORDER = 1
[Measures].[Percentage Margin]
  AS '[Measures].[Profit] / [Measures].[Sale Amount]',
  SOLVE_ORDER = 2
[Scenario].[Percentage Variance]
  AS '[Scenario].[Amount of Variance] / [Scenario].[Planned]',
  SOLVE_ORDER = 3
```

Even though Percentage Margin has a lower solve order number than the profit formula it depends on, it will still use the profit figure. After all, they'll never overlap because as members of the same dimension they are geometrically parallel! Figure 5.11 shows these four formulas and their inputs laid out on a grid, together with the formula that is actually in use for any given cell.

Calculated members for a cube's dimension may be defined at the server or at the client. Calculated members defined at the server will be visible to all client sessions that can query the cube, and can be used in any number of queries. A client can also define such calculated members as well. Clients and servers do this by using the second variation of the syntax for creating calculated mem-

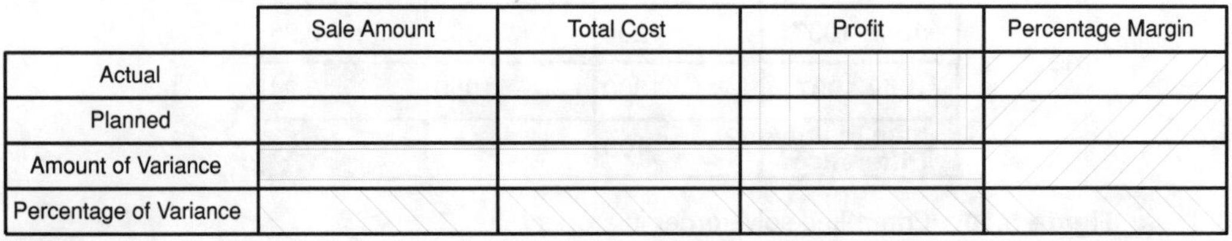

	Sale Amount	Total Cost	Profit	Percentage Margin
Actual				
Planned				
Amount of Variance				
Percentage of Variance				

Figure 5.11   Map of calculated member definitions and overlap on a grid.

bers: the CREATE MEMBER command. Calculated members defined with the CREATE MEMBER command must be named with the cube as well as the dimension that they are to be a part of. The CREATE MEMBER command is not part of a query that uses SELECT, but is its own statement. Other than that, the core syntax for naming the member and defining its formula and other properties is basically the same as a WITH-defined member. For example, the following MDX statement will create [Scenario].[Amount of Variance] on the Scenario dimension used by the [Sales Cube] cube:

```
CREATE MEMBER [Sales Cube].[Scenario].[Amount of Variance] AS '[Sce-
nario].[Actual] - [Scenario].[Planned]', SOLVE_ORDER = 1
```

This calculated member will only be visible to queries on the [Sales Cube] cube. Queries to other cubes, even if they also use the scenario dimension, will not be able to see this calculated member, just like they cannot see any other information about another cube. The CREATE MEMBER statement defines a calculated member for a dimension that can be used by any query (until the member is dropped or the client exits), and additionally will exist in the dimension's metadata visible through OLE DB for OLAP. (This metadata will only be visible on that client; that metadata will not be visible at the server or at any other client attached to that server.)

When a query uses calculated members, all solve order numbers from all the calculated members in the query are thrown together regardless of their source. A formula defined in the WITH section of a query as having solve order = 2 will be evaluated before a formula defined in a CREATE MEMBER statement as having solve order = 3. At the time a query is constructed, you can know the solve orders for all calculated members included in the cube definition on the server. However, when a database is constructed, you obviously cannot know the formulas used in queries and their solve orders. Furthermore, since solve orders are integer numbers, you cannot slip a calculated member into a query between two members whose solve orders are 1 and 2 by giving the new member a solve order of 1.5.

For these reasons, you may wish to leave gaps in the solve order numbers that are used for calculated members created as part of a cube's definition with OLAP Manager or through DSO. For example, the lowest-precedence number at the server might be 10, the next one 20, and so on. If you ever programmed in classic BASIC, this procedure should be familiar (remember line numbers running 10, 20, 30, etc.?). OLAP Services's solve order numbers can run up to 2,147,483,647, so you have plenty of headroom here. OLAP Services appears to ignore larger numbers and make them equivalent to zero.

The solve order of calculated members is one facet of the concept of formula application ranges. Basically, every formula that you will create will apply to some set of locations in your database. As far as OLAP Services is concerned, the formula that you define for a calculated member will be calculated over every cell in the database that intersects that member. This may or may not be what you want, depending on your circumstances. You may, at times, want some formulas to calculate differently depending on what level they are at in a dimension. Profitability may be calculated differently in different countries, for example, or a formula to compute GNP will not apply to a city by month level of data. We will explore techniques for controlling application ranges in depth in Chapter 9.

Named Sets

In addition to providing you with the ability to define calculations, MDX also enables you to define *named sets* that represent sets of interest. Named sets are a fairly powerful feature that can be used for several purposes. They can be used as placeholders to hold interesting products, ingredients, measures, and so on between one query and the next. They can also be used to greatly simplify the logic of a query by breaking up complex set operations into discrete units. They can also be used to simplify the substance of a total query by abstracting the logic used to generate the sets from a query template that uses the sets, and they may be used to increase the efficiency of a query's execution.

Named sets behave like any other sets in a query. The syntax for creating a named set is similar to the syntax for creating a calculated member, both in the WITH section of a query and in the CREATE SET command. For example, the following two queries return identical results:

```
SELECT
{ [Time].[1996] : [Time].[1998] } on columns,
{ [Measures].Members } on rows
FROM InventoryCube

WITH
SET [3 Years] AS '{ [Time].[1996] : [Time].[1998] }'
SELECT
{ [3 Years] } on columns,
{ [Measures].Members } on rows
FROM InventoryCube
```

We can also create the named set [3 Years] for use in multiple queries on the [InventoryCube] cube through the following CREATE SET statement:

```
CREATE SET [InventoryCube].[3 Years] AS
'{ [Time].[1996] : [Time].[1998] }'
```

Note that we needed to include the name of the cube in the name of the set when we created a named set that would be accessible by multiple queries. However, we did not need to include the name of any dimension. We also didn't include the name of a dimension in the WITH SET definition. Any set may have tuples of more than one dimension, but whether it is a set of one-dimensional tuples (members) or multidimensional tuples, it is not part of any dimension.

As with calculated members, a named set is defined within the scope of a single cube and cannot be referenced from another cube. Even if a dimension is used identically by two different cubes, a set in one cube that contains only members of that dimension cannot be used in a query on the other cube.

Unlike calculated members, named sets do not show up in any OLE DB for OLAP metadata. Like calculated members, however, named sets can be stored with a cube's definition on the server so that they can be easily accessed by client queries. In the initial release of Microsoft OLAP Services adding named sets to a cube definition can only be done through DSO programming. We provide an example of using DSO in Visual Basic to add named sets (and calculated members) to OLAP Services cubes in the source code for the "Calculated Member Editor" application found on the accompanying CD-ROM for this book.

The logic required to create a named set is executed once within the scope that it is defined in, and the resulting set is reused after that. This means that in addition to helping to clarify the logic involved in a query, named sets have the potential to greatly increase the efficiency of query execution. For example, in the following query the set [Top Custs] is evaluated once at the beginning of the query execution, and then the set of members that it results in is used for the sum, the count, and the formation of rows in the overall query:

```
WITH
  SET [Top Custs] AS
  'TopCount (
    [Customer].[Cust City].Members,
    25,
    ([Measures].[Profit], [Time].[1998])
  )'
  MEMBER [Measures].[Avg Sale] AS
  'Sum ([Top Custs], [Measures].[Sales]) /
   Count ([Topcusts] * { [Measures].[Sales] })'
SELECT
  { AddCalculatedMembers ([Measures].Members) } on columns,
  { [Top Custs] } on rows
FROM SalesCube
WHERE ([Product].[All Products])
```

Named sets are actually evaluated the first time they are used within a particular scope. For a WITH SET declaration within a query, this, of course, occurs at the commencement of the query (they are computed in the order in which they appear in the query). For a CREATE SET that a client issues in its session or connection, the set is calculated at the instant that the statement is executed. For a CREATE SET that is stored with the cube definition on the server, the set expression is actually evaluated the first time that the named set is invoked in a query.

For the sets that are defined at the session level (with CREATE SET statements retrieved from the cube definition on the server or created by the client application), the tuples that the set describes are cached until either the session is terminated or until a DROP SET statement is issued by the client. Yes, as with calculated members, it is possible to, within a client session, drop a set defined on the server. However, you should have a compelling design reason why your application does this, and the authors have not heard a guarantee from Microsoft that this is behavior that all future versions of OLAP Services will support.

MDX Queries: More Detail

Now that we've covered the components of MDX in some depth, let's return to MDX queries. We've taken a look at most of the parts of a query, but there are some that we haven't seen at all yet, including the following:

- axis numbering and ordering
- removing entirely empty slices from a query
- querying for member properties
- querying for specific cell properties

And the following two parts of MDX queries deserve some further explanation in this chapter:

- WITH Sections
- MDX Cube Slicers

Axis Numbering and Ordering

To use an abstract syntax notation, the core of a query is as follows:

```
[WITH set-or-member-declarations]
SELECT
  [axis-expression1 on axis1 [, axis-expression on axis2 . . .]]
FROM cube
[WHERE slicer]
```

Each axis expression can be a simple set expression or a complex set expression. You can specify from 0 to 64 axis expressions. If you specify 0 axis expressions, you probably will specify a slicer expression in the WHERE clause. You do not need to, but if you leave out the slicer you will get the global aggregate of the default measure, which is rarely of interest.

Each axis is numbered, starting at 0. The numbering of axes in the query corresponds with the positioning of the axis in the data structures that are related to the query results returned by the OLE DB for OLAP driver. You can refer to any axis by its number, as in axis(0) or axis(2). You can also refer to each of the first five axes by their aliases: COLUMNS, ROWS, PAGES, CHAPTERS, and SECTIONS, respectively. If a query uses only two axes, then the axis numbers that are used must be 0 and 1. If it uses only three axes, then the axis numbers that are used must be 0, 1, and 2. In general, if a query returns N axes, then axis numbers 0 through N-1 must be used. They also must be used in order: axis(0) or COLUMNS must be the first axis listed, axis(1) or ROWS must be the second axis listed, and so on. Skipping numbers will generate an MDX parser error. For example, `SELECT . . . on Axis (0), . . . on Rows, . . . on Axis (2) FROM Cube` is fine. However, `SELECT . . . on Axis (0) , . . . on Axis (2), . . . on Columns FROM Cube` is not fine because it gets them out of order. Finally, `SELECT . . . on Rows , . . . on Axis (2) FROM Cube` skips an axis (`axis(0)` or `Columns`). Since you must get the order right, there really is no purpose to using the `axis(n)` or tokens for rows, columns, and so on apart from the fact that they force you to document how an application is to receive the result.

Removing Empty Slices from a Query Axis

It is quite possible that a query will result in some of the tuples along an axis generating entirely empty slices along the result. For example, consider the following query:

```
SELECT
{ Filter (
  [Geography].[State].Members,
  ([Measures].[Unit Sales], [Time].[1995],
  [Product].[All Products]) > 3000)
} on columns,
{[Product].[Snow Shovels], [Product].[Sidewalk Salt], [Product].[Suntan
Lotion]} on rows
FROM Sales
WHERE ([Measures].[Revenue], [Time].[July-1997])
```

This query will include all states in which more than 3,000 units of all products together were sold and three products of interest (snow shovels, sidewalk salt, and suntan lotion), for the time slice of July 1997. Clearly, if the states returned for the Geography dimension are within 450 miles of the equator, there are going to be a lot of empty product by geography tuples across the result set. Less whimsically, in any given month most of your customers may not make any purchases, so asking for individual customer-by-month-level sales will result in an unpredictable pattern of missing intersections across products.

You can have Microsoft OLAP Services suppress entirely empty result slices from a query by using the NON EMPTY keywords. When NON EMPTY is specified on an axis, any tuples on that axis that correspond to entirely empty slices of data within the result set are removed from the result set before they are delivered to the client. For example, the query

```
SELECT
NON EMPTY { [Geography].[Nashville, TN].Children } on columns,
{ CROSSJOIN (
   { [Product].[Category].Members},
   { [Outlets].[Direct], [Outlets].[Small Retail] }
   ) } on rows
FROM Sales
WHERE ([Measures].[Units Sold], [Time].[July 3, 1999])
```

will return only those children of Nashville for which at least one Product category had a non-empty Units Sold measure on July 3, 1999. Notice that the Geography members are included or excluded here as determined by slices formed from the other axes of the query. NON EMPTY operates on a querywide basis, so in this way it is different than Filter(). You could construct Filter() expressions to remove empty tuples from sets that represented the axis queries, but these filters would have to employ cross-joins of all sets from all other axes, including the query slicer. Using NON EMPTY is much more convenient.

Querying for Member Properties

Within an MDX query, you can also query for member properties defined for members in a cube. A member property is defined for a single level of a dimension, while the axes of a query are sets that may contain multiple dimensions. However, OLE DB for OLAP and MDX allow the properties to be included on the axis anyway. On whatever axis a dimension is mapped to, you can query one or more member properties for each of the dimensions and levels as well as the identities of the members. If a member is repeated in a result axis, its related member property value will be repeated too.

You specify the member properties that you wish to have returned on an axis by using the PROPERTIES keyword in the axis specification. For example, the following will query for the zip code and hair color of customers returned in the query:

```
SELECT
{ [Customer].[Akron, OH].Children }, PROPERTIES
[Customer].[Individual].[Zip Code],
[Customer].[Individual].[Hair Color] on columns,
{ [Product].[Category].Members} on rows
FROM Sales
WHERE ([Measures].[Units Sold], [Time].[July 3, 1999])
```

Properties can be identified either by using the name of the dimension and the name of the property, as with the zip code property just given, or by using the unique name of the dimension's level and the name of the property, as with the hair color property.

NOTE

While the values of properties requested with PROPERTIES statement in an MDX query are returned, along with all other result information, in the Dataset object returned by OLE DB for OLAP, it is up to the client application to retrieve and utilize this information from the Dataset. For example, after running an MDX query using the "MDX Sample" application distributed with OLAP Services, double-clicking on a member name in the results pane will bring up a dialog that will include the values of any properties requested in the MDX query. For an example of using the PROPER-TIES statement in MDX queries with ADO and Excel VBA, see the "writeback.xls" workbook on the accompanying CD-ROM.

There are two general types of properties that can be queried for. One type is the member properties that you defined for the dimension as a whole. The other type is intrinsic member properties that exist for all members. The intrinsic member properties are named KEY, NAME, and ID, and every level of every dimension has them. For example, the KEY property of a Product dimension's SKU level is named [Product].[SKU].[KEY]. The member key property contains the values of the member keys as represented in the dimension table. The member name property contains the values of the member names as represented in the dimension table. The ID property contains the internal member number of that member in the dimensionwide database ordering.

When property names between levels of a dimension are ambiguous, you can get ambiguous results if you query for member properties on the axis of a query. For example, every layer of an organizational dimension may have a Manager property for each member above the leaf. Consider the following query fragment:

```
SELECT { Descendants ([Organization].[All Organization],
[Organization].[Junior Staff], SELF_AND_ABOVE }
PROPERTIES [Organization].[Manager] on columns
  ...
```

When the query is executed, OLAP Services will return the specific Manager property for only that one level. It is not a good idea to rely on whatever level that would happen to be. Members belonging to that level will have a valid [Manager] value; members belonging to other levels won't. Suppose that, instead, you queried for each level's properties independently, as with the following:

```
SELECT { Descendants ([Organization].[All Organization],
[Organization].[Junior Staff], SELF_AND_ABOVE } PROPERTIES
```

```
[Organization].[Executive Suites].[Manager],
[Organization].[Middle Managers].[Manager],
[Organization].[Junior Staff].[Manager] on columns
 ...
```

In this case, the property for each level at each level's member will arrive appropriately filled in (and be empty at members of the other levels). (However, when you access properties in member calculations, there won't be any ambiguity. Suppose, for example, that some calculated member referred to `[Organization]` `.CurrentMember.Properties` (`"Manager"`). (We explain this function in Chapter 7.) The lookup of this value is done on a cell-by-cell basis, and at each cell the particular manager is unambiguous [though the level of manager to which it refers may change]. For this case, you can easily and simply reference member properties on multiple levels that share the same name.)

WITH Section

Earlier in the chapter we took a brief look at the WITH section of an MDX query. We'll finish our description of it here. The WITH section of a query is the location where all definitions of calculated members and named sets that are specific to the query are made. Both calculated members and named sets may be defined within a single WITH section. For example, the following is fine MDX:

```
WITH
SET [3 Years] AS '{ [Time].[1996] : [Time].[1998] }'
MEMBER [Measures].[Avg Value Returned] AS
'[Measures].[Units Returned]/ [Measures].[Value Returned]', SOLVE_ORDER
= 10
SELECT
{ [3 Years] } on columns,
{ [Measures].[Units Returned], [Measures].[Avg Value Returned] } on rows
FROM InventoryCube
```

The order of members and sets does not matter so long as no set or member is referred to before it is defined. As you can see, it is the presence of each SET or MEMBER keyword that ends any definition and begins the next, and the appearance of the SELECT keyword ends the WITH section and begins the axis/cell specifications.

Querying Cell Properties

Querying for specific cell properties is fairly tightly bound to the programming layer that retrieves results from a query. In keeping with the non-programming thrust of this book, we won't cover all of the programming details here. However, we will explain the basic model that querying for specific cell properties supports and how an application might use it.

Every query is a specification of one or more result cells and, most frequently, one or more members of one or more dimensions. Much as each member is able to have one or more related properties, each result cell also has more than one possible related result property. If a query specifies no cell properties, then three properties are returned by default: an ordinal number that represents the index of the cell in the result set, the raw value for the cell, and the formatted textual value for the cell. If the query specifies particular cell properties, then only the cell properties actually specified are returned to the client. We discuss formatting the raw value into text in the section "Precedence of Display Formatting with Calculated Members" in Chapter 6. The ordinal cell index value is germane to client tools that are querying the data that has been generated through OLE DB for OLAP. There are other cell properties that can be queried for, which can be specified for any measure or calculated member in the cube. The full list of cell properties and how they are used in OLE DB for OLAP and ADO is found in Appendix A.

The way to specify cell properties in a query is to follow the slicer (if any) with the CELL PROPERTIES keywords and the names of the cell properties. For example, the following query

```
SELECT
{ [Measures].[Units Returned], [Measures].[Value Returned]} on columns,
{ [Time].[1997], [Time].[1998]} on rows
FROM InventoryCube
CELL PROPERTIES FORMATTED_VALUE
```

returns to the client only the formatted text strings that correspond to the query results. Generally speaking, clients that render their results as text strings (e.g., spreadsheet-style report grids) will be most interested in the formatted values. Clients that render their results graphically (e.g., in bar charts where each height of each bar represents the value of the measure at that intersection) will be most interested in the raw values. Other properties available in Microsoft OLAP Services allow string formatting, font and color information to be stored and retrieved for measures and calculated members. This gives you server-side control over useful client rendering operations.

Our discussion of CREATE MEMBER in Chapter 7, a reference chapter on MDX functions and operators, describes how to specify the various cell properties that should be associated with calculated members. In Chapter 6, we describe how calculated members influence cell properties in queries. In Chapter 4, we described how to set these properties for base measures.

MDX Cube Slicers

Astute readers may by now have noticed a remarkable logical similarity between the slicer clause of a cube query and an axis, albeit one whose interpretation is limited to a single tuple. In fact, this similarity is real. The primary reason for using the slicer is as a convenience and convention for the software portions of a client that interpret the data structures returned as a result of executing the query. If you think of the query result as a sub-cube of the original cube being queried, the chief advantage of a slicer is that it essentially parks unnecessary dimensions on the side. They aren't lost for most client queries. In the OLE DB for OLAP API, they are placed on a special edge in the IMDDataset structure resulting from an MDX query, and a front end will hopefully relay the slicer tuple information to the user. However, the number of (non-slicer) result edges implies to the client the number of dimensions in which it should lay out its reporting framework. (When an MDX query results in a regular OLE DB rowset, dimensional information placed in the slicer is indeed lost. See "Closing the Loop from OLAP Services back to the Warehouse" in Chapter 12 for more details.)

For example, the following two queries are identical in substance as well as being virtually identical in what they return to the client:

```
SELECT
{ [Measures].Members } on columns,
{ Time.Members } on rows
FROM cube
WHERE ([Product].[Ceiling Tiles], [Store].[Lincoln, NE])


SELECT
{ [Measures].Members } on columns,
{ Time.Members } on rows,
{ ([Product].[Ceiling Tiles], [Store].[Lincoln, NE]) } on pages
FROM cube
```

Ordinarily, clients would expect to lay out the first version of the query as a 2-D grid that has a product and store as context. Clients would expect to lay out the second version as a 3-D grid that has only one tuple on one of its axes.

Complex Slicers

Slicers need not be composed of simple base members from the cube. For example, it is perfectly fine to have the slicer include a calculated member from more than one dimension, including the measures dimension:

```
WITH
MEMBER [Measures].[Avg Sales per Employee Hour] as '. . .'
MEMBER [Time].[Sum to Date] AS '. . .'
SELECT ...
FROM ...
WHERE ([Measures].[Avg Sales per Employee Hour], [Time].[Sum to Date])
```

More advanced still would be a query that took the first member of a sorted set with the Item() operator and used that as its slicer, as in

```
CREATE SET SalesCube.OrderedProducts AS 'ORDER(
     [Product].[Product Family].Members,
     ([Measures].[Profit], [Time].[1997], [Customer].[All Customers],
BDESC)
)'

WITH
SELECT ...
FROM SalesCube
WHERE (OrderedProducts.Item (0))
```

(.Item() takes a set on its left side and an index, based at zero, as its argument, and it returns the tuple at that position in the set. CREATE SET creates a named set that can be referenced in a query like any other set.) Since OLAP Services evaluates the WHERE clause prior to any sets, you cannot use an item defined in a WITH . . . SET definition as a slicer in a query.

Sets in the Slicer

According to the MDX specification, it is also acceptable for the slicer expression to contain a set of tuples rather than a single tuple. Although the expression may contain a set, OLAP Services will only return a single tuple of data as the slicer by aggregating the result cells found for that tuple along the set. (The release of Microsoft OLAP Services you are using may or may not support this functionality.) The aggregation OLAP Services performs will be as if the MDX Aggregate() function were used: each base measure will be aggregated across the set by its associated aggregation function. (See Chapter 7 for information on the Aggregate() function.)

For example, the following two queries are basically equivalent:

```
SELECT
{ [Measures].[Sales], [Measures].Units } on columns,
{ Stores.[Las Vegas, NV], Stores.[San Ysidro, CA] } on rows
FROM Cube
WHERE { ([Time].[1997], [Product].[Rain Coats]),
([Time].[1997], [Product].[Umbrellas]) }

WITH
Member [Product].[CrossDimAggregate] AS
'Aggregate( { [Product].[Rain Coats], [Product].[Umbrellas] } )'
SELECT
{ [Measures].[Sales], [Measures].Units } on columns,
{ Stores.[Las Vegas, NV], Stores.[San Ysidro, CA] } on rows
FROM Cube
WHERE ( [Time].[1997], [Product.[CrossDimAggregate] )
```

These two queries will generate the same cell results at the client. However, the second variation returns the name of the calculated member to the client in the resulting slicer information while the first returns the tuples that composed the aggregate.

What MDX Sorely Lacks

Despite the fact that a number of vendors outside of Microsoft have reviewed MDX substantially, it lacks one important feature that most other successful computer languages have, including SQL, COBOL, C/C++, Lisp, APL, Java, Basic, FORTRAN, and various OLAP development languages. That feature is the ability to embed comments in a query! For a language that exists solely to be generated and interpreted by a machine, you might think comments are not necessary. However, we expect that MDX will need to be generated and maintained by human beings for the foreseeable future. We also find MDX to be a useful language for expressing multidimensional selection and calculation semantics between human beings. Unfortunately, all annotations must be maintained outside of a query if a computer is to interpret the query. In this book, we do not invent a comment syntax with which to annotate query logic. However, we do hope that the second edition of this book includes a description of an implemented comment syntax instead of this comment on MDX!

Summary

We have now covered the basics of MDX queries and expressions. We have gone over all of the components of a query, how we can refer to metadata in queries, what the MDX data model is, and some of the functions that are commonly used in queries. We have also seen how calculated members in a database relate to expressions in queries. With all these points fresh in our minds, we are ready to explore MDX in greater depth. In Chapter 6, we take a look at the role context plays in evaluating a query, how calculations use and generate data types, and how NULLs (or missing data) gets treated in queries.

Context and Data in MDX Evaluation

N ow that we have explored the basics of MDX queries, we need to turn our attention to the way MDX queries and statements actually get evaluated. Context and interpretation are the two major themes of this chapter.

Although context isn't everything, it is important. Every portion of a query has a particular context within the cube space, which affects how dimensions that are not explicitly referenced in any step are interpreted. This impacts how you actually compose queries and calculations in MDX. The interpretation of invalid data, missing data (NULLs), and invalid members is another important area that we will cover in this chapter. The cubes that you build in Microsoft OLAP Services will usually have many cells that contain no data, and your queries will need to deal with both invalid data and invalid members.

Every cell that is obtained from a query has a set of properties associated with it. One such property is the type of data that results in a query for that cell, and another is the formatted string version of that value as well as rendering information like font name. In this chapter, we will take a look at how the context of calculated members affects these cell properties.

So far, we have hardly discussed the concept of data types in MDX expressions at all, apart from the distinction between numbers, strings, Boolean conditions, and empty cells. In this chapter we will discuss the data types that MDX calculations take on in OLAP Services. The relevance of the data types used in calculations depends on your application, in that you can readily put cells into a calculation and report values out of them and usually get a suitable answer. However, depending on your application, you may need to precisely control the data types that are used. For example, external functions that use SetToArray() must deal with the exact data types of the calculations involved in them. (Considerations to be taken into account when using external functions are described in Chapter 14).

As in Chapter 5, we will generally not make distinctions between Microsoft OLAP Services and the local PivotTable Service in this chapter, but instead refer simply to OLAP Services. Our primary goal in this chapter is to provide guidance on how to construct and use MDX queries and statements, so we hope to avoid unnecessary confusion by referring to the product as a whole instead of specific subsets of the product. See Chapter 2 for a discussion of the role of the PivotTable Service in Microsoft OLAP Services and Chapter 11 for an in-depth discussion on the relationship between the PivotTable Service and OLAP Services in processing queries.

Cell Context and Resolution Order in Queries

The process of answering a query involves resolving the sets that comprise each of the axes and the member of the slicer and then filling in the cells at each intersection of members from each axis and the slicer. Resolving the sets that make up each axis will very often require OLAP Services to perform calculations against cells that are formed from base or calculated members. At every point in the preparation of the set of result cells, there is a context for calculations that determines what you need to say to reference the cell data you are interested in using.

For example, referring to our earlier typical cube example that has dimensions of measures, time, customers, and products, consider the following query:

```
WITH
  MEMBER [Measures].[Margin Percent] AS
'[Measures].[Sales] / ([Measures].[Sales] - [Measures].[Costs])'
  SET [GoodBets] AS
'Filter( [Customer].[City].Members, [Measures].[Margin Percent] > 0.1)'
SELECT
  { [Measures].[Sales], [Measures].[Margin Percent] } on columns,
  { CrossJoin ([GoodBets], [Product].[Product Category].Members) } on
rows
FROM
  SalesCube
WHERE
  ([Time].[Q1 1997])
```

There's more going on in this query than meets the eye; key things are left unsaid in several places. Let's walk through the parts of this query and explore how a query is answered. Keep in mind its basic skeleton, which is as follows:

```
WITH
   MEMBER
   SET
SELECT
      { axis set 0 } on COLUMNS,
      { axis set 1 } on ROWS
FROM
      cube
WHERE
   (slicer)
```

The first relevant element in the query is the FROM clause, which names the cube. Naming the cube implies that all of its dimensions will be involved in one way or another in the query. Any dimension that is not explicitly mentioned in the cube will implicitly be referenced in the slicer at the default member (which will be the All member, or an arbitrary member in the top level of the dimension if there is no All level). Naming the cube, therefore, implicitly sets the default member of every dimension in the cube to be the All member of that dimension, unless it is otherwise modified by some other part. Another way of thinking of this is that the default tuple for any cell in the cube is as follows:

```
([Customers].[All Customers], [Time].[All Time],
 [Products].[All Products], [Measures].Arbitrary Measure).
```

The default measure is usually the one that was picked first when the cube was defined.

The next relevant element is the WHERE clause. The slicer specifies a tuple from one or more of the dimensions of the cube. Dimensions mentioned in the slicer will not end up on any of the other axes of the result cube. The members that are specified override the implicit default members on those dimensions. In this case, the default tuple is now as follows:

```
([Customers].[All Customers], [Time].[Q1 1997],
 [Products].[All Products], [Measures].Arbitrary Measure).
```

The next relevant items are any member and set definitions between the WITH and the SELECT. No calculations will be performed when defining the member [Measures].[Margin Percent]. However, calculations will be performed during the definition of the set [GoodBets]. After the whole MDX statement is parsed, the tuples of each named set that is defined in the WITH . . . section are determined according to the order of the dependencies between them, which will roughly correspond to the order in which they appear (if set A uses the results of set B and set C, OLAP Services with resolve sets B and C before set A).

When the set declaration appears, none of the cells have been computed yet. The expression `Filter( [Customer].[City].Members, [Measures] .[Margin Percent] > 0.1)` returns a set that is formed out of members from the customer dimension, but it returns them based on the calculated values associated with the cells. The current context to this point is as follows:

```
([Customers].[All Customers], [Time].[Q1 1997],
[Products].[All Products], [Measures].Arbitrary Measure).
```

During the evaluation of the Filter() function, the `[Customer].[City].Mem-bers` term overrides the [All Customers] member in the context, and the `[Measures].[Margin Percent]` overrides the [Measures].Arbitrary Measure. As a result, the set of cells that will be evaluated and compared with 0.l can be defined as follows:

```
CrossJoin( [Customer].[City].Members, { ([Time].[Q1 1997], [Prod-
ucts].[All Products], [Measures].[Margin Percent] } ).
```

You can think of this context for evaluation of cell values as "within the context of the Filter() operator." After OLAP Services completes the evaluation of cell values within the Filter() context, the context returns to ([Customers].[All Customers], [Time].[Q1 1997], [Products].[All Products], [Measures].Arbitrary Measure) and the following set is returned for use within the SELECT clause:

```
{ [Customer].[Tucson, AZ], [Customer].[Laredo, TX],
[Customer].[Honolulu, HI] }.
```

Once OLAP Services has processed all of the set declarations and member definitions, it processes the SELECT clause. Within the SELECT clause, OLAP Services processes the sets for each axis in turn. The process of creating the sets for each axis is similar to the process for creating the set in the WHERE clause. Across the columns, the set of measure members is spelled out as follows:

```
{ [Measures].[Sales], [Measures].[Margin Percent] }.
```

Down the rows, the set of tuples is determined by taking the CrossJoin() of our three cities with every member of the product category level. Each axis is independent of the others; the columns do not form an additional context for the rows and vice versa.

Now that OLAP Services has determined the sets for each axis, both in dimensionality and with respect to the exact set of tuples in each, it calculates the cells. Each cell is defined entirely by a member of each of the four dimensions; every one will have its time member set to [Time].[Q1 1997] and will have a different ([Customer], [Product], [Measure]) component.

For each cell in the result set, if more than one of the members defining the cell is a calculated member, OLAP Services will determine the correct formula to use by selecting the formula for the member with the highest associated solve order number. The context for the evaluation of the cell will be the ([Time], [Customer], [Product], [Measure]) tuple that identifies the cell (this is similar to way the overall query started off with a single cell as its context).

Cell Context in Set Functions

The example in the preceding section showed the cell context that is generated within a Filter() expression. This cell context extends to all functions that operate over a set, including aggregation functions. For example, let us say that in a similar query we see the expression `Sum( [Geography].[State].Members, [Measures].[Units Manufactured] * [Measures].[Cost Per Unit])`. Within the execution of the Sum(), OLAP Services sets the [State] portion of the context for evaluating `[Units Manufactured] * [Measures].[Cost Per Unit]` to each [State] member in turn. We need to take the sum of units manufactured over states and months, which we can express as follows:

```
Sum( [Geography].[State].Members, Sum( [Time].[Month].Members, [Mea-
sures].[Units Manufactured] * [Measures].[Cost Per Unit])).
```

In this expression, for each [State] member, OLAP Services takes a sum of units times costs over months. Within the second Sum(), the [State] and [Month] context for evaluating [Units Manufactured] and [Cost Per Unit] is set to each ([State], [Month) tuple in turn.

TIP

If you are going to perform sums in MDX over two or more dimensions, then you should create a series of nested sum expressions rather than an MDX expression that performs a sum over a single CrossJoin. For example, use
```
Sum( [Geography].[State].Members, Sum( [Time].[Month].Members,
[Measures].[Units Manufactured] * [Measures].[Cost Per Unit]))
```
rather than
```
Sum( CrossJoin ([Geography].[State].Members, [Time].[Month].Mem-
bers), [Measures].[Units Manufactured] * [Measures].[Units Manu-
factured] * [Measures].[Cost Per Unit]). Numerically, both of these will
```
lead to the same result, but the sum of sums will be much more efficient. We cover efficiency issues for MDX queries in Chapter 11, on optimizing databases and queries.

Infinite Recursion: A Frequent "Gotcha" Related to Calculation Context

When you are defining calculated members, you have to take into account the concept of the current context along the dimension in which the calculated member is placed. This includes the measures dimension, which has a current member just like every other dimension. For example, the following calculated measure definition will not quite work, though it is syntactically correct:

```
MEMBER [Measures].[Avg Sale] AS
'Sum (Descendants ([Geography], [Geography].[City]), [Measures].[Sales])
/ Count (Descendants ([Geography], [Geography].[City]), EXCLUDEEMPTY)'
```

This may look like a perfectly good definition of an average (dividing a sum by a count), but it will not work. When OLAP Services calculates the [Measures].[Avg Sale] member, although the sum is quite clear, the count cannot be evaluated! When values are being calculated for the count, the current measure is [Measures].[Avg Sale]. When the cells formed by

```
{ Descendants ([Geography], [Geography].[City]) }
```

intersect with the current measure in that context, OLAP Services will go into infinite recursion in its attempt to determine whether the set is empty. To evaluate whether any [Measures].[Avg Sale] cell is empty or not OLAP Services needs to evaluate it by this formula, which will require recursive reevaluation ad infinitum. If you were going to include empty cells using INCLUDEEMPTY, then it wouldn't really matter what measure you chose; the algorithm employed by Microsoft OLAP Services will just count the cells without testing them, and it will work fine.

The solution to this problem is to be cognizant of the cell context. OLAP Services does not flag a potential infinitely recursive calculated member when it is defined, but you will notice it when the cell returns an "ERR" instead of a value or NULL. OLAP Services will also set an appropriate text message inside the error information retrieved by the client for this cell, indicating the presence of infinite recursion. Usually, when you are performing a SUM/COUNT over the same set of non-measure tuples, you are performing the SUM and the COUNT over the same measure. We can remedy this by cross-joining the non-measures tuples with the measure of interest to get the right set of cells.

Stylistically, you may wish to consider the equivalence of the following three ways of phrasing the calculation. First,

```
WITH
  MEMBER [Measures].[Avg Sale] AS 'Sum (Descendants ([Geography],
  [Geography].[City]), [Measures].[Sales]) / Count (CrossJoin
  ({[Measures].[Sales]}, Descendants ([Geography], [Geography].[City]),
EXCLUDEEMPTY)'
```

Second,

```
WITH
  MEMBER [Measures].[Avg Sale] AS 'Sum (CrossJoin ({[Measures].[Sales]},
```

```
Descendants ([Geography], [Geography].[City]))) / Count (CrossJoin
({[Measures].[Sales]}, Descendants ([Geography], [Geography].[City]),
EXCLUDEEMPTY)'
```

Third,

```
WITH
  SET [CellSet] AS 'CrossJoin ({[Measures].[Sales]},
  Descendants ([Geography], [Geography].[City]))'
  MEMBER [Measures].[Avg Sale] AS 'Sum ([CellSet]) / Count ([CellSet])'
```

The first of these variations simply sums sales over the city members and divides by the count of the non-empty tuples that were formed by cross-joining those tuples with the sales measure. The second variation cross-joins the city members with the sales measure in both the SUM and the COUNT; when the set is summed, the set specification includes the measure whose values are to be summed over the cities. The third variation does the same thing but encapsulates the definition of the set into a named set. This means that the cross-join is only performed once when the query is evaluated.

TIP

If you want to supply a set to a function (for example, an aggregation like Sum(), Max(), Correlation(), etc.) and you want the cells of a specific measure to be used in the function, simply cross-join the measure with the set. Then, even if the current context includes a different measure, your specific measure's cells will be used.

Non-Data: Invalid Numbers, NULLs, and Invalid Members

When performing queries and calculations, we will frequently need to deal with data that isn't valid as well as the empty space in our cubes where data could be but isn't. There are three sorts of non-data that we might encounter when evaluating queries: invalid numbers, NULLs (or empty cells), and invalid member specifications (which we have also seen referred to as NULL members). Let us take a look at each of these.

Invalid Calculations: Divide by Zero and Numerical Errors

Even though the result of a divide-by-zero is not a valid number, Microsoft OLAP Services does not treat it as an empty value. In some instances, you can test for the results of a divide-by-zero—or for a floating-point overflow caused by other means—by comparing the cell value with (1 / 0). For example,

```
iff (1.0e+40 * 1.0e+40 = (1/0), "Overflowed", "Didn't Overflow")
```

multiplies a very large double-float value by itself and will cause an overflow condition. When performing a the comparison, OLAP Services will consider the overflow value as being equal to (1/0), so the expression will always return the string Overflowed. Be aware, however, that this test is dependent upon how the processor of the machine OLAP Services is installed on handles different types of numeric errors. Different CPUs (different generations of Intel CPUs, or the Compaq/Digital Alpha CPU) may return different values, and different causes of overflow may cause different values to appear. In short, you may not be able to effectively test for an overflow condition for any given calculation.

Note that OLAP Services will never detect overflow in integer calculations. If you add 2,000,000,000 to 2,000,000,000 in a small-integer calculation, you will not get 4,000,000,000 as a result but rather 1,852,516,354. BigInt calculations are extremely unlikely to overflow; if 2,000,000,000 input cells each contribute a value of 2,000,000,000 to a sum, the result will still not overflow. Numerical errors trapped by external function libraries frequently raise an ActiveX Automation error rather than return a bogus value. When this happens, the evaluation of the cell will halt, and it will neither be empty nor have a value of any type.

Semantics of Empty Cells

Given the usual sparseness of data in a multidimensional data set, empty cells are frequently the rule rather than the exception. When you are looking at a data set as a set of cells within a big CrossJoin of all dimensions, you will see a lot more empty cells than there were NULLs in the underlying fact tables. The reason for this, of course, is because not every consumer or supplier participated in every type of transaction at every possible time period with every possible geographical location. You can also wind up with empty cells in your data set because the values for measures in the underlying fact table had NULL values.

Microsoft OLAP Services has default semantics for handling empty cells in an MDX expression, which differ somewhat from the default semantics for handling NULLs in SQL. OLAP Services also extends standard MDX with a NULL operator, which can be used to return an empty or NULL value from a formula. (Since MDX has an operator called IsEmpty() and OLAP Services has a "NULL" operator to make a cell empty, no clear terminology is laid out for us to use. We will therefore use both "NULL" and "empty" in our discussion here.) The MDX that OLAP Services provides does not, however, provide any operators for determining whether a cell is empty because the underlying table column values were NULL or because rows were not present for that dimensional combination. There are also no standard ways in a dimensional OLAP model for an application to signify whether an empty cell could possibly have had a value or not (such as the invalidity of a "how many months pregnant" condition for a male patient).

According to the OLE DB for OLAP specification of MDX semantics, empty cells are treated almost identically to -0 in a numerical context and as an empty string in a string context. That is, in a numerical context, they add, subtract, multiply, and divide as though they were zero. In an ascending sort, they will sort before zero and after the negative number that has the smallest magnitude. In a string context, concatenating a string with an EMPTY will result in the original string, and empty cells that have a string type will sort immediately before cells that have a real empty string for a value. That is, the following sets of values are sorted according to the MDX specification:

- Numbers: -10, -1, -0.00001, NULL, 0, 0.00001, 1, 10

- Strings: NULL, "", "a", "ab", "z"

Microsoft OLAP Services does not allow cell values to have a Boolean data type, so there is no need to define a Boolean interpretation of NULL. Since iif() must return a numeric or string value, the expression iif([cell] > 5, true , NULL) and [cell2] > 6 will not parse because it treats the result of iif() as a Boolean. Thus, in OLAP Services we don't have to consider the case in which NULL enters into a Boolean expression.

OLAP Services's interpretation of the MDX semantics varies a little bit from the OLE DB for OLAP specification in that the result of a calculation that involves empty cells may be NULL or it may not be NULL. A NULL value will be treated as zero when it is combined with a non-NULL value in a calculation, but a calculation that involves only NULL values will be regarded as NULL. Let's use as an example the following calculation:

```
([Measures].[Sales] - [Measures].[Costs] ) / [Measures].[Costs]
```

If Sales and Costs are both present, we will get a value in return; if Sales are 10 and Costs are 8, then (10 - 8) / 8 = 0.25. If Sales is present but Costs is not, the expression would be evaluated as (10 - 0) / 0, and the floating-point overflow value (with a typical string representation of "-1.INF") will be returned. If Costs are valid but Sales are not, the expression would be evaluated as (0 - 8) / 8 = -1. However, if neither costs nor sales are valid, the expression will return an empty value.

In a comparison, a NULL will be equal to zero in all circumstances. That is, the expression iif (NULL = 0, ..., ...) will always return the result of the if-true expression. Of course, NULL = NULL is true, and (NULL <> NULL) is always false. Don't fall into the trap of comparing a value with NULL directly, as with iif ([Measures].[Units Sold] = NULL, ...). The NULL will be silently converted into a zero if the [Units Sold] reference is present. If the [Units Sold] reference is NULL, perhaps a NULL will actually be compared to a NULL (which will result in true). The result will be exactly as if you compared [Units Sold] with 0.

If you include any constants in a expression, the expression will always return a result because any empty cell value will be combined with a non-empty value (the constant) as a result. For example, a growth projection formula of `(1.5 * ([Time].[Q2 1998] + [Time].[Q3 1998]))` will return zero if the given measure does not have a value at either [Q2 1998] or [Q3 1998]. It will return 1.5 times the sum of the values that are present, if any are. If we break this down into pieces, the expression `([Time].[Q2 1998] + [Time].[Q3 1998])` will have a NULL result if all of the cells are empty, but `(1.5 * (EMPTY))` will be treated as 1.5 * 0.

Keep in mind that the Sum() of values from cells that are defined as calculated results will be the same whether the cells return zero or NULL. However, if you are calculating averages based on the count of non-empty cells, you will need to pay attention to the averages of calculated members. The result of Avg() over an empty set returns a floating-point overflow (divide-by-zero), not a NULL.

You should also note that the initial release of Microsoft OLAP Services only performs the IsEmpty() operation on cells. Properties and the results of functions on members like *member*.UniqueName can have no result (see the following section on invalid locations). However, if you attempt to use IsEmpty() on these members it will result in a parser error. Hopefully, this will change in a later version or service release. The workaround for this problem is to declare a calculated member that returns the value of the property or name and then to test whether that value is empty.

Invalid Locations

There is another way that non-information may need to be dealt with in MDX: when invalid tuples or empty sets are specified. These can arise in a variety of ways. Microsoft OLAP Services has a very simple logic for dealing with them, which you will need to account for when you are constructing ranges using the colon (:) operator.

An empty set or tuple arises whenever you request a member or members that just aren't there. For example, take a time dimension whose leaf level is months and whose first month is January 1997. Since there are no children to January 1997, the set expression `[Time].[Jan 1997].Children` will return an empty set. The MDX parser will treat it as a set, and the set can be combined with other sets, as in `{ [Time].[Jan 1997], [Time].[Jan 1997].Children}`. However, the `[Jan 1997].Children` term will contribute zero members to the resulting set. Similarly, the member expression `[Time].[Jan 1997].PrevMember` specifies a non-existent member. A set that combined this non-existent member with other members, such as `{ [Time].[Jan 1997], [Time].[Jan 1997].PrevMember }` will only result in the members that were actually present in the dimension metadata (`{[[Time].[Jan 1997]]}`, in this case). If the geography dimension had [City] as its leaf level, then the tuple specification (`[Geography]`.`[Atlanta GA].FirstChild, [Time].[Jan 1997].PrevMember`) would result in an invalid tuple (as would (`[Geography].[Atlanta GA]`, `[Time].[Jan -1997].PrevMember`). This is so because if only one member in a tuple specification is invalid, the entire tuple is.

References to invalid members, tuples, or sets can occur in queries for a variety of reasons. Only valid locations can return results, however, so you will not get valid values back from invalid locations— only NULL. There really are two contexts in which invalid locations can spring up: when a set is being specified and when a tuple is being specified. We've just talked about the case in which a tuple is being specified; let's take a look at sets next.

When a set is being specified, it will ultimately form the range over which a set of values will be evaluated. This is true whether the set is the axis of a query, is a set created by CREATE SET or WITH SET, or is specified in a calculated member as input to an aggregation function. As the set specification is evaluated, valid tuples are included, and invalid ones will not appear. If the set specifies one valid member and one hundred invalid members, only one member will be in the final set, and all values (cell or property) that are evaluated relative to that will be related to the one member. Thus, OLAP Services prevents invalid member references (which will lead to invalid tuples) from contributing empty cell values to calculations like Count() and Avg().

It is important to understand the behavior of invalid members when they are used with the colon operator (:) provided by Microsoft OLAP Services. (This behavior may change in later releases .) When you specify a range in MDX in which one member is valid and the other is not, the resulting range will extend to the edge of the database's ordering of members on the level of the valid member. For example, consider a time level that has the twelve months January through December in calendar order. The range `{ [March] : [January]`.`PrevMember }` specifies a valid member on the left and an invalid member on the right. The set that results will be { [March] : [December] }. A symmetric form of this, `{ [December].NextMember : [April] }`, specifies an invalid member on the left and a valid member on the right; with a resulting range of { [January] : [April] }. If an invalid member is specified on both the left and the right side of the colon, then the result is an empty set. Common usage of MDX functions like .Lag(), .Lead(), Cousin(), and ParallelPeriod() will frequently result in sets that are formed with one invalid member. Part of the utility of Cousin() and ParallelPeriod() is that comparable ranges from multiple levels can be specified with one simple operator, and the byproduct of constructing ranges with them (like `ParallelPeriod (. . .) : [Time].CurrentMember`) is that some ranges may not mean what you want them to mean.

You can use iif() to directly test for the existence or non-existence of members as well as use indirect means. A direct test would be asking whether the member itself is empty. An indirect test would be to test the count of tuples from one member in a dimension back to the edge of the dimension. For example, if you want to calculate a six-month moving average only where at least six months exist over which to calculate it, you can count the number of tuples stretching from the current member backwards and only return the average if there are six of them, as the following expression does:

```
iif (
     Count( LastPeriods (6, [Time]), INCLUDEEMPTY ) >= 6,
     Avg(LastPeriods (6, [Time]), [Measures].[Volume Traded]),
     NULL
)
```

The best way to test for the existence of a member is to test for an invalid member reference, as with

```
iif (
     NOT IsEmpty ([Time].CurrentMember.Lag (119)),
     Avg([Time].Lag(119) : [Time], [Measures].[Volume Traded]),
     NULL
)
```

For some reason, the first release of OLAP Services requires that the argument to the IsEmpty() function be a cell, not an expression (though the MDX specification requires that any expression be allowed to be used there). An alternative approach is to compare the name to an empty string, although you have to beware of empty member names (hopefully, you don't have any in your time dimension):

```
iif (
     [Time].Lag (119).UniqueName <> "",
     Avg([Time].Lag(119) : [Time], [Measures].[Volume Traded]),
     NULL
)
```

Alternatively, if using IsEmpty() appeals to you more, you can define a cell expression that returns the following unique name:

```
WITH MEMBER [Measures].[Time-name] AS '[Time].UniqueName'
iif ( NOT ISEMPTY( [Measures].[Time-name], [Time].Lag (120) ), ..., ...)
. . .
```

The same principle of extended ranges is true for the ranges constructed with ParallelPeriod() and Cousin(). For example, even if there is no sibling of a quarter-level time member that is two quarters back, or no year at all that could be the ancestor of a parallel period two years back from the current time member, because there is a range specification that involves the current member, Microsoft OLAP Services will construct a range that stretches from the current member to one end or the other of the level, depending on which side of the colon the invalid member reference is on.

Precedence of Cell Properties with Calculated Members

There is one more aspect of context that we have not yet talked about: that of a single cell and a calculated member chosen as having precedence for that cell. When a calculated member is used to define the value of a cell, it defines the values for every aspect of that cell. Not only does that include the raw numerical quantity for the cell but all associated properties for that cell as well. In combination with the data types of the cells that go into calculating the cell, the formula itself will determine the data type of the raw value that is returned to the client or passed to an external function. The other properties of a cell, including textual display formatting and font-rendering information, will be those that are also defined for the calculated member. In the following sections we explore each of these areas.

Precedence of Display Formatting with Calculated Members

Let's revisit the trivial query introduced at the beginning of Chapter 5, this time with formatting applied. Assuming that our sales and costs are formatted to return zero decimal places, we will see the results shown in Figure 6.1 if we ask for June-to-July difference to two decimal places and that "Margin Pct" be formatted as a percentage to one decimal place:

```
WITH
MEMBER [Measures].[Margin Pct] AS '([Measures].[Sales] -
[Measures].[Costs]) / [Measures].[Costs]', SOLVE_ORDER = 1,
FORMAT_STRING = '#.00'
MEMBER [Time].[June to July] AS '[Time].[July 1998] -
[Time].[June 1998]', SOLVE_ORDER = 2, FORMAT_STRING = '#.0%'
SELECT
   { [Measures].[Sales], [Measures].[Costs], [Measures].[Margin Percent]
} on columns,
   { [Time].[June 1998], [Time].[July 1998], [Time].[June to July]} on
rows
FROM TrivialCube
WHERE ( [Stores].[Downtown] )
```

As you can see from Figure 6.1, the cell formatting defined in the calculated member that calculates the cell is the formatting that is applied to the value of the cell. The PivotTable Service itself takes on the chore of performing the formatting, so your clients will not need to devote any logic to this task. Font

		Measures		
		Sales	Costs	Margin Pct.
Time	June-1997	1200	1000	20.0%
	July-1997	1300	1050	23.8%
	June to July Difference	100.00	50.00	3.8%

Figure 6.1 Overlapping calculated members with cell formatting.

choice, size, style, and color information can also be specified by the calculated member; whether this information is used is up to the client application.

Data Types from Calculated Cells

It is a simple matter to describe the rules for the data types that are returned for calculations involving valid data and that return a valid result. The data type for the result of a calculated member depends on the formula as well as the types of cells that it uses as inputs. The following rules are used in MDX calculations:

- Two integers added, subtracted, or multiplied together result in an integer. If one integer is BigInt-sized, then the result will be BigInt size.
- An integer added to, subtracted from, or multiplied by a floating-point number in any way results in a floating-point number. The result will be the size of the floating-point number (single-float or double-float).
- Any number divided by any other number results in a double-float result.
- The data type of the value returned by Count(), Rank(), or .Ordinal is a 32-bit integer.
- The data type of the value that is returned by Max() and Min() is the largest type of any of its inputs (the maximum of an integer and a single float is a single float, even if the integer is the larger of the numbers; the maximum of a double float and any other type is a double float).
- The Sum() of an empty set or of a set of entirely empty cells is an empty value. The Avg() of an empty set or a set of entirely empty cells is a divide-by-zero overflow.
- Any values calculated by an aggregation operator other than those listed in the preceding rules (including Sum(), Max(), etc.) are returned as a double float. All values that are input to the aggregation operator are converted to a double float prior to aggregation, so if you take the sum of a large number of integers the aggregation operator will not overflow as the sum passes the 2,147,483,647 limit on a 32-bit integer.

There are no conversion rules for strings. They may be concatenated with other strings within Microsoft OLAP Services, but otherwise they are simply passed into functions and/or returned from functions. Although a Boolean result cannot be used in a context that expects a number, calculated members can be defined with a formula that just performs a logical operation, as follows:

```
CREATE MEMBER [AccountCube].[Measures].[Indebted] AS '[Measures].[Bor-
rowed] > [Measures].[Assets]'
```

Microsoft OLAP Services will convert the Boolean result into a 32-bit integer, with a true result represented by 1 and a false by 0.

Thus, even though a measure may have a defined data type, if the formula of some calculated member has precedence at a cell, the data type returned for the cell is defined by the calculation. For example, suppose an inventory units measure is defined as having an integer type and there is the following scenario variance member:

```
[Scenario].[Budget Pct. Variance] AS
'([Scenario].[Actual] / [Scenario].[Budget]) -1'
```

In this case, the result of any ([Scenario].[Budget Pct. Variance], [Measures].[Inventory Units]) tuple is going to be a double float (unless yet another calculation has precedence for that cell).

Summary

In this chapter, we have covered the topics of context in a query, the properties that are affected by the cell-by-cell calculation of members within a query, and the way in which OLAP Services handles missing and invalid data in a query. Combined with the base of MDX knowledge we gained in Chapter 5, these factors allow us to begin understanding all aspects of a query that are relevant to a client. In Chapter 7, on MDX function and operator reference, we enumerate all of the functions and operators of OLAP Services's MDX implementation, any of which we are now ready to use in any kind of query and predict what its semantics will be.

MDX Function and Operator Reference

Now that we have covered the basics of MDX, we can fully explain all the functions and operators that OLAP Services provides for expressions and commands. This chapter forms a reference for the MDX operators and commands used in queries and calculations. Although reading a reference chapter may sound boring, if you are still just learning MDX you may find it helpful to scan through the various functions described here just to see what capabilities you have at your disposal. In this book, we will use only a fraction of these functions to illustrate principles and specific analyses, so your ability to create appropriate applications will depend in part on your understanding of all of the functions we describe in this chapter.

Where appropriate, we have included figures that illustrate the behavior of operators that perform members, tuple, and set selection based on metadata. This chapter is organized into the following major sections:

- Numerical calculations (including aggregation functions)
- Comparison, logical, and conditional operators
- OLAP metadata
- Strings and name functions
- String and name operators
- Array creation
- MDX DDL statements

In addition to the MDX operators and functions presented in this chapter, there is also a large set of functions that return members and sets based on hierarchical relationships. We provide an illustrated reference for these functions in Chapter 8.

The lists of functions provided at the beginning of each section in this chapter show the function's name, and in the text beneath we provide a synopsis of the arguments to the function (if any) as well as what the function returns and whether or not the function/operator is particular to Microsoft OLAP Services. Operators that are extensions to the general MDX specification are marked with an asterisk (*).

Numerical Calculations

Arguably, the most important function of Microsoft OLAP Services is to deliver the results of numerical calculations to clients. In this section, we'll explore the numerical calculations available in MDX. OLAP Services builds in the basic four numerical operators:

+	addition
-	subtraction and unary negation
*	multiplication
/	division

OLAP Services also natively provides a set of aggregation and statistical operators, which we discuss in the next section, "Aggregation Functions." Although there are many more functions that one could want (modulus remainder, integer portion, logarithms, etc.), OLAP Services does not build them in. To use these additional functions, you need to exploit the *user-defined function (UDF)* facility, which allows the use of functions that are separate from OLAP Services. For example, the Visual Basic for Applications (VBA) function library is installed with OLAP Services and is automatically registered for use, so a large subset of the functions it provides may be used with OLAP Services, version 1. Similarly, if you use Microsoft Excel, the Excel function library is also automatically registered for use, and many of its functions may be used by OLAP Services as well. We cover how to create and use function libraries in more depth in Chapter 14.

Aggregation Functions

This section discusses all of the aggregation functions provided by Microsoft OLAP Services. All of the aggregation functions provided are listed in Table 7.1.

Table 7.1 Aggregation Functions

EXTENSION	SYNOPSIS
	Aggregate (set [, numeric xpression])
	Avg (set [, numeric xpression])
	Correlation (set, y numeric expression [, x numeric expression])
	Count (set [, INCLUDEEMPTY | EXCLUDEEMPTY])
	Covariance (set, y numeric expression [, x numeric expression])
	CovarianceN (set, y numeric expression [, x numeric expression])
	LinRegIntercept (set, y numeric expression [, x numeric expression])
	LinRegPoint (x slice numeric expression, set, numeric value expression [, numeric expression])
	LinRegR2 (set, y numeric expression [, x numeric value expression])
	LinRegSlope (set, y numeric expression [, x numeric expression])
	LinRegVariance (set, y numeric expression [, x numeric expression])
	Max (set [, numeric value expression])
	Median (set [, numeric value expression])
	Min (set [, numeric value expression])
	Rank (tuple, set)
	StdDev (set [, numeric value expression])
*	StdDevP (set [, numeric value expression])
*	StDev (set [, numeric value expression])
*	StDevP (set [, numeric value expression])
	Sum (set [, numeric value expression])
*	Var (set [, numeric value expression])
	Variance (set [, numeric value expression])
*	VarianceP (set [, numeric value expression])
*	VarP (set [, numeric value expression])

Aggregate (*set [, numeric value expression]*)

This function aggregates the cells formed by *set* according to the default aggregation operator for any measures in context. If a numeric value expression is provided, then this function sums the expression's set of values over the cells. In the event that the cells are of a measure that aggregates by COUNT, MIN, or MAX, then COUNT, MIN, or MAX, respectively, is the aggregation operation used; otherwise, the aggregation operation used is summation. Although you may specify an expression to be evaluated by this function, this function does not work if you use calculated members as its inputs. (If a calculated member "M" has a higher SOLVE_ORDER than a calculated member on a different dimension that is performing the Aggregate(), then "M" will use the results of the aggregating member.)

This comes in handy when you have a set of different measures with different aggregation rules that are all being queried for. Calculated members performing period-to-date aggregations as well as aggregations on other dimensions will often be best constructed out of this operator. (Essentially, this is the implicit operation carried out within OLAP Services's hierarchies.) Consider the following calculated member:

```
CREATE MEMBER [Time].[MonthsOf1998ToDate] AS
'Aggregate ( {[Time].[Jan 1998] : [Time].[May 1998]} )'
```

When combined with a summing measure, this member will yield the sum of its values over the range of January through May 1998. When combined with a measure aggregating by MAX, this member will yield the MAX of its values over that same time period.

Avg (*set [, numeric expression]*)

This function takes the average of the non-empty values found across cells in the set. If a *numeric expression* is supplied, then its values are averaged across the cells in the set. Note that the average is formed out of the sum of the cells divided by the count of the non-empty cells. If you wish to take the average over all cells, treating empty as zero, then you can either create a numeric value expression that converts missing to zero or take the Sum() over the set divided by the Count() of the set, including empty cells.

Avg() over an empty set returns a double-length floating-point overflow value, not a NULL value.

Correlation (*set, y numeric value expression [, x numeric value expression]*)

This function calculates a correlation coefficient between x-y pairs of values. The y numeric expression is evaluated over the set to get the y values for each pair. If the x numeric expression is present, then it is evaluated over the set. Otherwise, the cells formed by set are evaluated within the current context, and

$$\frac{n\sum_{i=1}^{n} x_i y_i - \sum_{i=1}^{n} x_i \sum_{i=1}^{n} y_i}{\sqrt{n\sum_{i=1}^{n} x_i^2 - \left(\sum_{i=1}^{n} x_i\right)^2}\sqrt{n\sum_{i=1}^{n} y_i^2 - \left(\sum_{i=1}^{n} y_i\right)^2}}$$

their values are used as the x values. The formula for the correlation coefficient is as follows:

If either the y or the x numeric expression is a logical or text value, or if the value is NULL, then that tuple and its related values are not included in the correlation. Zero values for y and x are included.

```
Count (set [, INCLUDEEMPTY | EXCLUDEEMPTY])
```

This function counts the cells in the range formed by *set* (as opposed to counting the tuples in *set*). Without the INCLUDEEMPTY flag, only non-empty cells are counted; with the flag, all cells are counted. INCLUDEEMPTY is the default.

```
Covariance (set, y numeric expression
[, x numeric expression])
```

```
CovarianceN (set, y numeric expression
[, x numeric expression])
```

These functions calculate the statistical covariance across x-y pairs of values. The y numeric expression is evaluated over the *set* to get the y values for each pair. If the x numeric expression is present, then it is evaluated over the *set*. Otherwise, the cells formed by *set* are evaluated within the current context, and their values are used as the x values. The biased population formula for covariance is as follows:

$$\frac{\sum_{i=1}^{n} (\bar{x} - xi)(\bar{y} - yi)}{n}$$

Covariance() calculates the population covariance and uses the biased population formula (dividing by the number of x-y pairs). CovarianceN() calculates the sample covariance and uses the unbiased population formula (dividing by the number of x-y pairs minus 1). If either the y or the x *numeric value expression* is a logical or text value, or if the value is NULL, then that tuple and its related values are not included in the correlation. Zero values for y and x are included.

```
LinRegIntercept (set, y numeric expression
[, x numeric expression])
```

This function returns the intercept of the linear regression line calculated from the given data points (where the regression line intersects 0). For the linear equation y = ax + b, which will be determined over some set of y and x, the values of the y numeric expression are evaluated over *set* to get the y values. If the x numeric expression is present, then it is evaluated over the *set* to get the values of the x axis. Otherwise, the cells formed by *set* are evaluated within the current context and their values are used as the x values.

Once the linear regression line has been calculated, this function returns the x-intercept of the line (represented by b in the equation y = ax + b). Also see the other LinRegXXX functions.

```
LinRegPoint (numeric expression, set,
y numeric expression [, x numeric expression])
```

This function returns the value of the calculated linear regression line y = ax + b for a particular value of x. For the linear equation y = ax + b, which will be determined from a set of y and x values, the values of the y *numeric expression* are evaluated to get the y values. If the x *numeric expression* is present, then it is evaluated over the set to get the values of the x axis. Otherwise, the cells formed by *set* are evaluated within the current context and their values are used as the x values.

Once the linear regression line has been calculated, the value of y = ax + b is calculated for the value given in the x *slice numeric expression* and returned.

```
LinRegR2 (set, y numeric expression
[, x numeric expression])
```

This function returns the statistical R^2 variance of the given data points to the linear regression line calculated from them. For the linear equation y = ax + b, which will be determined over some set of y and x, the values of the y numeric expression are evaluated to get the y values. If the x *numeric expression* is present, then it is evaluated over the set to get the values of the x axis. Otherwise, the cells formed by *set* are evaluated within the current context and their values are used as the x values.

Once the linear regression line has been calculated, this function returns the statistical R^2 variance between the points on it and the given points. See also the other LinRegXXX functions.

```
LinRegSlope (set [, y numeric expression
[, x numeric expression])
```

This function returns the slope of the linear regression line calculated from the given data points. For the linear equation y = ax + b, which will be determined over some set of y and x, the values of the y *numeric expression* are evaluated to get the y values. If the x *numeric expression* is present, then it is evaluated over the set to get the values of the x axis. Otherwise, the cells formed by *set* are evaluated within the current context and their values are used as the x values.

Once the linear regression line has been calculated, this function returns the slope of the line (represented by a in the equation y = ax + b). See also the other LinRegXXX functions.

`LinRegVariance (`*set, numeric expression*
`[, `*numeric expression*`])`

This function returns the variance of fit of the calculated linear regression line to the actual points given for it. For the linear equation $y = ax + b$, which will be determined over some set of y and x, the values of the y *numeric expression* are evaluated to get the y values. If the x *numeric expression* is present, then it is evaluated over the *set* to get the values of the x axis. Otherwise, the cells formed by *set* are evaluated within the current context and their values are used as the x values.

Once the linear regression line has been calculated, this function returns the statistical variance between the its points and the given points. See also the other LinRegXXX functions.

`Max (`*set* `[, `*numeric expression*`])`

This function returns the maximum value found across the cells of the *set*. If a *numeric expression* is supplied, then the function finds the maximum of its non-empty values across the set.

`Median (`*set* `[, `*numeric expression*`])`

This function returns the median value found across the cells of the *set*. If a *numeric expression* is supplied, then the function finds the median of its values across the set.

`Min (`*set* `[, `*numeric expression*`])`

This function returns the minimum value found across the cells of the *set*. If a *numeric expression* is supplied, then the function finds the minimum of its values across the set.

`Rank (`*tuple, set*`)`

This function returns the (one-based) index of the tuple in the *set*. If the tuple is not found in the set, Rank() returns 0.

`StdDev (`*set* `[, `*numeric value expression*`])`

`StdDevP (`*set* `[, `*numeric value expression*`])`

`StDevP (`*set* `[, `*numeric value expression*`])`

`StDevP (`*set* `[, `*numeric value expression*`])`

These functions return the standard deviation of a numeric expression evaluated over a set. If the numeric value expression is not supplied, these functions evaluate the set within the current context to determine the values to use. The formula for obtaining the standard deviation is as follows:

$$\sqrt{\frac{\sum_{i=1}^{n} (\bar{x} - x_i)^2}{n}}$$

StDev() calculates the sample standard deviation and uses the unbiased formula for population (dividing by n-1 instead of n). On the other hand, StDevP() calculates the population standard deviation and uses the biased formula (dividing by n). StdDev() and StdDevP() are aliases of StDev() and StDevP(), respectively.

Sum (*set* [, *numeric value expression*])

This function returns the sum of values found across all tuples in the *set*. If numeric value expression is supplied, then it is evaluated across *set* and its results summed, otherwise *set* is evaluated in the current context and the results summed.

Var (*set* [, *numeric value expression*])

Variance (*set* [, *numeric value expression*])

VarianceP (*set* [, *numeric value expression*])

VarP (*set* [, *numeric value expression*])

These functions return the variance of a numeric expression evaluated over a set. If the *numeric expression* is not supplied, these functions evaluate the set within the current context to determine the values to use. The formula for obtaining the variance is:

$$\frac{\sum_{i=1}^{n} (\bar{x} - x_i)^2}{n}$$

Var() calculates the sample variance and uses the unbiased population formula (dividing by n-1), while VarP() calculates the population variance and uses the biased formula (dividing by n). Variance() and VarianceP() are aliases of Var() and VarP(), respectively.

Note that you can create your own aggregation functions using the user-defined function (UDF) facility in combination with Microsoft OLAP Services operators like SetToArray() and SetToStr(). Later, in Chapter 9, on MDX application topics, we will also explore how to simulate logical aggregations.

Comparison, Logical, and Conditional Operators

Microsoft OLAP Services supports most of the comparison, logical, and conditional operators specified in the full MDX specification. The comparison operators supported by OLAP Services are shown in Table 7.2.

When OLAP Services compares a NULL expression with a non-NULL expression, the NULL is treated as zero. That is, `NULL = 0`, `NULL < 0.00001`, and `NULL > -0.000001` will all evaluate as true. If you test a cell as being equal to NULL (as in `iif ([Time].[1995] = NULL, "EMPTY", "FULL")`), a zero value in one cell will compare as being equal to a NULL for another cell. Only use IsEmpty() if you want to perform this comparison (or CoalesceEmpty(), which we describe at the end of this section).

OLAP Services supports the following logical operators:

expr AND *expr*   True if both expressions are true, false otherwise.

expr OR *expr*   True if either expression is true.

NOT *expr*   True if *expr* is not true, false otherwise.

expr XOR *expr*   True if either of the expressions is true but not both of them, and false otherwise.

Logical operators require that there be a logical expression on either side. Numerical and string expressions are not implicitly converted to logical values (and measures may not be of Boolean type in OLAP Services). Therefore, the following is valid:

```
((([Reject Count] < 100) AND ([Reject Count] > 0))
```

and the following is not valid:

```
((([Reject Count]  100) AND ([Reject Count]))
```

Table 7.2   Comparison Operators

EXTENSION	OPERATOR	MEANS
	<	Less than
	>	Greater than
	<=	Less than or equal to
	>=	Greater than or equal to
	<>	Not equal to
	=	Equal to
IsEmpty(*expr*)		True if *expression* is NULL.

Table 7.3   Conditional Operators

EXTENSION	RETURNS	SYNOPSIS
	string, number	iif (*search_condition, true_part, false_part*)
	string, number	CoalesceEmpty (*value expression* [, *value expression . . .*])

OLAP Services also supports the following two conditional operatorsListed in Table 7.3.

The first release of Microsoft OLAP Services does not support the MDX CASE . . . WHEN . . . END conditional construct in either of its forms.

iif (*search_condition, true_part, false_part***)**

This function evaluates *search_condition*, which needs to be a logical value. If the result is true, then the *true_part* expression is evaluated and returned. If the result is not true, then the *false_part* expression is evaluated and returned. The iif() function can either take numerical expressions for true part and false part and return a number, or it can take string expressions for true part and false part and return a string.

Note that since the search condition must contain a logical expression that involves comparison operations and NULL cells compare as equal to zero, the result of the search condition will not be NULL. However, either the true part or the false part may evaluate to NULL, in which case NULL will be the result when that condition is met.

CoalesceEmpty (*value expression* [, *value expression . . .*]**)**

This function evaluates the first value expression listed. If it is not NULL, then the value of that expression is returned. If it is NULL, then the second value expression is evaluated and returned if it is not NULL. Each subsequent expression, if present, is evaluated in turn; if the last one is NULL, the entire operator returns NULL.

CoalesceEmpty() can either take all number-valued expressions and return a number or it can take all string-valued expressions and return a string.

Specifying Tuples and Sets

Table 7.4 lists the functions and operators that provide the basic primitives for specifying tuples and sets in MDX.

SetToStr (*Set***)**

This function constructs a string from a set. It will frequently be used to transfer a set to an external function that knows how to parse the string, even though

Table 7.4 Basic Tuple and Set Primitives

EXTENSION	RETURNS	SYNOPSIS
*	string	SetToStr(*Set*)
*	set	StrToSet(*String Expression*)
*	string	TupleToStr(*Tuple*)
*	tuple	StrToTuple(*String Expression*)
*	tuple	Set.Current
	tuple	*member*
	tuple	*(member [, member . . .])*
	set	*{ tuple or set [, tuple or set . . .] }*
	set	*member : member*

the string is syntactically suitable for OLAP Services to parse into a set. OLAP Services constructs the string as follows: the first character is "{" and the last character is   "}." Between the braces, each tuple is listed in order. A comma and a space separate each tuple from the next name. If the set contains only one dimension, then each member is listed using its unique name. If the set contains more than one dimension, then each tuple begins with an open parenthesis (" (") and ends with a closing parenthesis (")"). The unique name of the member from each dimension is listed in the order of the dimensions in the set, separated by a comma and a space. For example, in a time dimension that has three years, the expression

```
SetToStr ([Time].[Year].Members)
```

would yield the following string:

```
"{[Time].[All Times].[1998], [Time].[All Times].[1999], [Time].[All
Times].[2000]}"
```

Moreover, the expression

```
SetToStr ( {([Time].[1998], [Customer].[Northeast]), ([Time].[1999],
[Customer].[Southwest])} )
```

yields the following string:

```
"{([Time].[All Times].[1998], [Customer].[All Customers].[Northeast]),
([Time].[All Times].[1999], [Customer].[All Customers].[Southwest])}".
```

Fairly large strings (greater than 16K) will take significant time to create, and the first release of OLAP Services was released with problems that led to the truncation of strings. The further down the hierarchy the members are, the longer and more numerous their unique names will be. So, you may need to perform your own performance evaluations when using this function.

StrToSet*(String Expression)*

This function constructs a set from a string expression. This will frequently be used to transfer a set specification returned by a UDF back to the MDX statement. The string must be a syntactically valid MDX set specification relative to the cube in whose context it is executed. For example, the set of all years in a time dimension that has three year-level members could be created by passing either of the following strings into StrToSet:

```
"{[Time].[All Times].[1998], [Time].[All Times].[1999], [Time].[All
Times].[2000]}"
"[Time].[Year].Members"
```

TupleToStr*(Tuple)*

This function constructs a string from a tuple. This will frequently be used to transfer a tuple specification to an external function. If the tuple contains only one dimension, the unique name for its member is placed in the string. (In this use, it is identical to Member.UniqueName.) If the tuple contains more than one dimension, OLAP Services constructs the string as follows. The string begins with an open parenthesis (" (") and ends with a closed parenthesis (" ("). In between the parentheses, the member's unique name is placed in the string for each dimension in the order they follow in the tuple. Each member is separated by a comma and a space. For example, the expression

```
StrToTuple ( (Time.[1997], Customer.[AZ]) )
```

which uses names that are not quite the members' unique names, might return the following string: "([Time].[All Times].[1997], [Customer].[All Customers].[Southwest].[AZ])"

StrToTuple*(String Expression)*

This function constructs a tuple from a string expression. This will frequently be used to transfer a tuple specification that is returned by an external function back to the MDX statement. The string must be a syntactically valid MDX tuple specification relative to the cube in whose context it is executed. For example, the following two strings would give identical results in the customer dimension, where [AZ] is a child of [Southwest], in that both would result in the Southwest region member:

```
"[Customer].[Southwest]"
"[Customer].[AZ].Parent"
```

(Set).Current

This function returns the current tuple from a set within an iteration over the set. Conceptually, this is the same as Dimension.CurrentMember, except that set.Current is only valid while there actually is an iteration occurring over the set. Also, it only returns a full tuple from the set as opposed to the dimension's member from the current tuple in that set.

(member [, member . . .])

member added to list

Tuples can be explicitly constructed by listing members from one or more dimensions, separated by commas, and enclosing that dimension or dimensions within parentheses. If only one dimension is present in the tuple, the parentheses can be omitted as well. Any member specification will work, not just explicitly named members. For example, the following examples are all tuple specifications:

```
[Time].[1997]
([Time].[1997])
([Time].[1997], [Customer].[All Customers])
([Time].[1997], {[Customer].Members}.Item (0))
```

Note that when a function requires that a tuple be one of its arguments within parentheses, the parentheses must be placed around the tuple as well as within. For example, the following would be a correct tuple specification to be passed to TupleToStr():

```
TupleToStr( ([Time].[1997], [Customer].[All Customers]) )
```

Trying to create an empty tuple with `()` will result in a syntax error.

{ tuple or set   [, tuple or set . . .] }

Sets can be explicitly constructed by enclosing one or more tuples or sets with the same dimensionality within curly braces ("{" and "}"). Each tuple or set specification must be separated from the next by a comma. For example, the following are all sets:

```
{ [Time].[1997] }
{ ([Time].[1997], [Customer].[All Customers]) }
{ [Time].[All Time], [Time].[Year].Members, { [Time].[Quarter].Members
}}
```

The first two are sets of one tuple each, and the last one is a set comprised of one member and two sets in order. Note that in the last example, the second set within it is also enclosed in curly braces. This is not required, and it does not affect the interpretation in any way. Although an empty set is not usually of much practical use, it may be created with an empty pair of curly braces.

member : member

This operator constructs a set from two members and uses the two members as endpoints. The two members must be on the same level; if they are not, a parse error will occur. Using the database ordering of the members in the dimension, all members between the endpoints will be included. It is not an error for the two members to be the same (i.e., {[Time].[1998] : [Time].[1998]}).

In the first release of Microsoft OLAP Services, if the member on the right-hand side of the colon is earlier in the database ordering than the member on the left, a range is constructed from the left-hand member to the last member on the level. If only one member is invalid and the other is valid, a range is constructed from the valid member to the end of the level. An invalid left-hand member creates a range from the first member in the level, and an invalid right-hand member creates a range to the last member in the level. If both are invalid, an empty set is returned.

Basic Set-related Operators

MDX also provides set-related functions that give you a great deal of power in terms of refining the sets specified by other operators. The basic set functions are listed in Table 7.5. Since "sets" in MDX may contain duplicate members, the following functions contain options for retaining or removing duplicates, as appropriate:

Table 7.5 Basic Tuple and Set Primitives

EXTENSION	RETURNS	SYNOPSIS
	set	Union (*set1, set2* [, ALL])
*	set	*set1 + set2*
	set	Intersect (*set1, set2* [, ALL])
	set	Except (*set1, set2* [, ALL])
*	set	*set1 − set2*
	set	Distinct (*set*)
*	set	Head (*Set* [, *Count*])
*	set	Subset (*Set, Start* [, *Count*])
*	set	Tail (*Set* [, *Count*])
	set	CrossJoin (*set1, set2*)
*	set	*set1 * set2*
	set	Generate (*set1, set2* [, ALL])
	set	Extract (*set, dimension* [, *dimension* . . .])
*	member	*tuple*[.Item](*index*)
	tuple	*set*[.Item](*index*)
	tuple	*set*[.Item](*string expression* [, *string expression* . . .])

```
Union (set1, set2 [, ALL])
```

```
set1 + set2
```

This function returns the union of the two sets. The ALL flag controls whether duplicates are retained or eliminated; by default they are not. When duplicates of each tuple are eliminated, the first instance of each tuple is retained according to the order in which it appears. The effect of this function is that *set2* is appended to *set1*, and then all copies of each tuple are removed after the first instance of that tuple in the appended version. When duplicates are retained, any duplicates in the *set1* are retained, and any additional copies in *set2* are also retained. The effect of the union is that *set2* is appended to *set1*. For example, the expression

```
Union (
   { [Customer].[AZ].[Phoenix], [Customer].[AZ].[Scottsdale],
     [Customer].[KS].[Pittsburg], [Customer].[AZ].[Phoenix] },
   { [Customer].[NM].[Albuquerque], [Customer].[AZ].[Phoenix],
     [Customer].[AZ].[Scottsdale], [Customer].[AZ].[Phoenix]
)
```

yields the following set:

```
 { [Customer].[AZ].[Phoenix], [Customer].[AZ].[Scottsdale],
[Customer].[KS].[Pittsburg], [Customer].[NM].[Albuquerque] }
```

The expression

```
Union (
   { [Customer].[AZ].[Phoenix], [Customer].[AZ].[Scottsdale],
     [Customer].[KS].[Pittsburg], [Customer].[AZ].[Phoenix] },
   { [Customer].[NM].[Albuquerque], [Customer].[AZ].[Phoenix],
   [Customer].[AZ].[Scottsdale], [Customer].[AZ].[Phoenix] }
   , ALL
)
```

yields the following set:

```
 { [Customer].[AZ].[Phoenix], [Customer].[AZ].[Scottsdale],
[Customer].[KS].[Pittsburg], [Customer].[AZ].[Phoenix],
[Customer].[NM].[Albuquerque], [Customer].[AZ].[Phoenix],
[Customer].[AZ].[Scottsdale], [Customer].[AZ].[Phoenix] }
```

Microsoft OLAP Services also provides "+" as an alternate way of specifying Union(). Duplicates are removed from the resulting set. The expression Set1 + Set2 + Set3 is equivalent to Union (Set1, Union (Set2, Set3)).

```
Intersect(set1, set2 [,ALL])
```

The ALL flag controls whether duplicates are retained or eliminated. When ALL is not specified, only the unique tuples appearing in *set1* that also appear in *set2* are returned. When ALL is specified, then duplicated tuples in set1 that appear anywhere in *set2* are returned. If there are duplicates of tuple in *set2*, only the duplicates that exist in *set1* will end up in the resulting set. The members are returned in the order in which they appear in set1. For example, the expression

```
Intersect (
  {[Customer].[AZ].[Phoenix], [Customer].[AZ].[Scottsdale],
    [Customer].[KS].[Pittsburg], [Customer].[AZ].[Phoenix]},
  {[Customer].[NM].[Albuquerque], [Customer].[AZ].[Phoenix],
    [Customer].[AZ].[Scottsdale], [Customer].[AZ].[Phoenix]},
)
```

yields the following set:

```
{ [Customer].[AZ].[Phoenix], [Customer].[AZ].[Scottsdale] }
```

The expression:

```
Intersect (
  {[Customer].[AZ].[Phoenix], [Customer].[AZ].[Scottsdale],
    [Customer].[KS].[Pittsburg], [Customer].[AZ].[Phoenix]},
  {[Customer].[NM].[Albuquerque], [Customer].[AZ].[Phoenix],
    [Customer].[AZ].[Scottsdale], [Customer].[AZ].[Phoenix]},
    , ALL
)
```

yields the following set:

```
{ [Customer].[AZ].[Phoenix], [Customer].[AZ].[Scottsdale],
[Customer].[AZ].[Phoenix]}
```

Except (*set1, set2* [, ALL])

set1 – set2

The Except() function removes all elements from *set1* that also exist in *set2*. The ALL flag controls whether duplicates are retained or eliminated. When ALL is specified, duplicates in *set1* are retained, though any tuples matching them in *set2* are discarded. When ALL is not specified, no duplicates are returned. The members returned are determined by the order in which they appear in *set1*.

Microsoft OLAP Services also provides "-" as an alternate way of specifying Except(). Duplicates are removed from the resulting set. The expression Set1 – Set2 is equivalent to Except (Set1, Set2).

Distinct (*set*)

This function removes any duplicates from the set. The first instance of each tuple is retained in the order in which it appears.

Head (*Set* [, *Count*])

This function returns a set of the first *Count* elements from the given set. The order of elements in the given set is preserved. If *Count* is omitted, the number of elements returned is 1. If *Count* is less than 1, an empty set is returned. If the value of the *Count* is greater than the number of tuples in the set, the original set is returned.

Subset (*Set, Start* [, *Count*])

This function returns up to *Count* elements from *set*, starting at *Start*. The *Start* index is zero-based (like Rank()): the first element in the set is at index 0, and the last is at one less than the number of tuples in the set. If *Count* is not specified or is greater than the number of elements in the set following *Start*, all elements from *Start* to the end of the set are returned. If *Count* is less than 1, then an empty set is returned.

Tail (*Set* [, *Count*])

This function returns a set of the last *Count* elements from the given set. The order of elements in the given set is preserved. If *Count* is omitted, the number of elements returned is 1. If *Count* is less than 1, an empty set is returned. If the value of the *Count* is greater than the number of tuples in the set, the original set is returned.

CrossJoin(*set1, set2*)

set1 * *set2*

These functions return a set formed out of the Cartesian product of the two sets. The two sets must represent different dimensions. Microsoft OLAP Services will signal an error if the same dimension appears in either of them. CrossJoin() only takes two sets as arguments. However, since it takes sets as input and returns a set as its output, you may nest multiple CrossJoins to take the Cartesian product of three or more dimensions. Following the same rules used for composing tuples by hand, the order of the dimensions in the resulting tuples is the same as the order of dimensions in the set arguments. Using an asterisk between two sets, as with (*set1* * *set2*), is a OLAP Services-specific synonym for CrossJoin(). The expression *set1* * *set2* * *set3* is the same as *CrossJoin(set1, CrossJoin(set2, set3))*.

Generate(*set1, set2* [,ALL])

Generate() iterates over each tuple in *set1*, and for each element in *set1* it puts every element specified by *set2* into the result set. The dimensionality of the result set is the dimensionality of *set2*. If ALL is specified, then duplicate result tuples are retained. If ALL is not specified, duplicates after the first are removed. *Set1* and *Set2* may be composed of completely different dimensionality, or they may be composed of exactly the same dimensionality. When set2 is a relatively static set of members, this function behaves much like CrossJoin(). Generate() gains its iterative power when *set2* is an expression that depends on the current member or tuple in *set1*. We will explore several examples of this later in this chapter.

Extract(*set, dimension***[,** *dimension* **. . .])**

This function behaves as an opposite to the CrossJoin() function. The resulting set consists of tuples from the extracted dimension elements. For each tuple in the given set, the members of the dimensions listed in the arguments are extracted into new tuples. Since this could result in a great deal of redundancy, this function always removes duplicate from its results.

*tuple***[.Item](*index*)**

This function returns the member at the *index* position within the tuple. The index is based at 0. For example, ([Product].[Jackets], [Time].[1996]).Item (0) is [Product].[Jackets], and ([Product].[Jackets], [Time].[1996]).Item (1) is [Time].[1996]. We indicate that ".item" is optional because it is the default operator. The following are equivalent:

```
Tuple(index)
Tuple.Item(index)
```

*set***[.Item](*index*)**

*set***[.Item](*string expression***[,***string expression* **. . .]**
)

The first variation of the `Item` operator returns the tuple at the *index* position within the set. The index is based at 0. For example, consider

```
{ [Time].[1996], [Time].[1997] }.Item (0) is [Time].[1996]
{ [Time].[1996], [Time].[1997] }.Item (1) is [Time].[1997]
```

The second variation returns the first tuple in the set whose name is matched by the string expressions. There can be only one string expression containing a complete tuple specification in string form or one string specification for each dimension. The order in which the members are specified, first to last across the string expressions and across the tuple in a single string expression, must match the order of dimensions in the set. If some member from the strings is not found in the metadata when the expression is parsed, then a parse error results. If the member is found in the metadata but not in any tuple in the set then an empty tuple is returned. For example, the following two item specifications are identical:

```
Crossjoin ([Time].[Year].members,
[Customer].[State].Members).Item( "[1997]", "[FL]")
Crossjoin ([Time].[Year].members,
[Customer].[State].Members).Item( "([1997], [FL])")
```

Note that in the tuple specifications, member expressions can be used as well as named members. For example, the following are also equivalent to the two-item specifications just given:

```
Crossjoin ([Time].[Year].members,
```

```
[Customer].[State].Members).Item( "[1998].lag(1)", "[FL]")
Crossjoin ([Time].[Year].members,
[Customer].[State].Members).Item( "([1997].[Q1].Parent, [FL])")
```

We indicate ".Item" as being optional because it is the default operator. The following are equivalent:

```
Set(index)
Set.Item(index)
```

Remember: If you are trying to use Rank() to pick out an index for Item(), that Rank returns a 1-based index, and you will need to subtract 1 from it to use it with Item().

Data-based Filtering of Sets

The functions listed in Table 7.6 all filter the tuples of a set based on associated data values.

Filter (*set, search condition*)

Filter returns those tuples of set for which the search condition (a logical expression) is true. If none are true, an empty set is returned. The tuples in the resulting set follow the same order in which they appeared in the original set.

BottomCount (*set, index* [, *numeric expression*])

TopCount (*set, index* [, *numeric expression*])

TopCount() returns the top *index* items found after sorting the set. The set is sorted on the *numeric expression* (if one is supplied). If there is no *numeric expression*, the cells found in the evaluation context are used. The Bottom-Count() function is similar to TopCount(), except that it returns the bottom *index* items. TopCount() returns elements ordered from largest to smallest in

Table 7.6 Data-based Functions Filter

EXTENSION	RETURNS	SYNOPSIS
	set	Filter (*set, search* condition)
	set	BottomCount (*set, index* [, *numeric expression*])
	set	TopCount (*set, index* [, *numeric expression*])
	set	BottomPercent (*set, percentage, numeric expression*)
	set	TopPercent (*set, percentage, numeric expression*)
	set	BottomSum (*set, value, numeric expression*)
	set	TopSum (*set, value, numeric expression*)

terms of the cells or expression used; BottomCount() returns them ordered from smallest to largest. Any duplicate tuples are retained during sorting, and those that make the cutoff are retained.

These functions always break the hierarchy. If members from multiple levels are combined in the set, then they are all treated as peers. If there are duplicate values for some of the cells in *set*, these functions may pick an arbitrary set. For example, suppose the set of values (when sorted) is as follows:

Fruit	Value
Strawberries	12
Cantaloupes	10
Peaches	8
Apples	8
Kiwis	8
Bananas	4

In this case, selecting the top three or bottom two fruits based on value will cause an arbitrary choice to be made at the value of 8. The results are function-ally equivalent to Head(Order(set, numeric value expression, BDESC), *index*) and Head(Order(*set, numeric value expression*, BASC), *index*).

`BottomPercent (set, percentage, numeric expression)`

`TopPercent (set, percentage, numeric expression)`

TopPercent() returns the top *percentage* tuples of *set*, based on *numeric expression* if specified. The cells or expression are summed over the set, and the top set of elements whose cumulative total of the *numeric expression* is at least *percentage* is returned. *Percentage* is a numeric expression. For example, using the sorted set of fruits and values, `TopPercent( fruit, 50, Value)` will result in { Strawberries, Cantaloupes }. Strawberries is 24 percent of the total, Cantaloupes + Strawberries is 44 percent of the total, and Peaches would push the set over the 50 percent limit to 56 percent.

BottomPercent() behaves similarly, except that it returns the bottom set of ele-ments whose cumulative total from the bottom is less than the specified per-centage. TopPercent() returns elements ordered from largest to smallest in terms of the cells or expression used; BottomPercent() returns them ordered from smallest to largest.

The percentage is specified from 0 to 100 (not 0 to 1.0). These functions always break the hierarchy. Like TopCount() and BottomCount(), they may pick an arbitrary cutoff when some cells have the same values. Any duplicate tuples are retained during sorting, and those that make the cutoff are retained. Note that these functions do not have anything to do with taking tuples in the top or bottom percentile ranges according to the statistical definition of percentiles.

`BottomSum (set, value, numeric expression)`

`TopSum (set, value, numeric expression)`

TopSum() returns the subset of *set*, after sorting it, such that the sum of the cells (or numeric value expression, if supplied) is at least value. This function always breaks the hierarchy. For example, given the sorted set of fruits and values, `TopSum(fruit, 24, value)` would return { Strawberries, Cantaloupes }. Strawberries' 12 is less than 24, Strawberries + Cantaloupes is 22, while adding Peach's 8 to the 22 would push it over the limit of 24 to 30. The BottomSum() function behaves similarly, except that it returns the bottom set of elements whose cumulative total from the bottom is less than the specified value. TopSum() returns elements ordered from largest to smallest in terms of the cells or expression used; BottomSum() returns them ordered from smallest to largest.

These functions always break the hierarchy. Like TopCount() and Bottom-Count(), they may pick an arbitrary cutoff when some cells have the same values. Any duplicate tuples are retained during sorting, and those that make the cutoff are retained.

Ordering Sets

The need to put tuples into a particular ordering arises frequently in OLAP applications. The functions listed in Table 7.7 provide ordering for sets.

`Hierarchize (set)`

Hierarchize() returns the set that it is given after it puts all the members in each dimension into hierarchical order. Within each level, members are put into their database ordering. Children are sorted to immediately follow after their parents. When the tuples are composed of more than one dimension, they are sorted primarily on the first dimension, then on the second dimension, and so on. Any duplicate tuples are retained.

Table 7.7   Ordering Functions

EXTENSION	RETURNS	SYNOPSIS
	set	Hierarchize (*set*)
	set	Order (*set*, {*string_expression* | *numeric expression*}[, ASC | DESC | BASC | BDESC])

```
Order(set, {string_expression | numeric expression}
[, ASC | DESC | BASC | BDESC])
```

Order() returns the set that it is given after it sorts it. If a numeric or string value expression is provided, then that is used to sort the tuples; otherwise, the values of the cells in context are used. This function also takes an optional flag to indicate how to sort. The default ordering is ASC (ascending without breaking the hierarchy).

Order() has two modes for sorting: breaking hierarchy and preserving hierarchy. The BASC and BDESC options break the hierarchy, while ASC and DESC do not. When the hierarchy is broken, the values associated with each tuple in the set are treated as peers, and the set is ordered only by the values. When the hierarchy is preserved, a more complex ordering algorithm is used, which can lead to very useful results.

Preserving Hierarchy: Set Containing One Dimension

When the set consists only of one dimension's worth of members, sorting and preserving the hierarchy orders each parent before its children. At each level of members from the top down, the children of each parent are sorted relative to each other. For example, the product hierarchy for a fictional fishcake manufacturer is shown in Figure 7.1 and the units shipped per product are shown in Figure 7.2. Ordering these members while preserving the hierarchy would give us the orderings shown in Figure 7.3. There is an extra sophistication in the sorting process that is not immediately evident. Let us imagine that the cate-

Category	Product Name
Premium	Ancient Mariner
Premium	Gobi Crab Cakes
Premium	Moby Dick
Premium	Neptunes Glory
Diet	Silver Scales
Diet	Thin Fins
Standard	Anglers Choice
Standard	Briny Deep
Standard	Gill Thrill
Standard	Mako Steak-o

Figure 7.1   Sample product hierarchy.

gory-level members [Standard], [Premium], and [Diet] were not part of the set being queried, while the ProductName members still were. Therefore, the category-level [Units] value does not come directly into play when the set is ordered. However, when sorting without breaking hierarchy, the [Units] value is still calculated at each parent member when Microsoft OLAP Services is trying to figure out how to order the groups of children relative to their cousins.

For example, suppose that the following set of product names was ordered by Units: { [Product].[Briny Deep], [Product].[Anglers Choice], [Product].[Ancient Mariner], [Product].[Gobi Crab Cakes], [Product].[Thin Fins]}. The ordering shown in Figure 7.4 would be returned.

Preserving hierarchy: set containing multiple dimensions

When the set consists of multiple dimensions, the tuples are sorted such that the hierarchical ordering of the first dimension in the tuples is the primary ordering. According to this ordering, within each member of the first dimension the members of the second dimension are sorted. Within each ([member from dim 1], [member from dim 2]) tuple, the members of the third dimension are sorted, and so on. For example, let us expand our example to include some customers and time periods and order the cross-join of

Product	Units
Ancient Mariner	221,871
Gobi Crab Cakes	223,351
Moby Dick	200,745
Neptunes Glory	210,745
Premium	856,274
Silver Scales	425,604
Thin Fins	434,482
Diet	860,086
Anglers Choice	207,662
Briny Deep	201,443
Gill Thrill	209,962
Mako Steak-o	215,521
Standard	834,588

Figure 7.2   Units shipped in hierarchy.

ASC

Product	Units
Standard	834,588
Briny Deep	201,443
Anglers Choice	207,662
Gill Thrill	209,962
Mako Steak-o	215,521
Premium	856,274
Moby Dick	200,745
Neptunes Glory	210,745
Ancient Mariner	221,871
Gobi Crab Cakes	223,351
Diet	860,086
Silver Scales	425,604
Thin Fins	434,482

DESC

Product	Units
Diet	860,086
Thin Fins	434,482
Silver Scales	425,604
Premium	856,274
Gobi Crab Cakes	223,351
Ancient Mariner	221,871
Neptunes Glory	210,745
Moby Dick	200,745
Standard	834,588
Mako Steak-o	215,521
Gill Thrill	209,962
Anglers Choice	207,662
Briny Deep	201,443

Figure 7.3 Hierarchy preserved in ordering.

```
{ [Product].[Briny Deep], [Product].[Anglers Choice],
[Product].[Mako Steak-o] }
```

with

```
{ [Time].[Quarter 2], [Time].[Quarter 3] }
```

with

```
{ [Customer].[Supernaturalizes Food Service], [Customer].[Hanover Dis-
tributors], [Customer].[Subcommittees Anticipates Farms] }.
```

The ordering and values shown in Figure 7.5 will appear. The products are arranged in order of decreasing quantity over year and customer parent. For each product, the quarters are arranged in order of decreasing quantity based on that product and customer parent. For each (Product, Time) tuple, the customers are arranged in order of decreasing quantity. Where tuples are tied (at

ASC

Product	Units	Parent's Units
Briny Deep	201,443	834,588
Anglers Choice	207,662	
Ancient Mariner	221,871	856,274
Gobi Crab Cakes	223,351	
Thin Fins	434,482	860,086

DESC

Product	Units	Parent's Units
Thin Fins	434,482	860,086
Gobi Crab Cakes	223,351	856,274
Ancient Mariner	221,871	
Anglers Choice	207,662	834,588
Briny Deep	201,443	

Figure 7.4. Hierarchy preserved in ordering set without parents.

			Qty.
Mako Steak-o	Quarter 2	Subcommittees Anticipates Farms	119.00
		Supernaturalizes Food Service	87.00
		Hanover Distributions	64.00
	Quarter 3	Hanover Distributions	185.00
		Supernaturalizes Food Service	151.00
		Subcommittees Anticipates Farms	105.00
Anglers Choice	Quarter 3	Hanover Distributions	181.00
		Supernaturalizes Food Service	179.00
		Subcommittees Anticipates Farms	
	Quarter 2	Supernaturalizes Food Service	127.00
		Hanover Distributions	73.00
		Subcommittees Anticipates Farms	
Briny Deep	Quarter 3	Subcommittees Anticipates Farms	213.00
		Supernaturalizes Food Service	
		Hanover Distributions	
	Quarter 2	Subcommittees Anticipates Farms	204.00
		Supernaturalizes Food Service	
		Hanover Distributions	

Figure 7.5   Hierarchy preserved in ordering set with multiple dimensions.

the blank cells), the original ordering of the tuples is retained rather than the dimension's ordering (which was alphabetical).

Measure Values

Microsoft OLAP Services provides two functions to assist in the accessing of data values for a measure as listed in Table 7.8.

measure[.Value]

The .Value operator returns the value of the specified measure at the location formed by the current members of all other dimensions in context. We show this operator as optional because it is the default operator on a measure in a calculation or query context. Note that the initial release of OLAP Services generates a syntax error whenever you actually try to use .Value. If you leave it off, you get

Table 7.8   Measure Value Reference Functions

EXTENSION	RETURNS	SYNOPSIS
	string or number	*measure*[.Value]
*	number	ValidMeasure (*Tuple*)

the value of the measure anyway since the default interpretation of a measure is to take its value. This operator exists simply as a specific counterpart to the other functions that return aspects of a member, like .Name (which would return the name of the measure).

ValidMeasure(*Tuple*)

This function returns the value of the measure specified by the tuple where the measure has been projected to a meaningful intersection in a virtual cube. When a virtual cube joins two or more regular cubes that have different dimensionality, all base data values in the virtual cube are found at the ALL levels of each dimension that is not shared by all cubes. You can always reference these base data cells by explicitly qualifying the measure reference to the ALL level of each dimension (for example, ([Measures].[Employee Count], [Product].[All Products], [Customer].[All Customers])). This function is a convenience because you do not need to explicitly reference all of the dimensions that are not relevant to the measure.

The tuple may contain members from any dimensions of the virtual cube (and it does not need to have a measure in it). Any members for non-common dimensions for the measure are projected to the ALL member. Any members for dimensions that are in common are used to locate the value returned. The function can be used with regular cubes, but in that case it does nothing to change the location of reference for the measure.

Property Values

Microsoft OLAP Services eschews the MDX standard syntax for referencing property values within an MDX expression. The function listed in Table 7.9 is provided for accessing property values in an MDX expression:

`member.Properties ( property name)`

The property name may be a string expression. Generally, this will be a constant string (like "Zip Code"), but it may also be a string-valued expression, such as a string returned by an external function. The property name string expression will be evaluated cell by cell every time the property reference is.

Table 7.9 Property Value Reference Function

EXTENSION	RETURNS	SYNOPSIS
*	string	*member*.Properties (*property name*)

OLAP Metadata

The operators and functions described in this section return non-member metadata information. Note that while the result of a cell cannot be a metadata item such as a dimension or level, the dimension, level, or other metadata object that is returned by one of these functions can itself be used as the subject of another operator or function. The name and unique name operators listed in Table 7.10 may be used in any context that calls for a string. Thus, the expression [Geography]. CurrentMember.Level.Name takes the name of the level of the current member in the geography dimension.

Hierarchy.Dimension

This function returns the dimension that the hierarchy is in. Since Microsoft OLAP Services semantically treats different hierarchies as different dimensions, this function is essentially a "no-op" in the first release.

Table 7.10 OLAP Metadata Functions

EXTENSION	RETURNS	SYNOPSIS
*	Dimension	*Hierarchy*.Dimension
*	Dimension	*Level*.Dimension
*	Dimension	*Member*.Dimension
*	Dimension	Dimensions(*Numeric Expression*)
*	Dimension	Dimensions(*String Expression*)
*	Hierarchy	*Level*.Hierarchy
*	Hierarchy	*Member*.Hierarchy
*	Level	*Member*.Level
*	Level	Levels(*String Expression*)
*	Level	*Dimension*.Levels(*Numeric Expression*)
*	String	*Dimension*.UniqueName
*	String	*Level*.UniqueName
*	String	*Member*.UniqueName
*	String	*Dimension*.Name
*	String	*Hierarchy*.Name
*	String	*Level*.Name
*	String	*Member*.Name
*	Number	*Level*.Ordinal

Level.Dimension

The function returns the dimension that contains *Level*.

Member.Dimension

This function returns the dimension that contains *Member*.

Dimensions(*Numeric Expression*)

This function returns the dimension whose zero-based position within the cube is *Numeric Expression*. Note that the measures dimension is always Dimensions(0), while the order of the other dimensions depends on the order in which they were added to the cube when it was being constructed (and/or modified).

Dimensions(*String Expression*)

This function returns the dimension whose name is given by *String Expression*.

Level.Hierarchy

This function returns the hierarchy that contains the level. Since OLAP Services semantically treats different hierarchies as different dimensions, this function is essentially equivalent to .Dimension.

Member.Hierarchy

This function returns the hierarchy that contains the member. Since OLAP Services semantically treats different hierarchies as different dimensions, this function is essentially equivalent to .Dimension.

Member.Level

This function returns a member's level.

Levels(*String Expression*)

This function returns the level whose name is given by *String Expression*. It is typically used with user-defined functions (UDFs) that return a name. The string expression can be any expression that results in a level reference. For example, the string "[Time].[Year]" will result in the year level of the time dimension. However, the string "[Time].Levels(1)" in a time dimension where the year level is the first one down from the root level will also result in the year level. (See the following description for the *Dimension*.Levels() function as well.)

Dimension.Levels(*Numeric Expression*)

This function returns the dimension level specified by *Numeric Expression*. The number is zero-based, starting at the root level. If the levels of the [Time] dimension are [All], [Year] and [Month], then [Time].Levels(0) returns the [Time].[All] level, and [Time].Levels(2) returns the [Time].[Month] level.

Dimension.UniqueName

This function returns the unique name of a dimension.

Level.UniqueName

This function returns the unique name of a level.

Member.UniqueName

This function returns the unique name of a member.

Dimension.Name

This function returns the name of the dimension.

Hierarchy.Name

This function returns the name of the hierarchy.

Level.Name

This function returns the name of the level.

Member.Name

This function returns the name of the member.

Level.Ordinal

This function returns the zero-based index of the level in the cube. The root level of a cube is number 0, the next level down (if there is one) is number 1, and so on. There is no MDX function that yields the number of levels in the cube.

String and Name Functions

Microsoft OLAP Services does not provide very many string-handling primitives. It builds in a few, but if you want to perform additional string manipulations, then external function libraries are the way to go. In this section we list all of the built-in functions and operators that can operate on strings as data values and return strings. Most of these were treated in earlier sections, but we repeat them here in Table 7.11 for convenience.

There is only one string-related function that we have not yet described, so we will describe it here. The others are described elsewhere in the chapter.

Table 7.11 String and Name Functions

EXTENSION	RETURNS	SYNOPSIS
*	string	+
	bool	<
	bool	>
	bool	<=
	bool	>=
	bool	<>
	bool	=
	bool	IsEmpty(*expr*)
	string	IIF(*search_condition, true_part, false_part*)
	string	COALESCEEMPTY(*value expression* [,*value expression . . .*])
*	string	*Dimension*.UniqueName
*	string	*Level*.UniqueName
*	string	*Member*.UniqueName
*	string	*Dimension*.Name
*	string	*Hierarchy*.Name
*	string	*Level*.Name
*	string	*Member*.Name
*	member	Members (*string*)
*	string	SetToStr(*Set*)
*	set	StrToSet(*string*)
*	string	TupleToStr(*Tuple*)
*	tuple	StrToTuple(*string*)

+   (String concatenation)

Instead of using the standard MDX string concatenation operator "||", OLAP Services uses "+". That is, the expression

```
"ho " + "ho " + "ho"
```

is valid and yields "ho ho ho", while the expression

```
"ho " || "ho " || "ho"
```

is not accepted.

Array Creation

Microsoft OLAP Services provides one special function for communicating with external functions via arrays, as shown in Table 7.12.

```
SetToArray (Set [, Set . . . ][, Numeric or String
Expression])
```

The SetToArray() function creates an array as a COM Variant type that holds an array of values. The only use for this function in the first release of OLAP Services is to pass the constructed array to an external function that is defined as taking an array.

The constructed array will hold values of only one type (which might be, for example, long integer, single float, double float, or string). That type is determined by the type of the first value that is actually placed into the array. The dimensionality of the array that is created is determined by the number of sets that appear as arguments to SetToArray(). If the optional *numeric or string expression* is provided, it is evaluated over the cross-join of the sets, and the values are placed in the array. If the *numeric or string expression* is not provided, then the cross-join of the sets is evaluated in the current context, and the results obtained are placed in the array.

MDX DDL Statements

Microsoft OLAP Services also provides a set of DDL statements to create metadata entities for use in queries and expressions. We explain them in this section. (OLAP Services also provides a syntax for creating cubes within the PivotTable Service. We do not discuss that syntax in this book.)

```
CREATE MEMBER cube-member-name AS 'expression' [, optional-property . . .]
WITH MEMBER member-name AS 'expression' [, optional-property. . .]
DROP MEMBER cube-member-name [,cube-member-name . . .]
CREATE SET cube-set-name AS 'expression'
WITH SET set-name AS 'expression'
DROP SET cube-set-name [,cube-set-name . . .]
```

Table 7.12 Function with Arrays

EXTENSION	RETURNS	SYNOPSIS
*	Array (internal, as COM Variant)	SetToArray (*Set* [, *Set* . . .][, *Numeric or String Expression*])

The OLE DB for OLAP specification also specifies ALTER MEMBER and ALTER SET constructs, but these are not implemented in the first release of OLAP Services.

```
CREATE MEMBER cube-member-name AS 'expression'
[, optional-property . . . ]
```

```
WITH MEMBER member-name AS 'expression'
[, optional-property . . . ]
```

The CREATE MEMBER statement is a client-side DDL statement that defines a new calculated member in the PivotTable service. The calculated member is defined within the context of a particular cube, so the name of the member must also be qualified with the name of the cube. Like any other calculated member, the expression may reference any MDX function, including user-defined functions (UDFs). It may also reference other members created with the CREATE MEMBER statement. Members created through the CREATE MEMBER statement are accessible in member-related metadata through OLE DB for OLAP.

Following the expression itself, one or more optional properties may be defined. The properties that you may define are as follows:

```
SOLVE_ORDER = positive-integer-number
FORMATSTRING = 'Microsoft-Office-cell-format'
FORE_COLOR = 'color-code'
BACK_COLOR = 'color-code'
FONT_NAME = 'font-name'
FONT_SIZE = 'font-size'
FONT_FLAGS = 'font-flags'
```

For example, the statement

```
CREATE MEMBER [Production].[Measures].[Avg Failure Cost] as '[Mea-
sures].[Failure Cost Sum Per Incident] / [Measures].[Failure Incident
Count]', SOLVE_ORDER = 10, FORMATSTRING = '#.##'
```

creates the calculated measure [Avg Failure Cost] as the ratio of total failure incident cost to count of incidents, specifies its SOLVE_ORDER number as 10 and indicates that wherever this formula is used to calculate cells, the result should be formatted with two decimal places.

Microsoft OLAP Services uses the SOLVE_ORDER property when it calculates values for cells related to a calculated member. The PivotTable Service uses the FORMATSTRING property, if provided, to format the data values into character strings. The other properties are specified and stored as character strings and are provided to the client in response to queries that explicitly reference cell properties. The OLE DB data types of these properties as they are delivered back to the client are as follows:

Property	Type
FORMAT_STRING	DBTYPE_WSTR
FORE_COLOR	DBTYPE_UI4
BACK_COLOR	DBTYPE_UI4
FONT_NAME	DBTYPE_WSTR
FONT_SIZE	DBTYPE_UI2
FONT_FLAGS	DBTYPE_I4

For more information on creating programs that use cell properties, refer to the developer's documentation for OLE DB for OLAP.

Within a CREATE MEMBER statement, the SESSION keyword is supported to make explicit the fact that the created member is valid for the OLE DB session in which the statement was issued. In the first release of OLAP Services, there is no difference between using SESSION or leaving it out. For example, the expression

```
CREATE SESSION MEMBER [Production].[Measures].[Failure rate] AS
' . . .'
```

explicitly creates the member within the scope of that single session, while

```
CREATE MEMBER [Production].[Measures].[Failure rate] AS
' . . .'
```

implicitly creates the member within the session.

The only difference between WITH MEMBER and CREATE MEMBER is that the scope of a member created with WITH MEMBER is limited to the query that contains the WITH MEMBER statement. A member created by WITH MEMBER will be invisible to any other query in any other session, and it will not be accessible as part of the OLE DB for OLAP metadata.

Multiple members may be defined in one CREATE MEMBER statement. After the CREATE and optional session scope identifier each member's definition is listed in order. For example, the following expression creates two members in the Production cube:

```
CREATE
    MEMBER [Production].[Measures].[Failure rate] AS ' . . . ',
SOLVE_ORDER = 10, FORMATSTRING = '#.##'
    MEMBER [Production].[Scenarios].[VarianceOverTrials] AS '. . . ',
SOLVE_ORDER = 20, FORMATSTRING = '#.##%', FONT_NAME = 'Times New Roman'
```

Note that you do not separate the different MEMBER definitions with commas.

You cannot define a calculated member to have the same unique name as another member in the cube, either base or calculated. If you want to redefine a calculated member, use DROP MEMBER to discard it first and then execute

CREATE MEMBER. Also, note that you can use WITH MEMBER to create a member whose name is identical to a member created with CREATE MEMBER. If you request all calculated members in their scope with AddCalculatedMembers(), you will get both of them; if you request a member by that specific name, you will only get the results of the WITH MEMBER definition.

DROP MEMBER *cube-member-name* **[,** *cube-member-name* **. . .]**

The DROP MEMBER statement removes one or more calculated cube members and all associated definitions. When more than one calculated member is to be dropped, each name is separated by a comma. When a calculated member is dropped, it disappears from the member-related metadata accessible through OLE DB for OLAP. For example, the statement

```
DROP MEMBER
   [Production].[Measures].[Failure rate],
   [Production].[Scenarios].[VarianceOverTrials]
```

drops the two named members.

You may drop members whose CREATE MEMBER statements were part of the database (stored at the server). You may also drop members that have other calculated members defined on them, and no warning is issued. The definitions of the dependent calculated members remain, but they are internally invalid and will return a #ERR cell value when they are included in a query. In Microsoft OLAP Service, version 1, it is not ever possible to return the dependent members to a valid state, even by re-creating the dropped input member.

CREATE SET *cube-set-name* **AS** *'expression'*
WITH SET *set-name* **AS** *'expression'*

The CREATE SET statement is client-side DDL that defines a set in the Pivot-Table Service. For CREATE SET, the set is materialized immediately upon execution of the statement. The set is defined within the context of a particular cube, so the set name must be qualified with the name of the cube. Since there is no query context around it, the default cell context for all data references in the definition (such as those required by ORDER, FILTER, and so on) is the default member from each dimension in the cube. However, the association of the created set with the cube means that the cube name is not required in order to qualify any of the metadata references within the set specification.

For example, the following statement creates a one-dimensional set of products in the Production cube. The set is defined as the top twenty product assemblies in terms of 1998 failure costs across all production lines:

```
CREATE SET [Production].[ProblemProducts] AS 'TopCount
([Product].[Assemblies].Members, 20, ([Measures].[Failure cost],
```

```
[Time].[1998], [Production Lines].[All Production Lines]))'
```

The set definitions in CREATE SET statements can invoke any MDX functions, including external functions. They can also involve any other sets currently defined on the cube, and any calculated members defined on the cube.

Within a CREATE SET statement, the SESSION keyword is supported to make explicit the fact that the created member is valid for the OLE DB session in which the statement was issued. In the first release of OLAP Services, there is no difference between using SESSION or leaving it out. For example, the expression

```
CREATE SESSION SET [Production].[Hot Items] AS ' . . .'
```

explicitly creates the set within the scope of that single session, while

```
CREATE SET [Production].[Hot Items] AS ' . . .'
```

implicitly creates the set within the session.

The only difference between WITH SET and CREATE SET is that the scope of a set created with WITH SET is limited to the query that contains the WITH SET statement. The set will be invisible to any other query in any other session. Multiple sets may be defined in one CREATE SET statement. After the CREATE and optional session scope identifier each definition is listed in order. For example, the following expression creates two named sets in one statement:

```
CREATE SET
   [Production].[ProblemProducts] AS ' . . . '
   [Production].[StellarProducts] AS ' . . . '
```

In CREATE SET, if the named set already exists, OLAP Services will generate an error message. You need to issue a DROP SET to drop the set before you create a new set with that name. If a set defined with WITH SET in a query shares the same name as a set defined with CREATE SET, then the query will use the set defined by WITH SET. Suppose one set created with CREATE SET is defined as using tuples from another set that was created with CREATE SET and then the first set is dropped. In this case, the second set is still valid because its members were materialized when the CREATE SET was issued.

DROP SET *cube-set-name* **[,** *cube-set-name* **. . .]**

The DROP SET statement removes one or more named sets from a cube. When more than one named set is to be dropped, each name is separated by a comma. For example, the following drops two named sets from the production cube:

```
DROP SET
[Production].[ProblemProducts],
[Production].[StellarProducts]
```

You may drop sets whose CREATE SET statements were part of the database (stored at the server). Dropping a set that was used to create another set has no effect on that other set.

Summary

In this chapter, we have described most of the MDX functions and operators supplied by Microsoft OLAP Services. These include the basic arithmetic, aggregation, set manipulation, tuple manipulation, and DDL for calculated members and named sets. Between Chapters 8 and 14, we will describe the remainder of them, including functions for performing dimensional referencing and using externally defined functions.

CHAPTER 8

MDX Dimensional Reference Functions

M DX dimensional reference functions are a class of functions that return members and sets in some relation to the current member in the calculation context. They are very important to queries and calculations, because much of the power of an OLAP database derives from its ability to reference data within a dimensional context. In this chapter, we focus on them specifically, individuating them from the other set- and member-related MDX functions that are available. The semantics for some of these functions are straightforward; for others they are complex or subtle.

The figures included in this chapter show what member or set of members the various MDX dimensional reference functions select for any given member in a calculation context. In these figures, members are represented by boxes. The current member in context (the starting point for the reference) is shown with a heavier line than the other members. If a single member is the target, that member is shaded in. A set of members is represented by shading surrounding all the members in the set. A legend describing this style of diagram is shown in Figure 8.1.

The first part of this chapter, "Context-free and Context-dependent Sets of Members," is organized according to where the target members of the MDX dimensional reference functions are relative to the current member in the calculation context:

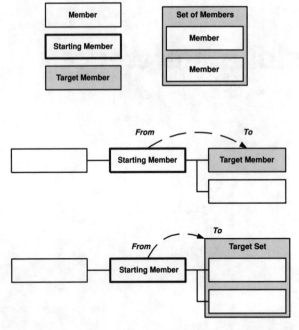

Figure 8.1 Diagram form for referencing operation illustrations.

- Anywhere (not affected by the context)
- At the same level as the current member
- At a lower level than the current member
- At a higher level than the current member

The second part of the chapter, "MDX Drill-related Functions," describes a set of MDX dimensional reference functions that are useful for manipulating sets for the purposes of drilling down and up within hierarchies.

At the beginning of each section presenting the various types of MDX dimensional reference functions, we first list the functions by name, and then in the text that follows we provide a synopsis of the arguments to the function (if any) as well as what the function returns and whether or not the function/operator is particular to Microsoft OLAP Services. In the lists throughout the chapter, Functions that are extensions to the general MDX specification are marked with an asterisk (*).

Context-free and Context-dependent Sets of Members

OLAP Services provides three functions that return the set of members associated with a metadata scope, which are listed in Table 8.1.

Table 8.1 Metadata Scope Members' Functions

EXTENSION	RETURNS	SYNOPSIS
	set	*dimension*.Members
	set	*hierarchy*.Members
	set	*level*.Members

`dimension.Members`

`hierarchy.Members`

`level.Members`

Each of the variations of the .Members function returns the set of all members within the scope of the given metadata object in the database's default order. Figure 8.2 shows the scope of the members operator. Dimension.Members, shown in Figure 8.2a, returns the members of the entire dimension and includes the All member of the hierarchy if present. Since in OLAP Services a hierarchy is implemented as a dimension, the *hierarchy*.Members function is also shown in Figure 8.2a. Level.Members, shown in Figure 8.2b, selects all members in the specified level.

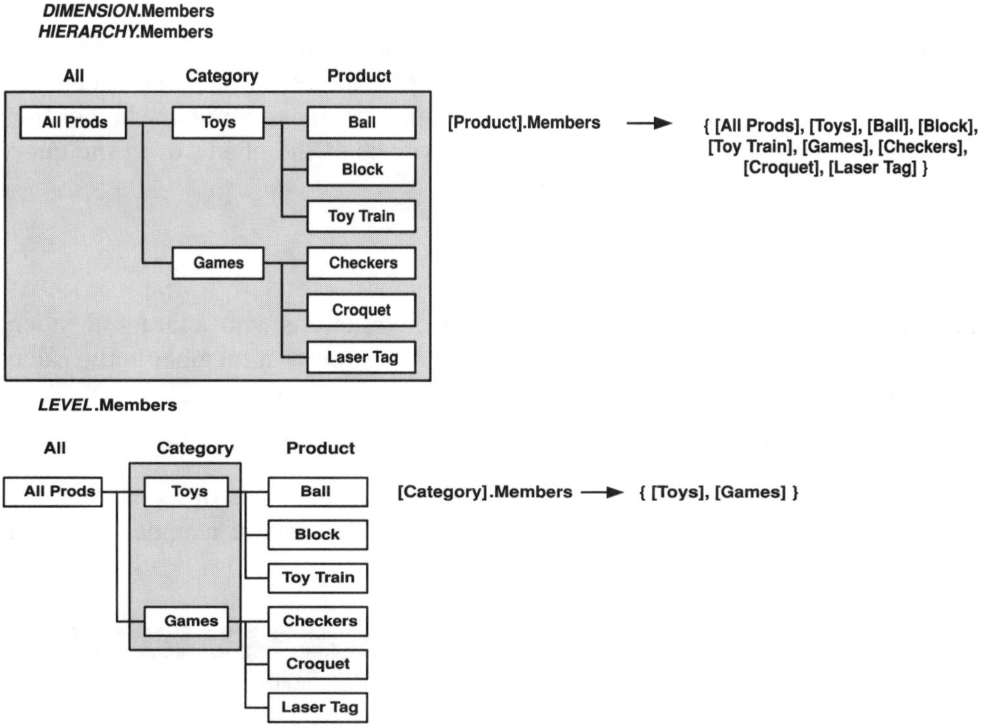

Figure 8.2 Members selected by .Members operator.

Table 8.2 Calculated Member Set Functions

EXTENSION	RETURNS	SYNOPSIS
*	set	AddCalculatedMembers (*set*)
*	set	StripCalculatedMembers (*set*)

OLAP Services also provides two functions that deal with calculated members in the set listed in Table 8.2.

AddCalculatedMembers (*set*)

By default, when a set of members is specified using a function that retrieves a set based on metadata (like .Members, .Children, Descendants(), etc.), only base members are returned even though calculated members may be within that range. The AddCalculatedMembers() function adds in all of the calculated members that are siblings of the members specified within *set*. Each calculated member that was not already in the set is added in database order after its last sibling member in the *set*. The set is limited to only one dimension. Note that this function adds all calculated members defined, whether they were defined by CREATE SET at the server or at the client, or in the query through WITH MEMBER.

StripCalculatedMembers (*set*)

The StripCalculatedMembers() function returns the members of set after removing all the calculated members. The set is limited to only one dimension. Note that this function removes all calculated members defined, whether they were defined by CREATE SET at the server or at the client, or in the query through WITH MEMBER.

Context-free Individual Members

There are three MDX dimensional reference functions whose target members are not affected by where they are relative to the current member in the calculation context. These are listed in Table 8.3.

dimension.DefaultMember *hierarchy*.DefaultMember

Each of these returns the default member for the dimension or hierarchy. If the dimension has an All level and member, then the default member is the All

Table 8.3 Context-free Member Functions

EXTENSION	RETURNS	SYNOPSIS
	member	*dimension*.DefaultMember
	member	*hierarchy*.DefaultMember
*	member	Members (*String Expression*)

member. If the dimension does not have an All member, then an arbitrary member from its top level will be the default member.

Members (*String Expression*)

This function returns the member whose name is given by String Expression. (Yes, it only returns a single member, even though its name is plural.) The most common use for this function will be to take a string from a user-defined function (UDF) that identifies a member and convert it to a member. For example, consider a UDF named UDF_GetMySalesTerritory on the client that returned the member name for the user's sales territory. Given this UDF, the following expression,

```
([Measures].[Sales], Members ( UDF_GetMySalesTerritory() ) )
```

would refer to the sales value for that user's sales territory.

Same Level

There are nine MDX dimensional reference functions in which the target members are at the same level as the current member in the calculation context, listed in Table 8.4.

dimension[.CurrentMember]

This function returns the current member in that dimension. "Current" is relative to the context that the calculation is taking place in. That context may be the axis of a query being executed or a Generate() function within that query. We indicate that .CurrentMember is optional. The default operator applied to a dimension is .CurrentMember.

Note that the MDX specification states that .CurrentMember may be applied to any set to return the current tuple. The first release of Microsoft OLAP Services

Table 8.4 Same-level Member Reference Functions

EXTENSION	RETURNS	SYNOPSIS
	member	*dimension*[.CurrentMember]
	member	*member*.PrevMember
	member	*member*.NextMember
	member	*member*.Lag(*index*)
	member	*member*.Lead (*index*)
	member	*member*.FirstSibling
	member	*member*.LastSibling
	member	Cousin (*member, ancestor_member*)
	member	ParallelPeriod ([*level*[, *index*[, *member*]]])

restricts the application of this operator to a set that has a single dimension—which will then return a single member. The .Current operator is applied to an arbitrary set to retrieve a tuple.

member.`PrevMember`

member.`NextMember`

.PrevMember gives the previous member along the level implied by the member, while .NextMember gives the next member along the level implied by the member. Figure 8.3 shows examples of .PrevMember and .NextMember. Note that these functions return the next or the previous member within the same level regardless of whether the new member shares the same parent or not.

member.`Lag` (*index*)

member.`Lead`(*index*)

.Lead() returns the member that is index members after the source member along the same level, and .Lag() returns the member that is index members before the source member on the same level. .Lead(0) and .Lag(0) each result in the source member itself. Lagging by a negative amount is the same as leading by the positive quantity, and vice versa. Figure 8.4 shows examples of .Lead() and .Lag().

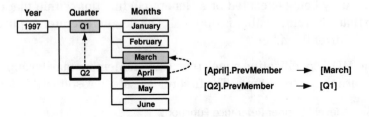

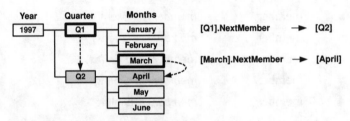

Figure 8.3   .NextMember and .PrevMember.

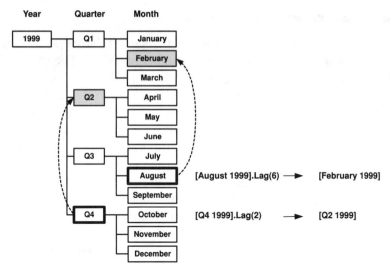

Figure 8.4   .Lag() and .Lead().

member.FirstSibling *member*.LastSibling

Figure 8.5 shows the behavior of the member.FirstSibling and member.LastSibling operators. The first child of a parent is its own first sibling, and the last child is its own last sibling. If there is no parent, then the first member in that level is the first sibling and the last member in the level is the last sibling. For example, the All member of a dimension is its own first and last sibling. In a dimension without an All level, the first member of the top level is the first sibling of all members at that level, and the last member of the top level is the last sibling of all members at that level.

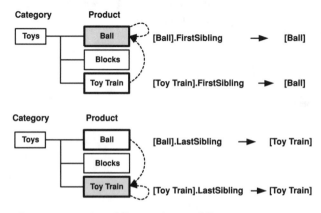

Figure 8.5   .FirstSibling and .LastSibling.

Cousin (*member, ancestor_member*)

This function returns the member that has the same relative position under a specified ancestor member as the initial member specified. The Cousin() function is best understood by walking through its algorithm. Figure 8.6 shows the behavior of the Cousin() function. From each level from the *member*'s level to the *ancestor_member*'s level, Cousin() tracks which sibling it is related to under its ancestor at that level. [March 1998] is the third child of the first child of [1998]. The same path is then followed from the *ancestor member* down to the level of *member*. [March 1999] is the third child of the first child of [1999]. Because of the straightforwardness of this algorithm, it works best when you can guarantee the same number of descendants under each ancestor. For example, it is likely that years, quarters, and months or days, hours, and minutes can be used with Cousin(),because each of these triples has a fixed relationship within itself. However, a cousin of January 31 in February will not exist because February will not have a thirty-first day.

ParallelPeriod ([*level*[, *index*[, *member*]]])

This function is similar to the Cousin() function. It takes the ancestor of *member* at *level* (call it "ancestor"); then it takes the sibling of ancestor that lags by *index* (call it "in-law") and returns the cousin of *member* among the descendants of in-law. Figure 8.7 illustrates the process of finding the parallel period. ParallelPeriod (level, index, member) is equivalent to Cousin(member, Ancestor(Member, Level).Lag(index).

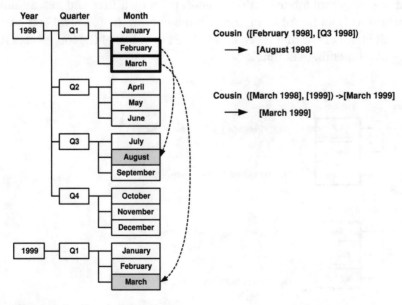

Figure 8.6   Cousin() function.

Table 8.5 Functions Referencing sets as the same level as the given member.

EXTENSION	RETURNS	SYNOPSIS
	set	PeriodsToDate([*level*[, *member*]]))
	set	WTD ([*member*])
	set	MTD ([*member*])
	set	QTD ([*member*])
	set	YTD ([*member*])
	set	LastPeriods(*index*[, *member*])

OLAP Services provides 6 functions for referencing sets of members at the same level as the given members, which are listed in Table 8.5.

```
PeriodsToDate ([level [, member]]))
```

This function returns a set of members at the level of member, starting at the first descendant under member's ancestor at level and ending at member. If neither level nor member is specified, then the default member is the current member of the cube's time-typed dimension, and level is the parent level of that member. If the level is specified but the member is not, then the dimension is inferred from the level, and the current member on that dimension is used. The function is identical to the following:

```
{ Descendants(Ancestor(member, level), member.Level).Item (0) : member }
```

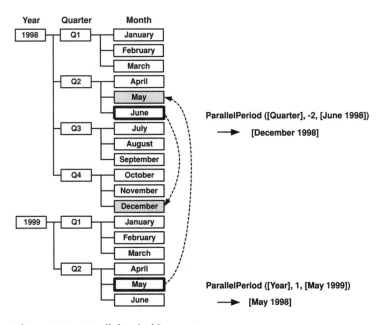

Figure 8.7 ParallelPeriod() operator.

If *member* is omitted, and no dimension in the cube is marked as being Time-typed, the statement will parse and execute without error. However, when a client attempts to retrieve a cell calculated in part by the PeriodsToDate() function, a cell error will occur.

The behavior of PeriodsToDate is shown in Figure 8.8.

`WTD ([member])`

WTD() is the equivalent of PeriodsToDate() with the level set to "Week." If *member* is not specified, it defaults to the current member of the time-typed dimension. If there is no time-typed dimension in the cube, or if it does not have a level tagged as a "Week," then a parser error results.

`MTD ([member])`

MTD() is the equivalent of PeriodsToDate() with the level set to "Month." If *member* is not specified, it defaults to the current member of the time-typed dimension. If there is no time-typed dimension in the cube, or if it does not have a level tagged as a "Month," then a parser error results.

`QTD ([member])`

QTD() is the equivalent of PeriodsToDate() with the level set to "Quarter." If *member* is not specified, it defaults to the current member of the time-typed dimension. If there is no time-typed dimension in the cube, or if it does not have a level tagged as a "Quarter," then a parser error results.

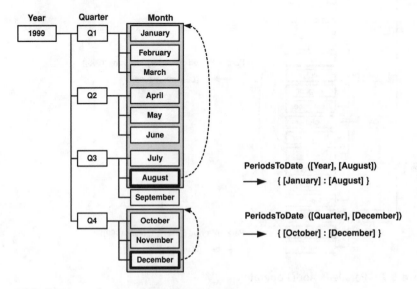

Figure 8.8 Behavior of PeriodsToDate().

`YTD ([`*`member`*`])`

YTD() is the equivalent of PeriodsToDate() with the level set to "Year." If *member* is not specified, it defaults to the current member of the time-typed dimension. If there is no time-typed dimension in the cube, or if it does not have a level tagged as a "Year," then a parser error results.

`LastPeriods(`*`index`*`[, `*`member`*`])`

This function returns the set of *index* periods from member back to the member lagging by *index* – 1 from member. This is equivalent to

```
{ member.LAG(index - 1) : member }.
```

If *member* is not specified, then it defaults to the current member of the time-typed dimension in the cube. If *member* is omitted, and no dimension in the cube is marked as being Time-typed, the statement will parse and execute without error. However, when a client attempts to retrieve a cell calculated in part by the LastPeriods() function, a cell error will occur.

The behavior of LastPeriods() is shown in Figure 8.9.

Referencing Lower Levels

The operators listed in Table 8.6 select a member or a set of members further down in the hierarchy:

member`.FirstChild`

member`.LastChild`

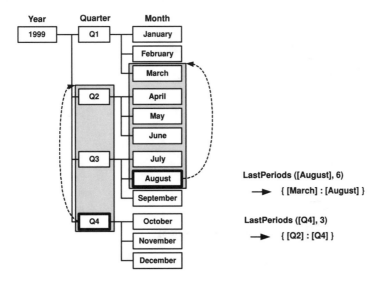

Figure 8.9 Behavior of LastPeriods().

Table 8.6 Lower-level Reference Functions

EXTENSION	RETURNS	SYNOPSIS
	member	*member*.FirstChild
	member	*member*.LastChild
	member	OpeningPeriod([*level*[, *member*]])
	member	ClosingPeriod([*level*[, *member*]])
	set	*member*.Children
	set	Descendants (*member*, *level* [, *desc_flags*])

These functions return the first child or last child of the member according to the database ordering of the child members. They are illustrated in Figure 8.10.

```
OpeningPeriod([level [, member]])

ClosingPeriod([level [, member]])
```

The OpeningPeriod and ClosingPeriod operators are essentially first-descendant and last-descendant operators that are intended primarily to be used with the time dimension, though they may be used with any dimension. The OpeningPeriod function returns the first member among the descendants of *member* at *level*. For example, `OpeningPeriod(Month, [1991])` returns `[January, 1991]`. If no member is specified, then the default is the current member of the time-type dimension in that cube. If no level is specified, then it is the level immediately below that of *member*. OpeningPeriod (*level*, *member*)

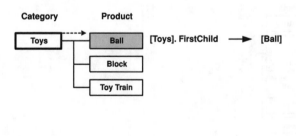

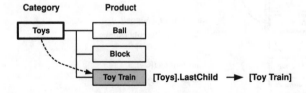

Figure 8.10 .FirstChild and .LastChild.

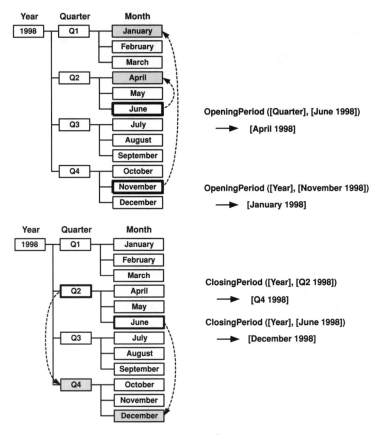

Figure 8.11 OpeningPeriod() and ClosingPeriod().

is equivalent to Descendants(*member, level*).Item(0). ClosingPeriod() is very similar, only it returns the last descendant instead of the first descendant. OpeningPeriod() and ClosingPeriod() are illustrated in Figure 8.11.

If *member* is omitted, and no dimension in the cube is marked as being Time-typed, the statement will parse and execute without error. However, when a client attempts to retrieve a cell calculated in part by the OpeningPeriod() or ClosingPeriod() function, a cell error will occur.

member.Children

This function returns the children of the given member. member.Children is equivalent to {*member*.FirstChild : *member*.LastChild}. As you might expect, if you apply member.Children to a leaf member, the result is no members. Figure 8.12 illustrates the behavior of the .Children function.

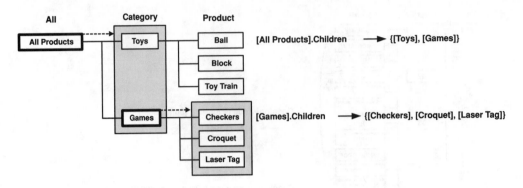

Figure 8.12   member.Children.

Descendants (*member, level* [, *desc_flags*])

This function returns a set of descendants of the given member using the given level as a reference point. The desc_flags parameter is used to pick from the many possible sets of descendants. Figure 8.13 illustrates the behavior of the Descendants () operator. The flags are as follows:

- SELF
- AFTER
- BEFORE
- BEFORE_AND_AFTER
- SELF_AND_AFTER
- SELF_AND_BEFORE
- SELF_BEFORE_AFTER

"SELF" refers to the level listed as the second argument and means to take the members at that level. "AFTER" refers to the level or levels that appear below the level listed as the second argument. "BEFORE" refers to the level or levels that appear above the level listed and below the member given as the first argument. The BEFORE_AND_AFTER, SELF_AND_AFTER, SELF_AND_BEFORE, and SELF_BEFORE_AFTER flags combine these basic options as shown in Figures 8.13d through 8.13g. If no flag is specified, the default behavior is SELF.

Table 8.7   Referencing Higher Levels

EXTENSION	RETURNS	SYNOPSIS
	member	*member*.Parent
	member	Ancestor(*member, level*)

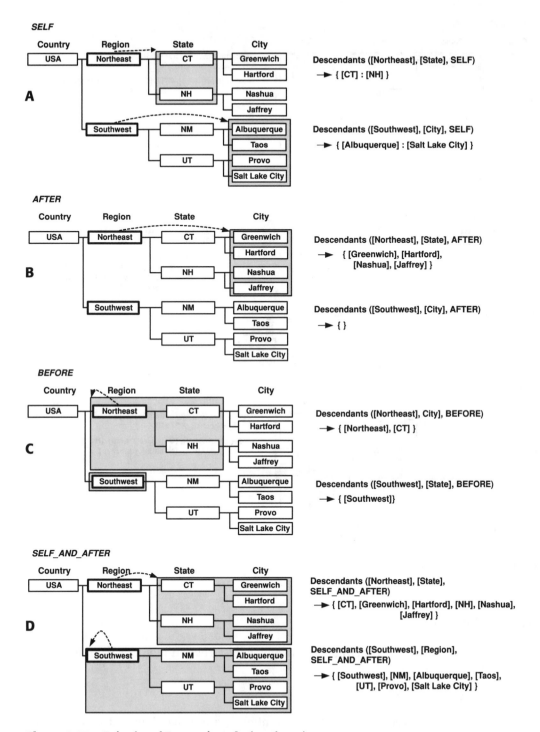

Figure 8.13 Behavior of Descendants(). *(continues)*

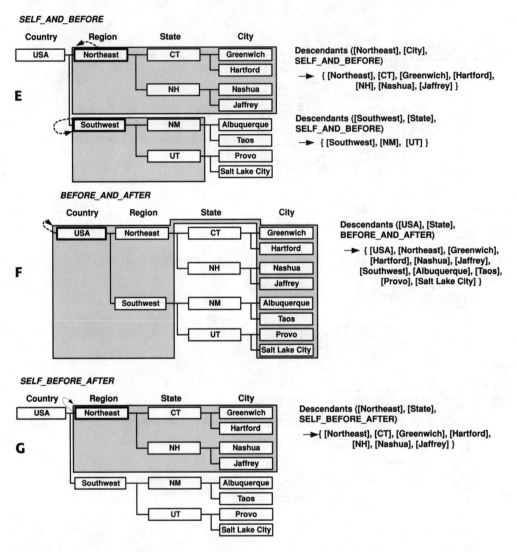

Figure 8.13 (Continued)

Higher Levels

The operators listed in Table 8.7 each select a related member from higher up in the hierarchy.

*member.*Parent

This function returns the source member's parent member, if it has one. The behavior of Parent() is shown in Figure 8.14.

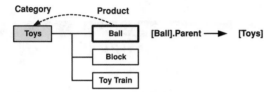

Figure 8.14 Behavior of .Parent.

Ancestor(*member, level*)

This function finds the source member's ancestor at the target level. If the target level is the level of the source member, then the source member is returned. The behavior of Ancestor() is shown in Figure 8.15.

MDX Drill-related Functions

The set of MDX operators listed in Table 8.8 are separated because they are particularly useful to simple browser operations. There are no absolutes, of course; these may also be useful for generating tuples for arbitrary sets within queries and CREATE SET statements.

Note that these operators generally assume a precise relationship among their members. The DrillDown*XXX()* functions add members or tuples into a set in hierarchical order, and the DrillUp*XXX()* functions assume that this hierarchical order is present in their operation. These functions may be used to perform some of the useful work of drilling up and down that a GUI would expose, particularly in conjunction with CREATE SET and ALTER SET statements.

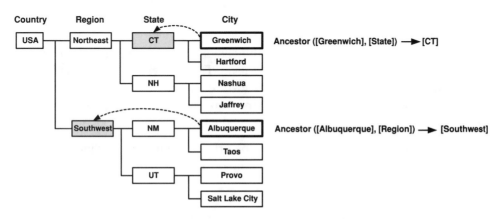

Figure 8.15 Behavior of Ancestor().

Table 8.8 MDX Drill-related Functions

EXTENSION	RETURNS	SYNOPSIS
	set	DrillDownLevel (*set* [, *level*])
*	set	DrillDownLevel (*set,,index*)
	set	DrillDownLevelBottom (*set, index* [,[*level*] [, *numeric value expression*]])
	set	DrillDownLevelTop (*set, index*[, [*level*] [, *numeric value expression*]])
	set	DrillDownMember (*set1, set2* [, RECURSIVE])
	set	DrillDownMemberBottom (*set1, set2, index* [, *numeric value expression*][, RECURSIVE]])
	set	DrillDownMemberTop (*set1, set2, index* [, [*numeric expression*][, RECURSIVE]])
	set	DrillUpLevel (*set* [, *level*]])
	set	DrillUpMember (*set1, set2*)
*	set	ToggleDrillState (*set1, set2* [, RECURSIVE])
*	set	VisualTotals (*set, pattern*)

The semantics of the following functions is among the most complex of any functions in the MDX dimensional reference, so we will illustrate them with the same diagramming style that we used for member and set references earlier:

DrillDownLevel (*set* [, *level*])

This function returns a set resulting from a particular drill-down operation performed by the function. The *Set1* can be of arbitrary dimensionality; *set2* must be of only one dimension. When the level argument is specified, all members or tuples in *set* that are in *level* are drilled down onto the next lowest level (if there is one). When the level argument is not specified, only those members or tuples that are at the lowest level in the first dimension of the set are drilled down, and they are drilled down to the next lower level. The behavior of DrillDownLevel() is shown in Figure 8.16. All children are inserted immediately after their parents; otherwise, the order is preserved. If *level* is specified but there is no member at level in the set, then the given set is returned without modification.

If one or more children of a member to be drilled down on immediately follows a parent in *set*, then that parent will not be drilled down on.

DrillDownLevel (*set,, index*)

This variation is a Microsoft OLAP Services-specific extension to DrillDownLevel(). It allows the dimension to be drilled down on by leaving the level field empty and providing a zero-based dimension index to specify which dimension

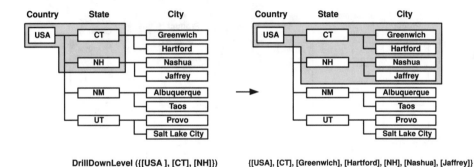

DrillDownLevel ({[USA], [CT], [NH]})

{[USA], [CT], [Greenwich], [Hartford], [NH], [Nashua], [Jaffrey]}

Figure 8.16 DrillDownLevel().

you should drill down on. This is really only useful when *set* has tuples with more than one dimension. The first dimension to drill down on is at index 0, the second dimension is at index 1, and so on. As with the rules for the standard version of DrillDownLevel(), tuples containing the lowest-level members of that dimension are drilled down on.

DrillDownLevelBottom (*set, index* [,[*level*]

[, *numeric expression*]])

Similar to DrillDownLevel() and DrillDownLevelTop(), this function drills down all members in *set* that are at the specified level, if *level* is provided (or the lowest level of members that are present in the set if *level* is not provided). However, instead of returning all children, this function returns only the bottom *index* members or tuples. The *set* can be of arbitrary dimensionality. The ranking is determined through the *numeric expression*, if one is provided, or through the values of cells found in the default context when the set is evaluated, if the *numeric expression* is left out. Figure 8.17 illustrates the behavior of DrillDown-LevelBottom(). As with DrillDownLevel(), if a member at *level* is immediately followed by one of its children, it will not be drilled down on.

DrillDownLevelTop (*set, index* [, [*level*]

[, *numeric expression*]])

Similar to DrillDownLevel() and DrillDownLevelBottom(), this function drills down all members in *set* that are at the specified level, if *level* is provided (or the lowest level of members that are present in the set if *level* is not provided). However, instead of returning all children, this function returns only the top *index* members or tuples. The *set* can be of arbitrary dimensionality. The ranking is determined through the *numeric expression*, if one is provided, or through the values of cells found in the default context when the set is evaluated, if the numeric value expression is left out. Figure 8.18 illustrates the behavior of Drill-

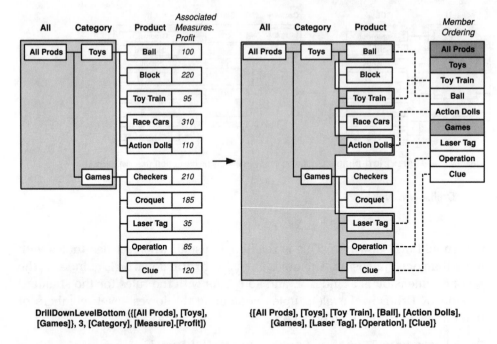

DrillDownLevelBottom ({[All Prods], [Toys], [Games]}, 3, [Category], [Measure].[Profit])

{[All Prods], [Toys], [Toy Train], [Ball], [Action Dolls], [Games], [Laser Tag], [Operation], [Clue]}

Figure 8.17 DrillDownLevelBottom().

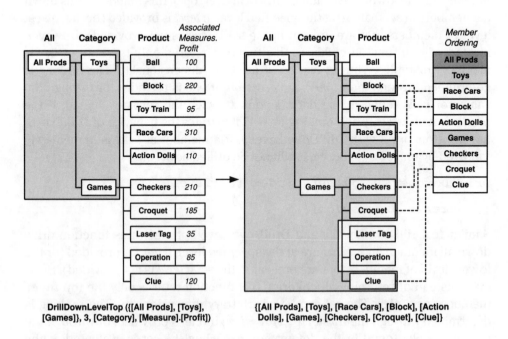

DrillDownLevelTop ({[All Prods], [Toys], [Games]}, 3, [Category], [Measure].[Profit])

{[All Prods], [Toys], [Race Cars], [Block], [Action Dolls], [Games], [Checkers], [Croquet], [Clue]}

Figure 8.18 DrillDownLevelTop().

DownLevelTop(). As with DrillDownLevel(), if a member at *level* is immediately followed by one of its children, it will not be drilled down on.

DrillDownMember (*set1, set2* [, RECURSIVE])

This function returns a set that is formed by drilling down one level on each member in *set1* that is present in *set2*. *Set1* can be of arbitrary dimensionality; *set2* must be of only one dimension.

If *set1* contains tuples, this function will return a set that is formed by drilling down each tuple in *set1* that has a matching member from *set2* in it. If RECURSIVE is not specified, then only one pass through *set1* is performed, matching each member or tuple with each member in *set2*. If RECURSIVE is specified, then the set resulting from the first pass is again matched with each member in *set2*, and so on until no more members in the set being constructed are found in *set2*. Figure 8.19 illustrates the behavior of DrillDownMember().

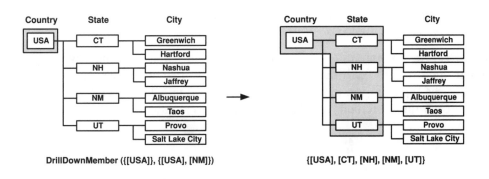

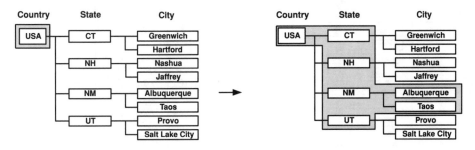

Figure 8.19 DrillDownMember().

```
DrillDownMemberBottom (set1, set2, index
[, numeric expression][, RECURSIVE]])
```

Much like DrillDownMember, this function returns a set that is formed by drilling down one level on each member in *set1* that is present in *set2*. However, it returns the bottom *index* children for a parent rather than all children. *Set1* can be of arbitrary dimensionality; *set2* must be of only one dimension.

If *set1* contains tuples, this will return a set that is formed by drilling down each tuple in *set1* that has a matching member from *set2* in it. If RECURSIVE is not specified, then only one pass through *set1* is performed, matching each member or tuple with each member in *set2*. If RECURSIVE is specified, then the set that results from the first pass is again matched with each member in *set2*, and so on until no more members in the set being constructed are found in *set2*. At each step of drilling, the bottom *index* child members or tuples are returned instead of all children. The ranking is based on the *numeric expression*, if specified; otherwise, values from the set of children are evaluated in the current context, and those results are used. Figure 8.20 illustrates the behavior of DrillDownMemberBottom().

```
DrillDownMemberTop (set1, set2, index
[, numeric expression][, RECURSIVE]])
```

Like DrillDownMember(), this function returns a set that is formed by drilling down one level on each member in *set1* that is present in *set2*. However, it returns the top *index* children for a parent rather than all children. *Set1* can be of arbitrary dimensionality; *set2* must be of only one dimension.

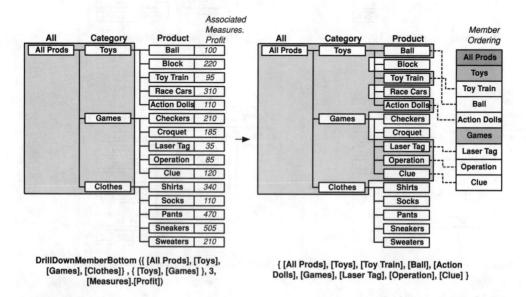

DrillDownMemberBottom ({ [All Prods], [Toys], [Games], [Clothes]} , { [Toys], [Games] }, 3, [Measures].[Profit])

{ [All Prods], [Toys], [Toy Train], [Ball], [Action Dolls], [Games], [Laser Tag], [Operation], [Clue] }

Figure 8.20   DrillDownMemberBottom().

If *set1* contains tuples, this will return a set formed by drilling down each tuple in *set1* that has a matching member from *set2* in it. If RECURSIVE is not specified, then only one pass through *set1* is performed, matching each member or tuple with each member in *set2*. If RECURSIVE is specified, then the set that results from the first pass is again matched with each member in *set2*, and so on until no more members in the set being constructed are found in *set2*. At each step of drilling, the top *index* child members or tuples are returned instead of all children. The ranking is based on the *numeric expression*, if specified; otherwise, values from the set of children are evaluated in the current context, and those results are used. Figure 8.21 illustrates the behavior of DrillDownMemberTop().

DrillUpLevel (*set [, level]*])

This function strips away all members in the set that are below the given *level*. If the *level* is not provided, then it is assumed to be one level higher in the hierarchy than the level of the lowest-level member(s) in *set* (the lowest-level members in the set are removed). Figure 8.22 illustrates the behavior of DrillUpLevel(). A set returned by DrillDownMember() or DrillDownLevel() will be suitable for cleanly drilling up with this function.

DrillUpMember (*set1 , set2*)

This step strips away members in *set1* that are descendants of members in *set2*. Figure 8.22 illustrates the behavior of DrillUpMember(). *Set1* can contain tuples of arbitrary dimensionality; *set2* must contain only members of one dimension.

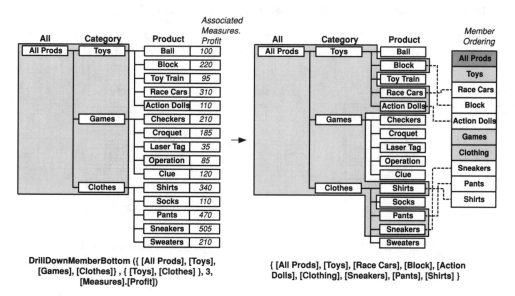

DrillDownMemberBottom ({ [All Prods], [Toys], [Games], [Clothes]} , { [Toys], [Clothes] }, 3, [Measures].[Profit])

{ [All Prods], [Toys], [Race Cars], [Block], [Action Dolls], [Clothing], [Sneakers], [Pants], [Shirts] }

Figure 8.21   DrillDownMemberTop().

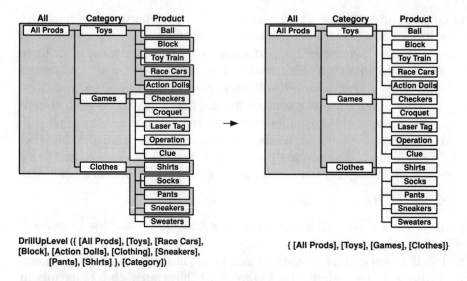

DrillUpLevel ({ [All Prods], [Toys], [Race Cars], [Block], [Action Dolls], [Clothing], [Sneakers], [Pants], [Shirts] }, [Category])

{ [All Prods], [Toys], [Games], [Clothes]}

Figure 8.22   DrillUpLevel().

Note that only descendants that are immediately after the ancestor member in *set2* are stripped away. If an ancestor member specified in *set2* is not present in *set1*, any descendants will remain. Descendants that precede the ancestor or that appear after another member that is not a descendant has intervened will not be stripped away. A set returned by DrillDownMember() or DrillDownLevel() will be suitable for drilling up cleanly with this function. Figure 8.23 illustrates the behavior of DrillUpMember().

ToggleDrillState (*Set1, Set2* [, RECURSIVE])

Returns a set in which those members or tuples in *set1* that are drilled up are drilled down and those members or tuples in *set1* that are drilled down are

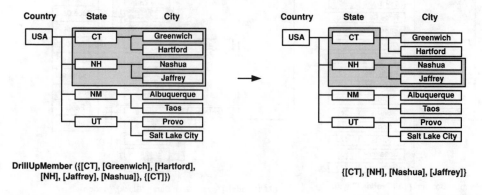

DrillUpMember ({[CT], [Greenwich], [Hartford], [NH], [Jaffrey], [Nashua]}, {[CT]})

{[CT], [NH], [Nashua], [Jaffrey]}

Figure 8.23   DrillUpMember().

drilled up. This function combines the operations of DrillUpMember() and DrillDownMember(). *Set1* can contain tuples of arbitrary dimensionality; *set2* must contain only members of one dimension. A member or tuple in *set1* is considered drilled down if it has any descendant immediately following it and is considered drilled up otherwise. When a member is found without a descendant immediately after it, DrillDownMember() will be applied to it, with the RECURSIVE flag if the RECURSIVE is present.

VisualTotals (set, pattern)

This function returns a set that includes dynamically created calculated members that total up the given descendants for an ancestor. The function accepts a set that can contain members at any level from within one dimension. (The set can only include members from one dimension.) When a parent member is followed by one or more of its children in the given set, or an ancestor by one or more of its descendants, the function replaces that parent or ancestor member with a synthesized member that totals the values taken only from the children or descendants that follow it in the set. The name of the synthesized member is formed from the pattern given in the pattern argument. The order of appearance of members is important: a parent that is to be replaced by a synthetic visual total must appear immediately before its children. The sets created by the DrillDownXXX functions are likely to fit VisualTotal()'s member ordering requirements.

The synthesized members are named using the text from the pattern string. Wherever an asterisk appears in the string, the name (the simple name, not the unique name) of that parent member is inserted. A double asterisk (**) causes an asterisk character to appear in the name.

Consider the following VisualTotals() expression, which contains numerous parents and ancestors (its results as shown in Figure 8.24):

```
WITH
MEMBER [Measures].[AvgPrice] AS '[Measures].[Total] / [Measures].[Qty]',
FORMATSTRING = '#.00000'
SET [Rowset] AS 'VisualTotals (
{
[Time].[All Time].[1997].[Quarter 1],
[Time].[All Time].[1997],
[Time].[All Time].[1997].[Quarter 1].[January],
[Time].[All Time].[1997].[Quarter 1].[February],
[Time].[All Time].[1997].[Quarter 2],
[Time].[All Time].[1997].[Quarter 2].[May],
[Time].[All Time].[1997].[Quarter 2].[June],
[Time].[All Time].[1997].[Quarter 1],
[Time].[All Time].[1997].[Quarter 2],
[Time].[All Time],
```

```
[Time].[All Time].[1997].[Quarter 1].[January].[Jan 01, 1997],
[Time].[All Time].[1997].[Quarter 1].[January].[Jan 02, 1997]
}
, "vt *")'
SELECT
{ {[Measures].[Qty], [Measures].[Total], [Measures].[AvgPrice} } on
axis(0),
{ [Time].[All Time].[1997].[Quarter 1], [Rowset]
} on axis(1)
FROM cakes03
```

This highlights some of the useful aspects of VisualTotals() and also some of its quirks, which you will need to watch out for. Looking at the Qty measure for [vt 1997], the value 5,965,904 is the sum of values found for January, February, [vt Quarter 2], [Quarter 1], and [Quarter 2]. In other words, [vt Quarter 2] was not double-counted with [May] and [June]. You do need to be careful in how you place descendants, however: [Quarter 1] and [Quarter 2] are included in the total without regard to the fact that their descendants have already been incorporated into the total. (You may also notice a bug in the totaling algorithm: the visual totals created for the [Total] measure do not add up correctly. Hopefully, this has been fixed by the time you read this.)

The bottom three rows of the VisualTotals() expression just presented show that VisualTotals() can work against ancestors and descendants of arbitrary depth: The [All Time] member is the higher-level member in the dimension,

	Qty	Total	Average Price
Quarter 1	1,811,965.00	44,166,000.00	24.37464
vt 1997	5,965,904.00	133,988,515.00	22.45905
January	620,829.00	16,343870.00	26.32588
February	572,194.00	13,863,990.00	24.26447
vt Quarter 2	1,186,056.00	23,660,064.00	19.94852
May	614,945.00	12,267,870.00	19.94954
June	571,111.00	11,392,190.00	19.94743
Quarter 1	1,811,965.00	44,166,000.00	24.37464
Quarter 2	1,774,860.00	35,934,600.00	20.24644
vt All Time	39,239.00	1,220,641.19	31.10786
Jan 01, 1997	16,127.00	492,969.90	30.56799
Jan 01, 1997	23,112.00	727,671.30	31.48456

Figure 8.24 Sample results from VisualTotals().

while each day is at the leaf level. If you observe the values for the [AvgPrice] measure in the query, you can see that it is calculated after the visual totals, despite the fact that it is at solve order precedence 0.

Note that the synthetic members in the set returned by VisualTotals() are almost fully equivalent to calculated members created by other means. They cannot exist outside of a set as a calculated member, so they will not appear as metadata items through OLE DB for OLAP. They can be part of a set held in a CREATE SET statement and are treated as another calculated member by StripCalculatedMembers(). They can be filtered by name and unique name. They cannot, however, be referenced by a tuple reference in a formula since they are not entered into Microsoft OLAP Services's internal list of metadata objects.

Summary

In this chapter, we have covered the various functions provided by Microsoft OLAP Services that allow a query or command to reference dimensionally related members and sets. Through this chapter and Chapter 7, we have focused on describing how individual functions and operators work. Now that we have examined them in detail, in the next chapter we will turn our attention to applying them in queries to solve analytical problems.

MDX Application Topics

This chapter covers a variety of topics regarding the construction and use of MDX as well as some pointers on building databases that leverage the MDX constructs. This chapter aims to be a broader reference than any chapter titled "MDX for Insurance Claim Analysis" or "MDX for Manufacturing Quality and Process Optimization," for example, would be. Of course, detailed examples in insurance and manufacturing would be worthwhile, but this book and chapter are a bit more general in scope. Along the way, we show some ways that the various operators and functions of MDX can get used together.

The topics presented in this chapter are common and less common calculation and analysis techniques that a variety of applications will use, though different application domains may use different terminology for the same technique. For example, analyses of insurance claims, production quality control, and customer shopping preferences may all require calculation of an item's percentage contribution to an aggregated item. In insurance claim analysis, this calculation may be required to see which claimants, treatments, or plans consume the largest proportion of resources. In production quality control analysis, this calculation may be used to see which products or production steps produce the greatest proportion of defects. In customer shopping preference analysis, this calculation may be used to see which products contribute the highest proportion of profits for a customer or set of customers, or which customers are the proportionately highest volume shoppers for a store.

This chapter is divided into three main sections. The first is devoted to commonly required straightforward expressions, which describe bread-and-butter calculations required by many applications. The second section is devoted to more advanced expressions and analytical queries which will be used by more sophisticated applications and reports. In the last section of the chapter we will work through the construction of a detailed series of analytical queries. Working through all of the examples and techniques we provide in this chapter should give you a good grasp of the principles underlying their construction and the tools available for constructing whatever MDX you need to solve a particular problem.

Commonly Required Straightforward Expressions

In this first section of this chapter, we focus on some of the simpler and more frequently used calculations and types of expressions that applications require. These include the following:

- Ratio to parent
- Ratio to ancestor
- Ratio to [All]
- Percentage contribution to parent/ancestor/All
- Proportional allocation of one quantity based on ratios of another
- Unweighted allocations down the hierarchy
- Simple averages
- Weighted averages
- Mixing aggregations: sum across non-time, average/MIN/MAX along time
- Mixing aggregations: sum across non-time, opening/closing balance along time
- Rolling averages
- 52-week high/low
- Carryover of balances for slowly changing values
- Reporting of last entered balance (as opposed to balance for last time descendant)

Each of these calculations is a fairly generic operation that many applications require, regardless of their analytical domain (finance, manufacturing quality, shipping, consumer behavior). They are also more expressions and types of calculations than they are whole analytical queries. We discuss more sophisticated analytical queries in the next section of the chapter, "Advanced Manipulations:

Queries and Expressions." We will now discuss in order each of the expressions presented in the preceding list.

Ratios between Levels in a Hierarchy

RATIO TO PARENT

RATIO TO ANCESTOR

RATIO TO [ALL]

PERCENTAGE CONTRIBUTION TO PARENT/ANCESTOR/ALL

PROPORTIONAL ALLOCATION OF ONE QUANTITY BASED ON RATIOS OF ANOTHER

Each of these five types of calculations involves taking the ratio of some measure at one level to the measures aggregate at higher level and returning the result to a different measure at the lower-level location. The calculated measure that uses this formula will specifically name the measure it is taking the ratio of. Using a payroll expense cube with a typical geography dimension as an example, we find the following examples:

Ratio to parent
```
[Measures].[Payroll Total] /
([Measures].[Payroll Total], [Geography].Parent)
```

Ratio to ancestor
```
[Measures].[Payroll Total] /
([Measures].[Payroll Total], Ancestor ([Geography],
[Geography].[State])
```

Ratio to [All]
```
[Measures].[Payroll Total] /
([Measures].[Payroll Total], [All Geographies])
```

For brevity, we leave out the *Dimension*.CurrentMember operator from these examples. Listing the dimension name by itself in a context that expects a member implies the current member along that dimension. The *ratio to parent* will be valid at every level except the top level in the dimension because there is no parent for the members there. The *ratio to ancestor* will be valid at every level from the ancestor's level (where the ratio's value will simply be 1, unless the total was 0) down to the leaf level. The *ratio to [All]* will be valid everywhere in the dimension. It is a special case of ratio to ancestor, but it will be slightly more efficient to phrase this special case as the "ratio to the [All]" member than as the "ancestor of the current member at the All level."

Given a ratio between a measure and its value at some ancestor, you can perform proportional allocation of any other measure based on that ratio. The measure being allocated is likely to come from a higher level than the target locations, although it could come from the same level. For example, budgeting models frequently allocate costs from a higher level down based on head count or anticipated sales. Suppose that you need to allocate a budgeted rent quantity to arrive at a calculated rent per person, given your headcount aggregated up a geography dimension. The following calculated measure would perform the allocation of budgeted rent based on headcount:

```
CREATE MEMBER [Measures].[Allocated Rent Budget] AS
'([Measures].[Rent], [Geography].[All Geographies]) *
[Measures].[Headcount] / ([Measures].[Headcount], [All Geographies])'
```

At the [All Geographies] member, the allocated rent budget should be equal to the total rent budget. Assuming that head count has summed evenly up all levels, at each state in the Geography.State level the allocated rent budget should be proportional to that state's head count compared to the total organization's head count. At each city, the allocated rent budget should be proportional to that city's head count compared with the cities in that state. That budget should also be proportional to the city's head count compared with the total organization's head count.

UNWEIGHTED ALLOCATIONS DOWN THE HIERARCHY

You may also need to allocate values for some measure down a hierarchy, but in proportion to the number of children under a parent rather than in proportion to some other measure's values. For example, measures that were input by quarter may need to be spread out to days. In this case, the ratio is simply going to be the reciprocal of the number of days in each quarter. In general, to get the ratio you simply divide 1 by the number of descendants under the ancestor of the current member in that dimension. For example, to allocate from the quarter level of the Time dimension down to a lower time level, the ratio would be expressed by the following:

```
(1.0 / Count (Descendants (Ancestor ([Time].CurrentMember,
[Time].[Quarter]), [Time].CurrentMember.Level, SELF), INCLUDEEMPTY))
```

Notice that we use the Member.Level operator to get the level of the current member in the time dimension. For clarity, we also explicitly list the default SELF option for Descendants().

Averages

SIMPLE AVERAGES

WEIGHTED AVERAGES

Since Microsoft OLAP Services does not provide the ability to pre-aggregate data by averaging, a frequent idiom you will use will be to calculate an average by explicitly taking the ratio of a measure that represents a sum with a measure that represents a count. Since the measures often represent the same concept aggregated two different ways, their names will often be related, as in

```
[Measures].[Sales Sum] / [Measures].[Item Count]
```

If you need to take a simple average over values associated with a set of cells, you can use the MDX Avg() function, as with the following example:

```
WITH
    SET [Best5Custs] AS 'TopCount ([Customer].[Individual].Members, 5,
[Measures].[Profit]'
    MEMBER [Customer].[Avg Over Best] AS 'Avg ([Best5Custs])'
SELECT
    { [Measures].[Sales], [Measures].[Units], [Measures].[Profit] } on
columns
    { [Products].[Category].Members } on rows
FROM Sales
WHERE ([Customer].[Avg Over Best])
```

This query returns a grid of three measures by N product categories. The sales, units, and profit measures are each averaged over the five best customers in terms of total profit. The mechanics of this query are diagrammed in Figure 9.1. Notice that we left the expression to be averaged by the Avg() function unspecified in the [Avg Over Best] calculation. Leaving it unspecified is the equivalent of saying,

```
([Measures].CurrentMember, [Products].CurrentMember ,...)
```

When we calculate weighted averages, we are usually trying to take the average of some ratio (like price per share of stock) weighted by some quantity of the quotient (like number of shares traded). What we want to calculate is the aver-

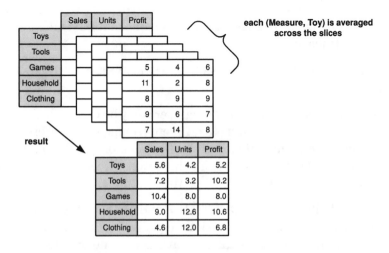

Figure 9.1 Calculated aggregate member as a slicer.

age of the product of these two things. As far as the calculation architecture of OLAP Services is concerned, the most efficient overall way to calculate the average of the product would be by performing the multiplication into yet another measure in the fact table, and then summing it and counting it through the implicit aggregations. Assuming that this was not done for us (there are a variety of things that we might have wanted to have precalculated that weren't), we can still do it effectively. For example, the expression

```
Avg(
  CrossJoin(
    Descendants ([Industry].CurrentMember, [Industry].[Company], SELF),
    Descendants ([Time].CurrentMember, [Time].[Day], SELF)
  )
  ,([Measures].[Share Price] * [Measures].[Units Sold])
)
```

will calculate this weighted average.

There is a difficulty lurking in this formulation, however. The greater the number of dimensions we are including in our average, the larger the size of the cross-joined set. We can run into performance problems (as well as intelligibility problems) if the number of dimensions being combined is large. Moreover, we should account for all dimensions in the cube or we may accidentally involve aggregate [share price] values in a multiplication, which will probably be an error. So, if you are setting up a database for others to use and some measures, such as prices, are ratios, do try to anticipate the ways in which the measures will be used.

Different Aggregations along Different Dimensions

In this section, we will discuss aggregating along the time dimension using a different function than along the other dimensions. There are two basic cases that we will discuss: taking the average, min or max along time, and taking the opening or closing balance along time.

MIXING AGGREGATIONS: SUM ACROSS NON-TIME, AVERAGE/MIN/MAX ALONG TIME

Depending on the data you are aggregating, there may be cases where you want the measures to aggregate according to different techniques in different dimensions. For example, measures that represent populations, including both people and inventory, will typically sum in all dimensions except time and they will aggregate across time by average, MIN, or MAX.

OLAP Services's built-in SUM, COUNT, MIN, and MAX aggregations for base measures aggregate along all dimensions equally. To take an average over time of sums over non-times, we take the average of the precalculated sums over the averaging period. We must be careful to define the averaging period as being the span of time members from the time level at which the data entered the cube. Otherwise, we will be dividing by either too many time periods or too few. To take the MIN or MAX over time of sums over non-time, we simply need to take the MIN or MAX over the time period. We can do each of these by using the Descendants() function, which will return the appropriate set.

For many applications, we are going to find that the measure for which we wish to take the average of sums will already be implicitly summed up to the current level. In this case, we can simply divide the sum we find by the number of time periods over which the data entered the cube. For example, in a human resources-related cube, our Headcount measure represents a population. Assuming that the head count number is input at the week level of time, to calculate average and maximum aggregate head counts for the enterprise we would need to use the following query:

```
WITH
MEMBER [Measures].[Aggregated Headcount] AS
'[Measures].[Headcount] / Count (Descendants ([Time].CurrentMember,
[Time].[Week], SELF)'
MEMBER [Measures].[Max Headcount] AS
'Max (Descendants ([Time].CurrentMember, [Time].[Week], SELF), [Mea-
sures].[HeadCount])'
 . . .
```

MIXING AGGREGATIONS: SUM ACROSS NON-TIME, OPENING/CLOSING BALANCE ALONG TIME

For inventory balances, we are frequently also interested in opening and closing amounts in any time period. This can be expressed straightforwardly in MDX. The OpeningPeriod() and ClosingPeriod() functions give us direct references to the appropriate members. For example, the following defines a measure that represents the closing inventory balance for any time period:

```
CREATE MEMBER [InventoryCube].[Measures].[Closing Balance] AS
'([Measures].[Inventory],
ClosingPeriod ([Time].[Day], [Time].CurrentMember))'
```

From whatever time member we are at in any time level, we can find the last day-level member that corresponds to that time in the hierarchy, and the value is taken from that member. Since this is not really an aggregation function (it selects from a single member, not over a range), it executes quickly even though it is not pre-aggregated.

If you are looking to calculate the last balance found in a time range in which not all of the data has been filled in (i.e., the last balance so far in the quarter since we only have data for October and November), look ahead to the section "Carryover of balances for slowly changing values" for techniques for carrying over balances for slowly changing values.

Moving Aggregates within a Level

ROLLING AVERAGES

52-WEEK HIGH/LOW

These two calculations are part of a general class of calculations that we will call *moving aggregates*, in which a measure is aggregated over a sliding window of members within a level. (Pareto, or 80/20, analysis is related to moving aggregates, but in Pareto the window is fixed at one end and grows toward the other.) We will talk about techniques for related calculations in the "Pareto analysis and cumulative sums" section.

In a moving aggregation, the important technique is to construct a range within the level whose endpoints are relative to the current member. MDX gives us several functions and operators to construct these with: *Dimension*.CurrentMember lets us reference the current member; the colon (:) implies a range between two endpoints; and .Lag(), .Lead(), PrevMember(), NextMember(), Cousin(), and ParallelPeriod() all let us reference members that are related to the current member. Note that to use these MDX member-referencing operators and functions we assume that the ordering of members within the hierarchy corresponds with the ordering our sliding window will follow. For the time dimension, this will be generally true.

Let's go through some examples. Consider the following two expressions:

```
Avg( [Time].CurrentMember.Lag(5) : [Time].CurrentMember, Measures.
[Volume Traded])
```

```
Avg( LastPeriods (6, [Time].CurrentMember), [Measures].[Volume Traded])
```

These expressions easily take the rolling average over a six-period time range: from the current time through the time five units back (0, 1, 2, 3, 4, and 5 units away makes six periods altogether). The expression

```
Avg( {[Time].CurrentMember.PrevMember, [Time].CurrentMember,}
[Measures].[Volume Traded])
```

takes the average of the current period and the prior period.

Notice that each of these three expressions is taking either a six-period or two-period average, not a six-month or two-day average. The level at which these averages are being calculated is determined by the context they are being evaluated at. If the first expression we gave is being calculated for a month-level cell then it will create a six-month average, and if it is being calculated for a year-level cell it will create a six-year average.

We can control that behavior in a couple of ways. If the measure being calculated truly needs to be a six-month average, we can control the function so it is only evaluated at the month level (read the section titled "One formula calculating different things in different places [also called 'formula application ranges']" later in this chapter to learn how to do this). If the measure really means "Average over the last half-year's worth of data at this level," then we can use the ParallelPeriod() or Cousin() functions to set this up for multiple levels at the same time.

If we have a half-year level in our database, we can be direct, as with the following two expressions:

```
Avg( { ParallelPeriod ([Time].[HalfYear], 1, [Time].CurrentMember) :
[Time].CurrentMember }, [Measures].[Volume Traded])
```

```
Avg( {ParallelPeriod ( [Time].[HalfYear]) : [Time].CurrentMember },
[Measures].[Volume Traded])
```

The second of these examples is terse but adequate, in that the 1 and Time.CurrentMember are the default arguments for ParallelPeriod. If we don't have a half-year level but we do have quarters, then we can be a little less direct:

```
Avg( { ParallelPeriod ([Time].[Quarter], 2, [Time].CurrentMember) :
Time.CurrentMember }, [Measures].[Volume Traded])
```

This works as well since two quarters create the same distance as one half year. A 52-period high can be computed at the week level with the following:

```
Max ({ [Time].Lag(51) : [Time] }, [Measures].[Share Price])
Max ({ LastPeriods (52, [Time]) }, [Measures].[Share Price])
```

If your calendar uses years and weeks, you may have some 53-week years to deal with inconsistency between weeks and years. ParallelPeriod() will not work when you are looking for the fifty-third week of one year in a parallel year that has only 52 weeks, so you wouldn't want to use it for that purpose.

Recall as well from the "Invalid Locations" discussion of Chapter 6 that when there is no time period 52 weeks ago or two quarters ago, we will get ranges of time members in our sets that may or may not be what we want.

Filling in Blanks

There are occasions where you need to look up the most recently entered value for a non-time dimensional slice, such as the size of the most recent purchase made by a customer. The following section explains techniques for creating carryover of balances and reporting of the last entered balance.

CARRYOVER OF BALANCES FOR SLOWLY CHANGING VALUES

REPORTING OF LAST ENTERED BALANCE (AS OPPOSED TO BALANCE FOR LAST TIME DESCENDANT)

Sometimes, records in a fact table represent the attainment of a certain state, for example, an account balance or a salary level. Rather than posting these records every time period, these records will only appear when the state is attained. Your application would like to use the value that is relevant for the time period of evaluation, yet the last record for that kind of balance may have been posted that month, one time period ago, two time periods ago, or more.

You can get around this problem within Microsoft OLAP Services, but it may be worth your time to perform the logic in SQL so there actually is a value for each month. This is because whenever the slowly changing value is used as the input for a calculation (especially one that is then aggregated), the calculations will be performed in cache at run time. When the calculation is then aggregated, as a calculation involving a tax rate, price, or salary would be, the performance of the query may be quite bad.

There are actually two very different ways to perform the reference for balance carryover for slowly changing values: by a recursive calculated member function and by using set expressions. The most practical method in terms of calculation speed is the recursive function. (We do not know whether to recommend recursive functions as a general style because we do not know how deep the stack that the recursion relies on is. It seems to be deep enough for most applications.) The set expression technique is instructive for examining issues in expression construction, however. But let's look at the recursive calculation first.

Our goal is to find the most recent value for a cell if there is not one available in the current cell. This means we need to test whether the current cell is empty or not, and if it is empty we need to check the previous cell. To efficiently reference the previous cell, we should put this calculation into its own calculated measure that searches the last found value of the measure we are interested in. A calculated member that almost does this to our liking is as follows:

```
WITH MEMBER [Measures].[Last Update of Price] AS
'iif (NOT IsEmpty ([Measures].[Price]),
  [Measures].[Price],
  ([Measures].[Last Update of Price], [Time].PrevMember)
)'
...
```

The reason this calculated member is almost but not quite adequate is that if the value for [Price] at the first time member along this level were itself empty, the formula would reference the value for a non-existent member. This would make the cell reference for [Measures].[Price] empty and trigger a recursive reference for another non-existent cell from another non-existent member. Since MDX does not intrinsically distinguish between invalid locations and empty cells, we need to wire the appropriate logic into the expression. We can do this by testing whether the time member itself is empty, as in the following expression:

```
WITH MEMBER [Measures].[Last Update of Price] AS
'iif (NOT IsEmpty ([Measures].[Price]),
  [Measures].[Price],
```

```
    iif (NOT IsEmpty ([Time].PrevMember),
      ([Measures].[Last Update of Price], [Time].PrevMember),
      NULL
    )
  )'
  ...
```

Since we expect that some value will usually be found before the searching operation runs off the edge of the dimension, we place the clause that tests for the edge of the dimension after the test for a valid cell value. Either way, [Last Update of Price] now returns values corresponding to the most recent change of price at the level which the measure is requested. We have organized the logic of this to emphasize the cases where we have data or valid time members. If we wanted to increase the speed of the query, we could re-phrase it so as to eliminate the NOT calculations.

Now, let us see how we would express this using set expressions. A set-based strategy would be to filter out all empty cells and then isolate the last one. A search expression that makes no assumptions about where data can be found and performs these two steps is the following:

```
Tail(
  Filter( PeriodsToDate([Time].[All]),
    NOT IsEmpty ([Measures].[Price])
  )
  , 1
)
```

If you are assured that every N time periods will contain one record, then you can search through that many periods with .Lag() or LastPeriods(), as with

```
Tail(
  Filter( LastPeriods (12, [Time].CurrentMember),
    NOT IsEmpty([Measures].[Price])
  )
  , 1
)
```

Since each of these options returns a set of 1 tuple, you will need to do something to turn it into a single value. The .Item() function will extract this one tuple, which expands our expression. The full member definition for [Last Update of Price] becomes the following:

```
WITH MEMBER [Measures].[Last Update of Price] AS
'Tail(
  Filter( PeriodsToDate([Time].[All]),
    NOT IsEmpty([Measures].[Price])
  )
  , 1
).Item (0)'
  ...
```

Regardless of how we defined it, using our last found value in queries is straightforward. Using it to calculate further values is also straightforward, but possibly costly. Let us assume that we have an adequate [Last Update of Price] measure. Using it to compute, say, `[Dollars Sold] AS '[Units Sold] * [Last Update of Price]'` will almost certainly require that we aggregate it. And performing aggregations of leaf-level cells in MDX can be expensive. The aggregation function will need to incorporate potentially all leaf-level cells, which will be expensive with one or more large dimensions:

```
WITH MEMBER [Measures].[Dollars Sold] AS
'Sum (Descendants ([Time].CurrentMember, [Time].[Month],
   Sum (Descendants ([Geography].CurrentMember, [Geography].[Store],
    Sum (Descendants ([Products].CurrentMember, [Products].[SKU]),
     ([Measures][Units Sold] * [Measures][Last Update of Price])
   )))'
...
```

This assumes that sales only vary by time, geography, and product. If sales vary by other dimensions, then those dimensions must all have aggregations in the formula for Dollars Sold as well.

Note that the difficulty with these carryover calculations is more in tractability than logic. OLAP Services provides a much more convenient environment for expressing the logic of [Last update of price] than SQL. And in your specific environment, the system which feeds you transaction data may currently only track changes to price (or salary, tax rate, etc.) However, the larger the number of dimensions involved in calculations that use this value and the larger the number of members in these dimensions, the greater the challenge of maintaining them and the greater the resources required to calculate them. Furthermore, other applications in your overall decision-support environment may well benefit from having these values explicitly maintained at every time period. For example, data mining tools tend to have very weak dimensional logic, and their ability to discover patterns based on rates or balances over time will be enhanced if the rates or balances are explicit in the database. You may wish to refer to the section "Closing the Loop: Writing Analytical Results Back to the RDBMS" in Chapter 12 for techniques that would allow you to use OLAP Services to perform the transformation of last-balance information into tables that would pre-aggregate quickly.

An issue related to reporting the last entered balance is determining the last time period for which data is actually available. A cube may use a time dimension with months for the entire year, but while the year is in progress the last month for which data is available will not be the last month for the year. One solution for this is to use an external function to retrieve from an external source the last time period for which that data was stored. (We discuss this use for an external function in Chapter 14.) Another plausible solution, entirely in MDX, would be to scan the leaf level of the time dimension for the last non-empty time member at the All level of every other dimension. Once the cube has been processed, at every time member for which data has been entered there will exist an aggregate value at the intersection of that time member with the All member for every other dimension. So, requesting the last time member for which there is an all-product, all-store, all-customer (etc.) sales value present would give you the last time member for which you have data at all.

Advanced Manipulations: Queries and Expressions

Now that we have seen a variety of common operations expressed in MDX, let us turn our attention to more advanced expressions and queries. The expressions and queries in this section are oriented more toward the composition of whole analytical queries, and the principles that go into constructing them are useful for constructing all manner of sophisticated analyses, even if the particular examples we present in this section do not address the applications you are going to build.

The types of expressions and queries we are going to explore in this section are as follows:

- Report totals-to-parent, totals-to-ancestor
- Percentage contribution to report totals
- Hierarchical sorting that skips levels in the hierarchy
- Including all tuples with tied ranking in sets
- Pareto analysis and cumulative sums
- Drilling down from virtual dimensions
- One formula calculating different things in different places (also called "formula application ranges")
- Logical aggregations (ForAny, ForEach, ForNone)

After we work through these expressions and queries, in the next section we will apply the same principles for using MDX we discuss here in a complete series of analytical queries.

Ratios between Levels for Members in a Report

REPORT TOTALS-TO-PARENT, TOTALS-TO-ANCESTOR

PERCENTAGE CONTRIBUTION TO REPORT TOTALS

Some reports need to provide a subset of children or a subset of descendants for a member, along with a total of those children or descendants. For example, for a group of interesting customers within a sales region, we want to see summary values for them at the city and state level. In addition to seeing the summary values, we want to see the influence of each of them as a percentage of all the interesting customers in that group. OLAP Services will provide intrinsic aggregation of all children to their parent (and all descendants to their ancestors), but this may include many descendants that are not part of the query. (In a query of this sort, in MDX we are really creating a proxy set of levels and ancestor members whose names are the same as the database's but who represent a different and interesting subset of the original dimension.)

VisualTotals() is an OLAP Services-specific function that will give us the report total to a parent member, which makes some of this process easy when only parents and children are involved. In essence, VisualTotals() returns a set that includes a new calculated member as a part of it, defined within VisualTotals(). For example, the query

```
SELECT
{ [Measures].[Sales], [Measures].[Costs] } on columns,
{ [Customer].[Fargo, ND], VisualTotals ({
    [Customer].[Fargo, ND],
    [Customer].[Fargo, ND].[C#4521772],
    [Customer].[Fargo, ND].[C#2329384],
    [Customer].[Fargo, ND].[C#3847321]
}, "Total in *") } on rows
FROM Shipments
```

would generate a straightforward report of three customers in Fargo, North Dakota, and their total sales and costs, along with the database total for Fargo, North Dakota, for contrast. The result would appear as shown in Figure 9.2. This approach is expedient when we only want the total values for children values, grouped according to their hierarchy. VisualTotals() will also let us total up descendants farther away than children and in fact will allow us to use descendants at multiple levels without double-counting their results. Using VisualTotals() is very convenient because it does not require us to devote any logic to the creation of calculated members:

```
WITH
SET [InterestingCustomers] AS ' {
    [Customer].[Fargo, ND].[C#4521772],
    [Customer].[Fargo, ND].[C#2329384],
    [Customer].[Fargo, ND].[C#3847321]
}'
MEMBER [Customer].[Explicit Total in Fargo, ND] AS
'Aggregate ( [InterestingCustomers] )'
SELECT
{ [Measures].[Sales], [Measures].[Costs] } on columns,
{ [Customer].[Fargo, ND], [Customer].[Explicit Total in Fargo, ND],
[InterestingCustomers] } on rows
FROM Shipments
```

	Sales	Costs
Fargo, ND	25,000	18,000
Total in Fargo, ND	9,000	8,850
C#4521772	6,000	7,000
C#2329384	2,000	1,000
C#3847321	1,000	850

Figure 9.2 Report totals versus VisualTotals.

However, when we wish to calculate percentage-of-total contributions for each customer in our [InterestingCustomers] set, we do need to create calculated members. This is because the member total created by VisualTotals does not have a name that we can reference in our query. When the query is parsed, the name has not yet been generated, and though we could form the expression (sales / [Total in Fargo, ND]), the MDX parser will not know what member it corresponds to since it will not exist until later.

The percentage-to-total calculation does not belong in the customer dimension. It is best suited to the measures dimension, on a measure-by-measure basis. For example, consider the following query:

```
WITH
SET [InterestingCustomers] AS ' {
     [Customer].[Fargo, ND].[C#4521772],
     [Customer].[Fargo, ND].[C#2329384],
     [Customer].[Fargo, ND].[C#3847321]
}'
MEMBER [Customer].[Explicit Total in Fargo, ND] AS
'Aggregate ( [InterestingCustomers])'
MEMBER [Measures].[Percent to Report Sales Total] AS
'Sales / (Sales, [Customer].[Explicit Total in Fargo, ND])'
SELECT
{ [Measures].[Sales], [Measures].[Costs],
[Measures].[Percent to Report Sales Total] } on columns,
{ [Customer].[Fargo, ND], [Customer].[Explicit Total in Fargo, ND],
[InterestingCustomers] } on rows
FROM Shipments
```

We can use this approach of creating a named set, a calculated member on the same dimension, and one or more calculated measures for any set of members that aggregate into one member only. More difficult, however, is when we wish to see a set of descendants and their contributions to ancestors for more than one ancestor. For example, we may have a set of interesting customers in North Dakota, South Dakota, Minnesota, and Wisconsin. Our last approach would run into a few complications when we try to extend it. The [Percent to Report Sales

Total] measure hardwires the Fargo, North Dakota, ancestor member within it. We would need to add a separate percentage measure for each ancestor, which is an ugly solution. It would create a set of 4 measures, each of which would only have a valid intersection with one of the four state-level members, something we would prefer to avoid. In addition, we would need to do other things like generate multiple sets of interesting customers, one for each Explicit Total pseudo-parent.

We can avoid this ugliness if we +create a new calculated report total measure and use some of the set manipulation functions provided in MDX. Let's say that we have a set of interesting customers in three different states:

```
SET [InterestingCustomers] AS ' {
     [Customer].[Fargo, ND].[C#4521772], [Customer].[Fargo,
ND].[C#2329384],
     [Customer].[Pierre, SD].[C#8212633], [Customer].[Pierre,
SD].[C#1012233],
     [Customer].[Hibbing, MN].[C#71236931], [Customer].[St. Cloud,
MN].[C#3492945],
 }'
```

Let's also say we wish to get the sum of sales and costs within each of these customers' states, along with the percentage contribution of each customer to that total. We do need to include the ancestor members within the query. If we are starting only with a set of customers, we can do that with Generate() (since Ancestor only works on members, not on sets). A hierarchized set to be used as one axis of the query could be obtained from a random set of customers with the following query:

```
SET [rowset] AS 'Hierarchize (
  [InterestingCustomers],
  Generate ([InterestingCustomers], { Ancestor([Customer].CurrentMember,
[Customer].[State]) } ))'
```

The real heart of the query is in the calculated measures that compute the report total of the sales and cost measures. Each is similar. The one for sales looks like this:

```
MEMBER [Measures].[Report Total Sales] AS 'Sum (
Intersect ([InterestingCustomers],
Descendants ([Customer].CurrentMember, [Customer].[Individual Customer])
), [Measures].[Sales])'
```

At each customer member, we take the individual customer(s) that correspond to that customer member. Intersecting that with our customers of interest gives us only the interesting individual customers that are under our customer member. (Or it will give us the interesting customer back, if one of the customers is our current member.) For each state-level member, the sum over that set gives us the report total sales for the interesting customers within that state.

Since we are using real state-level members to organize our report total sales, we can simply take the ratio of individual customer sales to the ancestor's Report Total Sales to obtain our percentage of total, as in the following:

```
MEMBER [Measures].[Sales Percent of Report Total] AS '[Measures].[Sales]
/ ([Measures].[Report Total Sales], Ancestor ([Customer],
[Customer].[State])'
```

So, the whole query rolled together would be as follows (excluding the details of the individual customers), with the query's result shown in Figure 9.3:

```
WITH
SET [InterestingCustomers] AS '. . .'
SET [Rowset] AS 'Hierarchize ([InterestingCustomers],
  Generate ([InterestingCustomers],
    { Ancestor([Customer].CurrentMember,
[Customer].[State]) } ))'
MEMBER [Measures].[Report Total Sales] AS 'Sum (
Intersect ([InterestingCustomers],
  Descendants ([Customer].CurrentMember,
    [Customer].[Individual Customer])), [Measures].[Sales])'
MEMBER [Measures].[Report Total Costs] AS 'Sum (
Intersect ([InterestingCustomers],
  Descendants ([Customer].CurrentMember,
    [Customer].[Individual Customer])), [Measures].[Costs])'
MEMBER [Measures].[Sales Percent of Report Total] AS '[Measures].[Sales]
/ ([Measures].[Report Total Sales], Ancestor ([Customer],
[Customer].[State])', FORMAT_STRING = '#.00%'
MEMBER [Measures].[Cost Percent of Report Total] AS '[Measures].[Costs]
/ ([Measures].[Report Total Sales], Ancestor ([Customer],
[Customer].[State])', FORMAT_STRING = '#.00%'
```

	Report Total Sales	Report Total Costs	Sales Pct of Report Total	Cost Pct of Report Total
MN	15,500	10,500	100.00%	100.00%
C#3492945	3,500	4,500	22.58%	42.86%
C#7123693	12,000	6,000	77.42%	57.14%
ND	8,000	8,000	100.00%	100.00%
C#2329384	2,000	1,000	25.00%	12.5%
C#4521772	6,000	7,000	75.00%	87.5%
SD	10,300	6,500	100.00%	100.00%
C#1012233	5,800	3,000	56.31%	46.15%
C#8212633	4,500	3,500	39.69%	53.85%

Figure 9.3 Full report totals and percent total results.

```
SELECT
{ [Measures].[Report Total Sales], [Measures].[Report Total Costs],
[Measures].[Sales Percent of Report Total], [Cost Percent of Report
Total] } on columns,
{ [Rowset] } on rows
FROM Shipments
```

Hierarchical Sorting That Skips Levels in the Hierarchy

The hierarchical sorting provided by the Order() function is very convenient when we wish to display data sorted within all hierarchical relationships. Sometimes, however, we may wish to sort by hierarchical relationships but not use all levels in the hierarchy. For example, we may use a geography dimension in a cube that has levels of state, city, and store. If we sort our geography members hierarchically by profit per unit, we will get each store sorted per city and each city sorted per state, whether or not those intermediate levels are in the report. How, in a report, can we sort each store per state, leaving out the cities?

The answer is to break apart the sorting so we are sorting the cities within each state independently. The Generate() function provides us with the iterative framework we need to do this. The first set can be our set of states, and the second set can be an expression that sorts the descendants of the current member of the first set:

```
Generate(
  { [Geography].[State].Members },
    Order(
       { Descendants( [Geography].CurrentMember, [Geography].[Store],
       SELF) },
       [Measures].[Profit Per Unit],
       BDESC
  ) }
)
```

It is important, of course, to specify BDESC or BASC rather than ASC or DESC. In a report where we wish to hierarchically represent the states with the stores, we can add them into the second set for Generate():

```
Generate(
  { [Geography].[State].Members },
  { [Geography].CurrentMember,
    Order(
       { Descendants( [Geography].CurrentMember, [Geography].[Store],
SELF) },
       [Measures].[Profit Per Unit],
       BDESC
  )
```

```
      }
   )
```

As an aside, the default hierarchical ordering always places parents before children, whether the sorting is ascending or descending. We can use the same sort of construct we just gave to put our states after their children, in a typical subtotal format:

```
Generate(
   { [Geography].[State].Members },
   { Order(
      {Descendants([Geography].CurrentMember, [Geography].[Store], SELF)},
      [Measures].[Profit Per Unit],
      BDESC
      ),
      [Geography].CurrentMember
   }
)
```

Including All Tuples with Tied Ranking in Sets

There are several MDX functions that return ranked sets: TopCount(), Bottom-Count(), TopSum(), BottomSum(), TopPercent(), and BottomPercent(). They will return a particular number of tuples. If several tuples share the same associated value, the functions will each arbitrarily cut off at some tuple, though other tuples with the same associated data values might have been included in the result set as well.

It takes a surprising amount of MDX to include all those tuples with values that are tied with the value of the last tuple, and hence have a tied ranking. It would be easy if the process were procedural; however, given the declarative constructs we have, it is not. The strategy we can follow is to take the value associated with the last element in the set, filter the original set for the tuples that have this value, and union this filtered set with the ranked set. Since MDX preserves the ordering in the sets when they are unioned, the final set that is created will be in the correct order. This process involves several intermediate sets. The logic will be clearest and the evaluation most efficient if we can create named sets along the way. For example, to select the top 20 stores in terms of square footage, and include all ties at the 20th place:

```
WITH
SET [StartingStores] AS '{ [Geography].[Store].Members }'
SET [TopSet] AS 'TopCount ( [StartingStores], 20,
   [Geography].Properties ("square footage"))'
SET [TiedTuples] AS 'Filter ( [StartingStores],
   [Geography].Properties ("square footage") = TopSet.Item (Count
```

```
([TopSet]) -1) )'
SET [FinalSet] AS 'Union ([TopSet], [TiedTuples])'
. . .
```

Based on this example, the set FinalSet will contain at least 20 stores, and perhaps more.

Pareto Analysis and Cumulative Sums

When you query for parents and children, you can use Order() with ASC or DESC to preserve the hierarchy while sorting. For example, given the store and employee count data values shown in Figure 9.4, the following set expression will result in the ordering of stores shown in Figure 9.5:

```
ORDER( {[Store].[California], [Store].[California].Children,
[Store].[Nevada], [Store].[Nevada].Children},
[Measures].[Employee Count], DESC)
```

Now, let's say that for each of the children, we want the cumulative sum as we go from the first child in this ordering to the last child. This will essentially give us a Pareto analysis within each state. If we used the following expression,

```
[Measures].[Cum Employee Count] AS 'Sum ( {[Employee].FirstSibling :
[Employee].CurrentMember}, [Measures].[Employee Count])'
```

our results will be quite wrong. This is so because .FirstSibling is not relative to this ordering, even though .CurrentMember will be.

To get the cumulative sum for each of the children as we go from the first child in this ordering to the last, we will need to re-create the range of ordered children within our calculated member. We will also need to find our current tuple within the range, using Rank(), and we will need to create a range from the first

Store	Associated Employee Count
California	124
Sacramento	49
Los Angeles	72
Ukiah	3
Nevada	129
Reno	55
Las Vegas	62
Tahoe	12

Figure 9.4 Store and employee count data values.

Store	Associated Employee Count
Nevada	129
Las Vegas	62
Reno	55
Tahoe	12
California	124
Los Angeles	72
Sacramento	49
Ukiah	3

Figure 9.5 Store and employee count data results.

tuple in the set to the referent child's tuple, using Head(). The following expression gives us the proper ordering of members:

```
Order ( {[Employee].Parent.Children}, [Measures].[Employee Count], DESC)
```

We obtain the ranking of any tuple in that set with:

```
Rank ([Store], Set)
```

The Rank() term gives us the rank of the current store member within that set to use as our cutoff point for aggregating. In addition, the expression

```
Head( Set, Index)
```

gives us the subset to aggregate. We need to use the set once to get the members to aggregate over and another time to get them to rank over. Rolling it all together, we get:

```
MEMBER [Measures].[Cum Employee Count] AS '
Sum (
  Head(
    Order( {[Store].Parent.Children}, [Measures].[Employee Count],
BDESC),
    Rank (
      [Store],
      Order( {[Store].Parent.Children}, [Measures].[Employee Count],
BDESC)
    )
  ),
  [Measures].[Employee Count]
)'
```

A sample complete query would look like the following, with its results shown in Figure 9.6:

Store	Employee Count	Cum. Employee Count
Nevada	129	129
Las Vegas	62	62
Reno	55	117
Tahoe	12	129
California	124	253
Los Angeles	72	72
Sacramento	49	121
Ukiah	3	124

Figure 9.6 Cumulative employee counts.

```
WITH
MEMBER [Measures].[Cum Employee Count] AS '. . .'
SELECT
{ [Measures].[Employee Count], [Measures].[Cum Employee Count] } on
columns,
{ [Store].[Nevada], [Store].[Nevada].Children, [Store].[California],
[Store].[California].Children} on rows
FROM [Employee Cube]
```

The exact results for Nevada and California are dependent on the contents of their siblings, of course. If you want to only return results for [Cum Employee Count] at the city level and omit cumulative counts at higher levels, use the techniques we discuss for "One formula calculating different things in different places" later in this section.

For comprehensibility if nothing else, it would be highly desirable to abstract the Order(. . .) clause into one definition and two uses. Although for each store member the set could be different (since it will be evaluated for the children of multiple parents), within the sum it doesn't change. However, named sets are evaluated at the time they are parsed, not each time they are referenced, so we cannot use them here.

If constructing, maintaining, and executing this sort of MDX is less onerous to you than maintaining code in an ActiveX Automation language, then you can certainly do it in MDX. If you would rather maintain Automation-related code, then a UDF is the way to go. For example, with the following query you could call a UDF named PartialSum to take an ordered set of stores, an ordered set of values, and the name of the store to stop summing at:

```
WITH
MEMBER [Measures].[StoreUniqueName] AS '[Store].UniqueName'
```

```
MEMBER [Measures].[CumSum] AS
'PartialSum (
   SetToArray (Order( {[Store].Parent.Children}, [Measures].[Employee
Count], DESC), [Measures].[StoreUniqueName]),
   SetToArray (Order( {[Store].Parent.Children}, [Measures].[Employee
Count], DESC), [Measures].[Employee Count]),
   [Measures].[StoreUniqueName]
)'

    . . .
```

Notice that you need to create a dummy measure that contains the name of the current store member (which we called [Measures].[StoreUniqueName] in the example). The first release of Microsoft OLAP Services will generate a parser error if you try to access the unique name directly in SetToArray().

DRILLING DOWN FROM VIRTUAL DIMENSIONS

The members of a virtual dimension exist in an N − 1 hierarchical relationship with the members of the real level upon which it is based. However, because the virtual dimension is distinct from the real dimension you cannot directly drill down on it to the underlying real members. This is, however, something that you might wish to allow in an application if a virtual member's slice is interesting to the user. We can always directly drill down on the virtual dimension to the underlying real members since the real dimension will exist in a cube with the property's level enabled if the virtual dimension is used in that cube. Furthermore, the name of the member will be identical to the value of the corresponding member property. We simply filter the real dimension based on the property value that was to create the virtual dimension. The abstract template for this operation is as follows:

```
Filter( Set Of Real Members On Real Dimension, Member.Properties ("Prop-
   ertyName") = Virtual Dimension Member.Name)
```

Notice that we are comparing the member property values to the Name of the virtual member, not to the UniqueName. The unique name will have extra information in it (like the name of the virtual dimension) that isn't part of the property. For any particular virtual member, this doesn't give us any extra power. If we know the name of the virtual member, we know the property value to compare it with. (Properties whose values are dates, numbers, etc., may require a data type conversion since the name is always a text value. Nevertheless, the principle still holds.) Consider the following trivial example. With a product dimension and a virtual dimension whose members are formed out of the product color property, we can select only those products where

```
Filter ([Products].[SKU].Members, [Product].Properties ("Flavor") =
   [ProductSKU].[Zesty Garlic].Name)
```

However, we can do some powerful things with sets of virtual members when we are filtering on virtual members that are themselves determined in the course of the query. As an example, suppose we want to see the top-selling three flavors of marinara sauce, and for each of these we want to see in a report the product SKUs nested within them. If we simply cross-joined SKUs within flavors, we wouldn't get the association—we would get a grid with an awful lot of empty cells within it. We would once again use Generate() to provide the iterative framework. The following query would yield the result shown in Figure 9.7:

```
WITH
SET [Top3flavors] AS 'TopCount ([ProductSku].[ProductSku].Members, 3,
([Measures].[Unit Sales], [Time].[1997], [Store].[All Stores]))'
SET [Flavors and Skus] AS
'Generate (
  [Top3Flavors],
  CrossJoin ({ [ProductSku].CurrentMember } ,
      { [Product].[All Products],
Filter ([Product].[Sku].Members, [Product].Properties ("Flavor") =
[ProductSku].CurrentMember.Name)
      }
    )
)'
SELECT
{[Measures].[Unit Sales], Measures.[Dollar Sales] } on columns,
{ [Flavors and SKUs] } on rows
FROM SalesCube
WHERE ([Time].[1997])
```

			Unit Sales	Dollar Sales
All of This Flavor	Zesty Garlic	All Products	540,000	1,080,000
	Zesty Garlic	SKU 254	223,000	446,000
	Zesty Garlic	SKU 996	205,000	410,000
	Zesty Garlic	SKU 223	112,000	224,000
All of This Flavor	Tomato Alarm	All Products	350,000	700,000
	Tomato Alarm	SKU 105	180,000	360,000
	Tomato Alarm	SKU 099	50,000	100,000
	Tomato Alarm	SKU 313	120,000	240,000
All of This Flavor	Pesto Walnut	All Products	315,000	630,000
	Pesto Walnut	SKU 291	120,000	240,000
	Pesto Walnut	SKU 293	195,000	390,000

Figure 9.7 Virtual dimension drill-down report.

One Formula Calculating Different Things in Different Places

We have seen that calculated members create slices across all intersections of all other dimensions. Sometimes, however, we need a calculated member to give a different result depending on where in the hypercube it is being evaluated. How can we make one calculated member return two different things at two different places? The answer is to use a conditional function and the various properties of members, levels, hierarchies, tuples, and sets in a calculated member to test for the location where the members are being evaluated and then choose the correct formula to use for that place in the cube.

For example, if we wish to create a calculated measure that shows a three-month moving average of sales, but we don't want it to show any values for any level other than month, we can use the *Level*.Ordinal property to tell us at what level the formula is being evaluated:

```
iif (
  [Time].[CurrentMember].[Level].Ordinal = [Time].[Month].Ordinal,
  Avg( LastPeriods (3, [Time].CurrentMember), [Measures].[Sales]),
  NULL
)
```

Notice that the test for whether or not this formula is being evaluated at the month level is implemented as a test to determine if the level's ordinal (depth from the root level) is equal to the month level's ordinal. We could test to see if the level's name was "Month", or we could test for a hard-wired depth like 2. However, this seems to capture the best combination of efficiency (comparing numbers instead of strings) and grace (we know what [Time].[Month] refers to, while 2 would not be as easily understood). There is a maintenance issue here as well: If the dimension changed and a new level was inserted between the month level and the root, then the 2 would need to be updated to a 3.

Earlier in this chapter, we showed an example of how to spread quarter-level input values down to lower time levels based on the number of time periods in the quarter. The calculated measure that resulted would only show values at or below the quarter level and result errors above it. We can use the same sort of level testing to create one calculated measure that shows aggregated values above the month level and allocated values below the month level:

```
CREATE MEMBER [Competitor Earnings Rate] AS
'iif ([Time].[CurrentMember].[Level].Ordinal < [Time].[Quarter].Ordinal,
  [Measure].[Earnings],
  ([Measure].[Earnings] / Count (Descendants (Ancestor (
    [Time].CurrentMember, [Time].[Quarter]),
    [Time].CurrentMember. Level, SELF), INCLUDEEMPTY))
)'
```

Sometimes, you may find that you need to use a different formula depending upon what member you are evaluating a calculated member at. For example, a multinational corporation may use a slightly different net profit calculation depending upon the country in which it is performing the calculation. For our case, we can use the unique name or the name of a member. The following example demonstrates three different profit formulas, two of which are specific to a single country as exceptions to the general rule:

```
iif ([Geography].CurrentMember.Name = "Japan",
  [Sales] - [Deductible Expenses 1],
  iif ( [Geography].CurrentMember.Name = "Malaysia",
    [Sales] - [Deductible Expenses 2],
    [Sales] - [Deductible Expenses 3]
  )
)
```

Although the MDX specification provides the CASE . . . WHEN . . . construct, the first release of OLAP Services does not support it, so we need to resort to nested IF-THEN logic using iif(). Also, notice that you cannot simply ask whether or not the current member is equal to another member. That is,

```
[Geography].CurrentMember = [Geography].[All].[Japan]
```

is not valid MDX.

If you are using IF-THEN logic to specify a constant value based on member name, you might also think about putting that information into a table and using it either as a member property or as a measure. The less conditional the logic in a formula, the easier it is to comprehend and maintain over time. The numbers that you are specifying might be exceptions to a general rule, for example, commission rates to charge based on product. In that case, the logic of the formula would test for the special commission being empty or not and to use the special commission value if it is present or the default value if the special commission is absent.

Three types of tests you may wish to perform on the current member are as follows:

- Is it at a particular member or members?
- Is it at a particular level or levels?
- Is it at a descendant of a particular member?

To test whether the current member is at a particular level (or above or below a particular level, including the level of an arbitrary named level), compare the current member's level ordinal to the ordinal of the level you are interested in using *level*.Ordinal. To test whether the current member is a descendant of a particular member, you can check the name of the current member's ancestor at that level with the target ancestor's name, as with the following expression:

```
Ancestor( [Dimension], Member).UniqueName = Ancestor-Member.UniqueName
```

The six predicates you can use against the current member or its related information for this purpose are as follows:

- *Member*.Level.Ordinal
- *Member*.Level.Name
- *Member*.Level.UniqueName
- *Member*.Name
- *Member*.UniqueName
- *Member*.Properties ("*Property N*ame")

They work as shown in the following table:

`[Dimension].Level.Ordinal = Named_Level.Ordinal`	tests for being at level
`[Dimension].Level.Ordinal > Named_Level.Ordinal`	tests for being below level
`[Dimension].Level.Ordinal < Named_Level.Ordinal`	tests for being above level
`[Dimension].Currentmember.Uniquename = [Specific Member].Uniquename` `[Dimension].UniqueName = "Unique Name"`	tests for member equivalence
`[Dimension].CurrentMember.Properties ("External Property") = Value`	tests for arbitrary condition on property; can be applied to this purpose

Also, `Rank( [Dimension].CurrentMember, { member1, member2, . . . memberN } ) > 0` can be used to test for whether or not the current member is in the given set.

Logical Aggregations (For Any, For Each, For None)

You may want some queries to return a result that is essentially a logical aggregation: Are there any cells at lower levels where some condition is true? Is it true at every cell? True at none? Essentially, these would be logical OR and AND operators that take cell ranges as inputs rather than discrete cells. For example, we could look at a report of states by quarters and see if sales were below some threshold at any related store for any related week.

Although MDX doesn't provide a direct way to do this, we can do it indirectly and get some useful side benefits along the way. We can count the cells for which the condition is true and compare that number with the number of cells in the range. Counting the cells itself is done indirectly too. The Count() function only counts cells, but we can sum an expression over the cells, where the expression returns 1 if the expression is true and 0 otherwise. We know that the condition is true for some location if the sum is greater than 0, and we know it's true everywhere if the sum is equal to the count of cells in the range. Using the rules of logic, we also know it's true everywhere if its opposite condition has a sum of 0. A useful analytical byproduct of this approach is that we can say what percentage of the time the condition is true by taking the ratio of the sum to the count of cells in the range.

For example, the following would be a query to obtain the count of stores per week where the profit was less than half of the year's average for stores in that province of Canada and for all Canada's provinces and cities in 1999:

```
WITH
MEMBER [Measures].[Avg Profit] AS
'[Measures].[Profit] / [Measures].[Units Sold]'
MEMBER [Measures].[Condition Count] AS
'Sum (Descendants ([Geography], [Geography].[Store], SELF),
  Sum (Descendants ([Time], [Time].[Week], SELF),
    iif ([Measures].[Profit] <
         ([Measures].[Avg Profit], Ancestor ([Time], [Time].[Year]),
         Ancestor ([Geography], [Geography].[Province])),
    1, 0)
  ))'
SELECT
CrossJoin ({ [Time].[Quarter].Members }, { [Measures].[Profit],
[Measures].[Condition Count] } ) on columns,
{ Descendants ([Geography].[Canada], [Geography].[City],
SELF_AND_BEFORE) } on rows
FROM Sales
WHERE ([Time].[1999])
```

A Sample Analysis

MDX is rich enough to support advanced analytical queries. Indeed, once you have created a database schema for Microsoft OLAP Services and populated it with data, MDX provides many of the tools you will need to support complex analyses within queries. We will spend the next several pages rolling up our sleeves and using MDX to explore a useful set of questions related to the topic: What are the important products to our important customers? Although your applications may not be related to customers and products, a generalization of the analysis we discuss here is "What are the important factors to each of a set of interesting members?" This is a form of data mining, even though we are performing it in an OLAP tool. Within the framework of this analysis, we will explore set construction and the use of the Generate() and Extract() functions and make extensive use of named sets.

The dimensions of primary interest in this analysis are customer, product, and time. A familiar simple OLAP query to use as a starting point is "Who are our best customers?" If we are interested in the top ten customers in terms of total profitability in 1998, we may start with the set defined by the following:

```
TopCount ([Customer].[Individual].Members, 10,
([Measures].[Profit], [Time].[1998]))
```

A query that shows profitability for 1997 and 1998 for these customers is as follows:

```
SELECT
{ [Time].[1997], [Time].[1998] } on columns,
{ TopCount ([Customer].[Individual].Members, 10, ([Measures].[Profit],
[Time].[1998])) } on rows
FROM Sales
WHERE ( [Measures].[Profit] )
```

Now, this query is useful in its own right, but we want to go a bit deeper and learn about the products that these customers are buying. We can learn about the top three product brands (in terms of profit) that some customers are buying with the following expression:

```
TopCount ([Product].[Brand].Members, 3, ([Measures].[Profit],
[Time].[1998]))
```

Because this is along a separate dimension, we can put it on a different query axis than the customer dimension, or we can put it on the same axis as the customers with CrossJoin(). For example,

```
WITH
SET [Top3Prods] AS
'{ TopCount ([Product].[Brand].Members, 3,
      ([Measures].[Profit], [Time].[1998])) }'
SELECT
{ CrossJoin ([Top3Prods], {[Time].[1997], [Time].[1998]}) } on columns,
{ TopCount ([Customer].[Individual].Members, 10,
      ([Measures].[Profit], [Time].[1998])) } on rows
FROM Sales
WHERE ( [Measures].[Profit] )
```

However, this still doesn't tell us about the products that these top customers are buying. Regardless of the way products are oriented in the query or whether the product set is evaluated as a named set or within the body of the SELECT clause, the context in which the product set is evaluated is going to be at the All-customer member since that is the default member in the query context. What we want is the set of products that these customers are buying. We can explore a couple of different paths for determining this.

One path is to ask about the top three product categories over the entire set of top ten customers. To do this, we need to calculate profitability across the top ten customers. Calculating the top ten customers from the leaf level of a fairly large dimension takes significant CPU time because of the sorting involved, so we should use a named set to hold the result customer set. We can then sum across that directly or use a calculated member to hold the result:

```
WITH
SET [Top10Custs] AS
'{ TopCount ([Customer].[Individual].Members, 10,
     ([Measures].[Profit], [Time].[1998])) }'
MEMBER [Measures].[Top10profit] AS
'Sum (Top10Custs, [Measures].[Profit])'
SET [Top3Prods] AS
'{ TopCount ([Product].[Brand].Members, 3,
     ([Measures].[Top10profit], [Time].[1998])) }'
SELECT
{ CrossJoin ([Top3Prods], {[Time].[1997], [Time].[1998]}) } on columns,
{ TopCount ([Customer].[Individual].Members, 10,
     ([Measures].[Profit], [Time].[1998])) } on rows
FROM Sales
WHERE ( [Measures].[Profit] )
```

This helps us out. We are now looking at the top three products of the top ten customers, which will give us a better picture of those products and customers in particular. Although these customers could be a fairly homogeneous group, each of them may well be fairly different from the others. (They also may be pretty different from the average customer in terms of product preferences; we will explore that later in this section as well.) In terms of our individual customers' favorite product mixes, we can get even more precise than we have, but the MDX will require a quantum leap in sophistication.

Exploring possibilities that don't give us what we are looking for helps us understand the MDX that does give us what we need. MDX's tuple orientation allows us to take the top N tuples from a set from multiple dimensions. However, taking the top N tuples from a customer-product set, by cross-joining customers and products together, won't give us what we are looking for. We are interested in ten customers and three products for each customer. However, the top 30 customer-product combinations (TopCount (CrossJoin (. . .), 30, . . .) could be dominated by 30 products sold to the most profitable customer. The top 30 customer-products of the top ten customers isn't any better. Taking the top three products of the top ten customers involves somehow breaking it up among the customers, instead of cross-joining customer and product sets. The MDX function that allows us to do this is Generate().

If we are going to create a set named Top3ProdsOf10Custs, the basic template for this is going to be

```
WITH
SET [Top10Custs] AS
'{ TopCount ([Customer].[Individual].Members, 10,
      ([Measures].[Profit], [Time].[1998])) }'
. . .
SET [Top3ProdsOf10Custs] AS
'{ Generate ([Top10Custs], . . . )}'
```

Within the Generate() function, for each tuple in the set Top10Custs we want to find the top three products. The following looks tempting:

```
Generate ([Top10Custs], TopCount ([Product].[Brand].Members, 3,
    ([Measures].[Profit], [Customer].CurrentMember, [Time].[1998])))
```

But even that will not get us there. (The `[Customer].CurrentMember` is completely superfluous and is only included to clarify our interest in the operation. The current member of a dimension does not need mentioning in this context unless we are going to modify it or access something related to it.) It will get us partway there, but when we put it into a query the total result (as shown in Figure 9.8) isn't what we want:

```
WITH
SET [Top10Custs] AS
'{ TopCount ([Customer].[Individual].Members, 10,
      ([Measures].[Profit], [Time].[1998])) }'
SET [Top3ProdsOf10Custs] AS
'{ Generate ([Top10Custs], TopCount ([Product].[Brand].Members, 3,
      ([Measures].[Profit], [Time].[1998]))) }'
SELECT
{ [Time].[1997], [Time].[1998]} on columns,
{ [Top3ProdsOf10Custs] } on rows
FROM Sales
WHERE ( [Measures].[Profit] )
```

Our Generate() clause returned the right products but no customers. How do we get the customers in? The Generate() function returns a set with the dimensionality of the second set, not the first set. We cannot express

```
Generate( [Top10Custs],
{ [Customer].CurrentMember, TopCount ([Product].[Brand].Members, 3,
      ([Measures].[Profit], [Time].[1998])))
```

since that is syntactically and semantically illegal (we are mixing customer and product members in a single set). Using the following query we can, however,

	1997	1998
Gobi Crab Cakes	25,000	28,400
Silver Scales	24,500	26,900
Poseidon's Platter	21,100	19,000

Figure 9.8   Results of first try.

combine the customer member with the product set using the CrossJoin() function, which will give us the customer by product tuples that we want:

```
Generate ( [Top10custs],
  CrossJoin (
    {[Customer].CurrentMember },
    TopCount ([Product].[Brand].Members, 3,
      ([Measures].[Profit], [Time].[1998]))
    )
  )
```

At last, we have the tuples that we want (see Figure 9.9). Note that in this last
version of the query, we did need to reference the current member of the customer dimension in order to have the result set contain both customers and
products.

Analytically, this particular result is useful for the fairly arbitrary cutoffs that
we chose to define important products for important customers. Importance is
defined here as importance to our organization (we are looking at profitability,
not units, revenue, value of long-term contracts, etc.). The thresholds here are
very arbitrary, since we are choosing the top N products and customers. Choosing sets of customers and products based on their percentage contribution to

		1997	1998
Hudson Food Dists.	Gobi Crab Cakes	1,200	1,370
Hudson Food Dists.	Silver Scales	1,400	1,250
Hudson Food Dists.	Poseidon's Platter	1,100	1,000
Barbara, Levin Inc.	Gobi Crab Cakes	1,120	990
Barbara, Levin Inc.	Briny Deep	1,040	980
Barbara, Levin Inc.	Silver Scales	1,200	1,300
...	...	...	...

Figure 9.9   Results of desired query.

profits, revenues, and the like would be a less arbitrary choice, and these are equally easy. For example, for the set of customers that form our most profitable 10 percent, what are the most profitable 20 percent of the products they each buy? Replacing the TopCount() function in our expression with TopPercent() will give us the following:

```
SET [Top 10% of Custs] AS
'{ TopPercent ([Customer].[Individual].Members, 10,
      ([Measures].[Profit], [Time].[1998])) }'
SET [Top 20% Prods Of Top 10% Custs] AS
'{ Generate ( [Top 10% of Custs],
    CrossJoin ( { [Customer].CurrentMember },
      TopPercent ([Product].[Brand].Members, 20,
        ([Measures].[Profit], [Time].[1998])
      )
    )
  )
}'
```

This can lead us to several other useful related queries. For example, this expression gives us the products per customer. If our goal is to then focus on the production, distribution, or pricing of these products, we may be interested in removing the specific customers and looking just at the products. Each customer is likely to have products in common with other customers. In fact, it is not immediately obvious how many different products there are in this group. The set of customers is not known in advance of the query—how can we find out the number of products or the set of products?

The answer can be found by using the MDX Extract() function, which returns a set of selected dimensionality. We can use it to return the unique set of products from our selected customer by product tuples, as with the following expression:

```
SET [Top 10%'s Top 20 Products] AS
'Extract ([Top 20% Prods Of Top 10% Custs], [Product])'
```

Extract() returns only unique tuples, so we don't have to worry about finding duplicates. The products will be in a fairly arbitrary order, and we can sort them further if we want to. We can also take this set and count the tuples to find out how many products make up this group.

If our goal is to understand how these customers are or are not representative of our customers as a whole, we may want to compare the product mix purchased by the top 10 percent of customers with the product mix purchased by the average customer. Which brands that are in the top 20 percent by profitability for our top 10 percent of customers are also in the top 20 percent of profitability for all customers? Which ones are peculiar to the top customers? Which ones, if any, are among the most profitable products for all customers but not among the most profitable products for our top customers? If we are exploring customers and products by profitability, these are also important questions.

This last set of three questions could be answered in one query, and we will continue our train of thought to create it. There is one creative leap that we will make to put it together. The goal is to create a grouping of products into three different groups: those corresponding to only the top ten customers, those which correspond to both the top ten group and across all customers, and those that correspond only across all customers and not within the top ten. These three groups represent customer populations, and we will use three calculated members on the customer dimension to represent these groups. (If no products exist in one of these three groups, we will not have any product-customer group tuples that use that customer group, and that group will not appear in the query result.)

We need to construct two basic sets and then manipulate them to get the third. The first set, of top products for top customers, we have already created as [Important Products]. The second set, of top products across all customers, is similar:

```
SET [Top 20% Prods Across All Custs] AS
'TopPercent ([Product].[Brand].Members, 20,
    ([Measures].[Profit], [Time].[1998]))'
```

The trick will now be to create three divisions between those two sets. We need to pool them together before dividing them up, using the following expression:

```
SET [Product Union] AS 'Union ([Top 20% Prods Across All Custs],
[Top 10%'s Top 20 Products])'
```

(We could also create the same effect with the following expression:)

```
Distinct ({[Top 20% Prods Across All Custs],
    [Top 10%'s Top 20 Products] })
```

Now, we simply create three subsets using set functions in sequence:

```
SET [Top10 Only] AS
'Except ([Product Union], [Top 20% Prods Across All Custs])'
SET [Both Groups] AS
'Intersect ([Top 10%'s Top 20 Products],
    [Top 20% Prods Across All Custs])'
SET [All Customers Only] AS
'Except ([Top 20% Prods Across All Custs], [Product Union])'
```

The last step is to create the calculated members that will group these three subsets. "Calculated members" implies computation; what formula will calculate the cells within these sets without altering the contents of the cells?

We know that we want to use some sort of default member for this calculation. These members are on the Customer dimension, so a formula of [Customer]. [All Customer] will make sense. That formula will cause the values of each of the products to be taken from the [All Customer] member for whatever measure is being calculated. So, the three calculated members can each have a very simple formula:

```
MEMBER [Customer].[Top 10% Only Group] AS '[Customer].[All Customer]'
MEMBER [Customer].[Top 10% And All Group] AS '[Customer].[All Customer]'
MEMBER [Customer].[All Customers Only Group] AS '[Customer].[All
Customer]'
```

And we can create our final set of tuples for reporting on as follows:

```
SET [Report Tuples] AS '{
  CrossJoin ( { [Customer].[Top 10% Only Group] }, [Top10 Only] ),
  CrossJoin ( { [Customer].[Top 10% And All Group] }, [Both Groups] ),
  CrossJoin ( { [Customer].[All Customers Only Group] }, [All Customers
Only]) }'
```

When we put it all together, it forms the following (long) query, whose results are shown in Figure 9.10:

```
WITH
SET [Top 10% of Custs] AS
'TopPercent ([Customer].[Individual].Members, 10,
      ([Measures].[Profit], [Time].[1998]))'
SET [Top 20% Prods Of Top 10% Custs] AS
'Generate( [Top 10% of Custs],
  CrossJoin (
    {[Customer].CurrentMember},
    TopPercent ([Product].[Brand].Members, 20,
      ([Measures].[Profit], [Time].[1998])
    )
  )
)'
SET [Top 10%'s Top 20% Products] AS
  'Extract ([Top 20% Prods Of Top 10% Custs], [Product])'
SET [Top 20% Prods Across All Custs] AS
  'TopPercent ([Product].[Brand].Members, 20,
      ([Measures].[Profit], [Time].[1998]))'
SET [Product Union] AS
  'Union ([Top 20% Prods Across All Custs], [Top 10%'s Top 20%
Products])'
SET [Top10 Only] AS
  'Except ([Product Union], [Top 20% Prods Across All Custs])'
SET [Both Groups] AS
  'Intersect ([Top 10%'s Top 20% Products],
  [Top 20% Prods Across All Custs])'
SET [All Customers Only] AS
  'Except ([Top 20% Prods Across All Custs], [Product Union])'
MEMBER [Customer].[Top 10% Only Group] AS '[Customer].[All Customer]'
MEMBER [Customer].[Top 10% And All Group] AS '[Customer].[All Customer]'
MEMBER [Customer].[All Customers Only Group] AS '[Customer].[All Cus-
tomer]'
```

		1997	1998
Top 10% Only Group	Gobi Crab Cakes	25,000	28,400
Top 10% Only Group	Silver Scales	24,500	26,900
Top 10% And All Group	Poseidon's Platter	21,100	19,000
Top 10% And All Group	Mako Steak-o	18,300	21,000
All Customers Only Group	Atlantic Trench Mouthfuls	18,100	16,300

Figure 9.10   Results of full query.

```
SET [Report Tuples] AS '{
   CrossJoin ( { [Customer].[Top 10% Only Group] }, [Top10 Only] ),
   CrossJoin ( { [Customer].[Top 10% And All Group] }, [Both Groups] ),
   CrossJoin ( { [Customer].[All Customers Only Group] }, [All Customers
Only])
}'
SELECT
{ [Time].[1997], [Time].[1998] } on columns,
{ [Report Tuples] } on rows
FROM SalesInfo
WHERE ([Measures].[Profit])
```

Whew! Although this is an involved query, it is not as complex as it would have been if we had tried to perform the same operation in SQL against the original source tables!

Summary

Although we have discussed a number of topics in this chapter, we have used only a fraction of the MDX functions available. It would not be possible to exhaustively cover all applications and MDX techniques in any one book. Hopefully, this chapter has given you all of the conceptual tools you need to understand how MDX functions as a language and how Microsoft OLAP Services and MDX work together so you can construct as sophisticated an application as your situation requires.

CHAPTER 10

Maintaining Applications

The nineteenth-century British prime minister Benjamin Disraeli once remarked, "The only constant in politics is change." Similarly, OLAP systems will undergo constant change during life. One obvious change will be new data values for measures over time. Historical data will also require adjustment, and dimensions will change. New customers and new products may appear, and today's dimension hierarchy will mutate to reflect the structure of your organization tomorrow. For example, employees move to different departments, accounting practices change, and you may adjust product categories to reflect the changing nature of your business and markets. In this chapter, we will explain how to manage changes like these for an existing OLAP system. Specifically, we will explore the impact of changes on storage, queries, and calculations and introduce techniques for managing change effectively.

We will start by exploring basic data changes in general and the tools Microsoft OLAP Services provides to handle them in specific. We'll also discuss some strategies for efficiently handling changes in data and to dimension and cube structures. Throughout this chapter we'll also note the performance implications of various types of change. Some changes may affect run-time query performance, while others may affect the performance of maintenance tasks themselves. We leave a detailed discussion of system optimization in OLAP Services to Chapter 11, on optimizing databases and queries. Throughout the chapter, our discussions of processing assume that you have read the discussion of what processing does in Chapter 2.

The Nature of Change

The data and structures we analyze with our OLAP system change in many ways over time. We discuss changes that require the structural modification of dimensions or cubes at the end of this chapter in the section titled "Design Changes." We'll also cover other kinds of changes to a database, such as merging cube partitions, in later sections. In this section, however, we will focus on changes to data that affect the content of our dimensions and cubes. The nature of the changes to the data itself can have numerous ramifications, both straightforward and subtle.

Synchronizing Updates with the Data Source

At the most basic level, new information gets created over time that must be added to an OLAP system to maintain its relevance for analyses. Microsoft OLAP Services offers several mechanisms that allow you to handle new data in a straightforward way.

Your first concern is deciding how often to update your cubes to reflect new data. You may or may not control how and when the data sources for your OLAP system get updated, and, even if you do, the updates may not necessarily be on the same schedule as updates of your OLAP system itself. Data sources may be updated daily, while the kind of reporting and analysis you perform with your OLAP Services database may require that it get only monthly updates. With certain notable exceptions, it is not necessary for your OLAP Services database to match the update schedule of the data warehouse. It is up to you to determine how often to process your dimensions and cubes so new data is added as appropriate for the individual system.

The notable exceptions we just mentioned arise with fact data and cubes or partitions that use ROLAP or HOLAP storage. Because a MOLAP partition holds all of the data in MOLAP storage—both leaf and aggregate—changes in the data source are largely irrelevant. All precalculated aggregate values will always equal the sum (or count, maximum, or minimum) of their composite leaf values. MOLAP-stored data may not match the data in the source warehouse, but it will always be consistent within the context of the OLAP system. With HOLAP and ROLAP partitions, however, Microsoft OLAP Services utilizes data in the source fact table itself to answer all queries that it cannot resolve through precalculated aggregations. In particular, queries against the leaf-level combination of a cube will always go against the source tables. If data changes in the source, users may see inconsistencies between stored aggregates and lower-level data until aggregations are recalculated with a full process or a data refresh.

For example, consider a fact table and query results from a cube that has its HOLAP partition loaded and preaggregated (see Figure 10.1). The query retrieves data from precalculated aggregates for the (Customer, Quarter) level and from the raw fact table for all other level-combinations. After a period of time, new rows of data were added to the fact table for February's sales, and the record for Richard Williams for January was also corrected. The adjusted fact table and the results from a repeat of the original query appear in Figure 10.2.

As you can see, after the update to the fact table the month-level data retrieved for the State, City, and Customer values changed according to the contents of the updated fact table, while the values for the Quarter remained unchanged. It would be a bad idea to base an important decision on the inconsistent data between these levels. If the cube used MOLAP storage, however, the query results would match those in the first version of the table both before and after the data source update.

When using ROLAP or HOLAP storage, you should always be sure you know the update schedule for your warehouse and make sure you are notified about any unscheduled updates. In addition, you may want to control the set of records that are used in the cube or its partitions to avoid any consistency accidents. One way to handle this is to include a column in your fact tables that con-

Month	Customer ID	Customer Name	Sales
January	1	Meehan, Martin	3,000
January	2	Williams, Richard	3,500
January	3	Guber, Peter	3,500

State	City	Customer	January Sales	February Sales	Quarter 1 Sales
Massachusetts			10,000		10,000
	Boston		6,500		6,500
		Meehan, Martin	3,000		3,000
		Williams, Richard	3,500		3,500
	Cambridge		3,500		3,500
		Guber, Peter	3,500		3,500
		Samuelson, Leonard			

Figure 10.1 Fact table data and query results from HOLAP partition *before* fact table update.

tains some form of serial identifier so you can tag records as belonging to a specific update. The identifier could be a replication batch number, or it could be the time stamp indicating when the row was last inserted or modified. You would then combine this identifier with a WHERE clause in the relevant partition definition that filters records relative to this number and maintain that WHERE clause to reflect the correct set of records as the OLAP database is updated.

Note that modified data in the relational source database is not an issue for changes to dimensions. Because OLAP Services uses only its internal, processed dimension structures as its reference for dimension information, changes to data in dimension source tables will not be visible until you update the dimension structures in OLAP Services. Notice that the updated fact table in Figures 10.1 and 10.2 contains sales data for Paul Rodgers, while the query

Month	Customer ID	Customer Name	Sales
January	1	Meehan, Martin	3,000
January	2	Williams, Richard	1,500
January	3	Guber, Peter	3,500
February	1	Meehan, Martin	3,000
February	2	Williams, Richard	1,500
February	3	Guber, Peter	3,500
February	4	Samson, Leonard	1,500
February	5	Rodgers, Paul	500

State	City	Customer	January Sales	February Sales	Quarter 1 Sales
Massachusetts			8,000		10,000
	Boston		4,500	4,500	6,500
		Meehan, Martin	3,000	3,000	3,000
		Williams, Richard	1,500	1,500	3,500
	Cambridge		3,500	5,000	3,500
		Guber, Peter	3,500	3,500	3,500
		Samuelson, Leonard		1,500	

Figure 10.2 Fact table data and query from HOLAP partition *after* fact table update.

does not. Because the customer dimension was not updated in OLAP Services, the data for Paul Rodgers is not included.

WARNING

While the presence of an unrecognized dimension key in a fact table will halt the processing of a partition or cube, Microsoft OLAP Services will ignore unrecognized keys it encounters in the fact table when it satisfies queries. This is the case regardless of whether or not the cube is defined as joining to the dimension table through a cube dimension member key. Thus, it is possible for data that corresponds to entirely new members to enter into the underlying fact table and still get consistent results from queries. Inconsistent results come from records that correspond to new locations that are formed from existing members.

Including New Data

As we discussed in Chapter 2, you can include new data in cubes and dimensions by using an incremental update process instead of doing a full refresh or reprocess. An incremental update only adds selected records to a dimension or cube; it does not repopulate all data. In large cubes, an incremental update will save you a tremendous amount of time over a full data refresh or reprocess.

Incrementally updating the customer dimension presented in the example in Figures 10.1 and 10.2 would mean including the sales value for our new customer, Paul Rodgers, in the query. If we had a ROLAP or HOLAP partition, we would also see the sales values for Mr. Rodgers in result cells that are not satisfied from stored aggregates (see Figure 10.3).

If we now perform an incremental update on the cube so it includes only February data, we would see correct February values for all customers, even at the quarter level (see Figure 10.4). However, unlike new records in dimension tables, Microsoft OLAP Services will not know how to identify the new fact records on its own. In the incremental process step, we specify a WHERE clause on the fact table that identifies the records of interest (for example, WHERE date >= 'Feb 01 1999' and date < 'Mar 01, 1999').

Changing Existing Data

Changes to existing data can be problematic. Notice that the sales for Quarter 1 in our example still do not include the change in sales for Richard Williams. Microsoft OLAP Services offers no method for reloading only specific data sets. Incremental updates add to, rather than replace, our stored aggregates. In our cubes, existing values may be deleted or replaced with new values only by reloading all data for a given partition. For smaller cubes and dimensions, this

State	City	Customer	January Sales	February Sales	Quarter 1 Sales
Massachusetts			10,000	10,000	10,000
	Boston		4,500	4,500	6,500
		Meehan, Martin	3,000	3,000	3,000
		Williams, Richard	1,500	1,500	3,500
	Cambridge		3,500	5,500	3,500
		Guber, Peter	3,500	3,500	3,500
		Samuelson, Leonard		1,500	
		Rodgers, Paul		500	

Figure 10.3 Query after incremental dimension update.

presents little more than a minor inconvenience. For a cube that is based on a fact table with tens of millions of rows that may take upwards of eight hours to process, it presents a significant problem for maintenance! There are some tricks for getting around doing a full refresh or process, however. We'll explore them in greater detail in the section titled "Techniques for Managing Change."

Changes to Dimension Data

As with new fact data, you may include new members in a dimension by doing an incremental update of the dimension. Modifications to existing members, such as name changes or changes in location within the hierarchy, can be made only by fully rebuilding the dimension. Such changes to dimension data, how-

State	City	Customer	January Sales	February Sales	Quarter 1 Sales
Massachusetts			10,000	10,000	20,000
	Boston		4,500	4,500	11,000
		Meehan, Martin	3,000	3,000	6,000
		Williams, Richard	1,500	1,500	5,000
	Cambridge		3,500	5,500	9,000
		Guber, Peter	3,500	3,500	7,000
		Samuelson, Leonard		1,500	1,500
		Rodgers, Paul		500	500

Figure 10.4 Query after incremental cube update.

ever, present more complex issues for our maintenance strategy than those for fact data alone because modifications to existing dimension data will also require that we do a full reprocess of any cubes that use the dimension.

When processing a dimension, Microsoft OLAP Services creates and stores a unique identifier for every member in a dimension based on its unique position within the dimension. OLAP Services uses these internal identifiers, not the member keys or names, to reference members for all actions. The identifier contains complete information about the member and its ancestors, and, according to Microsoft, it is one of the fundamental building blocks that enable OLAP Services to store data efficiently and quickly respond to queries. If the hierarchy of members or the member order within a hierarchy change, the identifiers for the moved members (and all descendants of those members) would reflect invalid information about the member's position. The first version of Microsoft OLAP Services cannot modify existing identifiers. The only way to reflect changes to member position is to rebuild the dimension. And if a dimension is rebuilt, any cubes that use the dimension must also be fully reprocessed to synchronize the cube definitions with the new member identifiers. The current version of OLAP Services is also unable to modify member names or keys in existing dimension structures without rebuilding those structures (though member properties and their values may be modified without such a drastic impact).

In the examples in Figure 10.1 and 10.2, for instance, you may have noticed that the spelling for Leonard Samuelson's last name changed when the data source was updated. However, this change was never reflected in our queries. The only way for our database to recognize and reflect this change in the updated data source is to fully rebuild the customer dimension and then fully reprocess any cubes that use the dimension.

We must also consider how we wish to reflect dimensional change in our database. What if Peter Guber moves from Cambridge to Boston in March? How do we treat his sales? Dimensions whose members at any level represent individual people are notoriously dynamic, as we have a tendency to marry, die, cross state lines, and otherwise wreak havoc on orderly categorizations. Ralph Kimball calls this topic "Slowly changing dimensions" and divides our options into three logical types based upon how we wish to recognize prechange and postchange data. Given the wide acceptance of these classifications, we too will use them here.

One way to handle dimension change is to rewrite history. If a member's name changes or it changes position within the hierarchy, we want to view all historical data under the new name or position. Such dimension changes are classified as "Type 1." Implementing a Type 1 change, we would see January and

February sales for Peter Guber of Boston and either not see "Peter Guber of Cambridge" or see no data under "Peter Guber of Cambridge." Although it is conceptually straightforward, handling dimension change using the Type 1 method is a challenge for OLAP Services. To reflect the change of Peter Guber's city from Cambridge to Boston in our dimension table we must fully reprocess the dimension and as a result fully reprocess the cube regardless of partitioning. As we noted earlier, for large cubes this can take a great deal of time. If we want to reflect changes on a daily basis but our cube takes eighteen hours to process, full processing is clearly unacceptable.

Another way to deal with dimension change is to keep historical data under the old name or position in the dimension hierarchy and show current and future data using new member or member position. Such dimension changes are classified as "Type 2." Once Mr. Guber has moved, we would see any new sales data under "Peter Guber of Boston," while preserving January and February sales under "Peter Guber of Cambridge."

Type 2 dimensions are handled quite simply since we can add new members with only an incremental update of our dimension and cube. When Peter Guber moves, we simply add a new version of Mr. Guber as a new member with a new customer ID into the customer dimension table, with a parent member of Boston. Upon incrementally updating the customer dimension, OLAP Services adds the new Peter Guber under Boston but does not remove the old Peter Guber from Cambridge. Adding any new fact data in March with Mr. Guber's new ID causes January and February sales to appear with "Peter Guber of Cambridge" and March data with "Peter Guber of Boston."

The third way to handle dimensional change is to keep track of all changes in parallel for both backward and forward viewing. Implementing this type of change we would see all sales for Peter Guber for all periods whether we looked at him in Boston or Cambridge. To do this, we could add a new member for Peter Guber as we did with our Type 2 change. Our fact table will need to include sales figures for both Peter Gubers for all periods. The problem with this type of change is self-evident: if we have duplicate data for Peter Guber, once in Boston and again in Cambridge, we will see inflated values in Massachusetts. Because of the purely additive nature of OLAP services, this problem is unavoidable.

Implementing Change

Implementing change in Microsoft OLAP Services is handled differently for dimensions and cubes.

Dimensions

To update dimension data, select the dimension in the OLAP Manager, right click on the dimension, and select "Process," or choose "Process . . . " from the console "Action" menu. This opens the dimension processing dialog as shown in Figure 10.5.

As we mentioned earlier, dimensions may be either incrementally processed or fully rebuilt. Incremental updating adds any new members and updates the values for any member properties for all members. All of these changes are immediately visible to any client. Rebuilding the dimension does exactly what it implies. It completely rebuilds the structure of the dimension as stored internally by Microsoft OLAP Services. Because this modifies the unique member codes used by cubes, any and every cube that utilizes the dimensions must be fully reprocessed for changes to be visible. An affected cube's internal status is changed to indicate that it must be processed fully, and the cube's data cannot be queried by clients. Queries by clients that have an open connection to OLAP Services and that queried a cube before it was disabled will still return values if the query can be resolved by data in the client cache. Queries that request new data from the server, however, will return an error.

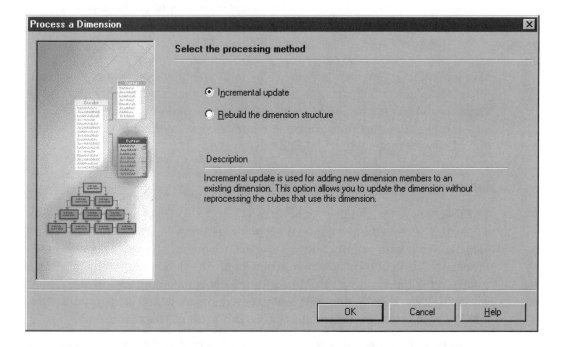

Figure 10.5 Dimension processing dialog.

Keep in mind that modifications to existing dimension members can affect existing calculations, both in front-end queries and in those stored with a cube as calculated members. We have not yet explained how members are referenced in MDX queries and calculated members. The naming of members is sensitive to the placement of a member in the hierarchy, including cases where a member's string of ancestors goes to the root of the hierarchy. OLAP Services has no mechanism to tell you before or after the fact whether a rebuilt dimension invalidates any existing calculated members.

Even incremental processing can affect cubes' aggregation design. As we noted earlier, OLAP Services's aggregation design algorithm determines optimal aggregations based on the amount of data in the fact table and the number of members in a dimension at any given level. If the number of members changes significantly, you may want to redesign aggregations for cubes that use the dimension. We cover aggregation design more fully in Chapter 11, on optimizing databases and queries.

Finally, private dimensions are processed when, and only when, a cube is fully processed. As we noted in Chapter 3, new members in private dimensions will not be visible unless the cube is fully processed. If the fact table contains data for any such new members, an "Unknown Dimension Member" error will indicate that the refresh or incremental update processing of the cube has failed.

Cubes

Microsoft OLAP Services allows us to incrementally update or completely refresh data in a cube in a way similar to that for dimensions. In the Enterprise version, OLAP Services also permits you to merge one or more cube partitions into another cube partition. We'll begin our discussion of implementing change for cubes with Incremental and Refresh updates.

Incremental and Refresh

The mechanics for updating cube data is similar to that for updating dimensions. To update data using the OLAP Manager console, select the cube in the console's tree pane, right click, and select "Process . . . " or select "Action | Process . . ." from the console menu (see Figure 10.6). "Process" fully processes a cube, rebuilding internal structures for the cube, including any private dimensions. "Refresh Data" completely rewrites existing data and aggregations. Only a full refresh or full process will update modifications to existing data.

"Incremental Update" allows you to merge a subset of fact data with existing data. Selecting incremental update starts the incremental update wizard. If this is the first time you have used the incremental update wizard you will see an

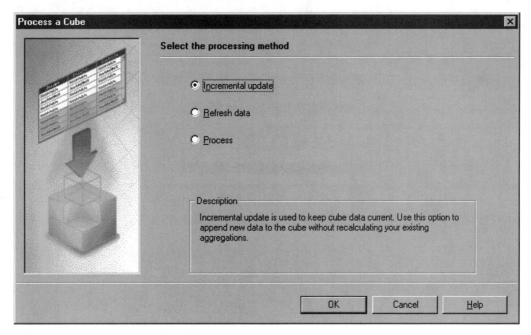

Figure 10.6 Cube processing dialog.

opening dialog that describes the wizard. Checking the "Skip This Screen in the Future" checkbox with your mouse will prevent the description dialog from being displayed in the future. If the cube has more than one partition, you will next be asked which partition you want to update, as shown in Figure 10.7 (as noted in Chapter 2, partitions can only be incrementally updated individually). Otherwise, you will be brought directly to a dialog where you can select the fact table that contains the new data (see Figure 10.8). By default, the wizard selects the fact table in the partition definition. In the last step (see Figure 10.9), you are given the opportunity to enter a filter expression.

You must exercise great care when selecting data for an incremental load. All data that is loaded incrementally gets added to existing data, which can potentially cause double-counting if it is not filtered accurately. Microsoft OLAP Services does not verify incremental data loads and will not warn you if your selection overlaps existing data. At the same time, the additive nature of incremental loading offers you a way to handle changes to historical data and to manage Type 1 changes to dimensions.

If you defined the updated partition with a WHERE clause, the WHERE clauses employed for incremental processing will be appended to the existing WHERE clause for the partition. OLAP Services keeps this combined clause with the

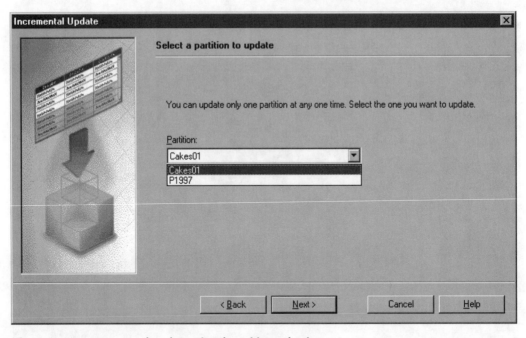

Figure 10.7 Incremental update wizard partition selection.

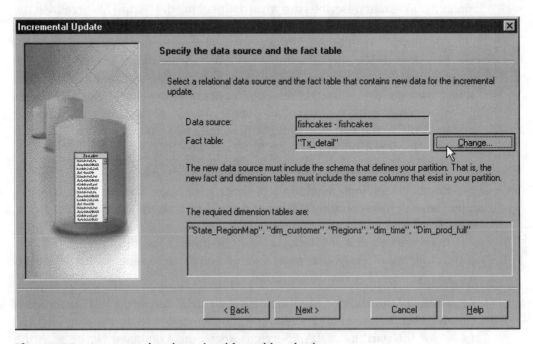

Figure 10.8 Incremental update wizard fact table selection.

partition definition, so any future refresh or processing of the partition will include the incremental data as well.

Continuing with the example we introduced in Figure 10.1 and 10.2, we will create a partition that filters the fact table to include only data for 1998. The WHERE clause may look something like this:

```
(fact.date between #1/1/1998# and #12/31/1998#).
```

To incrementally load new 1999 data that resides in the same fact table, we would use the following WHERE clause:

```
(fact.date between #1/1/1999# and #12/31/1999#).
```

When we look at the WHERE clause for the partition after we perform the incremental update, we'll see the following:

```
(fact.date between #1/1/1998# and #12/31/1998#) OR (fact.date between
#1/1/1999# and #12/31/1999#).
```

Note that if you use a different fact table than the one defined for the partition for an incremental load of a partition, the incremental data will *not* be included with a future cube refresh or full process. Microsoft OLAP Services maintains a reference to only a single fact table for a cube partition. When you are performing a refresh or full processing of a partition, OLAP services will not be aware of any other fact tables that you may have used in incremental loads and

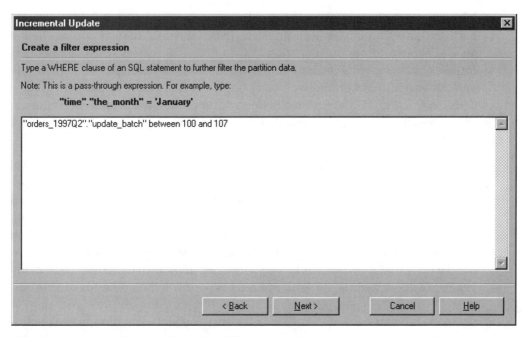

Figure 10.9   Incremental update wizard filter expression.

will load data only from the fact table in the partition definition. For example, suppose your cube is defined using a fact table named "sales" and you incrementally load data from another fact table named "sales_june". In this case, if you refresh the cubes data or fully process the cube, OLAP Services will only include the facts in the "sales" table.

One way to handle new data in a fact table that is different than the fact table defined for a partition is to append the new fact records to the partition's regular fact table (*after* you perform the incremental load for a ROLAP or HOLAP partition so as to avoid unsynchronized data). Alternatively, if the partition's fact table is based on a view, you can instead modify the view to UNION ALL data in both tables. Using either of these options will help you avoid using a WHERE clause in the partition definition, and the data will always be available in further processing.

Another way to handle incremental data in separate fact tables is to create unique partitions for each one. In fact, data that can be logically separated may be better suited for partitions. If you have the Enterprise version of SQL Server OLAP Services, and there is a good logical reason for keeping incremental data in separate tables, then go ahead and use partitions to efficiently manage the separate fact tables.

Merging Partitions

When partitions use identical aggregations, you may merge them into a single partition. Merging copies all aggregate data (and leaf data if you are using MOLAP storage) from one partition into another. This offers you a distinct performance advantage over modifying and processing a partition. We explore the performance differences between merging and redefining partitions in greater detail in Chapter 11. Here we will concentrate on the mechanics and things to watch out for. As with incremental updating, merging carries an inherent risk of data overlap.

When might you wish to merge partitions? Well, OLAP Services actually merges partitions when performing an incremental load on an existing partition (even in non-Enterprise versions). In an incremental load, OLAP Services creates a temporary partition with the same aggregation design as the existing partition, loads the new data from the data source into the temporary partition, and then merges the temporary partition into the existing partition. Suppose you want to build a cube that is based upon a very large fact table with data that spans many years. We know that most of our analysis is performed on data for the current year. To optimize query performance we could partition all prior year data in one partition and current year data in another. We include a filter in the historical partition so that it includes only data for prior years and define a slice for our current year partition based on the current year. With this arrangement we ensure that we have correct data in our cube and that queries requesting only current year data will only use the smaller current-year partition. Because of the large amount of data, the historical partition takes several hours to process. Throughout the year we refresh the data in our current-year partition so that it includes new monthly data–a task that, using incremental loads, generally lasts under an hour. At the end of the year we need to move the current-year data to the historical partition. Since the OLAP Services's incremental load process involves creating a temporary partition, it makes most sense to simply merge the partitions and create a new partition for new current year data.

To merge partitions, select a partition you wish to merge into another in the console tree pane, right click, and select "Merge . . . ". This brings up the partition merge dialog shown in Figure 10.10. Select the partition you wish to merge this partition into and click "OK." Microsoft OLAP Services will add the data in the first partition to the data in the second partition and then delete the first partition.

When you include partition merging in your maintenance strategy, pay close attention to slices and filters. Merged partitions will contain slices that use the nearest common member in the dimension hierarchy of the slices defined in the source partitions. If a slice is defined in both partitions using the same

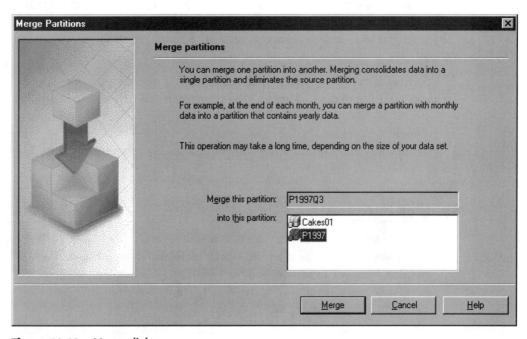

Figure 10.10 Merge dialog.

member for a given dimension, the merged partition retains that slice definition. If the slices for a given dimension are defined with different members, the merged partition will contain a slice definition for the nearest common parent. In cases where one partition identifies a slice for a specific dimension member while the other defines no slice for that dimension, the merged partition would contain no slice for that dimension (i.e., a slice on the All level for the dimension).

For example, if two partitions are sliced by January 1998 of the time dimension, the resulting merged partition will also contain January 1998 in its slice definition. If one partition contains a slice defined for January 1, 1998, and the other January 2, 1998, the resulting partition will be for the slice of January 1998. Should one of the partitions contain no explicit slice definition for the time dimension, the merged partition would contain no slice definition for the time dimension.

OLAP Services treats filters in a slightly different way. It will not attempt to determine a common parent in two filters. Instead, filters are concatenated with "OR" in merged partitions. For example, if one partition contains the filter (`"fact_basic"."trans_date" = #1/1/1998#`) and another contains (`"fact_basic"."trans_date" = #1/2/1998#`), the merged partition will contain (((`"fact_basic"."trans_date" = #1/1/1998#`)) OR ((`"fact_basic"."trans_date" = #1/2/1998#`))). Note that this means that if either partition contains no filter, the resulting partition will not contain a filter (i.e., `WHERE * OR ((`"fact_basic"."trans_date" = #1/1/1998#`))` is the same as no WHERE clause at all).

Again, Microsoft OLAP Services will not warn you if slices or filters in merged partitions overlap any other partitions. As we mentioned in Chapter 3, this slice and WHERE clause logic can lead to many possible overlap issues. For example, if you have partitions with slices defined for January, February, and March, respectively, March will be double-counted in the cube when you merge only the January and February partitions. If the time hierarchy contains quarters, the

Splitting Partitions

While Microsoft OLAP Services allows you to merge partitions, it offers you no direct way to split a partition into one or more different partitions. There is nothing, however, to prevent you from redefining an existing partition on a smaller slice and/or modifying the WHERE clause and then defining new partition(s) to include missing data.

merged partition will slice on Quarter 1 (the closest common parent for January and February). You can resolve this by adding a WHERE clause to the merged partition to include only January and February data or by eliminating the March partition.

Also pay close attention when you are merging partitions that use different fact tables. The merged partition will only contain a reference for the fact table of the destination partition. As a result, any future full refresh or process will include only data from that fact table. The only way to ensure data integrity in such a situation is to add the data from the fact table for the source into the fact table for the destination.

Techniques for Managing Change

We have discussed how changes to data affect a system. As we've seen, adding new data involves the relatively straightforward process of performing incremental updates on dimensions and cubes. Efficiently handling changes to existing data and slowly changing dimensions, however, is not straightforward. In this section, we detail some techniques for managing these types of change in OLAP Services. These techniques will help you avoid full processing where it would otherwise be needed.

All these techniques are based upon correction or adjustment transactions similar to those used in accounting. To prevent fraud, accounting rules do not allow the modification of historic values. Instead, adjustment transactions are appended in new records. This enables accountants to track every change, yet still see accurate current values. As we noted earlier, we need to be careful with incremental updates and the designing of partitions because OLAP Services does not prevent double loading. We can turn this risk into an advantage, however, by incrementally loading adjustment data. The "double-counting" will in fact provide us with correct current values without requiring us to perform a time-consuming full refresh or process.

These techniques require you to have a fair amount of control over your data source because they require you to add data to existing tables or create new tables. Some of these techniques may be accomplished with views. However, keep in mind that the complexity of a view can impact update performance because the view itself must be processed by the data source before OLAP Services can use the data to update a cube or partition.

The following techniques also *only* work for sum aggregate measures. Count, minimum, and maximum aggregate measures can't be modified with additional fact records. Count aggregation simply counts the number of fact records for a given intersection of dimension members. New fact records containing adjustments will only serve to increase the count value. Minimum and maximum aggregates would evaluate to the minimum and maximum values in a combined set of both the original and correction records (so a maximum measure value could never be decreased and a minimum measure value could never be increased using correction transactions).

To compensate for this problem, we might consider breaking out SUM into separate cubes and using a virtual cube for displaying all measures. With the sum cube we could incrementally load corrections in a fraction of the time required to fully process or refresh our cube containing counts. In practice, however, this approach offers us little real value. We still need to process our non-sum cube fully, and the removal of the sum measures would have only a minimal impact on the required processing time. The primary determinant of the amount of time that will be required to process any cube or partition is the number of dimension levels, members, and fact records there are. The number of measures has a minimal effect (in tests conducted by the author while writing this book, variations in the number of measures in a cube never had more than a 5 percent effect on overall processing time).

Correction Transactions

Measures in correction transaction records should be the difference between the existing and the new value. For example, if our Sales amount is currently 100, but we want to change it to 50, the correction transaction record should contain a Sales value of -50. Loading adjustments into an existing partition through an incremental update or creating a new partition based on the loading adjustments will result in correctly modified data in our cube for measures that sum.

When you are updating the data source, it's good practice to add correction transactions to their own tables before you incrementally update the partition. During the incremental update of our cube, using SQL against a smaller table containing only correction transactions should execute much faster than using SQL with a WHERE clause that filters out pre-existing data from a large fact table. Adding correction data to tables that are different from the ones used for partitions is particularly important if there could be a delay between the time when the data is added to the data source and the partitions are updated if the partitions are ROLAP or HOLAP. As we noted earlier, changes to facts in the data source can introduce inconsistencies between queried aggregate and leaf data for ROLAP or HOLAP partitions. If you are able to use multiple partitions, you can create partitions that are based upon the table that contains correction transactions.

If you do not create partitions for the correction records, you should update the fact table with any corrections once the correction records have been incrementally processed into the cube (again, for ROLAP or HOLAP partitions this is mandatory to avoid inconsistencies between aggregate and leaf data in queries). As we noted earlier, Microsoft OLAP Services does not track incremental loads from different tables. To ensure that correct values will be used in any future full refresh or process of the partition, we should update the fact table to include the corrections after we perform our incremental load. Although our goal with these techniques is to avoid a full refresh or process of a cube or partition, there is no guarantee that we will not have to perform a full refresh or process at some point in the future. For example, some design changes such as changing the name of a measure will remove existing aggregation designs and require us to design new aggregations and fully process a cube. We discuss design changes and their effects later in the chapter. Keeping a partition's fact table up to date with current values ensures that our cubes will always contain correct data. Once the corrections have loaded into a partition, you can use an SQL UPDATE . . . or INSERT INTO . . . to update existing fact table data or append the correction transactions as new records.

Moving Members and Their Data (Type 1 Dimension Change)

The ability to adjust historic data using correction transactions leads us to a method for efficiently handling Type 1 dimension change. You can use correction transactions to "zero out" existing data for a specific member and incrementally load historical and new data to a new member with the same name. This requires us to do several things:

1. Add a new member with the same member name but a new member key to the dimension's source table.

2. Incrementally update the dimension so it contains the new member.

3. Duplicate fact records for the old member using the member key value of the new member.

4. Create correction transactions that zero out fact values for the old member.

5. Incrementally load the data created in steps 3 and 4.

Let's illustrate this process with the example we used to describe Type 1 change at the beginning of this chapter. In this example, we have a simple cube of sales data that is dimensioned by customer with levels for state, city, and customer. In February, one of our customers, Peter Guber, moves from his home in Cambridge to a home in Boston. To handle this as a Type 1 change we first add a new record for Peter Guber and change the city from Cambridge to Boston, as shown in Figure 10.11. Incrementally updating our dimension adds the new Peter Guber to the hierarchy under Boston as shown in Figure 10.12. Next we need to duplicate Mr. Guber's data under his new member key and

Customer ID	Customer Name	City	State
1	Meehan, Martin	Boston	MA
2	Williams, Richard	Boston	MA
3	Guber, Peter	Cambridge	MA
2	Samson, Leonard	Cambridge	MA
3	Rodgers, Paul	Cambridge	MA
3	Guber, Peter	Boston	MA

Figure 10.11 Customer dimension table with new record for moved member.

create correction transaction records that zero out existing data under the old member key. As we recommended earlier, we'll put these correction transaction records into a new table with the following SQL, which will result in the data set shown in Figure 10.13:

```
INSERT INTO fact_corrections (month, customer_id, customer_name sales)
SELECT month, customer_id, customer_name, sales * -1
FROM fact_sales where customer_id = 3

INSERT INTO fact_corrections (month, customer_id, customer_name sales)
SELECT month, 6, customer_name, sales
FROM fact_sales where customer_id = 3
```

If we now incrementally load our cube using the fact data in this new table, we will see that all of the data for Peter Guber appears under his new city (see Figure 10.14). Finally, since we used a fact table that is different from the one

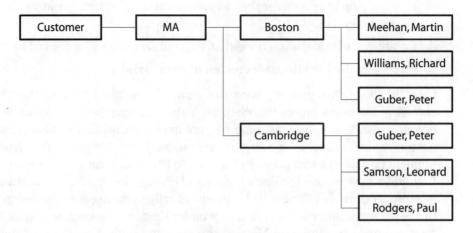

Figure 10.12 Customer dimension with new member.

Month	Customer ID	Customer Name	Sales
January	3	Guber, Peter	-3,500
February	3	Guber, Peter	-3,500
January	6	Guber, Peter	3,500
February	6	Guber, Peter	3,500

Figure 10.13 fact_corrections table after adding correction transactions.

assigned to our partition, we should add the records in our correction fact table to the original fact table to ensure that fully refreshing or processing our cube will include current values.

Note that these procedures do not remove Peter Guber in Cambridge from the cube. As shown in Figure 10.14, queries against the cube would include two Peter Guber members. This could become particularly confusing in queries that request only the members at the bottom level of the customer dimension. One way around this is to create calculated members for all of our measures that return NULL for Peter Guber in Cambridge. Querying only the calculated member measures and using NON EMPTY would eliminate the old member from results. It's desirable to make the calculated member formula more generic since updating calculated member formulas each time a customer moves could be quite burdensome. To do this, we can use a member property to tag moved members. The calculated member formulas can use the member property to

State	City	Customer	January Sales	February Sales	Quarter 1 Sales
Massachusetts			8,000	10,000	18,000
	Boston		8,000	8,000	16,000
		Meehan, Martin	3,000	3,000	6,000
		Williams, Richard	1,500	1,500	3,000
		Guber, Peter	3,500	3,500	7,000
	Cambridge		0	2,000	2,000
		Guber, Peter	0	0	0
		Samuelson, Leonard		1,500	1,500
		Rodgers, Paul		500	500

Figure 10.14 Query results after implementing Type 1 change with correction transactions.

return NULL for any customer tagged as "old." See Chapters 5 and 6 for more information on using MDX in calculated members.

Members Properties and Type 2 Dimension Change

Earlier in this chapter we showed that Type 2 dimensions were handled well with simple incremental updates of dimensions and cubes. To move a member while maintaining history, we simply add the member as a new record in the dimension table with its new parent, incrementally update the dimension to include the new member in the hierarchy, and incrementally load fact data to a new or existing partition.

However, changes to member properties will always be treated as Type 1 change since incrementally updating or rebuilding a dimension always replaces property values for all the members in a dimension with the properties in the dimension's source table. For example, consider a dimension that contains products that have a property of color. What if we want to evaluate the affect of a color change on a product's sales? By default, we won't be able to perform such an evaluation since all sales will only know of the property's current color.

Design Changes

Eventually, you will need to modify the actual design of your system. There are many changes you can make, and they all have ramifications. In this section we describe the various structural changes you can make to objects in Microsoft OLAP Services and the effects that such changes will have on other objects in your system.

For the most part, OLAP services handles such changes smoothly. However, as with the first release of any software, the implementation in OLAP Services is not flawless. For example, if we remove a level from a shared dimension and then process a cube that uses the dimension, OLAP Services will rebuild the dimension before processing the cube. If we change the member key column property for a dimension, which also requires us to rebuild the dimension, OLAP Services will only incrementally update the dimension if we process a cube that uses it. Many of these types of inconsistencies, which we discovered while writing this book, may be fixed through service packs by the time you read this, so we will not go into their minutia here. Instead, we will concentrate on the processes and the order in which these processes should be executed.

Figures 10.15 and 10.16 show the various changes that can be made to OLAP Services objects, the effects that a particular change may have on other OLAP Services objects, and any actions that should be taken to implement the change. For example, look for Add/Delete/Move Level in column 1 of Figure

Change	After Save	Recommended Dimension Action	Recommended Aggregation Action	Recommended Cube Action
Design Changes				
Member Count (Level)	Agg. Designs Dropped	Rebuild Dimension	Design Aggregations	Full Process
Member Key Column (Level)	Agg. Designs Dropped	Rebuild Dimension	Design Aggregations	Full Process
Add/Delete/Move (Level)	Agg. Designs Dropped	Rebuild Dimension	Design Aggregations	Full Process
Order By Key (Level)	Agg. Designs Dropped	Rebuild Dimension	Design Aggregations	Full Process
Name (Level)	Agg. Designs Dropped	Rebuild Dimension	Design Aggregations	Full Process
All Level (Dimension)	Agg. Designs Dropped	Rebuild Dimension	Design Aggregations	Full Process
All Caption (Dimension)	Agg. Designs Dropped	Rebuild Dimension	Design Aggregations	Full Process
Member Name Column		Rebuild Dimension		Full Process
Type (Dimension)		Rebuild Dimension		Full Process
Type (Level)		Rebuild Dimension		Full Process
Add/Modify/Delete Member Property (Level)		Incremental Update		
Unique Members (Level)				Refresh Data
Key Data Size (Level)				Refresh Data
Key Data Type (Level)				Refresh Data
Data Changes				
New Members		Incremental Update		Incremental Update
Delete/Modify/Move Members		Rebuild Dimension		Full Process
Member Property Change		Incremental Update		

Figure 10.15   Dimension design modifications.

10.15. In column 2 we see that adding, deleting, or moving a level causes OLAP Services to drop the aggregation designs in any cubes that use the dimension (but not the aggregations themselves). The third column tells us that we must rebuild the dimension to actually modify the dimension structure stored in OLAP Services. Column 4 tells us that we should design aggregations for dependent cubes. Finally, column 5 tells us that we should fully process those cubes and that fully processing one of the cubes will automatically rebuild the dimension.

Change	After Save	Recommended Aggregation Action	Recommended Cube Action
Design Changes			
Calculated Sets (Cube)			
Calculated Member (Cube)			
Display Format(Measure)			
Is Internal (Measure)			
Fact Table Size (Cube)		Design Aggregations	Full Process
Change Fact Table (Partition)		Design Aggregations	Full Process
Level Member Count (Private Dimension)		Design Aggregations	Refresh Data
Aggregation Prefix (Partition)			Refresh Data
Slice (Partition)			Refresh Data
Filter (Partition)			Refresh Data
Member Key Column (Level)			Refresh Data
Source Column (Measure)			Refresh Data
Schema Joins (Cube)			Refresh Data
All Caption (Private Dimension)			Full Process
Level Unique Member (Private Dimension)			Full Process
Type (Private Dimension)			Full Process
Level Type (Private Dimension)			Full Process
Level Member Name Column (Private Dimension)			Full Process
Level Member Key Type (Private Dimension)			Full Process
Level Member Key Size (Private Dimension)			Full Process
Level Order by Key (Private Dimension)			Full Process
Member Key Column (Private Dimension)			Full Process
Data Type (Measure)			Full Process
Aggregation Function (Measure)			Full Process
Dimension Aggregation Usage (Cube)	Agg. Designs Dropped	Design Aggregations	Full Process
Level Enable Aggregation (Cube)	Agg. Designs Dropped	Design Aggregations	Full Process
Add/Move/Delete Dimension (Cube)	Agg. Designs Dropped	Design Aggregations	Full Process
Level Disable (Cube)	Agg. Designs Dropped	Design Aggregations	Full Process
Add/Move/Delete/Rename measure (Cube)	Agg. Designs Dropped	Design Aggregations	Full Process
Name (Private Dimension)	Agg. Designs Dropped	Design Aggregations	Full Process
All level (Private Dimension)	Agg. Designs Dropped	Design Aggregations	Full Process
Level Names (Private Dimension)	Agg. Designs Dropped	Design Aggregations	Full Process
Data Changes			
New or Modified Data (Private Dimension)			Full Process
Facts Changed			Refresh Data
New Fact Records			Incremental Process

Figure 10.16   Cube design modifications.

Take extreme care when editing and processing OLAP Services objects. We cannot recommend strongly enough that you *plan out all design changes you may need to make before you edit even a single OLAP Services object.* As we noted earlier, rebuilding a dimension disables (prevents clients from seeing or querying) any cubes that use the dimension, which in turn disables any virtual cubes using those cubes. At the same time, fully processing a cube rebuilds any of its dimensions that have been edited and require rebuilding. In addition, processing a virtual cube fully processes any of the cubes it uses that require processing, which in turn rebuilds all of the cubes' dimensions that require rebuilding—which, in turn, may disable other cubes that use the rebuild dimensions!

As a final note, be aware that in the first release of Microsoft OLAP Services processing a cube via the console (right clicking on the cube with your mouse and selecting "Process" from the pop-up menu or selecting "Action|Process" from the console menu) without designing any aggregations for it actually does process the cube without any aggregations. If you are processing from the cube editor, on the other hand, the OLAP Manager warns you that you should create aggregations before processing.

Summary

In this chapter we discussed how data changes over time and the life cycle of OLAP systems in general and how to handle change in Microsoft OLAP Services databases in particular. OLAP Services handles some types of change (new fact and metadata) better than other types of change (changes to existing data and metadata). We've also showed how, in some circumstances, correction transactions can be used to efficiently handle changes to historical data. In Chapter 11 we'll explore ways to fine tune your OLAP Services database during the database design and creation process and over the lifetime of the database.

Optimization

Optimization is a complex process that combines objective facts and subjective decisions. There are some principles that work well in all circumstances, and others which depend on the needs of the particular application. It is up to you, the OLAP developer, to balance conflicting goals and to work within the restrictions placed on you by hardware, software, business requirements and logistics, and the data itself. In this chapter, we will walk you through optimization tasks and arm you with the principles you need to follow so you can make informed decisions about optimizing your OLAP database.

Not all databases need equal attention to optimization. A database that starts out small and will remain small will probably not need any attention at all. A database that starts out large or may grow large over time may need detailed optimization of many aspects. Just as with other aspects of database design, implementation and maintenance, optimization steps create resource overhead. So, choose degrees of optimization as you need them.

Optimizing Microsoft OLAP Services databases involves a number of different areas. One area involves interrelated decisions about the OLAP storage method and the stored aggregates to calculate. With OLAP Services Enterprise edition, the location, form, and logical relationship between storage partitions also enter into the equation. Another area involves the optimization of the RDBMS schema that underlies the OLAP database. A third area involves optimizing MDX queries and calculations. We approach optimization with three goals in mind—minimizing storage, minimizing processing time, and minimizing run-time query execution time. We want to minimize the amount of physical storage space for our databases because (1) we have only so much disk space available and (2) smaller storage consumed requires less I/O during processing and querying. Business requirements also limit the amount of time that is available for processing our cubes. A cube for analyzing daily sales patterns should not take 24 hours to process. And queries are how we obtain our analyses, so we are interested in how to make them perform efficiently. The whole point is to provide simple, flexible, and fast access to data.

We have organized this chapter to follow roughly the same order you would follow when building a database. We start with the data source and move on to the dimension and cube design, OLAP storage options, aggregations, query processing, MDX expressions, and finally touch on relevant server settings.

Data Source

Much of the performance of Microsoft OLAP Services depends on the level of optimization of the database that contains your source data. To create and populate dimensions and aggregations, OLAP Services must first retrieve relevant data from source tables. OLAP Services will also retrieve data from the fact source tables for queries made against partitions that use ROLAP or HOLAP storage. How quickly these tasks occur depends on how well the DBA for the data source has optimized the database.

The DSS Lab Environment

All of the optimization testing we did as research for this chapter took place at the DSS Lab in Cambridge, Massachusetts. SQL Server 7.0 and Microsoft OLAP Services were installed on a 4x400 MHz Pentium II Xeon server with four gigabytes (GB) of RAM. The data resided on a 900 GB Clariion FC5700 storage system accessed through a Fibre Channel interface. All processing query and storage comparisons found in this chapter were derived from tests performed using this hardware. For our examples based on the tutorials in Chapters 15 and 16 we used the same machine for both OLAP Services and the SQL Server data source. For large-scale optimization investigations we created a warehouse with a model that consisted of five dimensions (some both large and deep) loaded with various densities of data, and distributed the database among multiple RDBMS servers.

The detailed tuning of an RDBMS is a complex process and lies outside the scope of this book. The brand of server you use will greatly influence the degree to which you can optimize the data source and the steps that you will need to take to accomplish the optimization. You may not have control over your source database for logistical reasons, or it may be that organizational policy limits your control. Even if you don't know all the ins and outs of optimizing your RDBMS or don't have direct control, you should still make sure that, at a minimum, you have taken the actions described in the following sections. The things you can do to improve the performance of the RDBMS for use with OLAP Services are typical of the optimizing process for all data warehouses.

Indices

Microsoft OLAP Services creates the SQL that populates dimension structures and cube partitions by relying on the key columns that are defined for dimensions. Some of the SQL OLAP Services generates takes the form of SELECT DISTINCT queries for a dimension's joined set of tables. Indices on columns used for joining, and particularly unique indices or primary key constraints for dimension keys, enable the RDBMS to return the requested data to OLAP Services as efficiently as possible. You should create indices on all member key columns in dimension tables. For the fact table, you should create an index on the combined dimension columns for each fact table. For a database like Oracle8 or Red Brick, bitmap dimension indexes may be more appropriate. Note that it is not necessary to index member name or property columns because OLAP Services always utilizes internal dimension structures for this information. As a general rule, use compact join keys where possible: a 16-bit integer for low-cardinality dimensions, a 32-bit integer for high cardinality, or even an 8-bit integer for tiny dimensions.

Views versus Tables

As we have described throughout this book, views offer you tremendous flexibility in designing your dimensions and cubes. Keep in mind, however, the possible impact that views will have on performance. Since views are merely stored SQL queries, they are only as efficient as the SQL they use. A view that contains numerous joins or selects records based on non-indexed columns will not provide results as quickly as one with only a few joins that filter on only indexed columns. The data types of the join keys themselves will also have an impact, even for views with few table joins.

Views that are used for dimensions are not as great a concern as views used for fact tables. If a view for a dimension takes a long time to process, this only impacts the processing of the dimension itself. Once OLAP Services processes a dimension, it stores all metadata internally and uses only these internal structures when it processes cubes and queries.

Views can have a greater impact when they are used to provide facts for a cube, especially when you are using ROLAP or HOLAP storage. For example, consider a data source that contains facts in separate tables according to year. A simple way to build a cube for all years would be to base the cube on a view that uses "UNION ALL" to merge the tables. Depending upon the number of records in the tables, such a view could take several minutes, perhaps even an hour, to query. Using the view will affect MOLAP partitions only during processing, which may be perfectly acceptable. Using the view for ROLAP or HOLAP data, however, will have a dramatic effect on queries made against a partition that OLAP Services cannot satisfy through designed aggregations. In these cases, OLAP Services will use the performance-challenged view to return the appropriate result.

Some complex views may be obviated if you use partitions. Consider our earlier example of different fact tables that contain data for different years. In this case, creating a partition for each year by using the appropriate fact table as the source will accomplish the same goal as creating a single partition based upon a view using "UNION ALL." If you do not have the Enterprise version of Microsoft OLAP Services, your best option may be to create new fact tables.

Dimension and Cube Design

Dimension and cube schema design affects processing for all OLAP storage forms as well as the query speed against ROLAP and HOLAP partitions. We introduced many of these issues in Chapters 2 and 3 and, as promised, we will go into greater detail here.

Table Joins

In our discussion on optimizing the RDBMS data source earlier in this chapter we described how important it is to index key columns. By the same token, it is also important that you join tables in your cube schema *only* by indexed columns in order to take advantage of those indices.

TIP

Only join tables in dimension and cube schemata by indexed columns.

Key Data Type and Size

As we discussed in Chapter 3, the size of OLAP storage is affected by the Key Data Size and Key Data Type properties of dimension levels. Aggregations for a dimension level occupy less disk space if they have a member key that consists of a four-byte integer than if they have a member key defined as a ten-byte character string. This impacts ROLAP storage to a much higher degree than MOLAP or HOLAP. Differences in key data size and type in MOLAP and HOLAP are often mitigated by the compression OLAP Services uses in its own storage of data.

OLAP Manager will set the appropriate size and type when you create a dimension with the wizard and when you add a new level. However, OLAP Manager will not alter the original setting if you change the key column for a level by manually typing in a new key column source definition (as opposed to using the column selection dialog). For example, consider a time dimension created with the dimension wizard that contains levels for year, month, and day. If you were to add a quarter level to this dimension using the OLAP Manager dimension editor, the new level would initially have a key data type of "Date & Time" and a key data size of nine bytes. When you edit the Key Source Column property of the new level to identify quarters using the following SQL expression:

```
datepart ('q', "dimtable"."datecolumn")
```

the key data size and key data type will remain unaffected.

TIP

Always double-check the Key Data Type and Key Data Size properties for all the levels in a dimension.

WARNING

Verify the key data type and key data size before you process the dimension. Changing these will require that you fully reprocess the dimension and all the cubes that depend on it.

Unique Members

As we discussed in Chapter 3, if values for member keys are not unique within a dimension level, OLAP Services must also reference upper-level keys to retrieve correct data from a fact table. This can greatly affect cube processing. Figure 11.1 shows the SQL that is used to process a cube where the "Unique" Member property of the leaf level is set to false. Figure 11.2 shows the SQL that is used for the same cube with the Unique Member property of the time dimension's leaf level set to "True."

When the leaf level is not identified as having unique members, as in Figure 11.1, Microsoft OLAP Services must include all the required parent members to uniquely identify each fact. Note that the Unique Member property by itself

```
SELECT "customer"."cust_id", "product"."prod_id",
DatePart(year,"days"."date_id"),
DatePart(quarter,"days"."date_id"),
DatePart(month,"days"."date_id"), "days"."date_id",
"fact_basic"."sale", "fact_basic"."cost"
FROM "fact_basic", "customer", "product", "days"
WHERE ("fact_basic"."cust_id"="customer"."cust_id") AND
("fact_basic"."prod_id"="product"."prod_id") AND
("days"."date_id"="fact_basic"."trans_date")
```

Figure 11.1 SQL for processing a cube where the time dimension's leaf-level Unique Members property is False.

has a minimal effect on storage. Aggregations always include all the levels above the level defined for the aggregation (this allows the aggregation to satisfy queries against higher levels where there are no existing aggregations without joining to the dimension tables). Because of the fact that multiple levels' worth of keys are stored in each aggregate table, it is especially important to choose compact member keys for non-leaf levels in cubes using ROLAP storage. For MOLAP storage, OLAP Services identifies leaf-level facts through the unique code that is created for each leaf member when the dimension is processed.

Member Key Columns in the Cube Definition

As we discussed in Chapter 3, OLAP Services allows you to define the member key column for any dimension level in the cube schema independently of the member key columns identified in the dimension definition. When processing a cube, OLAP Services uses the member key columns from the cube to generate

```
SELECT "customer"."cust_id", "product"."prod_id",
"days"."date_id", "fact_basic"."sale", "fact_basic"."cost"
FROM "fact_basic", "customer", "product", "days"
WHERE ("fact_basic"."cust_id"="customer"."cust_id") AND
("fact_basic"."prod_id"="product"."prod_id") AND
("days"."date_id"="fact_basic"."trans_date")
```

Figure 11.2 SQL for processing a cube where the time dimension's leaf-level Unique Members property is True.

the SQL that is needed to retrieve data from the RDBMS source. By strategically assigning member key columns for all levels as close to the fact table as possible you minimize the number of joins in the SQL that is generated by OLAP Services to retrieve data. This results in more efficient processing because queries with few joins perform better than queries with many joins.

Let's continue our earlier example. If we change the member key for the leaf levels in our dimensions to the fact table columns instead of to the dimension table columns, Microsoft OLAP Services will use the SQL shown in Figure 11.3 when it processes the cube. This SQL performs no joins (unless the "fact table" is itself a view that performs joins) and will simply scan the table as quickly as possible.

Level Aggregations

It is possible to define specific aggregations for a partition using Decision Support Objects (DSO) (we'll go into this in greater detail later in this chapter when we discuss how OLAP Services designs aggregations). However, the OLAP Manager only offers a way to set boundaries on the aggregations that it will design through the aggregation analyzer. In a cube definition, shared and private dimensions have an "Aggregation Usage" property with options of "Standard," "Top Level Only," "Bottom Level Only," and "Custom." "Standard" tells OLAP Services to design aggregations as needed for any level in the dimension. "Top Level Only" and "Bottom Level Only" tell OLAP Services to only include aggregations that include the top or bottom level of the dimension. "Custom" allows you to turn aggregation on or off by specific level by using the level's "Design Aggregation" property. Figure 11.4 illustrates these relationships.

For example, in the tutorial in Chapter 16 we utilize MDX in a calculated member to get the counts of visitors to a store so we can answer such questions as "How many people purchased something from the produce department in March?" The MDX accomplishes this by requesting all customers with data for the submitted query and returning the count of members in the resulting set. Since every request for this calculated member will always result in a request

```
SELECT "fact_basic"."cust_id", "fact_basic"."prod_id",
"fact_basic"."date_id", "fact_basic"."sale", "fact_basic"."cost"
FROM "fact_basic"
```

Figure 11.3 SQL for processing a cube with an optimized schema.

a) Product leaf only, Geography leaf only

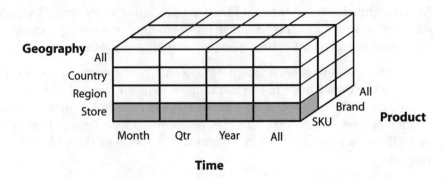

b) Custom: Time.Quarter, Time.All levels disabled

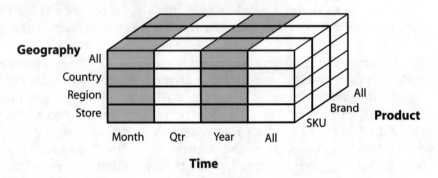

Figure 11.4 Relationship of levels with modified aggregation usage.

for leaf data in the customer dimension, aggregations for higher levels in that dimension will be useless. To optimize our overall application, we put the data for this count calculation in a separate cube and limit aggregations for the customer dimension to "Bottom Level Only." Using 100 percent performance as our goal in the aggregation wizard, OLAP Services creates seven aggregations that have an estimated size of 2.9 megabytes (MB) (with an actual size of 1.26 MB after processing). With aggregation usage for the customer dimension defined as "Standard," the aggregation wizard designed 555 aggregations with an estimated size of 80.4 MB (and an actual size of 7.71 MB after processing).

Calculated Members

Because calculated members are simply stored MDX expressions that OLAP Services executes when a query requests the calculated member, it's important that you understand the efficiency of the MDX used to define calculated members. For this purpose, we cover optimizing MDX expressions fully in its own section, "MDX Expressions," later in this chapter. It's important to point out here, however, that for those unavoidable cases in which one or more calculated members may impact performance, you may want to segregate the data that supports those members into distinct cubes, as demonstrated in the frequent shopper program tutorial in Chapter 16. Although the measure data is dispersed among different optimized cubes, you can provide a single view of all the cubes and put the calculated member(s) into a virtual cube. When OLAP Services submits a query to a virtual cube that requires data from multiple cubes, it will query the source cubes in parallel.

OLAP Storage Options

We described the differences between the three storage forms used by OLAP Services (MOLAP, HOLAP, and ROLAP) in Chapter 2. By understanding the basic architecture of these three storage forms you can get a good indication of how they perform relative to each other. Because the RDBMS creates, populates, and holds all aggregations for ROLAP partitions, we would expect these partitions to take longer to process and occupy more space than the other two forms. At the same time, we would expect MOLAP to take more time to process and to use more disk space than HOLAP because it will store leaf- data as well as aggregations.

To compare the three forms in greater detail, we built the Paid Claims cube described in Chapter 15 in the DSS Lab. We designed aggregations for all three storage forms with a performance target of 30 percent, which resulted in sixty-five aggregations. The table in Figure 11.5 shows the differences in processing time and the resulting storage requirements for all three forms.

As you would expect, ROLAP took the greatest amount of time to process and required the greatest amount of additional disk storage space (more than twice that of MOLAP, which contains leaf data as well as aggregations!). HOLAP took the least amount of time to process and required the least amount of storage space. MOLAP took slightly longer than HOLAP to process but was faster than ROLAP by a factor of over ten.

We have also conducted similar tests in the DSS Lab with much larger databases, which consisted of tens and hundreds of millions of fact table records with dimensions containing up to 200,000 members. The results of all the tests were similar to those for the Paid Claims cube shown in Figure 11.5. Processing ROLAP partitions generally takes anywhere from 10 to 15 times longer and requires 3 to 4 times the space of MOLAP partitions. The number of aggrega-

Starting RDBMS size: 10.690mb

Storage Form	Difference in Processing Time	Data Size (additional)
MOLAP	0%	3.180mb
HOLAP	-10%	0.345mb
ROLAP	1,019%	7.120mb

Figure 11.5 Processing and storage comparison of MOLAP, HOLAP, and ROLAP.

tions is the driving force for this difference, and the factor increases with the number of aggregations. HOLAP processing performance differs from MOLAP processing performance according to the amount of leaf data, and the difference in processing performance speed grows with the amount of leaf data. In general, a MOLAP partition will take only 10 percent to 20 percent longer to process than a HOLAP partition, despite the fact that it is two orders of magnitude larger.

Our understanding of the three storage forms also allows us to predict the behavior of queries against cubes. Queries that Microsoft OLAP Services can resolve through the data that resides in optimized OLAP Services structures should execute faster than queries that require OLAP Services to look to the RDBMS source data for resolution. Again we return to the DSS Lab for details. Figure 11.6 shows the performance of queries against one of the large cubes we mentioned earlier. The cube contained 5 dimensions. The dimensions included one customer dimension that had three levels below "All" and 5,000 leaf members and a product dimension that had five levels below "All" and 100,000 leaf members (and 12 to 30 million fact records). We designed aggregations based on a 10 percent performance benefit and created 17 aggregations. The first column in Figure 11.6 shows the amount of time it took OLAP Services to return results for a query that was satisfied directly by an existing aggregation. The second column shows the execution speed for a query that OLAP Services could resolve by aggregating existing aggregations. The last column shows the performance of a query that could only be satisfied by accessing leaf-level data.

Storage Form	Query Against Existing Aggregation	Query Requiring Aggregation of Existing Aggregation	Query Requiring Aggregation of Leaf Data
MOLAP	<1	<1	41
HOLAP	<1	<1	144
ROLAP	5	10	144

Figure 11.6 Query performance comparison (in seconds) of MOLAP, HOLAP, and ROLAP.

Performance Targets and the PivotTable Service Cache

You may notice that to test query performance we used the rather low performance target of 10 percent to design aggregations for our large cube. We did this to test raw data access. For a performance target of 10 percent, OLAP Services's aggregation analyzer designed 17 aggregations. With these aggregations it was fairly easy to devise MDX queries that OLAP Services could resolve only by aggregating leaf-level data at query time. For a 30 percent target the analyzer designed 38 aggregations. Although the number of aggregations was only a little more than doubled, a large number of level-combinations became supported by at least one aggregate!

Most meaningful queries will request data that is non-leaf in at least one dimension (otherwise, you might as well query the relational source directly). However, you may still find that the leaf levels of large dimensions are unsupported by aggregation. We discuss this in greater detail in the next section, "Aggregations." The effectiveness of the PivotTable Service and its client cache hindered our ability to easily gauge the time it takes OLAP Services to resolve queries according to storage form. When a complex query that required leaf data from our ROLAP partition executed for the first time, it took 144 seconds to return results. After that, resubmitting the query always returned results in under a second. Executing a second query that would summarize data in existing aggregations also returned results in under a second (because the PivotTable Service could provide results based on the data already in its local cache from the first query).

Because the "REFRESH CUBE" statement will not flush the cache if there are no changes at the server, we needed to shut down the ADO application that we created to time the query execution between each query so we could accurately determine how long OLAP Services took to return results! Although the aggregation analyzer and PivotTable services make it more difficult to test the raw data access time for OLAP Services, they clearly do their jobs well in terms of optimizing client query performance.

As Figure 11.6 shows, the lab experiments bear out our assumptions. Queries against data stored in Microsoft OLAP Services structures perform much faster (in less than a second when resolved through aggregations) than against relational structures, by factors of anywhere between three and ten. This is not the fault of the relational structures since they are fully indexed; it is just representative of the boost that specialized storage and access techniques bring to query processing.

Although ROLAP is significantly slower for both processing and querying and requires much more storage than either MOLAP or HOLAP, it does offer the advantage of allowing cubes and partitions to be distributed across servers. When we tested the first release of OLAP Services, ROLAP aggregations that contribute to a query result were accessed serially. For example, imagine a situation in which server KILLINGTON is the source for HOLAP or ROLAP partitions for 1995 and 1997, and CHAMONIX is the source for HOLAP or ROLAP partitions for 1996 and 1998. OLAP Services will satisfy a query that involves accessing the source tables for all four years by querying KILLINGTON for 1995, then CHAMONIX for 1996, then KILLINGTON for 1997, and finally CHAMONIX for 1998. However, MOLAP aggregations will be accessed in parallel—in fact, OLAP Services will provide intra-query parallelism when it accesses MOLAP partitions.

When you are deciding upon the storage form for cube partitions, the point at which one factor outweighs another is highly subjective and will depend entirely upon the specifics of the project: the amount of fact data, the number of aggregations, the available storage, and the number of queries to be executed. Clearly, OLAP Services's own storage and access is relatively efficient compared to a typical RDBMS source. Evaluating all of these factors together, the efficiency of MOLAP aggregations in terms of processing, storage, and query resolution generally outweighs the benefits of distributing storage (and even the parallel processing of queries among multiple cubes) provided by ROLAP. MOLAP is clearly the fastest storage form to retrieve from. But if physical limitations on disk space are a serious issue for you or if the performance of queries that require leaf-level data is clearly unimportant, then HOLAP provides a good compromise between MOLAP and ROLAP.

Aggregations

Now that we have examined the storage of aggregations, let's take a closer look at how to specify them. As we explained in Chapter 2, the Microsoft OLAP Services aggregation designer will design the same aggregations regardless of storage type. To summarize our discussion there, aggregations store precalculated aggregate values of a cube's measures at a specific level in each dimension in a cube. For a query that can be resolved through an existing aggregation, OLAP Services only needs to look up and return these aggregate values, with no runtime aggregation. If a specific aggregation does not exist, OLAP Services will try to resolve the query through the run-time aggregation of another existing stored aggregation. As our discussion of storage forms in the previous section showed, OLAP Services performs such run-time aggregation very quickly. For this reason, we don't need every possible aggregation to improve query performance. We only need to aggregate data to the levels we will usually query against. As pointed out in the earlier sidebar "Performance Targets and the PivotTable Service Cache," it doesn't take many aggregations before it becomes difficult to create queries that won't be resolved by one of them.

How OLAP Services Determines Aggregations

Although the OLAP Services aggregation designer will never create all possible aggregations, it will create aggregations that will improve performance for most queries. At the same time, however, it may also create many unnecessary aggregations or fail to create specific aggregations that could dramatically improve the performance of an application.

OLAP Services's aggregation analyzer (which is accessible as a DSO object) allows you to proceed step by step through the combinations of possible aggregations for a partition. After each step, it returns the estimated total size and the performance benefit percentage for the designed aggregations. The OLAP Manager's aggregation design wizard drives the analyzer and stops the process as soon as the requested size or performance targets are reached or the performance benefit reaches 100 percent (or you press the "Stop" button). The estimates that are returned after you perform each step in the analyzer are based on the size of the key columns and measures as well as on the number of possible records in a given aggregation. The heuristics of this process are proprietary, but we do know some details that will help us.

Estimated Aggregation Size and Performance

As you may have noticed, the estimates of aggregation size and performance benefits that OLAP Services makes in the aggregation analyzer are rarely accurate. However, they are useful for comparison purposes and as rough guides. A partition with an estimated performance benefit of 50 percent will probably answer more queries through aggregations (and thus with better "performance") than will a partition with an estimated performance benefit of 10 percent. At the same time, a partition with an estimated size of 5 MB will probably occupy more disk space than a partition with an estimated size of 1 MB.

The only way to determine if a partition provides satisfactory performance is to process it and issue queries against it. The only way to determine the real amount of disk space that a partition will occupy is to process it and look at the size of the partition file through the file system. OLAP Manager does display the actual size of all partitions in a cube through the metadata pane of its main window when the cube is selected in the tree pane. On the other hand, in terms of resource planning the actual values for estimated performance and size are not of much use.

One-third Rule

The aggregation analyzer will include a given aggregation in a partition's aggregation design only if the total possible number of records in the aggregation will be one-third or less of the number of records in the fact table (as set in the cube's "Fact Table Size" property). (This rule is a heuristic used by the first release of OLAP Services. It is significant enough to describe in this section. Of course, like any heuristic, it may be eliminated or substantially changed in later releases.) To determine the possible number of records in an aggregation, Microsoft OLAP Services simply multiplies the number of members for each dimension level that would define aggregation by each other. For example, Figure 11.7 shows the number of members in each level of each dimension in a fictitious cube. If the Fact Table Size property of the cube has a value of 2,400,000, OLAP Services will only design aggregations that contain no more than 800,000 records. The analyzer may design an aggregation that is defined for the All level of Customers and Stores and for the days level of time ($1 \times 1 \times 1,461 = 1,461$ possible aggregation records). It may even create an aggregation for the customer level of customers, the month level of time, and the All level of stores ($8,000 \times$

Dimension	Level	Member Count
Customers	All	1
	State	10
	City	25
	Customer	8,000
Time	All	1
	Year	4
	Quarter	16
	Month	96
	Days	1,461
Stores	All	1
	Store	5

Figure 11.7 Dimensions and the number of members in each level.

$96 \times 1 = 768,000$ possible aggregation records). However, the analyzer will not design an aggregation for the customer level of customers, the month level of time, and the store level of stores ($8,000 \times 96 \times 5 = 3,840,000$ possible aggregation records).

For some applications, you may want to "trick" the aggregation analyzer into creating more aggregations by increasing the "Fact Table Size" property of a cube. For example, some dimensions in a cube may be related and will *never* result in the mathematical maximum number of possible records in an aggregation. Imagine that our fictitious cube also contains dimensions derived from the customer dimension for Gender, Age Group, and Household Size, as shown in Figure 11.8. All of these dimensions relate to the facts through customers, and thus the total number of possible values for any given combination of customer-related dimensions can realistically be no greater than the number of customers (8,000). OLAP Services, however, does not take such dimension relationships into consideration when it designs aggregations. An aggregation that included the leaf level from all of the customer dimensions, the year level of time, and the All level of Stores could realistically contain only a maximum of 32,000 records. However, the analyzer will calculate that it could contain 3,360,000(!), and it will never create the aggregation based upon the value of the original Fact Table Size property of the cube. Increasing the Fact Table Size property to 10,080,000 would enable the analyzer to create such an aggregation.

Fact Table Size

When you are creating a cube in OLAP Manager, the value of the Fact Table Size property defaults to the size of the fact table that was used to create the cube (you must determine the appropriate value yourself when you are creating a cube through DSO). OLAP Manager does not change the value of the Fact Table Size property if you change the fact table for the cube. This can significantly affect aggregation design if you are developing your cube based upon a sample or an early data set. Before you design aggregations, be sure to base a cube's fact table size on the estimated size of the fact table in the production data source.

Level Aggregation Usage

As we mentioned earlier in this chapter, you can restrict the aggregations that are created with the analyzer through the Aggregation Usage property of dimensions. Be aware, however, that for a given performance/size goal Microsoft OLAP Services will not always necessarily create more of the aggregations that we need in place of the aggregations that it would create with standard aggregation usage. OLAP Services will only design aggregations that it determines will fit within the expressed goal.

Dimension	Level	Member Count
Customers	All	1
	State	10
	City	25
	Customer	8,000
Genders	All	1
	Gender	3
Age Groups	All	1
	Age Group	7
HH Sizes	All	1
	HH Size	5
Time	All	1
	Year	4
	Quarter	16
	Month	96
	Days	1,461
Stores	All	1
	Store	5

Figure 11.8 Dimensions and the number of members in each level.

To see this aggregation design behavior in action, we again look to the Customer Counts cube from the tutorial in Chapter 16. As we noted in our earlier discussion of this cube, with standard aggregation usage for all dimensions and a 100 percent performance goal, OLAP Services will design 555 aggregations with an estimated total size of 80.4 MB for this cube (resulting in 7.71 MB of

Identifying Aggregations

OLAP Services's aggregation analyzer names aggregations by the ordinal number of the level that was used in the aggregation for each dimension. Using the dimensions shown in Figure 11.8 as an example, an aggregation defined for the "State" level of Customers, the "Quarter" level of Time, and the "All" level of stores would be named "231," while an aggregation for the leaf of Customers, the "All" level of Time, and the leaf of Stores would be named "412." Knowing this, you can use DSO to identify the aggregations that were created in a partition. In the DSS Lab, we created a DSO application called the Partition Explorer that, among other things, shows the aggregations designed for an OLAP Services partition. To help optimize your OLAP Services applications we've included a copy of this utility on the CD-ROM that accompanies this book.

HOLAP storage after processing). With aggregation usage limited to bottom level only for the customer dimension, OLAP Services will only design 7 aggregations, with a total estimated size of 2.9 MB (and an actual 1.26 MB of disk space after processing for HOLAP storage). Comparing the list of created aggregations shown in Figure 11.9, we see that "bottom only" includes only one additional aggregation beyond those that were included for the bottom level of the customer dimension in the aggregations designed for "standard" usage. On the other hand, with a 50 percent goal, OLAP Services creates 11 aggregations for "standard" usage and 2 aggregations for "bottom only," with estimated sizes of 0.053 and 0.480 MB, respectively. As shown in Figure 11.10, none of the bottom-only aggregations are included in the standard list.

Optimizing Aggregations

As we mentioned earlier in this chapter, by using DSO it is possible to create specific aggregations for a partition without using the Microsoft OLAP Services aggregation analyzer. The Partition Explorer mentioned in the "Identifying Aggregations" sidebar will allow you to do just that. In case you are interested in experimenting, we've included sample code demonstrating the creation of specific aggregations through DSO on the CD-ROM that accompanies this book.

Although OLAP Services does not clearly offer a way to create specific aggregations, it does offer a method for influencing the aggregations designed by the analyzer. This method involves weighting the design according to the number of time-specific queries that have been made against a cube or partition. You can do this manually through DSO (again, sample code is included on the CD-ROM

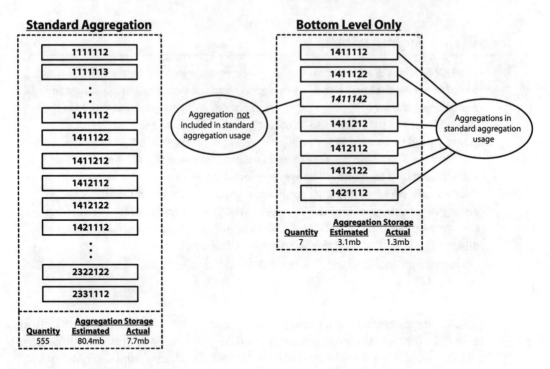

Figure 11.9 Aggregations for cubes with different level aggregation settings and 100 percent performance target.

if you are willing to experiment) or through OLAP Services's usage-based optimization wizard, which weighs aggregation design according to queries tracked by the server.

Tracking Aggregation Use

OLAP Services logs queries that it receives from client applications. By default, it includes only one out of every ten queries it receives. You can change the default, however, so that the query log tracks anywhere from every query to one out of every ten thousand queries. To change the setting in OLAP Manager, open the properties dialog for the server by right-clicking on the server in the tree pane of the OLAP Manager console and select "Properties." The sampling frequency setting is found on the "Query Log" tab. Logging can be completely turned off by un-checking "Sample Frequency." You may also clear the existing log by pressing the "Clear Entire Log" button.

OLAP Services by default maintains the log in a single Microsoft Access database named "msmdqlog.mdb," which is installed with OLAP Services. Queries are identified by the actual combination of dimension levels they request from

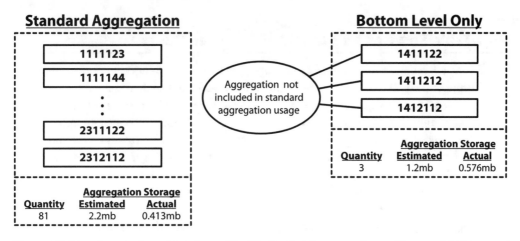

Figure 11.10   Aggregations for cubes with different level aggregation settings and 100 percent performance target.

different partition storage types. The actual MDX or SQL is not tracked, however. The log also includes information on the database and cube that the logged query accessed, who ran the query, when they ran it, and how long OLAP Services took to return results.

Although you can explore the log yourself using any tool that can read an MS Access database, OLAP Manager provides a usage analysis wizard that provides usage information from the log in a variety of formats. Unfortunately, the wizard only displays the reports on the screen. It offers you no way to print reports or save them to a file. By using the usage analysis wizard you can see the following information:

- Description of query based on the levels used in specific dimensions
- Duration of query execution
- Number of times the query was executed
- Most active users based on number of queries
- Distribution of queries for certain durations (0–5 seconds, 6–10 seconds, etc.)
- Distribution of queries per hour of day
- Distribution of queries per day

The wizard allows you to filter the data in these reports by day, duration, user, and number of times run. Because the wizard is rather straightforward, we won't provide specific examples illustrating its use here. You can launch the wizard by right-clicking on any cube or partition in the tree pane of the OLAP Manager console and selecting "Usage Analysis . . ." from the pop-up menu.

PivotTable Services and the OLAP Services Query Log

As we mentioned earlier in the chapter, the PivotTable Service will not submit a query to OLAP Services if it can resolve the query from cached data. As a result, the OLAP Services query log will never accurately reflect the number of times a client application executed a given query. For example, suppose a client application repeatedly requests a query or variations of a query that take several minutes to execute. In that case, only the first request will be logged because the PivotTable Service will resolve subsequent requests from cached data.

Although the query may be of tremendous importance to clients (reflected in the number of times they request it), the server will never accurately know that degree of importance, and the query may never be given the appropriate weighting in the optimization wizard. As a result, each client may always go through a lengthy "initialization" the first time it runs a particular query.

You have two options if it is vitally important for an application that aggregations be available to resolve specific queries. You can either manually "stack" the query log by duplicating records in the "Query Log" table in msmdqlog.mdb, or you can create the desired aggregation through DSO.

The Optimization Wizard

OLAP Manager's optimization wizard combines the usage analysis wizard and the aggregation design wizard. This enables you to influence the aggregations that are created by OLAP Services's aggregation analyzer according to selected queries that have logged by the server.

Regardless of how many times a specific query is logged, OLAP Services will not create an aggregation that would optimize the query if the aggregation could be greater than 1/3 of the cube's fact table size.

The wizard starts by allowing you to select the queries you wish to optimize, as shown in Figure 11.11. After entering selection criteria, the wizard shows you a list of logged queries that match the criteria. It also shows you the number of times they were run and the average time OLAP Services took to return results.

The following steps of the wizard are identical to those in the aggregation design wizard. First, the wizard asks whether you want to replace existing aggregations or add new ones. (This is a confusing question in the initial release of OLAP Services because, regardless of choice, OLAP Services replaces existing aggregations. However, by selecting "Replace Existing" you are also

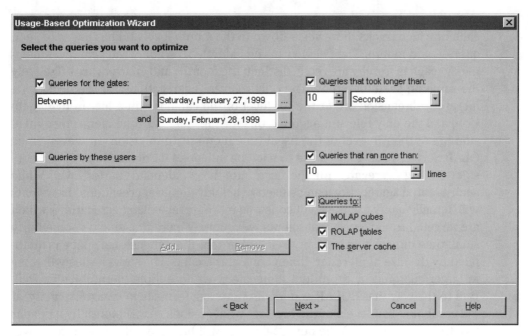

Figure 11.11   Usage Optimization Wizard query selection.

allowed to change the storage form.) Second, you enter performance targets and then design the aggregations. (Again, this is a bit confusing because the targets do not default to the defaults for the current aggregations, probably because you are actually always replacing those aggregations.) In the last step of the wizard you are given the option of either processing the cube or partition using the new aggregations or simply saving the aggregation design.

The usage optimization wizard will not always design new aggregations that will improve performance for identified queries. If a specific aggregation (or any other aggregations that would improve performance for the query) does not fit the given space or percent targets, the aggregation will not be created.

Optimizing Aggregations for Multiple Hierarchies

Since OLAP Services implements multiple dimensional hierarchies as multiple dimensions, the presence of multiple hierarchies in a cube expands the dimensional space considerably. Much of the dimensional space is irrelevant. This irrelevant space can cause a sub-optimal aggregation design to be created for the cube. We introduced this consideration in Chapter 3, and we explore it in more depth here.

For example, consider a cube with two time hierarchies (calendar and fiscal), each of which tracks three years down to the month level and has levels of year, quarter, and month. The fiscal year ends March 31, so only the year-level members in each hierarchy are really distinct; the months and quarters are effectively the same on each hierarchy. The only relevant aggregations for the fiscal time hierarchy-dimension are at the All level of the calendar time hierarchy-dimension, and the only relevant aggregations for the calendar time hierarchy-dimension are at the All level of the fiscal time hierarchy-dimension. However, since OLAP Services considers these to each be independent dimensions, it will consider storing aggregates for the fiscal month by calendar quarter level. While such a stored aggregation can be used to quickly derive aggregations that clients will actually query for, they will consume more storage than aggregations which are targeted to the levels that clients will query. We are focusing on some fairly small time dimensions here, but remember that the dimensional space is multiplied by the size of all other dimensions in the cube. The same issues will arise in larger customer and product dimensions with multiple hierarchies as well. Due to the way that ROLAP and MOLAP storage forms help control sparsity, at the combined leaf levels of the hierarchy-dimensions (fiscal month by calendar month in this example) the potential space will be large but no extra rows will be stored. For example, data for each fiscal month also exists for only one calendar month, so no significant extra storage will be required.

As pointed out in Chapter 3, the ideal set of level-combinations to use for stored aggregations in a cube with multiple hierarchies is the same set of level-combinations that would be valid if each separate hierarchy-dimension was used in a separate regular cube, and the cube that provided multiple hierarchies was a virtual cube. There are two ways to directly achieve this effect. One is by using regular cubes and virtual cubes in exactly this way. The other is by using one regular cube with multiple hierarchies, and using DSO to control the set of aggregations that is actually created. (The Partition Explorer tool included on the accompanying CD-ROM will allow you to delete and add specific aggregations to a cube.)

There are some trade-offs inherent in using virtual cubes to control the aggregations in a cube that uses multiple hierarchies. The major benefit is that each cube can be independently optimized, and can have an independent storage form. Since the query analyzer only considers queries against the underlying real cubes, the query analyzer will suggest aggregations that support the actual pattern of queries in each hierarchy (as opposed to trying to pick aggregations that might support multiple hierarchies somehow, when no queries actually touch more than one hierarchy). Also, since each regular cube is responsible for only one hierarchy, changes to only one hierarchy require re-processing only the related regular cube and the virtual cube. However, the cubes do prove more difficult to manage. You need one regular cube for each hierarchy-dimension, plus the virtual cube that ties them all together, which will all need to be maintained as a group. Also, since each base cube contributes its own set of measures to the virtual cube, you will want to add a set of calculated measures to merge them together. (See "Masking the Application Ranges" in Chapter 12 for a discussion of how to do this.) Also, if you have multiple hierarchies on more than one dimension, the number of base cubes involved increases geometrically. Remember that this discussion of optimization of aggregations only applies to regular dimensions. When you create a large number of hierarchies for multiple dimensions, the chances are good that most of them will be implemented as virtual dimensions, which do not cause aggregations to be stored in the first place.

Taking explicit control of the aggregations created in a single regular cube is the other way to achieve the highest level of aggregation optimization. As we explained in Chapter 3, the interface provided by the OLAP Manager for including and excluding level-combinations from having data stored for them is inadequate for restricting away the irrelevant combinations for multiple hierarchies. Through the Partition Explorer, you can delete irrelevant aggregations, and substitute related aggregations that will support the queries that you anticipate. As this book went to press, we had not completed our lab testing towards guidelines of how to choose the relevant aggregations and the performance trade-offs between the methods. Visit our Web site (http://www.dsslab.com) for updates on this issue.

Query Processing

Aggregations serve as the foundation of optimization with regard to queries against cubes and partitions in Microsoft OLAP Services. However, it is useful to understand where and how processing takes place and where data is cached when OLAP Services processes a query. After the PivotTable Service has parsed the MDX for a query or a CREATE SET statement, for each layer of calculation context the query is divided into internal queries against all of the partitions that will contribute data to the result. OLAP Services queries ROLAP partitions (and HOLAP partitions if the query requires leaf data) in serial and MOLAP and HOLAP partitions in parallel. It combines the result at the component that is performing the calculations.

We have been talking as if OLAP Services performs the calculations, without specifying either the PivotTable Service or the server as the location of calculations. The location for the calculations depends on whether or not the "large-level" limit was exceeded for the query. By default, OLAP Services defines a large level as 1,000 members. Using the default as an example, PivotTable Services would consider a query as requiring the aggregation of a large level if the results require the run-time aggregation of 1,000 or more members of a dimension level. If the query does not involve any large level, then all calculations occur at the client. If the query involves a large level, then the query is evaluated at the server (however, in tests it appears that the supporting data is also passed along to the client because subsequent variations on the query that used the same low level data were not forwarded to the server).

This issue of the location of calculations is particularly important for you to understand if you are making use of ROLAP or HOLAP partitions. An MDX query that cannot be satisfied from a stored aggregate and that does not cross the large-level threshold on members involved will cause the required records from the fact table to be aggregated in the PivotTable Service. This means that clients that make queries that involve lots of fact table aggregation will only require the OLAP Services server to spend a negligible amount of CPU and no measurable additional RAM to satisfy the query. The amount of work performed at the client may be significant, however, because even on an SMP client the PivotTable Service will devote only one thread's worth of processing to the task. It also means that the results will not be cached at the server, only at the client. If more than one client needs the same aggregated data, then each client will perform the same aggregation of leaf-level data. By adjusting the large-level threshold you will allow more of these queries to be handled and cached at the server. Whether this makes sense or not for your situation will depend on the mix of queries posed to your server.

MDX Expressions

We have discussed MDX expressions in detail in earlier chapters. How you formulate them can have a big impact on performance. In this section we will provide a rough outline of the ways MDX construction can impact performance. The most important topics are the resource requirements of large sets and query constructs that either force the query to be executed on the client or enable it to be executed on the server.

When the PivotTable Service executes queries, it behaves as though every set were fully materialized in memory prior to use. This introduces significant resource issues for both the client and the server. The server lets you tune the size of a "large level." The server will handle calculations that involve members from a single dimension level that are greater in number than this "large-level" size. Calculations that involve fewer members will be handled in the PivotTable Service at the client. Note that this issue affects the use of members from a single dimension. For example, the expression

```
Topcount ([Customer].[Individual Customer].Members, 50,
    [Measures].Sales)
```

will be evaluated at the server if the number of members in the [Customer].[Individual Customer] level is greater than this threshold, and at the client if it is less. However, this threshold is for members of a level, not tuples in a set. Assume that the threshold is set at 1,000 (the default). Suppose that you have 500 customers, which is safely below the threshold, and 100 product categories. Suppose also that you request the following:

```
Topcount (CrossJoin( [Customer].[Individual Customer].Members,
    [Product].[Category]), 50, [Measures].Sales)
```

You will get the top 50 customer-product tuples in terms of sales. In this case, the 50,000 combinations will be generated and examined on the client, perhaps pushing the memory consumed by the PivotTable Service past the limits of your machine.

There is no way for the client to make the request "Please execute this at the server; I don't have the resources here." (There is also no direct way for the client to make the request "Please execute this here; I don't want to tie up the server resources if I can't answer it myself." However, when the client connects, there is an OLE DB Connection property that allows the client to suggest a different "large-level" limit). There is an indirect way to specify that large calculations take place at the client, however. Named sets, which are instantiated at the client, are used at the client. If you first create a named set at the client that contains the large level's members, then using that set in a query will cause the query to be executed at the client. This is true for sets created by CREATE SET and also for sets created by WITH SET within the context of a query. Forcing the calculation to take place at the client also forces all of the required cell data to cross the network to the client.

To obtain good performance, you may need to rephrase very resource-intensive calculations. The key to rephrasing is breaking up an operation on a large set into a set of operations on smaller sets. For example, sums across multiple dimensions that are phrased as the sums of sums of individual dimensions will be less resource-intensive than will a single sum of a cross-join. That is, instead of this expression,

```
Sum (
  CrossJoin (
    Descendants ([Customer].CurrentMember,
      [Customer].[Individual Customer], SELF),
    Crossjoin (
      Descendants ([Time].CurrentMember, [Time].[Day], SELF),
      Descendants ([Product].CurrentMember, [Product].[Category], SELF)
    )
  ),
  [Measures].[Sales in Euros] *
  ([Measures].[Currency Conversion],
    Ancestor ([Geography], [Geography].[Country]))
)
```

you would want to express it as follows:

```
Sum (
  Descendants ([Customer].CurrentMember,
    [Customer].[Individual Customer], SELF),
  Sum (
    Descendants ([Time].CurrentMember, [Time].[Day], SELF),
    Sum (
      Descendants ([Product].CurrentMember, [Product].[Category], SELF),
      [Measures].[Sales in Euros] *
      ([Measures].[Currency Conversion],
        Ancestor ([Geography], [Geography].[Country]))
    )
  )
)
```

Another type of expression that might need to be optimized would be the following, as it potentially generates a huge set in memory:

```
TopCount (
  { [Customer].[Individual Customer].Members
  * [Time].[Day].Members
  * [Product].[Category].Members },
  50, [Measures].[Qty Returned]
)
```

It could be broken up into the following to get the same result:

```
TopCount (
  Generate (
    [Customer].[Individual Customer].Members,
    Topcount ({ [Customer].CurrentMember } *
      [Time].[Day].Members * [Product].[Category].Members,
      50, [Measures].[Qty Returned])
  ),
  50, [Measures].[Qty Returned]
)
```

This last expression means "for each customer, generate a top-50 set, combine all of these top-50 sets, and take the top 50 from them." The overhead of creating the larger number of smaller sets is less than the overhead of extracting the top 50 from the single larger set. For example, in a smallish database where Individual Customer has 934 members, Day has 365 members, and product category has 34 members, a 400 MHz four-way Pentium II Xeon server required 800 MB of RAM to answer the first formulation and around 15 minutes even when the data set was fully in cache. The second formulation took about 8 minutes at the server and about 10 MB of RAM.

Expressions that use new calculations defined by WITH MEMBER and that involve large levels will be calculated at the server. For example, the following expression will be calculated at the server:

```
WITH
MEMBER [Measures].[Avg Return Value] AS
'[Measures].[Credit Amt] / [Measures].[Qty Returned]'
SELECT
...
TopCount (
  Generate (
    [Customer].[Individual].Members,
    Topcount ({ [Customer].CurrentMember } *
      [Time].[Day].Members * [Product].[Category].Members,
      50, [Measures].[Avg Return Value])
  ),
  50, [Measures].[Avg Return Value]
) on rows
FROM SalesDetail
```

If the member was created at the client with CREATE MEMBER, then the query will be resolved at the client even if a level crosses the large-level threshold. For example, suppose [Client Avg Return Value] is defined with the following:

```
CREATE MEMBER [SalesDetail].[Measures].[Client Avg Return Value] AS
'[Measures].[Credit Amt] / [Measures].[Qty Returned]'
```

In this case, queries involving this member will be performed at the client.

The NON EMPTY clause on a result axis specification can only be executed after all cells have been resolved. In the first release of OLAP Services, the process of whittling down the return set to only NON EMPTY cells happens at the client.

This section can be summarized with the following general rules:

- You do need to determine what level of server resources you are willing to use to support client queries because this will impact your choice of default large levels. This will involve looking at the query mix and client machine resources. You can adjust the large-level settings so as to push more queries to the server or to the clients. Note that a client can also alter this setting for itself.

- The relationship between CrossJoin() and Generate() can be leveraged when operations that involve sorting and selection are involved. The relationship is as follows: CrossJoin(A, B) is equivalent to Generate(A, CrossJoin({A.Current}, B)).

- The commutative nature of SUM (and MIN and MAX) can be leveraged when operations that involve aggregating over multiple dimensions are involved. That is, Sum({A} * {B} * {C}, d) is equivalent to Sum({A}, Sum ({B}, Sum ({C}, d))). Operations involving Count() need to be treated a little differently: Count({A} * {B} * {C}) is equivalent to Sum ({A}, Sum ({B}, Count ({C}))).

Server Settings

A Microsoft OLAP Services server offers a few optimization settings that you can tweak to improve performance. These settings are described fairly well in Microsoft's online documentation for OLAP Services. We discussed the server's "Large level defined as" setting in great detail in the section titled "Query Processing," and we also discussed the query log sample frequency setting in the section on "Tracking Aggregation Use." In this section, we'll explore two more important server settings: "Read-ahead buffer size" and "Process buffer size."

OLAP Services uses the read-ahead buffer to hold data that is read from a partition (which will do when it is processing queries). The higher the setting, the more data OLAP Services can retrieve from disk at one time, thus reducing the number of disk accesses required.

The process buffer determines how much data OLAP Services will accumulate and process in RAM before it writes the results to disk when creating MOLAP aggregations. Process buffer size can have a tremendous impact on partition processing and can affect the amount of source data that can be read before OLAP Services begins creating aggregations and writing them to disk. As the amount of data that can be processed in RAM increases, the number of times OLAP Services has to write out processed data decreases.

Minimum Allocated Memory determines the minimum amount of memory that OLAP Services will request for exclusive use from Windows NT. This memory will always be available to OLAP Services regardless of the other activity on the server.

TIP Changes to server settings do not take effect until the next time OLAP Services starts.

Summary

Although the name "Microsoft OLAP Services" does not convey the same meaning as "OLAP database," the product does offer a set of optimization and tuning options that are entirely relevant to databases. We have explored a variety of ways for you to minimize storage and increase responsiveness for your applications given the requirements that are imposed by your applications and hardware environment. With appropriate planning and attention to details, you will be able to maximize the performance available from this first release of OLAP Services.

CHAPTER 12

Advanced Cube and Database Design

In Chapter 3, "Database Design Basics," we covered the fundamentals of designing dimensions and cubes as well as the structures of the tables that feed the database. These design basics will allow you to create databases that support an increasing number of analyses over time, but there are additional design topics you will need to know to create more advanced applications. The advanced design considerations we will cover in this chapter include:

- Line-item dimensions
- Closing the loop from OLAP Services back to the warehouse or operational systems
- Masking measure application ranges in virtual cubes through formulas

Line-item dimension techniques are required for many budgeting and financial analysis/reporting applications as well as for applications that use a large number of stored measures. Since a decision-support system (DSS) is used to inform actionable decisions, we need to be able to write analytical results back to an RDBMS so we can use the sets of interesting products, promotions, prices, and so on that we compile. Finally, if we have the ability to create the appearance of a single measure in a virtual cube for a set of measures from different base cubes we will be able to greatly simplify calculations and client queries on virtual cubes.

Line-item Dimensions

The definition of a measure is fairly general: it is any type of data that has a unit (such as dollars, packages, kilograms per square inch, and so on) associated with it. Some applications involve fewer distinct measures; others involve more. Financial applications that deal with accounting measures may use a large number, as would applications like business performance metric analysis. When an application uses a larger number of measures, it also will frequently require that they be structured in some hierarchical way that is akin to the structure of other dimensions. This allows end users to drill down from categorical summaries to subcategories to base-line items.

In OLAP Services, neither cubes that involve large numbers of measures nor sets of measures that you would like to treat hierarchically can be handled using the usual measures dimension. An OLAP Services cube (regular or virtual) is limited to 128 base measures, and these measures cannot have any hierarchy between them. Furthermore, in relational databases that involve large numbers of measures, like financial databases, the measures are likely to be defined by rows in supporting dimension tables, and the fact tables that contain related data are likely to reference each measure by a key value in a row rather than treat each measure as a column. The combination of the cube and dimension structure limitation on the one hand and the usual table formations on the other leads us to simply implement the "measures" as another dimension.

We first saw an example of a line-item dimension in the financial account hierarchy shown in Chapter 3, Figure 3.7. We show it again here in Figure 12.1. From an end user's perspective, a hierarchical set of measures can be very handily represented as a hierarchical dimension. Each parent measure usually represents a generalization or aggregation of its children, just as the parent members in other dimensions represent aggregations or generalizations of their children members. To create a hierarchical effect with the standard OLAP Services measures dimension, you would need to associate additional information with each measure and create a front-end tool that understands it. Since you cannot attach member properties to members of the measures dimension, you would have to do a great deal of work to mesh the functionality together.

Along with the return of the issue of turning the measures into a dimension, we also see the issue of irregular hierarchies raising its head again. Line-item dimensions are usually irregular, and there usually is no useful semantic naming we can give to any level apart, perhaps, from "leaf" and "root." We should also point out here that data is frequently input to a cube at multiple levels of a line-item hierarchy. When this happens, we need to combine the considerations for multiple levels of input data with the considerations for line-item dimensions. We will focus on the details that are specific to line-item dimen-

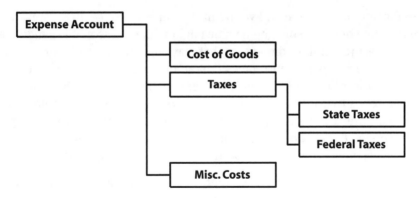

Figure 12.1 Typical line-item dimension hierarchy.

sions in this section, and simply point out that the two usually need to be considered in tandem.

Regular Dimension and Measures Dimension

If our measures are a "regular" dimension, what do we do with the "measures" dimension? When we put the measures into a line-item dimension, we still need a measures dimension to create the cube. We won't be able to change its name from "Measures" because that is hardwired into Microsoft OLAP Services. At the very least, you will end up with one measure whose name will roughly be "value" (or "amount"). In any case, its meaning will certainly be that. After you have factored out business unit, time, related product or process, scenario, and semantic measure (along with all of the other typically hierarchical dimensions), there aren't any other really useful concepts left with which to name the remaining member of the measures dimension. (This is also frequently what the fact table will use as a name for the column that holds the data values). In a regular cube with a line-item dimension, the line-item dimension will probably be called "Line Item" or "Account" or "Metric". Moreover, the measures dimension will probably have a single measure called "Value" or "Quantity" or "Amount." This will usually aggregate by summation. To help you calculate averages later, you may also have a second measure called "Count" or "Occurrences" with an aggregation function of COUNT.

Since you have moved the "measures" off of the measures dimension, it is logical to briefly consider moving some other small, non-hierarchical dimension onto the OLAP Services measures dimension. For example, databases that include accounting line items are frequently used for budgeting applications, and these typically have a Scenario dimension that is used to relate actual measurements to the given budget and to different types of forecasts. The Scenario dimension is generally non-hierarchical and would fit the bill here. Since an organization may have only one budget, a budgeted value might make a reasonable candidate for a second measure. Another dimension that may come to mind is a currency dimension since the number of currencies that an organization typically needs to deal with is far fewer than 128 (the limit on stored measures in a cube). Indeed, if the company tends to use directly only one or two currencies per customer, then the stored measures can be the local currency values, and calculations can perform the conversion to many other currencies (since a cube can have up to 15,000 calculated measures, far exceeding the 128 base measures allowed).

However, the idea of putting the members of a small non-measures dimension into the cube's measures dimension should usually be discarded shortly after you think of it. You should look at the subject of cube dimensionality from a systemic perspective as well as from the perspective of cube efficiency. It would work reasonably well if we could tell OLAP Services that the measures dimension for one cube was the scenario or currency dimension for another cube, but we cannot. We will still want to use a currency dimension that has a full complement of currency members so we can relate measurements in local units to currencies in specific units. We will still want a separate Scenario dimension so we relate actual facts to budgeted facts to various forecasts of facts. Putting these relationships into the measures dimension of one cube gives us no leverage for performing the same relations and calculations in the other dimensions for other cubes. Budgets and forecasts are frequently performed at a higher level of aggregation than the level at which the actual fact data is measured. Combining budgets and forecasts with actual data requires that you use a cube or cubes that are separate from the cube that holds the actual facts. When the actual is combined with the budget in a virtual cube, the measures from each cube will be segregated anyway.

One practical consideration to keep in mind when you are using line-item dimensions is how measures get formatted into text. Since there is only one measure, there is only one display format string shared among all of the lines, even though some may be currency amounts and some may represent unit amounts to different degrees of precision. One approach to deal with this and give different formats to different measures is to define a set of calculated measures, each of which simply displays the value measure in a different format. For example,

```
MEMBER [Measures].[CurrencyValue] AS '[Measures].[Value]',
FORMAT_STRING = '$#.##'
MEMBER [Measures].[UnitsValue] AS '[Measures].[Value]',
FORMAT_STRING = '#'
```

Another, more robust method is to store the format string in a member property. We can then use one calculated measure that returns the string that results when we format the value measure according to the property's value. We can do this using the external Visual Basic for Applications (VBA) library Format()

function. Assuming that we have a member property named Measure_Format that contains the correct format string for a measure, the following calculated measure returns the value properly formatted:

```
MEMBER [Measures].[FormattedValue] AS
'Format ([Measures].[Value],
 [Line Item].CurrentMember.Properties ("Measure_Format"))'
```

This function will work in this form so long as we do not need to specify optional calendar parameters for converting measures to a date string. However, it can also be easily extended to work in that case as well.

Representing Line Items

How do we represent our line items in the dimension? One of the attractions of the line-item dimension for cost and revenue accounting is that most line items and their categories form a neat hierarchy, in which each line item contributes to one and only one parent in that hierarchy, and the calculations are all additive. This is fairly straightforward when a line-item dimension consists purely of costs or of revenues, where all items only add up. However, as we mentioned in Chapter 3, in general accounting dimensions not all line items (accounts) will sum up. Costs and revenues will require that you take a difference to obtain gross profit. In an accounting line-item dimension, there will be many stages where you will need to take a set of differences. Examples include subtracting net costs from gross revenue to calculate adjusted gross revenue and subtracting other expenses from gross profit to calculate net profit. In addition, there may be all manner of ratios.

There are three identifiable levels of complexity for line-item dimensions that OLAP Services can handle directly:

- a flat dimension, with no hierarchical relations between the members (like the standard measures dimension)
- a hierarchy where all elements are only additive
- a hierarchy where elements may be both additive and subtractive

A line-item dimension can also provide the user with the ability to navigate ratios, products, and other calculations as though they were part of a computational hierarchy. These dimensions fall outside the scope of this book. Although it is possible to implement them with OLAP Services, they require significant system development in terms of the interrelationships between client interface, database design, external functions, and calculated members.

A Flat Line-item Dimension

In the simplest kind of line-item dimension, there is only one level that contains all members (and no All level). This line-item dimension will appear and behave very much like the standard measures dimension of a cube but one with the capabilities of a shared or private dimension. One of the attractive features of a flat line-item dimension as a dimension is that it can be shared by multiple cubes. The flat line-item dimension provides an elegant solution to the problem of measuring "explosion" in virtual cubes, where the total number of measures contributed from all of the base cubes exceeds 128. For example, 33 measures from each of four base cubes would require that you use a line-item dimension to combine them together into a single virtual cube, because they contribute 132 measures in total. In a virtual cube that combines other cubes that share the line-item dimension, each cube will only need to contribute a single "value" measure.

Simple Hierarchy: All Lines Aggregate to Parents

When all lines represent the same sort of quantity and there is a hierarchical relationship between them (as in a chart of cost accounts), then a single, simple hierarchy can provide you with the ability to aggregate cube measures up through the tree of line items as well as embedding hierarchical navigation paths directly in the dimension metadata. A line item dimension like this will usually be most naturally represented as a ragged hierarchy. You can create a balanced hierarchy to prepare these line-item dimensions by using the techniques we described in Chapter 3. Note that this will come at the expense of some redundant storage for values that are associated with high-level leaf members. For a typical cost hierarchy, however, the extra storage taken up ought not be a cause for concern.

Simple Hierarchy: Lines May Subtract from Other Lines

Microsoft OLAP Services does not embed any other calculation on base measures into its dimensions besides SUM, COUNT, MAX, and MIN. However, without too much work we can use a combination of arithmetical techniques and additional data to put subtraction into the hierarchy. A variation on these techniques is also illustrated in the tutorial presented in Chapter 15.

We will use the basic property of arithmetic that $A - B = A + (-B)$ to put the subtraction of values into the hierarchy. The most convenient way to convert a value to its negative is to multiply it by -1. To define each line item as being subtractive rather than additive to its parent, we can associate it with a sign multiplier value, which will be either 1 or -1 for each member. This multiplication would be done for each row as it enters into the cube, much as you would get total value by multiplying a price by a number of units.

If we were to only do this much, we would get correct results for the leaf-level members that were subtractive. However, non-leaf members that are subtractive would not be treated correctly. Once the values have been sign-adjusted at the leaf level, OLAP Services will only sum them up the hierarchy from the leaves. We have no opportunity to take each parent member and multiply the related value by its sign multiplier. We can, however, solve this problem by carrying the adjustment of signs one step further when bringing fact data into the cube. We can introduce a single calculated member to be used when queries and further calculations reference the aggregated values. (If we had separate debit and credit columns in the fact table, the solution to the design problem might look different. However, we will assume that this is not the case.)

The problem we are trying to solve is how to subtract the value for any parent node from its own parent. To solve this, we will continue to leverage the fact that $A - B = A + (-B)$. In the cases where we are trying to subtract B from A, we want to calculate B as $-B$ in the first place. That is, we need to prepare the data for aggregation such that parents which are to be subtracted from their parents are calculated with an inverted sign from the beginning. If we needed to treat this $(-B)$ as $(+B)$ for reporting or further analysis, we can flip its sign again in a calculated member. For example, if we are going to subtract 100 euros of costs from 122 euros of revenue to try to calculate our profit parent, we will want to calculate our costs in such a way as to arrive at -100 euros instead of $+100$ euros in the first place. When the sign multiplier is associated with the dimension as a member property, you can reference it in the following way (leveraging the VBA library function CInt()):

```
MEMBER [Measures].[Value Contribution] AS
'[Measures].[Value] *
CInt ([Line Items].CurrentMember.Properties ("Sign Multiplier"))'
```

How do we flip the signs? We need to create a second multiplier in addition to the first one we have already discussed. Let's call it the *adjusted* sign multiplier. The adjusted sign multiplier will only be used at the level(s) of the line-item dimension where data enters the cube (which could be only at the leaf level or it could be at all levels). When we are assigning an adjusted multiplier to a member, we need to look at its parent member's original multiplier. If the parent's original multiplier is $+1$, then the child's multiplier is unaffected. If the parent's original multiplier is -1, then the parent's adjusted multiplier would have been flipped, and the child's multiplier is itself flipped (either from 1 to -1 or from -1 to 1). When we carry this operation out from the root level and its members' children down to the lowest level of parents and their children, we will end up with a new set of multipliers. Figure 12.2 shows the effect of the transformation and how it works.

You will probably find it most convenient to (1) maintain this information in a parent-child hierarchy table (so each line is only described once) and (2) perform the creation of each of these multipliers in the SQL view(s) that convert(s)

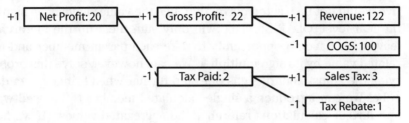

a) Original signs in hierarchy

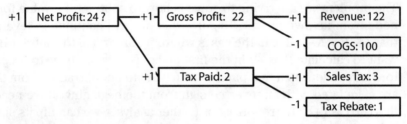

b) Problem: upper levels of hierarchy only sum

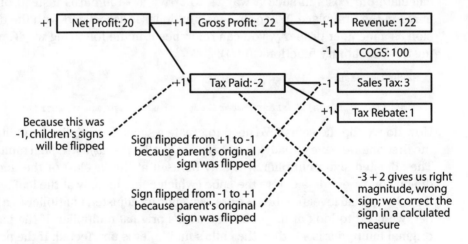

c) Signs flipped from parents to children

Figure 12.2   Transforming the sign multiplier down the line-item hierarchy.

the irregular hierarchy form into the leveled hierarchy table form required by OLAP Services. For each level, include the column for the multiplier from the previous level and the column for the current level. Multiplying the sign multiplier for the current level by the sign multiplier for the previous level will perform any flipping that has to be done. It will do this by using the arithmetic property that $-1 * 1 = -1$ and $-1 * -1 = 1$. The following SQL builds the top two levels (omitting the details for handling irregular hierarchies):

```
/* create top-level view */
CREATE VIEW Lines_L1
AS
SELECT
  member_key AS key_L1,
  member_name AS name_L1,
  multiplier AS multiplier_L1,
  multiplier AS AdjustedMultiplier_L1
FROM LinesTable
WHERE parent_key IS NULL

/* create second-level view */
CREATE VIEW Lines_L2
AS
SELECT
  LinesL1.key_L1 AS key_L1,
  LinesL1.name_L1 AS name_L1,
  LinesL1.multiplier AS multiplier_L1,
  LinesTable.member_key AS key_L2,
  LinesTable.member_name AS name_L2,
  LinesTable.multiplier AS multiplier_L2,
  (LinesTable.multiplier * Lines_L1.AdjustedMultiplier_L1)
    AS AdjustedMultiplier_L2
FROM LinesTable, Lines_L1
WHERE LinesTable.parent_key = Lines_L1.key_L1
```

For the multiplier to affect the rows of the fact table, you must join the dimension table with its multiplier values to the fact table by a view (since OLAP Services can only perform row calculations on a single fact table). This means that while your primary definition of the hierarchy will probably be in a parent-child table, for efficient joining you should materialize the dimension-level view into a dimension table. Within the fact view, the multiplication could be performed by the view and the result returned as a single-quantity column. Alternatively, the member multiplier and the measure value can be returned as separate columns and multiplied by the cube's measure link.

The technique we have just described is effective for embedding addition and subtraction between children of a parent. Ratios (the other important members of line-item dimensions) can usually be handled as ordinary calculated members. Since calculated members can be made to appear as children of a regular member, you can associate them with lines that are related to the ratios as well as place them in the top level of the dimension (by giving them no parent member). If you use calculated members for ratios, users will not be able to "drill down" on the inputs to the ratios in the same way they can for the sums and differences.

Closing the Loop: Writing Analytical Results Back to an RDBMS

The focus of OLAP is to support decisions about all kind of topics, such as which customers to attract or retain, which products to promote or discontinue, what prices to set, what quality levels to achieve, which employees to train or reward, and so on. Once an application is built, it may be used primarily by people who pose queries to it, digest the results they see, and probably ask other questions based on those results. Preparing a report to management or deciding which course of action to take may not require work on the part of the application beyond simply formatting the results. This would be an example of an "open-loop" application, so called because it delivers results in one direction only: from operational system to warehouse to user. Applications that are built to help determine what populations are of interest (such as which customers to retain, products to promote, etc.) or to calculate important parameters across these populations (like ideal product pricing) will also frequently need to close the loop and send data back to the warehouse or an operational system. For example, once we have identified a set of customers that we would like to send a particular promotion to, we will need to put that set in some RDBMS table so the mailing list can be generated. If we have calculated a new set of prices for our products because profits are too low, we will need to send new prices to the pricing tables. Microsoft OLAP Services only provides us with the ability to query data out of a cube, but we can enlist the aid of another component of SQL Server 7.0 to marshal the query result out of OLAP Services and into RDBMS tables— namely, DTS (Data Transformation Services).

We have not discussed DTS before this because it does not play a role in the dimensional design or the calculations of an OLAP system. However, it does play an important role in the full implementation of a closed-loop decision-support system (DSS) in OLAP Services and SQL Server. To do so, it relies heavily on OLE DB, which we have also not really described yet. We will briefly discuss OLE DB and DTS here so you can understand how they facilitate closing the loop. A detailed discussion of OLE DB would require us to talk about fairly low-level programming (for example, in C++), which is outside of our scope. By the same token, we will also only discuss the most relevant parts of DTS.

OLE DB and Tabular Results for MDX Queries

OLE DB (of which OLE DB for OLAP is a part) is a fairly general data-transport interface that is based on COM. An important interface abstraction in OLE DB is the *rowset*, which behaves conceptually like a table. A rowset has a set of columns, each of which has a name and a data type. A rowset also provides a software interface through which a client program can obtain rows of information from it. Because the results of an SQL query are in the form of rows and columns, they fit easily into the OLE DB rowset model. DBMS metadata, such as lists of tables, lists of columns, indexes, and the like, are also easily represented as rowsets. For the most part, OLE DB for OLAP uses the same mechanisms as general OLE DB. For example, it provides its own rowsets for an OLAP database's dimensions, hierarchies, levels, members, measures, cubes, and properties.

Although an MDX query specifies an N-dimensional result space, an OLE DB for OLAP client can specify two different formats in which to return the data when it submits the query. One format is as a multidimensional data set and the other is as a normal tabular rowset. The multidimensional data set is normally requested by an OLAP client because it retains the full dimensional layout of the query. Suppose the client requests that the results be returned in tabular form, even though the PivotTable Service is processing an MDX query. In this case, the client will receive a result data rowset that is almost indistinguishable from the result data rowset coming from any SQL query. There are some restrictions on what data comes back from an MDX query when it is requested as a rowset, which we will discuss in this section. In addition, the column names will not be like those from an SQL database. However, neither of these poses an obstacle.

DTS will request that the results to any query (SQL or MDX) be in tabular form. An important aspect of using DTS to get data out of OLAP Services is to understand how your MDX query ends up looking like a table. The OLE DB for OLAP specification documents the table layout. The process of laying out the tabular format is called "flattening" the result set. We will explain in this section which aspects of this you need to understand in order to use DTS. (If you are programming an application that will directly use OLE DB or ADO to retrieve the rows, you will want to refer to the programming documentation for OLE DB for OLAP and the PivotTable Service to get additional programming details.) Let's look next at how a query is mapped to tabular form.

Recall from Chapter 5 that an MDX query specifies results that are organized along a set of axes. Flattening orients the axes of the result set into rows and columns. There is a special division between axis 0 (the "columns" axis) and the other axes of the query. To prevent confusion between MDX "columns" and table columns, we will refer to the axes of an MDX result set as "axis 0" and "non-axis 0."

Axis 0

Each tuple from axis 0 will appear as its own column of the result rowset. For each of these columns, the column name will be formed from the unique names of the tuple's members, joined together by periods. For example, the following tuple on axis 0,

```
([Time].[All Time].[1965], [Geography].[USA].[IL].[Chicago])
```

would correspond to a column named:

```
[Time].[All Time].[1965].[Geography].[USA].[IL].[Chicago]
```

On each row of the resulting table, the columns for the axis 0 tuples will contain cell-related values. Since the actual cell values can be of any type and the type may change from row to row, the values will be returned as COM Variants. Only the cell values will be returned. If the query requests specific cell properties (as listed in Appendix A), the request will be ignored. Member properties cannot be returned for the dimensions of axis 0. An MDX query can request member properties for axis 0 without generating an error, but the request will be ignored.

Other Axes

The tuples for the non-axis 0 axes are essentially cross-joined together and placed in the result rows. The information that is returned for each dimension can be divided into two different cases depending on whether or not any properties have been specified in the query for the axis that contains the dimension (through the PROPERTIES . . . on *axis* clause).

When no properties have been specified on the axis, then for each dimension of each of the non-axis 0 axes there will be one result column for each level of that dimension from its root down to the lowest level of that dimension for which there will be a result member. (The All level, if it exists in a dimension, will not have a corresponding column.) Each column will have a name that consists of the level's unique name and "[CAPTION]," joined by a dot (.). For example, consider the use of a geography dimension that has country, region, state/province, and city levels. If a query only requests region members there will be one column for that dimension's region level and another for its country level. If a query results in a mix of country members, region members, and city members, there will be a column for each of the country, region, state/province, and city levels (even though no state/province was specifically requested). In the event that the members returned for any dimension are not all from the same level, some rows will have NULL member values. For example, using our geography dimension as just described, a query for

```
{[Geography].[France], [Geography].[France].[Bordeaux],
 [Geography].[France].[Bordeaux].[Cadillac]}
```

will produce the names for the following members in the rows:

[GEOG].[COUNTRY].[CAPTION]	[GEOG].[REGION].[CAPTION]	[GEOG].[STATE/PROVINCE].[CAPTION]	[GEOG].[CITY].[CAPTION]
France	<null>	<null>	<null>
France	West	Bordeaux	<null>
France	West	Bordeaux	Cadillac

Note that by the same token, the [Geography].[All Geography] member would be represented by a NULL in each column.

When any level's member properties are specified for an axis, there will be one column for each member property that is listed in the properties clause. Intrinsic properties like ID, KEY, and NAME can be requested, along with any member properties defined by the database. It is important to note that only the properties you list will have corresponding columns. For example, the following axis specification will only return a column for Manufacturer property values in the rowset:

```
CrossJoin ([Product].[Brand].Members, [Time].[Quarter].Members) PROPER-
TIES [Product].[Brand].[Manufacturer] on rows
```

If you also wanted a single column for each dimension's member names, you would need to specify the following:

```
CrossJoin ([Product].[Brand].Members, [Time].[Quarter].Members) PROPER-
TIES [Product].[Brand].[Manufacturer], [Product].Name, [Time].Name on
rows
```

Note that all slicer information is lost when an MDX query is flattened into a rowset. No member information will be returned for any dimensions that you fail to place on an axis. If it is important to retain the slice context for the cell data, place all relevant dimensions into an explicit axis of the query (for example, axis 2).

DTS Basics

DTS functions primarily as a data pump, moving and optionally transforming rows from one OLE DB data source to another. Although the DTS GUI is primarily oriented to sources of data that use SQL, it does not prohibit you from using a data source that speaks MDX (or any other language, for that matter). Although the DTS GUI provides special support for the construction of SQL queries, we will focus here on its use with Microsoft OLAP Services's MDX.

DTS executes *packages* that contain various nodes and arcs corresponding to the steps of a data transformation and movement process. Nodes can represent OLE DB data sources that function as sources or targets for rows. Nodes can also contain arbitrary language statements, such as SQL CREATE TABLE and UPDATE . . . WHERE . . . statements or MDX CREATE SET and USE LIBRARY statements. They can also contain more general function modules written in VBScript or JavaScript. Arcs can contain queries as well as mappings and transformations of output columns into input columns. They can also indicate precedence relationships for the purpose of establishing a sequence for operations carried out by the nodes they connect. As far as OLAP Services is concerned, DTS is just another client that attaches to the PivotTable Service, poses a query in MDX or SQL, and retrieves rows. Therefore, all integration issues (such as running the query or determining the destination table and the OLE DB source holding the table) are actually pushed to the DTS package. The minimum requirements for moving data from OLAP Services into an RDBMS is to set up one node for an OLAP Services data source and one node for an RDBMS data source and then connect them with a data transformation workflow arc.

To use OLAP Services as a data source for DTS, you must set up a data source node as a Microsoft Data Link connection instead of as an OLE DB for OLAP connection. (The OLE DB for OLAP connection will not provide a way for you to specify the database from which to query, which is a critical piece of information!). Configuring a Microsoft Data Link connection is analogous to setting up an ODBC data source: you specify the OLE DB provider, the location of the database, and the initial catalog to use. In the connection properties dialog, you click on the Properties button to bring up the Data Link's provider properties dialog, which is used to configure source databases for OLAP Services so you will recognize it and its options. Through the Data Link provider properties dialog, you specify "Microsoft OLE DB for OLAP services" as the provider, select the name of the OLAP Services server machine as the data source, and select the name of the database that you wish to query from as the initial catalog to use.

For space reasons, we will not go into the details of setting up a normal RDBMS connection for receiving the results of the query. For your target database, setting up a normal RDBMS connection would consist of choosing the correct OLE DB data source and picking out the right machine, database, catalog, and permissions for the target database. Finally, you would set up a "transform data" workflow connection from the query to the receiving connection. This is where most of the details appear. When you go to edit the properties of the workflow connection, you will see that the dialog is really configured for SQL queries. However, you can enter your MDX query into the "SQL Query" section, and it will be executed without any problems. Figure 12.3 shows a sample MDX query placed in that box. The destination table may or may not exist yet. If it doesn't, the Data Transformation Properties' "Destination" tab will give you the opportunity to define the table, and DTS will create a suggested table definition.

When you create the table in the DTS package, you will need to edit the names and data types for the suggested table definition. The default name suggestions will have dot-separated qualified names (like [Measures].[Qty] and [Customer].[Key]), which are illegal in SQL. The OLE DB column types for the cell value and member property columns of the flattened rowset will all be of type Variant, which the DTS GUI will suggest mapping to SQL types of BINARY (16). If you did not request member properties for an axis, the member captions will be suggested as nvarchar (128). You will want to edit these to be appropriate numeric, varchar, and date types. If any of the measures might have

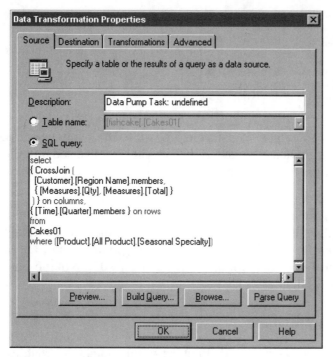

Figure 12.3 MDX query in "SQL Query" box.

empty cells or any member name columns might be empty for a resulting member, you must ensure that their columns are defined as NULL instead of NOT NULL. For example, the following MDX query requests a mixture of customer region names and state names, integer product keys, and a Qty measure that might be NULL:

```
SELECT
{ [Measures].[Qty] } on columns,
{ CrossJoin ( { [Customer].[Northeast],
        Descendants ([Customer].[Northeast], [Customer].[State]) },
[Product].[Brand].Members } PROPERTIES [Customer].[Region].Name,
   [Customer].[State].Name, [Product].Key on rows
FROM Shipments
```

This MDX query would generate the following suggested table definition (notice the lack of level identifiers in the customer dimension columns):

```
CREATE TABLE [dbo].[New Table] (
[Customer].[Name] binary (16)  NOT NULL
[Customer].[Name] binary (16)  NOT NULL,
[Product].[KEY] binary (16) NOT NULL,
[Measures].[Qty] binary (16) NOT NULL
)
```

You would edit this into the following:

```
CREATE TABLE [dbo].[CustProds] (
    [Customer Region Name] varchar (32) NOT NULL,
    [Customer State Name] varchar (32) NULL,
    [Product Key] integer  NOT NULL,
    [Measures Qty] integer  NULL
)
```

When the rows are actually transferred from the Microsoft OLAP Services rowset to the target database, each field value will be converted into the actual data type of the target table's column.

In the "Transformations" tab of Data Transformation Properties, you can adjust any links between the columns of the source rowset and the destination table. While we are on the subject of setting up the transformation properties, if you are sending the result to a table in SQL Server 7.0 you may also want to check the Keep Nulls and Table Lock options in the "Advanced" tab of the Data Transformation Properties dialog.

Example Query and Flow

Suppose our target is to create a mailing list of customers we wish to attract more business from and the products we believe we should promote to them. For example, for our 25 most profitable customers, we want to send them a set of coupons for their three favorite products. Because we want the information for these to appear in the rows, we will put them on axis 1. Since we are primarily interested in the set of customer members and their associated products, the choice of members from the other dimensions is arbitrary. We must pick something to fill into axis 0, so we will choose [Measures].[Sales].

What kind of information do we want for the customers and products? If we don't ask for any member properties for these dimensions, we will get their members' names back. However, to use the rows returned, we are probably going to have to join the result table to some other tables in our warehouse or operational system. One intrinsic property that we would like to leverage would be the member key values. Recall that the member key values are available in queries as the *dimension*.KEY and *level*.KEY properties. These values are specifically intended to be joined to the dimension tables, so we may as well leverage them.

Having decided on the information we want and the form we want it in, we will create a data link node, an RDBMS node, and a workflow arc between the two nodes. We will then fill the arc's workflow properties in. Figure 12.4 shows the query that was entered into the SQL Query area. The columns suggested by DTS for the result table are shown in Figure 12.5, along with the columns that we actually chose. We have no interest in the measure column in this query, so we do not put one in the table. Finally, we specify the mapping of source columns

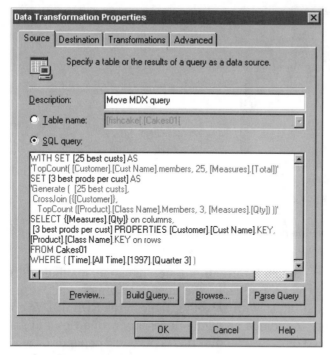

Figure 12.4 MDX query.

to table columns. We ensure that we are putting the customer and product keys into the right columns. Figure 12.6 shows what our mapping will look like.

That's it! Overall, our entire DTS package will look like any other, but the query to obtain our population of interest was much simpler than the equivalent SQL. When we run the package, the main transfer process will execute the query and insert the rows into the table that we have named as our target. This table can now be used as the basis for printing coupons or preparing an advertising circular to be mailed to the indicated customers.

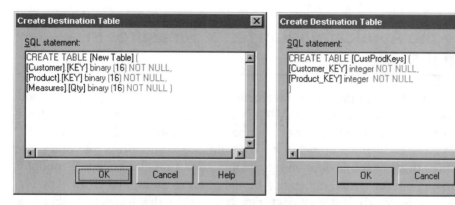

Figure 12.5 Columns suggested by DTS and specified by us.

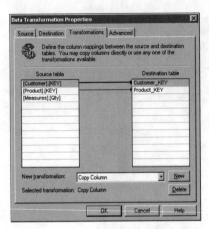

Figure 12.6 Ensuring the right mapping between columns.

If we have captured enough information (such as name, mailing address, and telephone numbers) as properties in the customer dimension, we might not need to join our result tables with any other table in the RDBMS. We could simply phrase the query to include all of the necessary properties and generate a table that will be used directly. Whether this is practical depends on several factors, but if you can have the information available then the process for using the analysis results can be simplified even further.

There may be other details that you want to attend to in the overall DTS package, but at this point you have a functioning query and the logic in place to create the table, execute the query, and pump the data in. Executing the package should give you an SQL table that can be integrated with other tables in any database, either in your warehouse or in your operational systems. You can also add any additional DTS steps to the transformation flow for your database. For example, you might add a step that creates indexes on the query result table, or you might add a step that schedules the result table to be replicated to remote databases.

Masking the Application Ranges of Measures in Virtual Cubes

Virtual cubes are an important mechanism for solving a variety of cube construction issues in Microsoft OLAP Services. Whether a cube is real (instantiated) or virtual, when an end user connects to that cube and begins navigating within it the conceptual model that we would like to support is that of a set of measures organized by common dimensions. For a regular cube this model is automatic, but for virtual cubes this model requires additional effort. The reason for this is that all the measures for each base cube that forms an input to the virtual cube are placed in parallel.

For example, a virtual cube for budget performance analysis may be based on two regular cubes, one holding actual data and another holding budget data. At least one of the regular cubes is associated with one slice of a Scenario dimension, so the budget analysis cube may use the Scenario dimension. Each of these cubes has identical dimensionality: time, geography, products, customers, and sales channels. Each of the cubes also has identical measures: units, sales, direct costs, and indirect costs. However, when the cubes are combined in the virtual budget analysis cube, there are two of every measure: two sales measures, two units measures, and so on. An MDS of the applicability ranges for the measures is shown in Figure 12.7a, and a sample report that compares actual to budget sales for a set of stores and months is shown in Figure 12.7b. As you can see, the display leaves something to be desired in terms of easy comprehensibility.

The duplication won't just create empty patches on a screen. Any inter-scenario calculations that are formed will need to involve not just different scenarios but different, related measures as well. This is something that query builders (human and software) will need to deal with over and over. The benefit of having a Scenario dimension is somewhat diminished if our measures are the major source of scenario identification. We cannot get away from dealing with this in the database, but we can at least hide it under a layer so that

a) MDS of measure application ranges

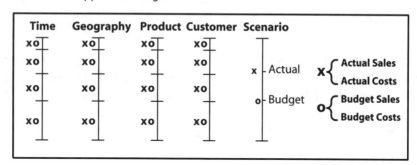

b) Query result for actual and budget sales

		1995		1996	
		Act. Sales	Bud. Sales	Act. Sales	Bud. Sales
Northeast	Actual	125		160	
	Budget		160		150
Southwest	Actual	110		140	
	Budget		130		110

Figure 12.7 Applicability range of measures within virtual cube created from identically dimensioned regular cubes.

end users and query builders alike deal with a cleaner dimensional model for the cube. To do this, we need to employ the following features and attributes in concert:

- Calculated measures
- Solve orders
- The IsInternal property of a measure
- The independence of a virtual cube's measure name from the corresponding base cube's measure name

The dimensionality of the cube is fine, and the members of all non-measures dimensions are also all fine. It is just the relationships between measures that we wish to alter. What we want to achieve is a set of calculated measures that each represent a single measure (like Units Sold) rather than independent measures that represent Actual Units Sold and Budget Units Sold. When someone is using the base cubes, they will see names for certain measures and expect to see those names in the new cube as well. When we define the virtual cube, we can redefine the names so they do not collide with our desired name. For example, the Units Sold measure from the Actual cube can be named "Actual Units Sold" in the virtual cube, and the Units Sold measure from the budget cube can be named "Budget Units Sold." Furthermore, we can use DSO to set the IsInternal property of each of these measures in the virtual cube so they do not appear in the metadata that a client can access. (They can still be used in queries and calculations; they will just have to be accessed by name.)

We then need to create a set of calculated measures, one for each measure duplicated in the base cubes. These calculated measures won't perform any calculations of note; they will just access the correct base measure for the particular scenario being accessed. For example, the formula for our calculated Units Sold measure would be as follows:

```
'iif ([Scenario].CurrentMember.Name = "Budget",
      [Measures].[Budget Units Sold], [Measures].[Actual Units Sold])'
```

We could also phrase this as a sum of the measures from the various cubes, as with

```
'Sum ({[Measures].[Actual Units Sold],
      [Measures].[Budget Units Sold]})'
```

Depending on how the values for the measures overlap in the virtual dimension's cell space, this may be exactly how you want to combine them. You should be aware that OLAP Services will need to query each base cube involved to create the sum. If there is only one correct base cube for the measure, then the logical test with iif()allows OLAP Services to search for the value only within the correct cube.

Finally, we need to pay close attention to our solve orders. Most if not all other calculations in this virtual cube that are generated by a client will come after this range-masking calculation, so we will want the solve order number associated with each of these calculated measures to be 0. We will therefore want all other calculated members on any dimension to have a solve order number of at least 1. As we noted in Chapter 4, solve order numbers can range up to more than 2,000,000,000, so adopting a practice in which all client solve orders start at, say, 1,000,000 will give you plenty of solve order headroom for both server-defined and client-defined calculated members.

When we are done, we will be able to browse a logical space whose MDS looks like that shown in Figure 12.8a. This logical space will result in reports that look like those shown in Figure 12.8b. The client no longer has to deal with empty spaces of measures when comparing actual to budget. Furthermore, the

a) MDS of altered measure application ranges

b) Query result for actual and budget sales, costs, and differences between actual and budget

		1995		1996	
		Sales	Costs	Sales	Costs
Northeast	Actual	125	80	160	190
	Budget	160	90	150	180
	Difference	-35	-10	10	10
	Percentage	-0.22	-0.11	0.07	0.06
Southwest	Actual	110	90	140	120
	Budget	130	90	110	140
	Difference	-20	0	30	-20
	Percentage	-0.37	0	0.27	-0.07

Figure 12.8 Applicability range of combined measures within virtual cube and sample report view from it.

budget absolute and percentage difference from actual formulas now looks like this:

```
CREATE MEMBER [Budget Performance].[Scenario].[Budget Difference With
Actual] AS '[Scenario].[Budget] - [Scenario].[Actual]'

CREATE MEMBER [Budget Performance].[Scenario].[Budget Percentage From
Actual] AS '[Scenario].[Budget] / [Scenario].[Budget Difference With
Actual]'
]
```

Summary

In this chapter, we have covered a few more of the advanced topics in the design and use of Microsoft OLAP Services cubes and databases. For many databases, making the data in a virtual cube appear more seamless to a client will be a bread-and-butter task and in that sense the range-masking calculated measure technique is more of a basic design pattern. The other two techniques we discussed—handling line-item dimensions and exporting query results as tables—involve somewhat more advanced interactions between cubes and database systems and will only be used for particular applications. Exporting query results back to the database involves viewing OLAP Services as just one piece of a larger system. We hope that you recognize other opportunities to exploit this point of view in your own applications.

CHAPTER 13

Security

Microsoft OLAP Services databases exist to make discoveries and decisions accessible to users, but securing the data within them is also an important consideration in their design. Not every organization will need extensive security on its databases, but most will need to keep some types of information private. This chapter discusses security features of OLAP Services, the implications of these features for database and cube designs, and some implementation considerations. The security model for the first release of Microsoft OLAP Services is, for the most part, extremely simple.

Security Architecture

Microsoft OLAP Services provides only two scopes for authorizing access: at the server level and at the cube level. Non-administrative users can be permitted or denied access to each cube within a database. Real cubes and virtual cubes are considered to be separate cubes, so the permissions granted for access to a real cube can be different from those granted to a virtual cube that incorporates that real cube. Permissions at a sub-cube level are not supported in the first release of OLAP Services. Administrative privileges will grant or deny administrative users the ability to perform any database management activity on each server individually.

For non-administrative access, privileges are granted by *roles*. A role is simply a category of user, and your categorizations will depend on your application and the organization that you are deploying the application for. A role can consist of a single user, NT groups, or both. A role-based security scheme allows groups of users with similar access needs to be efficiently represented in the security structure and granted access to databases and cubes as a group. OLAP Services's roles are similar to NT groups in this regard. Roles are kept on a database-by-database basis; if two or more databases have common roles between them, the role definitions must be copied from one database to the other(s).

For end-user access, there are two levels of permissions that can be specified on a cube: *read* and *read/write*. Read access gives the user the ability to perform all metadata and MDX queries on the cube. Read access also allows the user to modify values for leaf-level cells in a cube within his or her client session, but he or she will not be able to commit these changes to the server, even if the cube is write-enabled. Read/write access grants all the capabilities of read access as well as the ability to commit cell changes to the server on a write-enabled cube. Granting a user read/write access to a cube does not write-enable the cube. Neither read nor read/write access allows the user to affect the structure or content of a database (with the exception of write-back data), such as initiating the processing of dimensions or partitions. Roles are not declared to be read or read/write. Instead, you declare the use of a role in a cube to be read or read/write, so if a role has read/write access to one cube it only has read access to another.

There is no way to deny a user access to a Microsoft OLAP Services server. Although you can grant permissions on a cube-by-cube basis within a server, you cannot control permissions at a database level. OLAP Services's security scheme does not hide top-level database objects from unauthorized users. A user who connects to a server will be able to list all the databases on that server and all of the cubes for that database, even if that user does not have permissions to use any of those cubes. A user will only be able to browse the metadata of a cube and issue queries to the cube if he or she has permissions on it, however, so the only unauthorized objects he or she will be able to see are databases and cubes.

Administrative access is global to a server; there are no different levels of permissions. An administrative user can create, delete, and alter all database objects and properties on the server. This includes specifying security information within the database and processing dimensions and cubes. The administrator will be able to query all metadata and data out of every cube of every database on the server regardless of whether he or she has logged in on the server machine or on some other node of the network.

Authentication

Microsoft OLAP Services uses the Windows NT domain security for authorizing access. Thus, the users who are placed into roles are the users and groups recognized by the Windows NT domain security. The authenticated identity of the process that initiates a session at the PivotTable Service is the identity that access rights are checked against. For end users, this is generally their login identity, but it is also possible to have services that log in under a different identity than that of the user currently sitting at a workstation. For example, users accessing a Web interface would access the database using the identity of the Web server. OLE DB for OLAP and ADO MD each provide a mechanism for a client to specify authentication information such as username and password. However, the PivotTable Service will ignore this information in favor of the identity of the process. This is true even if the name and password that are specified are the username and password for an NT login.

Designing for Security

Although the security options in the first release of Microsoft OLAP Services are very limited, there are still a few ways that you can create varied access to stored information. Since you cannot restrict a user's access to a subset of a cube, you need to design cubes that as a whole provide only the information the user is allowed to see. Depending on the complexity of the cube(s) and how you need to restrict access, this will range from straightforward to nearly impossible. We won't go so far as to say absolutely impossible, but you will need to trade the costs of securing subsets of data off against the costs of creating and maintaining the applications in the first place. The brute-force method for creating restricted subsets of data is to create separate databases or cubes that contain only the data that a certain population is allowed to see. If you are willing to invest the redundant processing time, disk storage, and application maintenance that this requires, then you may find this a viable option.

Virtual cubes provide the major mechanism for restricting access to data without requiring that separate cubes be populated with aggregates. There are two ways that a virtual cube can restrict access to the data of a base cube: by hiding selected measures and by hiding levels of detail. The levels of detail removed from view can range from only the leaf level to hiding the entire dimension itself. For some applications and environments, this level of security will be perfectly adequate.

Other applications and environments may need to provide a finer granularity of security, and particularly the ability to restrict access on slices of data in a cube.

Imagine a cube of employee compensation data, with salary, bonus, and benefit measures; a time dimension; and an organizational dimension. Corporate managers can see all of the details for all divisions and departments. Divisional managers should be able to see the measures for their division and the departments within it. They may or may not be authorized to see companywide aggregates, but in any case they are not authorized to see the measures for other divisions. If the cube was constructed from partitions based on division slices, then permissions granted on a partition basis would help us toward the goal of restricting access on slices of data in a cube. Although we cannot restrict cube access to a slice, we can construct a similar partitioning scheme that builds a less restricted virtual cube out of more restricted base cubes.

When you use virtual cubes to implement security, either as restricted or combined views of other cubes, you do have a greater administrative burden. Not only must you coordinate the processing of virtual cubes with their base cubes, but you must also manage the replication of any desired calculated members from the base cube to the virtual cubes. You might think that one use of a virtual cube would be to simply suppress certain calculated members from a base cube without restricting the measures or levels. Remember, however, that there is nothing you can do in the calculated member defined in the cube that you cannot also do in the calculated member defined for a query.

Hiding Measures

When you create a virtual cube, you select the measures of the base cube or cubes that you wish to include in the virtual cube. All other measures of the base cube are completely unavailable in the virtual cube. This effectively hides those measures. For example, in the case of the employee compensation cube, some users may be allowed to see the salary, benefits, and bonus measures, while others are only allowed to see the salary and benefits measures. Including only the salary and benefits measures in the restricted virtual cube, and excluding the bonus measures, will keep them completely out of view. Figure 13.1 shows an MDS diagram of this schema. The "BoardMember" role has access to the equity bonus information, while the "Payroll Analyst" role only has access to the cash-related information.

Note that hiding measures is different from simply marking a measure as IsInternal. If a measure is marked as internal, it will not show up in the metadata reported either through OLE DB for OLAP or ADO MD, but an MDX query can still use it.

Moreover, the technique of hiding measures only works on measures that appear as part of a measures dimension. A line-item dimension (described in detail in Chapter 12, on advanced database and cube design) cannot use the

Base Cube

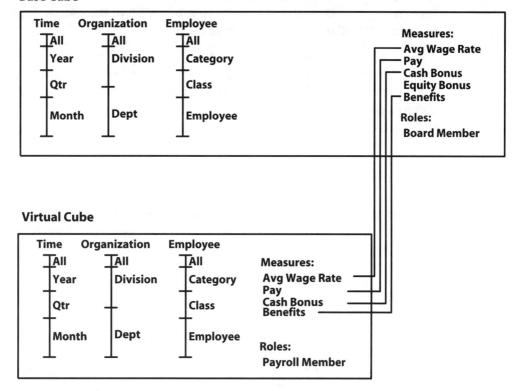

Figure 13.1 MDS of restriction by hiding measures.

technique because OLAP Services does not treat the line item dimension as a measures dimension.

Hiding Levels of Detail

The dimension levels that are enabled or disabled in a virtual cube are completely separate from the dimension levels enabled or disabled in its base cubes. When a level is disabled, it and its members do not appear in the metadata and cannot be referenced by MDX queries. If you need to restrict access to data below some dimension level for a class of users, you can exploit this feature to create a virtual cube that disables the requisite levels. The virtual cube will include all the measures that these users can see and will disable dimension levels from the leaf level of the dimension down to the lowest level that the restricted users can access. For example, an employee compensation base cube may contain salary and bonus information down to the department level. A virtual cube that disabled the department level would only allow access to salary and bonus information at the division level for users who needed to know something about the pay without knowing all of the details. Figure 13.2 shows an MDS diagram of this schema.

Entire dimensions can be suppressed from a base cube simply by excluding those dimensions in the virtual cube. Data queried from the virtual cube will come from an All-level aggregation of that dimension. For example, if the organization dimension were omitted from the restricted, virtual employee compensation cube, then the only salary and bonus information available to users of that cube would be company-wide information.

Hiding Slices

To restrict users' access to slices of data, we need to use a different tactic for employing virtual cubes than we used for hiding measures or levels. The structures of Microsoft OLAP Services support the ability to exclude measures and levels from a cube fairly directly. Although it doesn't let us exclude slices or par-

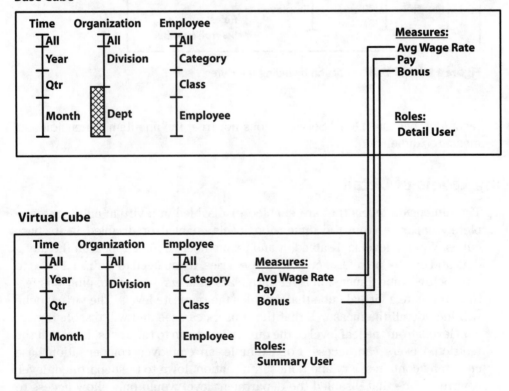

Figure 13.2 MDS of restriction by hiding levels.

titions, we can use the fact that virtual cubes allows us to include more than one cube to provide a degree of slice security. The trick will be to declare a single cube for each slice one which we want to provide a restricted view and then create a virtual cube that combines all the restricted views into a global cube that provides a less restricted view.

There are some caveats to this approach that we will state up front. First, there is a limit to the number of measures and slices that go into the final unrestricted cube. If each cube has only one measure, then no more than 128 separate slices can be combined. Second, to create the appearance of a unified single cube for the global, unrestricted cube, you will need to employ the technique called "masking virtual cubes' application ranges through formulas," which we described in Chapter 12, on advanced database and application design. If some slices overlap, the task of creating the necessary formulas or otherwise interpreting the measures will get more complex. (If slices overlap, you also have spent at least some redundant storage and processing on constructing the base cube because overlapping slices mean the same data has been processed and stored in two or more base cubes.) Third, each base slice cube will not see any high-level aggregates from other slices, only its own contribution at a higher level. This hiding slices technique is most tractable for slicing on one dimension only; slicing on more than one dimension creates a much greater administrative overhead.

Because the base cubes in this schema are meant to be combined into a single virtual cube, there is no significant difference in their dimensionality. The dimension on which the slices are defined must be shared between all of the cubes. This means that every user of the cubes will see the same dimensional information. A user looking at a cube whose data is restricted to the months, quarters, and year of 1995 will still see the full time dimension, including the months and years of 1994 and 1996, but with empty cells. The hiding slices technique offers no way to restrict access to the members and properties outside of the authorized slice, only to the data that goes into the cells.

Let us illustrate this technique with an example. Mighty Manufacturing is divided into four divisions: Big Tools, Middling Gears, Little Widgets, and Headquarters. The top management of each division will be allowed to see its division's compensation information, and the senior corporate management will be allowed to see the compensation information for all divisions. To implement this access, we need to create four different base cubes—one for each division—and one virtual cube. Each base cube will share the same time and division dimension, and the virtual cube will also expose these two dimensions. An MDS diagram of this scenario along with the various role permissions is shown in Figure 13.3.

Senior corporate management will probably want to deal with a simpler unrestricted cube that has three integrated measures rather than four sets of three

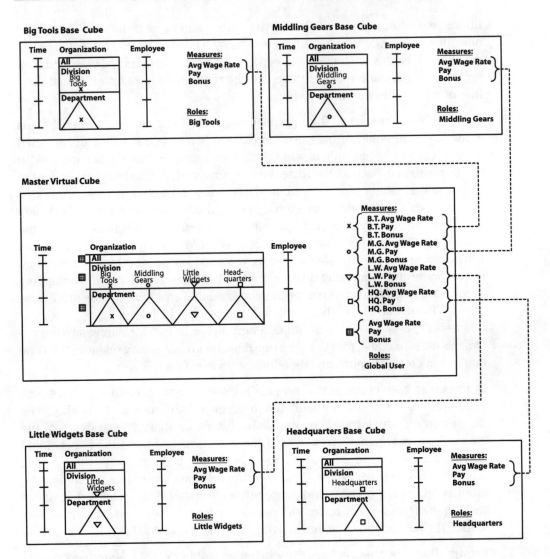

Figure 13.3 Diagram of cube slice security schema.

measures from each base cube. The MDS shows the addition of three calculated members. It also shows that the original measures have each been renamed and marked as internal to simplify the presentation of the cube.

Implementing Security

The OLAP Manager interface for setting up roles and adding them to databases is simple and straightforward. For any database, the Roles node in the database objects tree will expand to show all roles defined for the database. By right click-ing on it and choosing "New Role . . . " you will bring up a dialog that lists the roles defined for the database. Any of these can be selected and edited at any point; the editor allows you to add and remove NT users and groups through an interface similar to the one used for defining groups in the NT security scheme. Figure 13.4 shows the role-definition dialog being used to define a new role, "Fishcake Analyst." This same dialog is also used to edit existing roles.

For any cube, you can list the roles that have been assigned access to the cube at any time by expanding the Roles node under that cube's node in the database objects tree. Right clicking on the cube's Roles node and selecting "Manage Roles" from the context menu will bring up the dialog that allows you to add and remove authorized roles from the cube. From this same dialog you can specify for each role whether it will have read-only or read/write access to the cube. Finally, from this dialog you can also bring up the role-definition dialog to add new roles. Figure 13.5 shows an example of this dialog in use after the "Fishcake Analyst" role has been added with read-only permission to the Cakes01 cube.

"Under the hood" in DSO, there are database role objects (clsDatabaseRole) that each represent a named role and the set of NT groups and users assigned

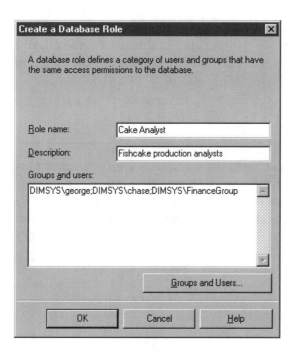

Figure 13.4 Role-definition dialog.

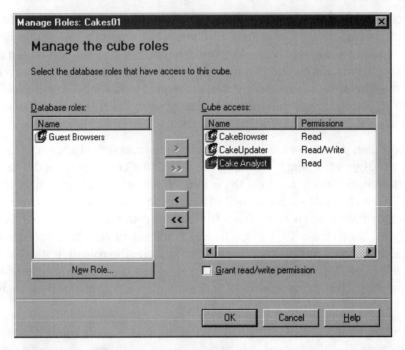

Figure 13.5 Role access-granting dialog.

to it. There are also cube role objects (clsCubeRole) that each represent the association of a database role with a cube. In this regard, the OLAP Manager appears to offer the full range of functionality provided by the underlying metadata object structure.

Summary

In this chapter, we have explored the intrinsic security features provided by Microsoft OLAP Services as well as the way virtual cubes can be employed to create different secure zones of data. We expect that as OLAP Services matures, additional features will be added to increase the available security options.

CHAPTER 14

Extending OLAP Services through External Functions

In this chapter we will discuss how to create libraries of external functions for use with Microsoft OLAP Services and illustrate possible applications for these libraries. Libraries of external functions are invaluable because while Microsoft OLAP Services implements a rich subset of the full MDX specification, and adds a number of its own functions and operators on top of it, MDX fails to cover all of the analysis functionality that a typical application will need. For example, simple operations, like rounding a value to a specified number of decimal places, are not present as primitives in the language. However, through use of libraries of external functions, any calculation you can express as a function call (within certain limits) can be used in MDX. This feature can be applied in many practical ways in any kind of application, in any sort of calculated member or named set.

Before we get started, let's clarify our terminology. Microsoft's OLAP Services documentation refers to what we call *external functions* as *UDFs* (user-defined functions). We use the term *external functions* because, for example, the function libraries for Excel and Visual Basic for Applications (VBA) fill in a large number of MDX gaps right out of the box, and yet they don't count as "user-defined." You may also purchase libraries from third parties or perhaps distribute libraries you create to others.

In this chapter, we will discuss how external functions are referenced in an MDX expression, what kinds of data they can accept and return, how to construct them (using Visual Basic as the example language), and the special MDX extension functions provided by OLAP Services that are particularly useful in conjunction with external functions. The chapter is organized into the following sections:

- Overview of using external functions with MDX
- Argument and return-type details
- MDX functions for use with external functions
- Additional considerations for external functions
- Loading and using libraries

We will illustrate these topics with several examples along the way. In Chapter 9, we described MDX calculations that would be less cumbersome if they were contained in an external function. In this chapter, we will explain how those calculations are implemented and provide additional examples.

Overview of Using External Functions with MDX

External functions and MDX operations work together. MDX constructs may prepare data as arguments to external functions, and all external functions may return data values that will be used by OLAP Services. We will therefore begin with a simple example to lay the groundwork for an understanding of how MDX and external functions interact. Suppose you are writing MDX expressions that require numerous percentage difference calculations. For example, you need to calculate Profit Percentage as '([Measures].[Sales] - [Measures].[Cost]) / [Measures].[Cost]' and you need to calculate Scenario Percentage Variance as '([Scenario].[Actual] - [Scenario].[Forecast]) / [Scenario].[Forecast]'. If you are working on a scenario analysis cube that is comparing the relative accuracy of twelve different forecasts to actual results, you may feel like encapsulating this in a single function that we'll call PctDiff(). We would use this function in expressions like 'PctDiff ([Measures].[Sales], [Measures].[Cost])' and 'PctDiff([Scenario].[Actual], [Scenario].[Forecast])'.

Calling external functions in Microsoft OLAP Services is usually done in just this format: the name of the function, an opening parenthesis, each argument in order and separated by commas, and then a closing parenthesis. (If the external function has no arguments, then you use an empty pair of parentheses. For example, the bare name PctDiff would be treated like a member or set name, while PctDiff() would be treated like a function.) For example, using our PctDiff() function, the complete syntax for creating our Scenario Percentage Variance member in a cube named Scenario Analysis would be as follows:

```
CREATE MEMBER
[Scenario Analysis].[Scenario].[Scenario Percentage Variance]
AS 'PctDiff([Scenario].[Actual], [Scenario].[Forecast])'
```

For OLAP Services to use external functions, they must come packaged in libraries of functions that are accessible through ActiveX Automation. More than one external function can reside in a library. Since external functions are by definition not a part of OLAP Services, you need to make it aware of them. With the exception of the Excel and VBA libraries, which are automatically loaded when your PivotTable Service starts up, you must tell OLAP Services to load the library or libraries that contain the functions before you use them. The basic MDX statement for loading a library is USE LIBRARY *"library-name"*. We will explain this in greater detail later in the chapter.

The easiest way to create an external function in Visual Basic (version 5.0 and higher) is to simply create, in an ActiveX DLL or other ActiveX library/executable type, a class with "GlobalMultiuse" instancing and then add public functions to it. For example, our PctDiff() function would be created with the following:

```
Public Function PctDiff (ByVal A As Double, ByVal B As Double)
As Double
PctDiff = (A - B) / B
End Function
```

This declares the function as taking two double-typed arguments and returning a double result, which is what we want. The key features of the class are that it must be global (not hidden or restricted) and that the functions to be used must all be public.

External functions are useful both for calculating cell values and defining named sets. Although you can use the results of any external function as a cell value, you can also use a string result to completely specify or partly specify a set by using the StrToSet(), StrToTuple(), and Members() functions. Many of the useful applications of external functions involve defining sets and tuples, such as slicers for queries.

Argument and Return-type Details

You can pass numbers, strings, and arrays of numbers or strings into external functions, and they can return either numbers or strings. The arguments for an external function can be declared to be number types, strings, arrays of numbers or strings, or variant types. If the type is specifically declared in the function signature (like double, integer, or string), the value passed from Microsoft OLAP Services for that argument will be coerced into that type when the function is called. For example, if our PctDiff() function takes two arguments of type double, and it is called with the value of an integer-type measure at some cell, then the integer will be changed into a double. If it is called with a string, such as a property value (which must be a string in OLAP Services), the first digit of the string will be converted into a number when the function is called. (You can use the Val() function, which is part of the VBA library, to convert the string into a number first. For example, PctDiff(Val("20"), Val("15")) will return 0.333.)

If the argument is a variant type, OLAP Services will pass the argument as its own internal type for the value. Depending on the actual type of the cell, the value that is received by the external function may be a 32-bit integer, a 64-bit integer, a single or double float, or a string. An empty cell passed to an external function will be received by the external function as an empty variant.

The return type of an external function is a little more restricted in scope. You can declare the return type to be a number, a string, or a variant. If you declare the type to be a variant, you can only return numbers from it—not strings or arrays. Also, in the first release of OLAP Services, if an external function returns an empty variant, the PivotTable Service will return an error condition for the calculation. That behavior may be fixed by the time you read this.

Passing Arrays of Values to External Functions

You can pass arbitrary-size arrays of values into external functions through the MDX extension function SetToArray(). Although the documentation for Microsoft OLAP Services indicates that SetToArray() only creates arrays of numbers, it will in fact create sets of strings as well, which makes it useful for scanning sets of member names and property values as well as for processing a set of numbers. SetToArray() is useful for creating all kinds of custom aggregator functions. For each tuple in the set that is passed to SetToArray(), OLAP Services will place a value in the array at the corresponding location in the array, so there will be one value in the array for each tuple in the set (with one exception case that we will describe later in this section), in the same order.

For example, consider the issues we examined in Chapter 9 regarding the construction of cumulative sums of members. We proposed an external function, PartialSum(), to perform this task. As envisioned there, PartialSum() takes three arguments: an array of values to sum across, an array of names corresponding to the values, and the name of the tuple at which summing should stop. In VB, we could code the function like this:

```
Public Function PartialSum (ByRef ArgVals() As Double, ByRef ArgNames()
As String, ByVal StopAt As String) As Double
Dim Start As Integer
Dim Finish As Integer
```

```
Dim i As Integer

Start = LBound(ArgVals, 1)  ' for safety
Finish = UBound(ArgVals, 1)

' initialize working sum to zero
PartialSum = 0
For i = Start To Finish
    ' add value for this tuple
    PartialSum = PartialSum + ArgVals(i)
    ' leave if we have encountered the stopping point
    If ArgVals(i) = StopAt Then Return
Next i

' If we get here, there is a problem
' leave the next two commented out in order to simply return the sum we
got
' PartialSum = 0
Err.Raise 9999

End Function
```

The function takes the lower and upper bounds of the array and loops through the argument value array, adding each value into the sum. (Although the documentation for OLAP Services does not discuss the lower-bound number for the array—does the array numbering start at 0, 1, or something else?—the numbering does consistently start at 0.) At each cycle through the loop, the function tests whether the current argument name is equal to the name at which the loop should stop, and when that condition is met the function returns the value. If the function does not encounter the name to stop at in the array of names, we have three possible choices: return the total across the entire set, return zero, or raise an error. We have chosen the most conservative approach in the code (to raise an error), but there are arguments to be made for either of the other two outcomes. We could then call this function in a query to generate cumulative sums, as with the following simple query, which would yield the result shown in Figure 14.1 as a spreadsheet grid and as a graph:

```
WITH
MEMBER [Measures].[Geog. Name] AS '[Geography].CurrentMember.UniqueName'
SET [Ordered States] AS 'Order ([Geography].[State].Members, [Mea-
sures].[Profit], BDESC)'
MEMBER [Measures].[Cum Profit] AS
'PartialSum (
    SetToArray ([Ordered States], [Geography], [Measures].[Profit]),
    SetToArray ([Ordered States], [Geography], [Measures].[Geog. Name]),
    [Geography].CurrentMember.UniqueName
)'
SELECT
```

```
{ [Ordered States] } on columns,
{ [Measures].[Profit], [Measures].[Cum Profit] } on rows
FROM
[Sales Cube]
```

The first release of Microsoft OLAP Services makes every value of the array have the same type. That is, arrays can be of numbers or text can be passed to functions, but OLAP Services cannot pass arrays of variants to an external function. If OLAP Services could pass variants, then we might be able to pass in a single two-dimensional array containing pairs of "(name, value)" and simplify our MDX a bit more. But the function is still handy enough as it is.

Notice that we passed the string array in by first declaring a measure to simply return the unique name of the current geography member and then using that as the value expression for SetToArray(). OLAP Services generates a parser error if you try to use any value expression that is not the value of a cell here, so we need to make sure to make it a cell value.

Because arrays are passed in COM variant types, we might think about passing accepting arrays in variant arguments. If we declare our array input to be of variant type, then we must understand how Microsoft OLAP Services prepares

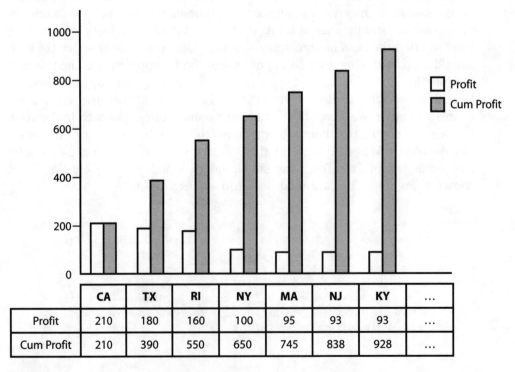

Figure 14.1 Result of cumulative sum query using external function.

the array in its native type. Recall from Chapter 6 how the data type for each cell is determined independently of the type of any other cell. When OLAP Services creates the array, it chooses the data type of the first value that it places into the array as the type for the array. If that value is a double, then the variant will contain an array of double-typed values. If that value is an integer, then the variant will contain an array of integer-typed values, and so on. If the first value is an empty cell, then an empty variant is passed rather than an array whose first element is zero. (Since the variant cannot itself contain an array of variants, no empty argument can be passed in an array.) Any value after the first value that is empty in OLAP Services will have a zero placed in the corresponding array position. Given the issues that handling the array data types entails, you may wish to declare your array arguments as being arrays of a specific type.

Raising an error was one of the options that we listed in the code for Partial-Sum() for the case when the stop-at name is not found. If your external function raises an error, then OLAP Services will immediately stop evaluating the formula and return an error condition for the cell instead of a value for it. A well-constructed client will somehow feed this information back to the user to let him or her know that something went wrong when the cell was calculated.

If you are paying attention to run-time performance (and that is a good idea), you may have already seen how the SetToArray() function can be made more efficient. Although a member's unique name will uniquely identify the member within the dimension, the member also has an intrinsic integer ID property. Having OLAP Services construct the array of integers is likely to be faster, and it will certainly be faster for our external function to test each of them to see if they are the last one to be processed. We can rewrite our function as follows:

```
Public Function PartialSum (ByRef ArgVals() As Double, ByRef ArgIDs() As
Integer, ByVal StopAt As Integer) As Double
Dim Start As Integer
Dim Finish As Integer
Dim i As Integer

Start = LBound(ArgVals, 1)  ' for safety
Finish = UBound(ArgVals, 1)

' initialize working sum to zero
PartialSum = 0
For i = Start To Finish
    ' add value for this tuple
    PartialSum = PartialSum + ArgVals(i)
    ' leave if we have encountered the stopping point
    If ArgIDs(i) = StopAt Then Return
Next i

' If we get here, there is a problem
' leave the next two commented out in order to simply return the sum we
```

```
got
' PartialSum = 0
Err.Raise 9999

End Function
```

Our function would be used in our sample query as follows:

```
WITH
MEMBER [Measures].[Geog. ID] AS
'[Geography].CurrentMember.Properties("ID")'
SET [Ordered States] AS 'Order ([Geography].[State].Members,
[Measures].[Profit], BDESC)'
MEMBER [Measures].[Cum Profit] AS
'PartialSum (
    SetToArray ([Ordered States], [Geography], [Measures].[Profit]),
    SetToArray ([Ordered States], [Geography], [Measures].[Geog. ID]),
    [Measures].[Geog. ID]
)'
SELECT
{ [Ordered States] } on columns,
{ [Measures].[Profit], [Measures].[Cum Profit] } on rows
FROM
[Sales Cube]
```

One subtle point to note regarding SetToArray() is how Microsoft OLAP Services constructs the array. Recall from Chapter 7 how an invalid tuple specification in a set specification ends up contributing no tuple to the set. For example, if a time dimension's month level starts with January 1997, then the set specification {[Time].[Jan 1997], [Time].[Jan 1997].PrevMember, [Time].[Jan 1997].NextMember } will result in a set of only two tuples (for January and February). When this set is used to materialize an array that is passed to an external function via SetToArray(), the set will only contain two values as a result. If you construct your sets using functions like .PrevMember, Cousin(), ParallelPeriod(), SetToArray(), LastPeriods(), and the like, you will need to code your external functions to take this into account.

MDX Functions for Use with External Functions

In addition to SetToArray(), which can only be used with external functions, there are a number of functions specific to OLAP Services's implementation of MDX that are most useful in combination with external functions. We list them in Table 14.1 and describe their utility in the following paragraphs. As in Chapters 7 and 8, each function is marked by an asterisk (*) since it is an OLAP Services extension to the MDX specification.

Table 14.1 MDX Functions useful with External Functions

EXTENSION	RETURNS	SYNOPSIS
*	string	SetToStr (Set)
*	string	TupleToStr (Tuple)
*	set	StrToSet (String Expression)
*	tuple	StrToTuple (String Expression)
*	member	Members (String Expression)
*	dimension	Dimensions (String Expression)
*	level	Levels (String Expression)

We will discuss most of these functions below. We leave application of the Dimensions() and Levels() functions to your imagination and application requirements.

SetToStr(), TupleToStr()

SetToStr() converts the given set specification into a string. It does not convert the values associated with the set's tuples into a string. The format of the string is simple and is fully described in Chapter 7. We could well have written Partial-Sum() so that it uses SetToStr() instead of an array of strings or member IDs. An external function that uses SetToStr() might be easier to write and might run faster if it uses SetToArray() instead of SetToStr()since the string will need to be parsed in the external function if the tuples are to be processed there. Tuple-ToStr() is similar except that it converts only a single tuple to a string.

Members(), StrToSet(), StrToTuple()

Suppose that we want to create an MDX query that always requested data for the current day, for example, by using it as a slicer in the query. If we are generating the query dynamically, we can create an MDX expression every time the query is accessed, which puts the current date into the slicer. However, we can get the same effect through a completely static query by using an external function that returns the name of the current month. For example, a query that always returned the year-to-date sales through the current month might be written as follows:

```
WITH
MEMBER [Measures].[Sales YTD] AS
```

```
'Sum (PeriodsToDate ([Time].[Year], Members (OurCurDate ())),
      [Measures].[Sales])'
SELECT
{ [Products].[Division].Members } on columns,
{ [Geography].[Regions].Members } on rows
FROM
[Sales Tracking]
WHERE ([Measures].[Sales YTD])
```

The logic that makes this query tick can be included in a single VB function that is 17 lines long, including white space. Assuming that the levels of the time dimension are [All], [Year], [Quarter], and [Month], the following VB code would return the appropriate name (assuming default time member names are used):

```
Public Function OurCurDate() As String
Dim TheDate As Date


TheDate = Date

' e.g. "[Time].[All Time].[1999].[Quarter 1].[February].[Feb 01, 1999]"
OurCurDate = "[Time].[All Time].[" & _
               DatePart("yyyy", TheDate) & _
        "].[" & _
          "Quarter " & Format(DatePart("q", TheDate)) & _
        "].[" & _
          Format(TheDate, "mmmm") & _
        "].[" & _
          Format(TheDate, "mmm dd, yyyy") & _
        "]"


End Function
```

In our own validation of this function, Microsoft OLAP Services did not recognize the simple name of the date (like [Time].[Feb 01, 1999]), so we also add the names of the ancestor members to create the complete unique name. We must take care that the name logic is in synch with the name logic of the dimension. For example, if we change the way the quarters are named so that Q1 of 1999 is renamed from [Quarter 1] to [Q1, 1999], then we need to update the function. (If we were generating MDX dynamically to insert the current month, we would have needed to update its code generator too, so there is no great need to keep naming priniciples in synch).

The major difference between Members() and StrToTuple() is simply that Members() returns a single member while StrToTuple() returns a tuple of arbitrary dimensionality. You could, of course, construct a tuple using multiple calls to Members(). For example:

```
(Members(MemberF1()), Members(MemberF2()))
```

specifies a tuple that combines the member whose name is returned by MemberF1() with the member whose name is returned by MemberF2().

StrToSet() returns an actual set, so it would be used in contexts in which StrToTuple() and Members() cannot be. You could, of course, express one-tuple sets as `{ StrToTuple(...) }` or `{ Members(...) }`. For example, the statement

```
CREATE SET [Production].[ProductsToAnalyze] AS
'StrToSet( MyEFThatReturnsAProductSetString(...))'
```

will generate a named set within the context of the production cube that you can use in any number of subsequent queries.

Additional Considerations for External Functions

Although the calling interface between an external function and Microsoft OLAP Services is reasonably restricted, there are few limits on what the external function does while it is executing. It may open and read files, read the registry, put up dialogs, interact with other programs, and so on. (One restriction to note: while the external function is executing, the OLE DB for OLAP session that is executing the MDX query or statement which calls the external function is blocked. This means that the external function cannot itself call back into OLAP Services on the same session.) A custom browser could expose a global class containing functions that, when called, reference cached metadata, user preferences, real-time data feeds, and so on. These will all be very application-specific, so we will not attempt to go through all of the possibilities here, but you may find that they make a great deal of sense for your own application.

One interesting use of an external function is to have an application combine its specific calculations with cube data in MDX queries. Your application may need to perform some amount of data processing that would be inconvenient in MDX queries and then combine the results with data in an OLAP Services cube. One way to perform the combining of the results would be to feed them into a fact table and process a cube that provides additional calculations on them. If the scale of the calculations is small enough (in terms of number of cells calculated and suitability to calculation in a client's session), it may make sense to have your application read its input data through MDX, perform its calculations, and then expose its results to further MDX calculations through an external function that references the results. Candidates for this approach would be any calculations that require iterative methods on the data from OLAP Services and return results that map to cells in the database.

Loading and Using Libraries

Libraries must be loaded by executing the USE LIBRARY statement (an extension to MDX). Like CREATE MEMBER and CREATE SET statements, this statement may be executed on the fly at the client or may be stored in a command object at the server and invoked when you connect to a database or cube. When you register a function library at the server through the OLAP Manager's calculated member builder, a USE LIBRARY statement for the library you chose gets saved in such an object.

USE LIBRARY Syntax

The USE LIBRARY statement takes the form,

```
USE LIBRARY [library-spec [, library-spec . . .]].
```

The USE LIBRARY statement controls the loading and unloading of external function libraries. Zero, one, or more than one library paths may be listed as arguments to the command, separated by commas. Each library spec is a string that contains either the directory path and file name of the file that contains the function library's type library or a class name that appears in the system registry and identifies the type library and the location of the executable code (.DLL, .OCX, .EXE). Executable files (.EXE or .DLL), ActiveX controls (.OCX), and type library files (.DLL, .OLB, .TLB) files are candidates. OLAP Services must find the type library of the function library to understand the functions, and these files all contain enough information for OLAP Services to find the type library information. You can specify the name of the class directly as well.

When one or more libraries are listed in the command, the specified files are examined and their applicable functions loaded. If the same function name exists in two or more files (either in the same statement or from one USE LIBRARY command to another) and that function name is used in an MDX expression, the first function with that name that was loaded is the version OLAP Services calls. For example, the following statement loads two external function libraries from DLLs:

```
USE LIBRARY
"D:\AppSystems\Bin\StatFunctions01.DLL",
"D:\AppSystems\Bin\FinanceFunctions02.DLL"
```

The following loads a library based on class name:

```
USE LIBRARY "EFStatsPackage.FunctionsClass1"
```

If USE LIBRARY is called without any library pathnames being listed, then all function libraries that are currently loaded become unloaded. There is no way to selectively unload libraries.

Loading the Library

Using the name of the file that contains the function class is a simple way to identify and load the library on a given machine. When you are creating a USE LIBRARY statement that may be executed on multiple client machines, you will run into the issue of exactly where the file has been installed to. For example, it may have been installed to a directory on the C:\ drive of one machine and the D:\ drive of another machine. When this may become an issue, the easiest solution is to obtain the class name and reference that is used in the USE LIBRARY statement. This is the technique that the OLAP Manager uses when it registers function libraries.

Remember that if you are distributing ActiveX DLL components to client machines, you must register them with COM on the client by running RegSvr32 as well as make the library available on that machine.

Disambiguating Duplicated Function Names

There is nothing to prevent you from loading two or more function libraries that each contain a function with the same name. Even when a single USE LIBRARY statement references multiple libraries, they are always loaded one at a time, so there is a clear ordering in terms of which library was loaded before or after which other library. When a function name is found in two or more libraries, the version that was loaded first is the one that is called if the function is simply called by name. For example, if library A and library B both contain a PctDiff() function and library B is loaded before library A, then the formula 'PctDiff ([Time], [Time].PrevMember)' will invoke library B's implementation.

You can explicitly qualify the name of the function so as to pick out the exact version that you wish to call, however. The syntax for this is to prefix the name of the function with the class ID of the library. If the class ID of library A is EFStatsPackage.FunctionsClass and the class ID of library B is EFFinancialPackage.FunctionsClass, then the formula

---

Class Names Generated in Visual Basic

Remember that when you create a class in Visual Basic, VB will prepend and underscore to the name of the class. If you create a VB project named EFStatsPackage, create within it a class called "FunctionsClass," and add a function named PctDiff() to that class, you would refer to the specific function within that class by EFStatsPackage!_FunctionsClass!PctDiff (...), not by EFStatsPackage!FunctionsClass!PctDiff (...).

```
'EFStatsPackage!FunctionsClass!PctDiff ([Time], [Time].PrevMember)'
```

will call the version of PctDiff() that resides in EFStatsPackage.FunctionsClass (our library A).

Summary

When we extend the calculation ability of Microsoft OLAP Services to include anything we can create an ActiveX function interface that makes it possible to directly satisfy application requirements that OLAP Services by itself cannot. In this chapter, we covered the mechanisms that you use to call into and receive results from an external function as well as how to register them for use with OLAP Services. We also looked at a set of examples to illustrate situations that these mechanisms can be applied in as well as how to implement them, so you can write your own with confidence. Many applications may have no need for them at all, but you may find they are the perfect technique for implementing the functionality your particular application needs.

CHAPTER 15

Tutorial 1:
Health Care Benefits Analysis

A s health care costs increase, benefits managers must continually look for ways to manage the cost of employee health care. One focus of their investigations is the use of health care services and accompanying costs. For example, are employees using more expensive out-of-network service providers? Do some hospitals admit people for longer periods than others for the identical treatment? Do some providers use more procedures than others for the same illness? With access to up-to-date, detailed claims data, benefits managers can get a better handle on where their health care dollars are going. Fortunately, the fictitious organization we illustrate in this chapter (we'll call it "Amalgamated Industries") has access to all such pertinent data.

In this tutorial we will create a Microsoft OLAP Services application for analyzing employee health care usage within Almagamated Industries. In addition to basic OLAP Services tasks, this tutorial will show you how to do the following.

In the section titled "Identify/Create Dimension Data Source Tables/Views" you will:

- Create a time dimension table from data in an existing fact table
- Handle dimensions with irregular or ragged hierarchies
- Handle data entering a cube at different levels of a dimension

In the section titled "Identify Calculations" you will:

- Use calculated members for semi-additive measures

Finally, in the section titled "Build the Virtual Benefits Cube" you will:

- Use virtual cubes to provide a consolidated view of data
- Use Decision Support Objects (DSO) to create calculated members in virtual cubes

Before beginning this tutorial you will need to create an SQL Server 7 database using the tables and data found in the Microsoft Access database named benefits.mdb from the CD-ROM that accompanies this book. You will also need to create an ODBC data source for the database on the server running Microsoft OLAP Services. Instructions for both of these tasks can be found in the "setuprdb.doc" file on the CD-ROM.

Analyze Needs

Before we even open the OLAP Manager console, we will start by examining how our "Almagamated Industries" currently analyzes health care benefits data and what its benefits managers need to do their jobs better.

Current Workflow

Today, all health care claims data for the company resides on a mainframe transaction database located off site. Although logistically Amalgamated has 20-hour high-speed access to the data, only three people in the IT department have the equipment and training required to make requests to the database. The DBAs in IT submit a series of stock reports every month, and the results are returned to the analysts in both ASCII text files and in printed form. The analysts then import the data into Excel or Access on their own workstations for further analysis. Analysts also regularly submit requests for custom reports to the DBAs who then submit queries to the database through batch jobs. The analysts generally receive the results of such custom requests within 24 hours.

Desired Model

The company's benefits managers and analysts are satisfied with the data they currently receive. Quite frankly, however, given how long it takes to get data and manipulate it for analysis they don't have the time to truly explore the data on an ad hoc basis and investigate whether new data will help them manage the company's health plans better. Thus, the first step everyone has agreed upon is to make sure the data is readily accessible to analysts. In addition, some common framework for the data will be created as a more coherent starting point for analysis in place of the existing multitude of disparate spreadsheets and desktop databases.

Several months ago Amalgamated began a "Universal Data Access" project, starting with the creation of an on-site data warehouse, part of which contains the benefits data. As a manager in the Universal Data Access project, you've become the company expert in decision support (having just read Erik Thomsen's *OLAP Solutions* [Wiley, 1998] and this book) and have been assigned the task of creating a separate data mart that benefits managers can use continuously without impacting the rest of the Amalgamated's access to the data warehouse.

Analyze Data

Our first task is to gain a full understanding of the data we have to work with. The data warehouse that holds our benefits data contains copious amounts of information about our organization. For the sake of clarity, we'll assume that we've already taken the time to identify the tables and data within the warehouse that are useful for our project. Our next step is to conduct a thorough review of the desired analyses to determine how we will use the data.

Identify Dimensions

Amalgamated's data warehouse contains three fact tables of interest to us: fact_population, fact_activity, and fact_claims. The facts are organized by various combinations of the following dimensions, which will allow for productive analysis of Amalgamated's healthcare benefits programs. Unless otherwise noted, all these dimensions consist of a single level of members for which analysts will want to see an aggregate total value:

Plan. The benefits plan that is providing coverage.

Employee class. The covered person's employment status—active, retired, and so on.

Provider. The health care provider submitting the claim.

Network status. Whether the claim was made by a provider inside or outside of the network of providers with which the company has established contracts.

MDC. Major Diagnostic Category—an industry-standard description of the problem being treated.

Service classification. The type of service provided. Services themselves can be grouped into Inpatient, Outpatient, and Drug categories. As such, the dimension should have two levels that aggregate to a single total.

Financial accounts. The financial account against which a claim was charged. Financial Accounts can be organized into multiple levels. We'll examine the levels in greater detail shortly.

Period. The date of the transaction. Data is organized by month, and analysts wish to explore the data by year, quarter, and month.

Note that at this point we're not yet concerned about the specific details regarding our dimensions. At this initial stage we want to establish the broad dimensionality of our data and verify that it will satisfy the analysis needs of our project. If the existing data lacked a required dimensionality, then it's best to correct the situation near the beginning of the project. If we discover further down the road that our data lacks some vital dimensionality, we would have to redo work we've already completed.

Identify Measures

Each of the fact tables contains different specific types of measures: populations, utilization, and claims. We discuss each of these in this section.

Populations

The population table contains membership information for our plans over time. This table organizes population figures by leaf-level members for "Plan," "Employee Class," and "Period" dimensions. The table contains two measures: Lives and Members.

Lives. This is the count of the total number of people covered by the plan. For example, my health care policy through work covers my wife and daughter as well as myself (three lives). Lives aggregate with summation across all dimensions except time. In the time dimension the value of lives at aggregate levels should be the ending balance in that period (the value of the last leaf level member below the aggregate level member instead of a sum of the leaf members). To obtain an ending balance amount at aggregate levels, we can use MDX in a calculated member as described in the section "Identify Calculations."

Members. These represent the count of the number of enrolled employees. For example, I am enrolled in a health care plan at work, contributing one enrolled member to this measure. As with Lives, "Members" aggregates through summation across all dimensions except time, in which the correct value is the ending balance for the period. We will also aggregate with SUM across time for use in some additional calculations (which we'll also get to shortly in the section titled "Identify Calculations").

Members or Members

Members is a standard term in the health care industry, and, of course, it is also a standard term in OLAP. To limit any confusion, throughout this tutorial we'll enclose *Members* in quotation marks when we are referring to plan members.

Utilization

The utilization table contains measures of health care services utilization. Data is available by leaf-level members for "Period," "Plan," "Employee Class," "Provider," "Network Status," "MDC," and "Service Classification" dimensions. We describe three measures—"Admissions," "Days," and "Services Provided"— in the following list. Note that "Admissions" and "Days" apply only to inpatient service classifications. "Services Provided" apply only to outpatient services and drugs. The Multidimensional Domain Structure (MDS) in Figure 15.1 clearly illustrates the dimensionality of the Utilization measures.

Admissions. This is the number of inpatient hospital admissions for plan members. "Admissions" aggregates by summation over all dimensions.

Days. The number of days covered individuals spent in a hospital. Days aggregates by summation over all dimensions.

Services provided. This is the count of outpatient services provided or prescriptions filled. It aggregates by summation over all dimensions.

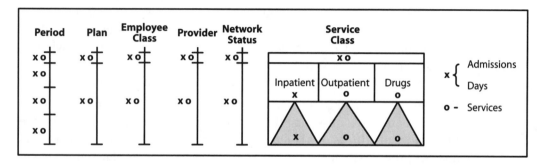

Figure 15.1   MDS of utilization.

Claims

The claims table contains the most important piece of information to our benefits managers: money. The table organizes the following amounts in terms of all of our previously defined dimensions:

Paid amount. Dollar amounts for claims paid. Aggregates by summation over all dimensions.

Submitted amount. Dollar amounts for claims made. Aggregates by summation over all dimensions.

Identify Calculations

We have already identified some major calculations by identifying how each of the base measures aggregates from the fact table. As we mentioned earlier, we'll need to use calculated members to provide ending-period values for "Members" and "Lives" at the levels in the period dimension that are above the leaf. As we described in Chapter 8, MDX has a special function `closingPeriod(level[,member])` that identifies the last sibling of a member with the same ancestor at a given level. If left out, member defaults to the current member of the time dimension. Thus, the formulas for our Calculated measures for "Members" and Lives, respectively, will be some variation of the following:

```
([Measures].[Members],ClosingPeriod([Time].[Month])) and
([Measures].[Lives],ClosingPeriod([Time].[Month]))
```

Although the basic measures provide a great deal of useful information, there are also a few standard calculations that benefits managers use repeatedly to analyze health benefit plans. We'll note the basic formulas here and provide the actual MDX expressions we'll use later in the section "Design Dimensions and Cubes".

Average Length of Stay (ALOS). This formula is determined by the following equation: Days/Admissions. This answers the question, "How long are patients who are covered under our benefits plans hospitalized?" Generally, the longer hospital stays are, the higher the costs. With the simple formula of days per admissions we can begin to compare how efficient each provider is in caring for patients covered under our benefits plans. We may also notice that the lengths of stay differ on a regular basis according to benefit plan.

Admissions per 1000 Members. This calculation is determined by the following equation: Admissions*1000/Cumulative "Members". Although the total number of admissions is interesting, for comparison purposes benefits managers prefer to look at a ratio of admissions to number of members to get a better "apples-to-apples" comparison. For example, a plan with 200 admissions out of 1,000 utilizes more health care services per member than does a plan with 500 admissions for 10,000 "Members". Note also that we use the cumulative members within the time frame being reviewed as opposed to the number of members at the end of the period.

Services per 1000 Members. This is calculated by Services*Cumulative "Members"/1000.

Days per 1000 Members. The formula for this is Days*Cumulative "Members"/1000.

Paid Amount per Member. This is calculated with the formula, Paid Amount/Cumulative "Members".

Submitted Amount per Member. The formula for this is Submitted Amount/Cumulative "Members".

Identify/Create Dimension Data Source Tables/Views

Most of the dimension information we require is available in the existing dimension tables in the company's data warehouse. The sole exception is the month of the transaction. However, we have a simple way of deriving the metadata for our period dimension. We know that the fact_population table contains every month we are using (since there is at least one member of at least one plan in every month). To create a time dimension, we can create a view in our data source that contains the unique dates in fact_population. We can do this using the SQL `SELECT DISTINCT fact_population.period FROM fact_population`. For your convenience we've included SQL for creating a view_period view in the sample database (along with the SQL for creating all other views required in this tutorial) on the CD-ROM that accompanies this book. Please see the document "setuprdb.doc" in the root directory for instructions on setting up the sample data source for this chapter in SQL Server 7 and Microsoft Access.

WARNING

Dimensions that are defined according to fact tables only reflect the state of the existing warehouse. However, you may remember from Chapter 3 that we generally recommend that you maintain separate time dimension metadata. We chose to use a fact table as the source of dimension data in this instance because in one of the several real-life projects that we based this tutorial on, the group developing the decision support system (DSS) was not permitted to create or modify tables in the relational data source, but it was permitted to create views. We include this method here to illustrate one of the ways in which you may work around organizational restrictions that may prevent you from using the "correct" method.

Plan, Employee Class, Provider, MDC, and Network Status all seem fairly straightforward and reside in their own tables. They follow a single table schema with a single ID column and a single description column. Similarly,

Service Classification follows a simple snowflake schema. There's one table containing a service type ID and description and a second table containing a service type ID, service class ID, and service class description.

Financial Accounts, however, appears to be a bit problematic. The table doesn't follow the star or snowflake schema required for dimension data by Microsoft OLAP Services. Instead, it has a parent-child hierarchy layout shown in Figure 15.2. We briefly mentioned the parent-child table format for metadata in Chapter 3, and it is used quite frequently in many data warehouse implementations. Most often the parent-child table design is used for dimensions with irregular or ragged hierarchies that do not fit cleanly into a star or snowflake schema and that avoid the use of null or redundant column values. Looking at the data, we can clearly see the hierarchy. Each member belongs to a level between 0 and 3, so we know there are 4 levels. The "parent_id" also coincides with the "account_id" of another member, which indicates the parent-child relationship that exists among the dimension's members.

Following the member-parent and level information, we can map out our dimension hierarchy as shown in Figure 15.3. Indeed, we see that some members have no children in lower levels. For example, "Deductible" has no children at any level, while "Pay" has three levels of children. As we explained in Chapter 3, we can transform such metadata to work with MS OLAP Services by using views that create "dummy" child members in lower levels for members that have no children. Figure 15.4 shows the SQL that could be used to create such a series of views.

We have one other problem besides Financial Accounts. Although paid claims enter through leaf members for any branch in the account dimension hierarchy, submitted claims do not. For example, our facts may include Submitted Amounts for "Pay" but Paid Amounts for one or more children of "Price Savings." In our current claim fact data, Submitted Amounts always enter through members in the top level of the account dimension, such as "Pay" or "Coordination of Benefits."

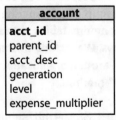

Figure 15.2 Account table schema.

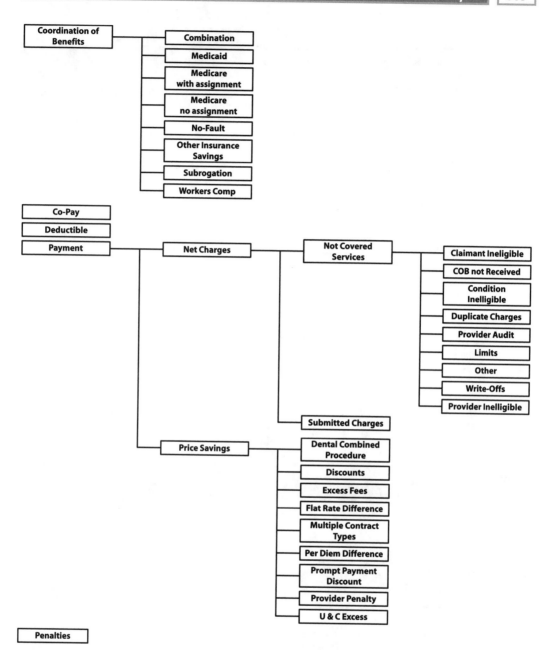

Figure 15.3 Account hierarchy for health care benefits data.

We have two basic options for handling this problem. One is to add a new column to our Account table that flags appropriate members as entry points and then use the flag value in views to extend the appropriate members to the leaf

```
CREATE VIEW dbo.view_acct_gen1 AS
SELECT acct_id, acct_desc
FROM account
WHERE ([level] = 3)

GO

CREATE VIEW dbo.view_acct_gen2 AS
SELECT parent_id, acct_id, acct_desc
FROM account
WHERE ([level] = 2)

GO

CREATE VIEW dbo.view_acct_gen3 AS
SELECT parent_id, acct_id, acct_desc
FROM account
WHERE ([level] = 1)

GO

CREATE VIEW dbo.view_acct_gen4 AS
SELECT parent_id, acct_id, acct_desc
FROM account
WHERE ([level] = 0)

GO

CREATE VIEW dbo.view_acct_extend_gen2 AS
SELECT
  parent_id = CASE
    WHEN view_acct_gen2.parent_id IS NULL THEN
      view_acct_gen1.acct_id
    ELSE view_acct_gen2.parent_id
  END,
  acct_id = CASE
    WHEN view_acct_gen2.parent_id IS NULL THEN
      view_acct_gen1.acct_id
    ELSE view_acct_gen2.acct_id
  END,
  acct_desc = CASE
    WHEN view_acct_gen2.parent_id IS NULL THEN
      view_acct_gen1.acct_desc
    ELSE view_acct_gen2.acct_desc
  END
FROM view_acct_gen1 LEFT OUTER JOIN
  view_acct_gen2 ON view_acct_gen1.acct_id = view_acct_gen2.par-
ent_id
```

Figure 15.4 SQL views that create members in lower levels for childless members.

```
GO

CREATE VIEW dbo.view_acct_extend_gen3 AS
SELECT
  parent_id = CASE
    WHEN view_acct_gen3.parent_id IS NULL THEN
      view_acct_extend_gen2.acct_id
    ELSE view_acct_gen3.parent_id
  END,
  acct_id = CASE
    WHEN view_acct_gen3.parent_id IS NULL THEN
      view_acct_extend_gen2.acct_id
    ELSE view_acct_gen3.acct_id
  END,
  acct_desc = CASE
    WHEN view_acct_gen3.parent_id IS NULL THEN
      view_acct_extend_gen2.acct_desc
    ELSE view_acct_gen3.acct_desc
  END
FROM view_acct_extend_gen2 LEFT OUTER JOIN
  view_acct_gen3 ON
  view_acct_extend_gen2.acct_id = view_acct_gen3.parent_id

GO

CREATE VIEW dbo.view_acct_extend_gen4 AS
SELECT
  parent_id = CASE
    WHEN view_acct_gen4.parent_id IS NULL THEN
      view_acct_extend_gen3.acct_id
    ELSE view_acct_gen4.parent_id
  END,
  acct_id = CASE
    WHEN view_acct_gen4.parent_id IS NULL THEN
      view_acct_extend_gen3.acct_id
    ELSE view_acct_gen4.acct_id
  END,
  acct_desc = CASE
    WHEN view_acct_gen4.parent_id IS NULL THEN
      view_acct_extend_gen3.acct_desc
    ELSE view_acct_gen4.acct_desc
  END
FROM view_acct_extend_gen3 LEFT OUTER JOIN
  view_acct_gen4 ON
  view_acct_extend_gen3.acct_id = view_acct_gen4.parent_id

GO
```

Figure 15.4   (continued)

level of the dimension. For example, in the SQL in Figure 15.4 we would modify the WHEN clause of our case statements to read something like the following:

```
WHEN ((view_acct_extend_gen4.parent_id IS NULL) OR
(view_acct_extend_gen4.acct_flag = 1))
```

Unfortunately, as we mentioned earlier, we don't have appropriate permissions in our warehouse to make such adjustments. Even if we did have such permissions, however, the safest action would be our second option: to make no assumptions about where current or future data may enter the hierarchy and to use union queries so every member has a matching child in the next level. Figure 15.5 shows the series of SQL views that do this.

Although the first option would be the most accurate in terms of the current state of our data, we need to keep in mind that our application will not exist

```
CREATE VIEW dbo.view_acct_1 ASSELECT
   account.acct_id,
   account.acct_desc,
   account.expense_multiplier
FROM dbo.account
WHERE dbo.account.[level]=3

GO

CREATE VIEW dbo.view_acct_2 AS
SELECT
   view_acct_1.acct_id as parent_id,
   view_acct_1.acct_id,
   view_acct_1.acct_desc,
   view_acct_1.expense_multiplier
FROM dbo.view_acct_1

UNION SELECT
   account.parent_id,
   account.acct_id,
   account.acct_desc,
   account.expense_multiplier
FROM dbo.account

HERE (account.[level]=2)
GO

CREATE VIEW dbo.view_acct_3 AS
SELECT
   view_acct_2.acct_id as parent_id,
   view_acct_2.acct_id,
```

Figure 15.5 SQL views that create default members for the parent at all levels.

frozen in the amber of time. We may want to use this dimension with other facts that enter at completely different members and/or levels at any point in the future. If we created our account dimension based upon the first option, fact entry-point changes would require us to rebuild the dimension (and thus fully reprocess all cubes that use the dimension). But if we allow for any possibility we will be able to simply load any new data incrementally, regardless of where it enters the dimension.

Identify/Create Fact Tables/Views

Most of the facts are straightforward. We find our population figures in the fact_population table, utilization data in the fact_utilization table, and claims data in the fact_claims data. We do notice one problem, however, when we

```
    view_acct_2.acct_desc,
    view_acct_2.expense_multiplier
FROM dbo.view_acct_2

UNION SELECT
    account.parent_id,
    account.acct_id,
    account.acct_desc,
    account.expense_multiplier
FROM account
WHERE (account.[level]=1)

GO

CREATE VIEW dbo.view_acct_4 AS
SELECT
    view_acct_3.acct_id as parent_id,
    view_acct_3.acct_id,
    view_acct_3.acct_desc,
    view_acct_3.expense_multiplier
FROM dbo.view_acct_3

UNION SELECT
    account.parent_id,
    account.acct_id,
    account.acct_desc,
    account.expense_multiplier
FROM account
WHERE (account.[level]=0)
GO
```

Figure 15.5   (continued)

take a closer look at the values in our claims table and in our account dimension hierarchy. Accounts do not always aggregate to their parent through addition; some aggregate through subtraction. For example, "Net Charges" equals "Submitted Charges" less "Not Covered Services." Yet the table stores only the positive values for all claims, regardless of how they may aggregate. Our account metadata, however, does contain a column called "Expense Multiplier" that has values of either 1 or -1. By multiplying the claim amount by the expense multiplier prior to aggregation we can ensure that the values aggregate with the appropriate function. Although we might consider Expense Multiplier to be a true member property, to use it with data values prior to aggregation we need to create a view of our facts that is joined to accounts.

Just as we can use SQL expressions to define measures in a cube, we can also do the actual multiplication either in the view or in the measure definition in our cube. Figures 15.6 and 15.7 show the SQL for defining these views. Which path to take is a "week or seven day" decision. In either case, the multiplication expression is included in the SQL that OLAP Services will use to query the data source when it updates cube data, and it will be performed by the data source.

We'll be able to reverse this process by using a calculated member so values display with the correct signs. We will describe the exact implementation in detail when we design the cubes that contain claims data.

```
CREATE VIEW view_fact_claims AS
SELECT
  fact_claim.provider_id,
  fact_claim.plan_id,
  fact_claim.empclass_id,
  fact_claim.mdc_id,
  fact_claim.svc_id,
  fact_claim.ns_id,
  fact_claim.Period,
  fact_claim.acct_id,
  fact_claim.PaidDateAmount as PaidAmount,
  fact_claim.ServiceDateAmount as SubmittedAmount,
  view_acct_4.expense_multiplier
FROM fact_claim
  INNER JOIN view_acct_4
    ON fact_claim.acct_id = view_acct_4.acct_id
```

Figure 15.6 SQL for a view of claim fact data including the account expense multiplier.

```
CREATE VIEW view_fact_claims AS
SELECT
  fact_claim.provider_id,
  fact_claim.plan_id,
  fact_claim.empclass_id,
  fact_claim.mdc_id,
  fact_claim.svc_id,
  fact_claim.ns_id,
  fact_claim.Period,
  fact_claim.acct_id,
  fact_claim.PaidAmount*view_acct_4.expense_multiplier
    AS PaidAmount,
  fact_claim.SubmittedAmount*view_acct_4.expense_multiplier
    AS SubmittedAmount,
  view_acct_4.expense_multiplier
FROM fact_claim
  INNER JOIN view_acct_4
    ON fact_claim.acct_id = view_acct_4.acct_id
```

Figure 15.7   SQL for a view of claim fact data including the account expense multiplier and performing the multiplication.

Design Dimensions and Cubes

The goal we have defined for this project is to provide our benefits managers with an easy-to-understand path to our existing data. We've matched the data in our warehouse to the analyses we wish to do and defined the required calculations. Now we'll begin the actual design of our Microsoft OLAP Services database with our dimensions.

Our facts come in three tables that do not share dimensionality. Since cubes can be based on only a single fact table, we'll begin our dimension with the assumption that we will be creating more than one cube. As we recommended in Chapter 3, such an assumption means that we should create all of our initial dimensions as shared dimensions. Shared dimensions allow us to use dimensions in any cube. Although our possible cubes may not use all of our dimensions, most of our dimensions may be used by two or more cubes. The account dimension could be an exception to this since it is only referenced by a single fact table (fact_claims). However, there's no reason to believe that we would not use the account dimension in some other cube at some point in the future and, at this point, there's a possibility that we might want to create two cubes from our fact table in this project.

As we also noted in Chapter 3, shared dimensions allow us to add new members over time without having to perform a full reprocess of our cube. Of all our dimensions, we know that periods will definitely grow over time. Providers will also most likely grow over time because a person covered by one of our plans can get sick anywhere in the world and go to any health care provider (which will most definitely submit a claim for any care it provides). The other dimensions may or may not change on any regular basis, but we know that we cannot rule out the possibility that they will change. Any possibility that a dimension will change gives you a strong reason *not* to create it as a private dimension since private dimensions are only modified when a cube is fully processed.

Most of our dimensions are simple single-level dimensions. Members have no properties other than name. Services are snowflaked in two levels: Category and Service. As we noted earlier, accounts have four levels. In the metadata, each member has properties of generation, level, and expense multiplier. Generation and level serve no purpose outside of defining the dimension hierarchy (and we used generation for just this purpose when we created the views upon which we will base our account dimension). Remember that we used the expense multiplier in the view of our claim facts to ensure correct aggregation. Blueprints for building our dimensions in Microsoft OLAP Services are shown in Figures 15.8 through 15.15.

In determining whether to create our dimensions as shared or private we began with the assumption that we will create more than one cube. Now we must confirm whether that assumption was correct. It's possible to create a single source for all of our facts by using a view that joins our three fact tables. However, because our facts do not share dimensionality, we could create a view that

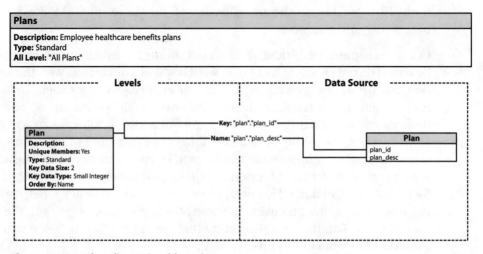

Figure 15.8 Plan dimension blueprint.

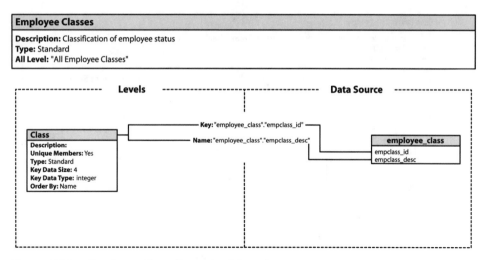

Figure 15.9   Employee Class dimension blueprint.

includes all of our facts only by using outer joins. This, in turn, would introduce unnecessary data sparseness into a cube. For example, population figures would be non-existent for "Service Classification" and "Account," yet aggregations would include empty cells for population measures for any Service Classification or Account member included in the aggregation. Based upon the dimensionality of our facts, at a minimum we should design three cubes: populations, utilization, and claims.

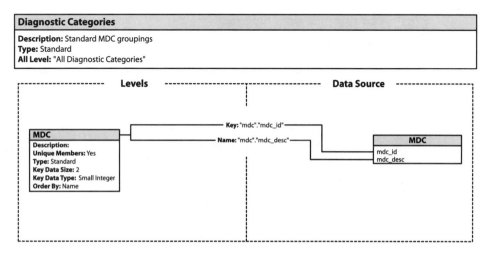

Figure 15.10   MDC dimension blueprint.

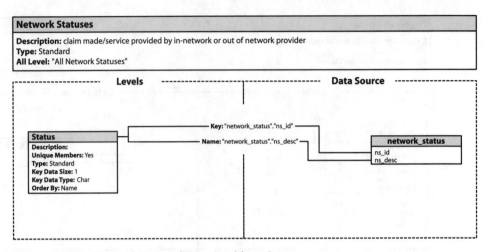

Figure 15.11   Network Status dimension blueprint.

Remember that for our claims data the two measures enter at different points in our account hierarchy. "Paid Claims" enters at the leaf level of the hierarchy, but "Submitted Claims" enters at the highest designed level in the dimension (the first level below any possible "All" level). For "Submitted Claims," any aggregations that are based on account dimension levels below the first designed level will be totally meaningless and will only serve to take up space and processing time. We can avoid this by separating paid and submitted claims into different cubes and restricting aggregation for the account dimension in the Submitted

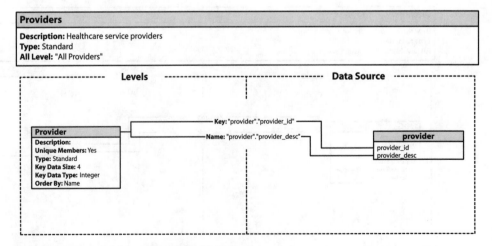

Figure 15.12   Provider dimension blueprint.

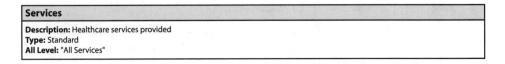

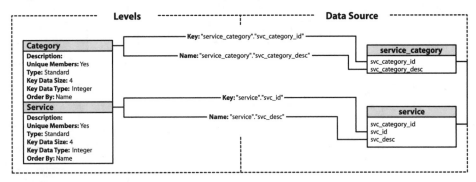

Figure 15.13   Service Classification dimension blueprint.

Claims cube to the first level or disabling lower levels in the dimension. We can optimize processing even further by using a separate view (fact_claims_submitted) for our Submitted Claims cube that includes only records from the

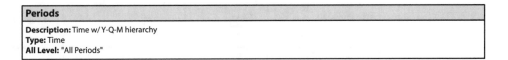

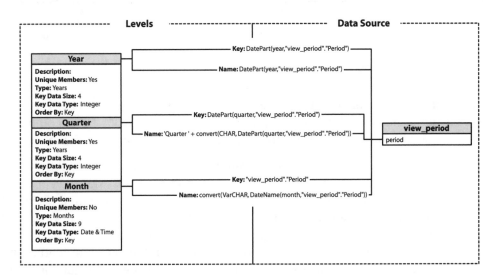

Figure 15.14   Period dimension blueprint.

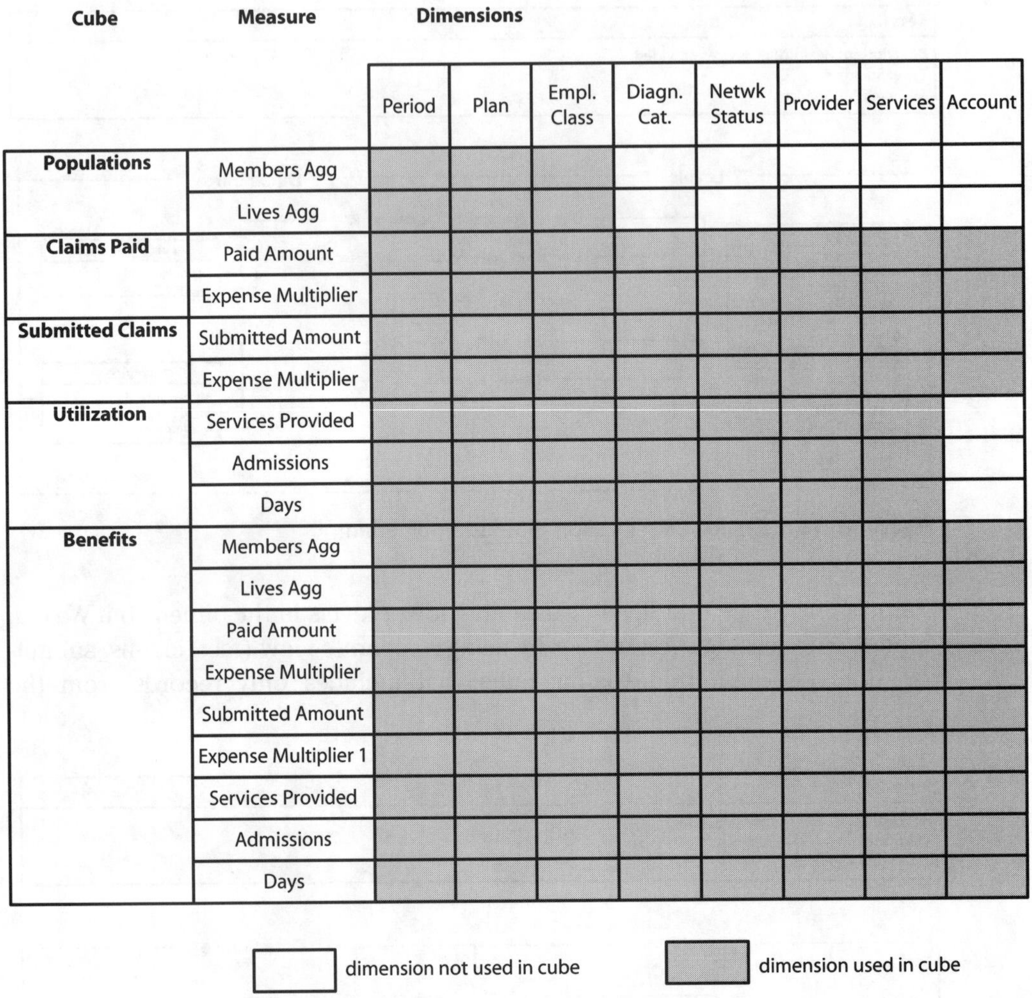

Cube	Measure	Period	Plan	Empl. Class	Diagn. Cat.	Netwk Status	Provider	Services	Account
Populations	Members Agg	▓	▓	▓					
	Lives Agg	▓	▓	▓					
Claims Paid	Paid Amount	▓	▓	▓	▓	▓	▓		▓
	Expense Multiplier	▓	▓	▓	▓	▓	▓		▓
Submitted Claims	Submitted Amount	▓	▓	▓	▓	▓	▓		▓
	Expense Multiplier	▓	▓	▓	▓	▓	▓		▓
Utilization	Services Provided	▓	▓	▓	▓	▓	▓	▓	
	Admissions	▓	▓	▓	▓	▓	▓	▓	
	Days	▓	▓	▓	▓	▓	▓	▓	
Benefits	Members Agg	▓	▓	▓	▓	▓	▓	▓	▓
	Lives Agg	▓	▓	▓	▓	▓	▓	▓	▓
	Paid Amount	▓	▓	▓	▓	▓	▓	▓	▓
	Expense Multiplier	▓	▓	▓	▓	▓	▓	▓	▓
	Submitted Amount	▓	▓	▓	▓	▓	▓	▓	▓
	Expense Multiplier 1	▓	▓	▓	▓	▓	▓	▓	▓
	Services Provided	▓	▓	▓	▓	▓	▓	▓	▓
	Admissions	▓	▓	▓	▓	▓	▓	▓	▓
	Days	▓	▓	▓	▓	▓	▓	▓	▓

☐ dimension not used in cube   ▓ dimension used in cube

Figure 15.15 Account dimension blueprint.

fact_claim table that enter the cube at the first designed level of the Accounts dimension. The document "setuprdb.doc" on the CD-ROM that accompanies this book contains instructions for creating the required views in SQL Server 7.

Next, we need to determine the functions that Microsoft OLAP Services uses when it aggregates the measures in our cubes. With the exception of the "expense multiplier" measure in our Paid Claims and Submitted Claims cubes, all measures aggregate using SUM(). We mentioned earlier, however, that we want to use the expense multiplier to reverse the multiplication we used to allow our claims measures to aggregate correctly along the account hierarchy. If we were to have the expense multiplier aggregate with the SUM() function, we'd see

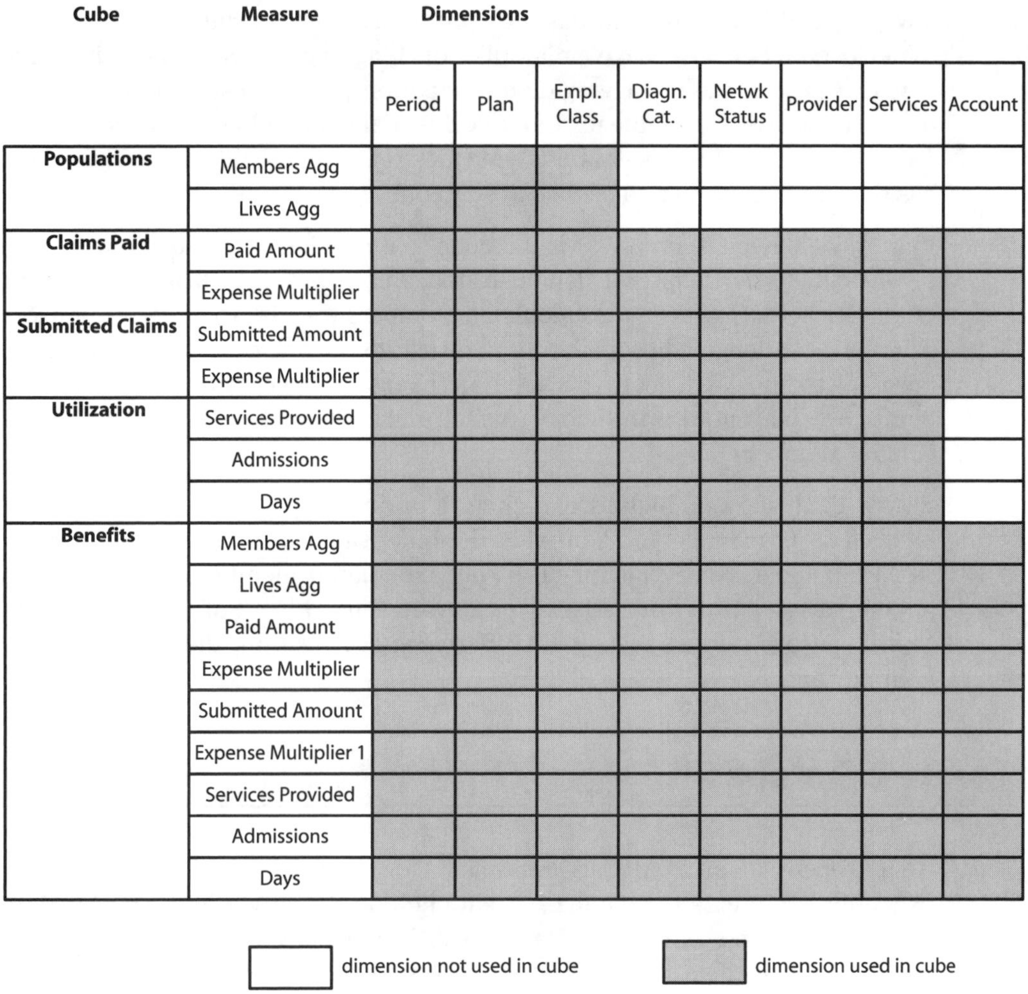

Cube	Measure	Dimensions							
		Period	Plan	Empl. Class	Diagn. Cat.	Netwk Status	Provider	Services	Account
Populations	Members Agg	▓	▓	▓					
	Lives Agg	▓	▓	▓					
Claims Paid	Paid Amount	▓	▓	▓	▓	▓	▓	▓	▓
	Expense Multiplier	▓	▓	▓	▓	▓	▓	▓	▓
Submitted Claims	Submitted Amount	▓	▓	▓	▓	▓	▓	▓	▓
	Expense Multiplier	▓	▓	▓	▓	▓	▓	▓	▓
Utilization	Services Provided	▓	▓	▓	▓	▓	▓	▓	
	Admissions	▓	▓	▓	▓	▓	▓	▓	
	Days	▓	▓	▓	▓	▓	▓	▓	
Benefits	Members Agg	▓	▓	▓	▓	▓	▓	▓	▓
	Lives Agg	▓	▓	▓	▓	▓	▓	▓	▓
	Paid Amount	▓	▓	▓	▓	▓	▓	▓	▓
	Expense Multiplier	▓	▓	▓	▓	▓	▓	▓	▓
	Submitted Amount	▓	▓	▓	▓	▓	▓	▓	▓
	Expense Multiplier 1	▓	▓	▓	▓	▓	▓	▓	▓
	Services Provided	▓	▓	▓	▓	▓	▓	▓	▓
	Admissions	▓	▓	▓	▓	▓	▓	▓	▓
	Days	▓	▓	▓	▓	▓	▓	▓	▓

☐ dimension not used in cube   ▓ dimension used in cube

Figure 15.16   Benefits cubes and their dimensions.

expressions like "500 * -10" when we attempted to back out the effects of our pre-aggregation multiplication for "Not Covered Services." (This represents the sum of claims for the ten children of "Not Covered Services" multiplied by the sum of the "expense multiplier" for those children). Aggregating "expense multiplier" with MAX(), however, would always result in the desired expression. For example, "Net Charges" equals "Submitted Charges" less "Not Covered Services." The MAX() value for the children of Net Charges would be 1 (the value of the expense multiplier in any transaction for "Submitted Charges"). This would result in the proper multiplication ("Net Charges" * 1). At the same time, multiplying "Not Covered Services" by the MAX() value of its children would also always result in a value that has the appropriate sign. Because all children of "Not Covered Services" have a multiplier of -1, aggregation sums negative numbers (because of the pre-aggregation calculation), which results in a nominally negative total. However, the maximum value of the multiplier for the children of "Not Covered Services" is -1. Multiplying these two values will return a value that has the appropriate sign to be displayed to our users.

Finally, we'll need to create a virtual cube that provides a unified view into all of our cubes. As Chapter 4 demonstrated, this is a simple task in Microsoft OLAP Services. However, the calculated members we wish to provide our users offer us a challenge whose solution we must go outside of the OLAP Manager interface to find. We'll get to this solution (using DSO to create calculated members in a virtual cube) at the end of this tutorial in the section titled "Adding Calculated Members."

Figure 15.16 shows a high-level depiction of our cubes and their dimensions. Figures 15.17 through 15.21 provide the blueprints for building the cubes in OLAP Manager. Note that for all of our calculated members the blueprints indicate a solve order of 0. Because the values used in all of the calculations have been pre-calculated by OLAP Services aggregation, the solve order is unimportant.

Create a Database

We'll keep all of our OLAP Services objects for this project in a database called "Benefits." To create the database, right click on the server in the OLAP Manager tree pane and select "New Database . . .". In the new database dialog, enter the name for the database and a short description, as shown in Figure 15.22.

Select a Data Source

To identify the data source, right click on the "Data Sources" folder in the OLAP Manager tree pane under the "library" folder for the Benefits database we just created and select "New Data Source . . .". If you followed the instructions in "setuprdb.doc" on the CD-ROM as recommended at the beginning of this chapter, you should already have created an SQL Server 7 database named "Benefits" containing the tables and views we need for our OLAP Services database. And you now have an ODBC data source for the database on a machine running OLAP Services. Select "OLE DB Provider for ODBC Drivers" from the provider tab of the data link properties dialog as shown in Figure 15.23 and click the button labeled "Next >>." On the connection tab of the dialog, select the data

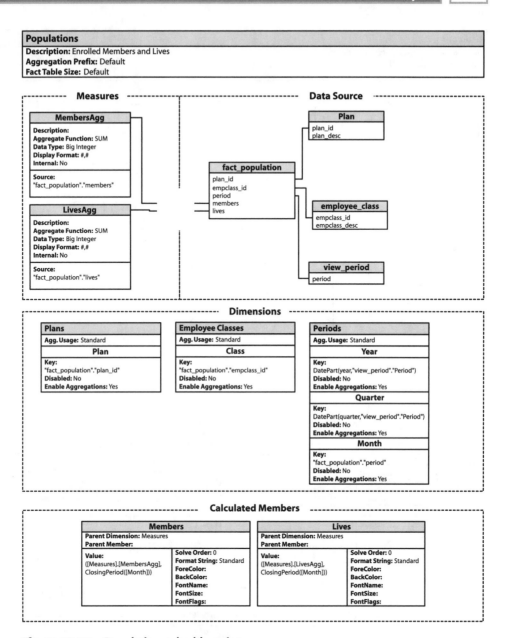

Figure 15.17   Population cube blueprint.

source name you used when creating the ODBC data source for the benefits database. Enter the log-on information required to connect to your SQL Server as shown in Figure 15.24. Click the "Test Connection" button to verify that you can indeed connect to the database and then click "OK" to save the data source.

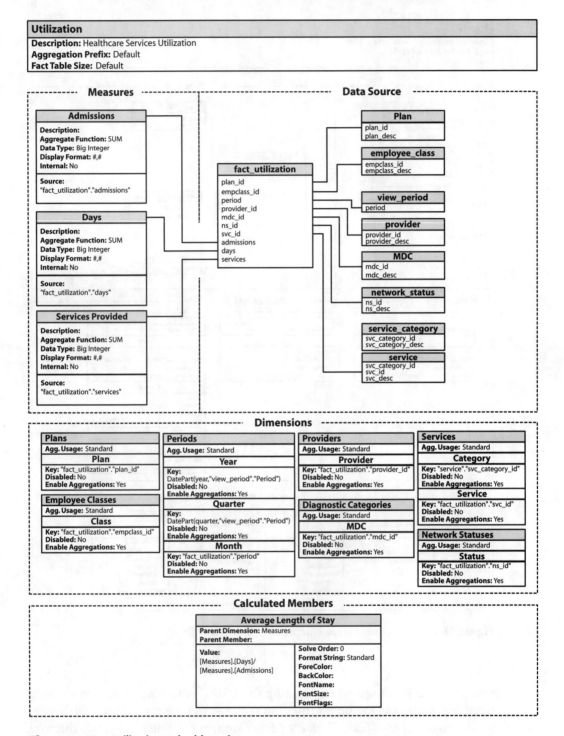

Figure 15.18 Utilization cube blueprint.

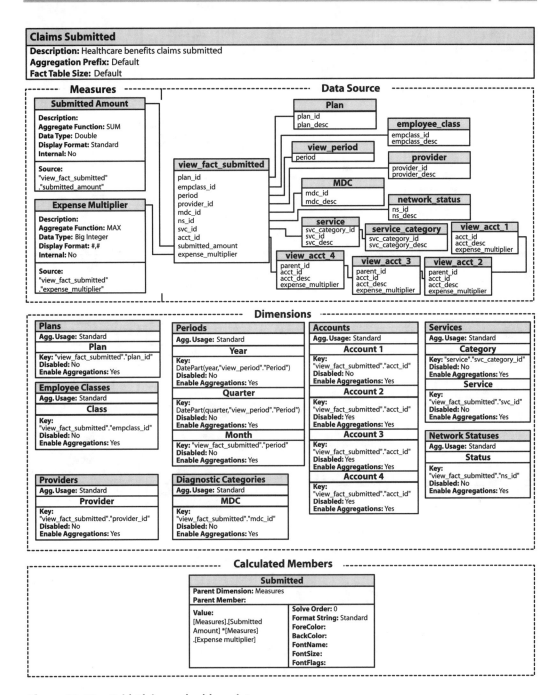

Figure 15.19 Paid Claims cube blueprint.

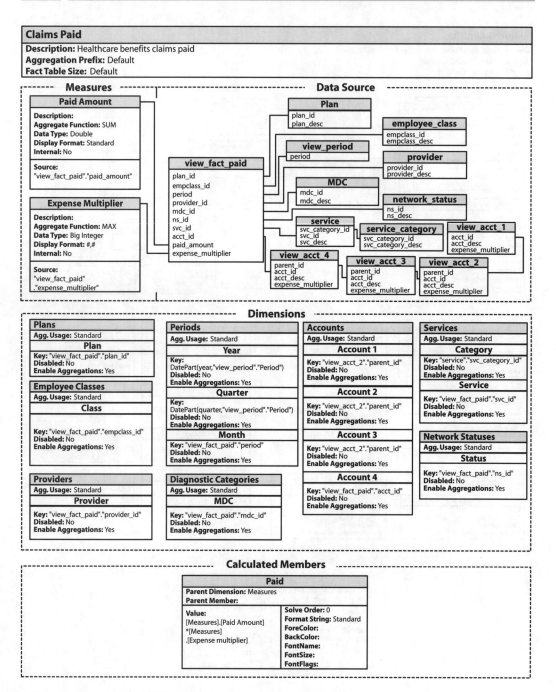

Figure 15.20 Submitted Claims cube blueprint.

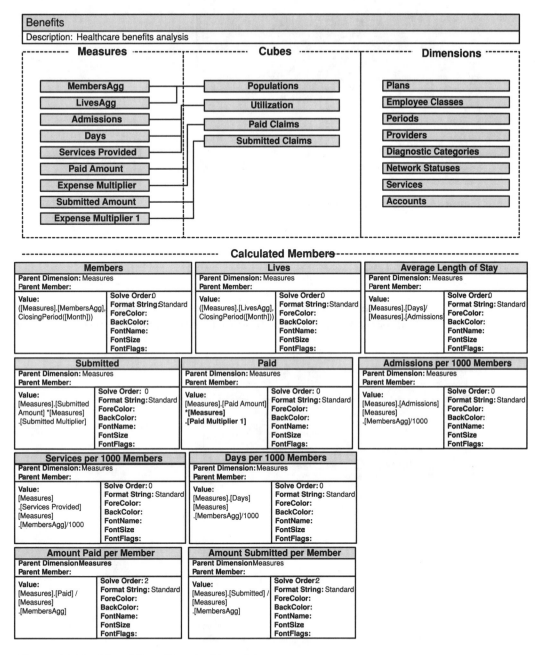

Benefits

Description: Healthcare benefits analysis

------- **Measures** ------- | ------- **Cubes** ------- | ------- **Dimensions** -------

Measures:
- MembersAgg
- LivesAgg
- Admissions
- Days
- Services Provided
- Paid Amount
- Expense Multiplier
- Submitted Amount
- Expense Multiplier 1

Cubes:
- Populations
- Utilization
- Paid Claims
- Submitted Claims

Dimensions:
- Plans
- Employee Classes
- Periods
- Providers
- Diagnostic Categories
- Network Statuses
- Services
- Accounts

------------ **Calculated Members** ------------

Members	
Parent Dimension: Measures	
Parent Member:	
Value: ([Measures].[MembersAgg], ClosingPeriod([Month]))	**Solve Order** 0 **Format String** Standard **ForeColor: BackColor: FontName: FontSize: FontFlags:**

Lives	
Parent Dimension: Measures	
Parent Member:	
Value: ([Measures].[LivesAgg], ClosingPeriod([Month]))	**Solve Order** 0 **Format String:** Standard **ForeColor: BackColor: FontName: FontSize: FontFlags:**

Average Length of Stay	
Parent Dimension: Measures	
Parent Member:	
Value: [Measures].[Days]/ [Measures].[Admissions]	**Solve Order** 0 **Format String:** Standard **ForeColor: BackColor: FontName: FontSize: FontFlags:**

Submitted	
Parent Dimension: Measures	
Parent Member:	
Value: [Measures].[Submitted Amount] *[Measures] .[Submitted Multiplier]	**Solve Order:** 0 **Format String:** Standard **ForeColor: BackColor: FontName: FontSize: FontFlags:**

Paid	
Parent Dimension: Measures	
Parent Member:	
Value: [Measures].[Paid Amount] *[Measures] .[Paid Multiplier 1]	**Solve Order:** 0 **Format String:** Standard **ForeColor: BackColor: FontName: FontSize: FontFlags:**

Admissions per 1000 Members	
Parent Dimension: Measures	
Parent Member:	
Value: [Measures].[Admissions] [Measures] .[MembersAgg]/1000	**Solve Order:** 0 **Format String:** Standard **ForeColor: BackColor: FontName: FontSize: FontFlags:**

Services per 1000 Members	
Parent Dimension: Measures	
Parent Member:	
Value: [Measures] .[Services Provided] [Measures] .[MembersAgg]/1000	**Solve Order:** 0 **Format String:** Standard **ForeColor: BackColor: FontName: FontSize: FontFlags:**

Days per 1000 Members	
Parent Dimension: Measures	
Parent Member:	
Value: [Measures].[Days] [Measures] .[MembersAgg]/1000	**Solve Order:** 0 **Format String:** Standard **ForeColor: BackColor: FontName: FontSize: FontFlags:**

Amount Paid per Member	
Parent Dimension Measures	
Parent Member:	
Value: [Measures].[Paid] / [Measures] .[MembersAgg]	**Solve Order:** 2 **Format String:** Standard **ForeColor: BackColor: FontName: FontSize: FontFlags:**

Amount Submitted per Member	
Parent Dimension Measures	
Parent Member:	
Value: [Measures].[Submitted] / [Measures] .[MembersAgg]	**Solve Order** 2 **Format String:** Standard **ForeColor: BackColor: FontName: FontSize: FontFlags:**

Figure 15.21 Virtual Benefits cube blueprint.

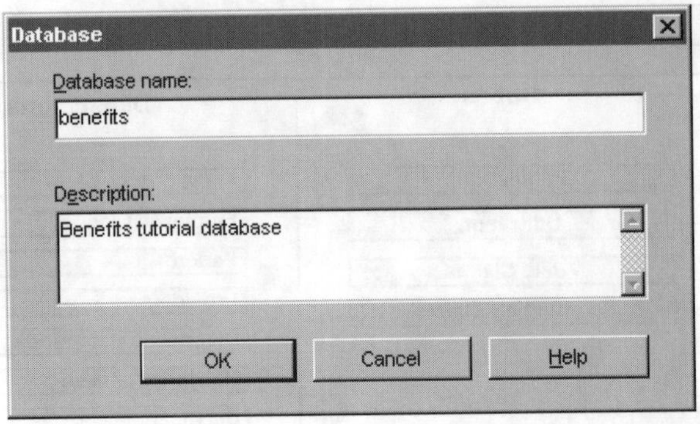

Figure 15.22 Creating a new database in OLAP Manager.

Build Dimensions

For all of our dimensions we'll start with the dimension wizard and then make any needed adjustments through the cube editor. By using the wizard we can

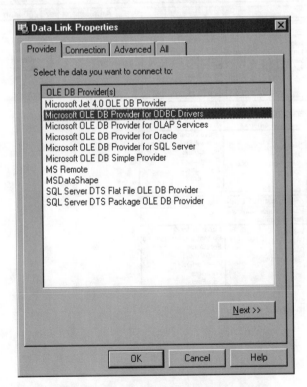

Figure 15.23 Selecting a data source provider.

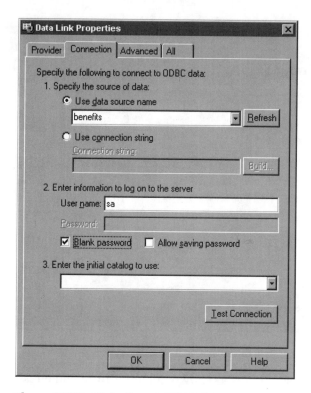

Figure 15.24   Selecting an ODBC data source.

build a basic dimension structure quickly and with little effort. To begin creating a dimension using the wizard, right click on the "shared dimensions" folder in the OLAP Manager tree pane below the Benefits database we just created and select "New Dimension . . .".

Building Single-table Dimensions

In this section, we'll walk through the process of building single-table dimensions using Plans. Because a single table contains all of our plan dimension information, select the star schema option as shown in Figure 15.25 and click "Next." Select the dim_plan table from the data source, as shown in Figure 15.26, and click "Next."

In selecting our dimension level, we have a choice between the ID and description columns. To minimize aggregation storage, we want to use plan_id as the member key column (4-byte integer versus 15-byte character). Since the wizard (and the editor, too, for that matter) creates a level that is based on a single column, we'll start with the plan_id column as shown in Figure 15.27 and change the member name column in the cube editor later on.

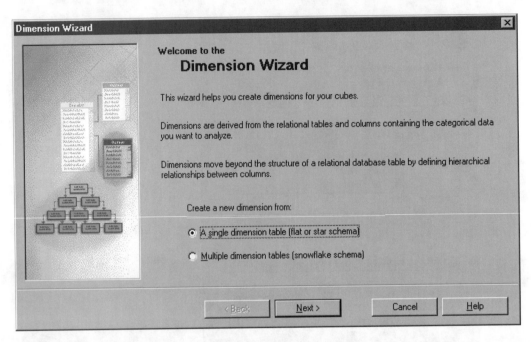

Figure 15.25 Dimension wizard selecting dimension schema.

Finally, name the dimension Plans as shown in Figure 15.28 and click "Finish." When the wizard finishes, OLAP Manager displays the dimension editor where

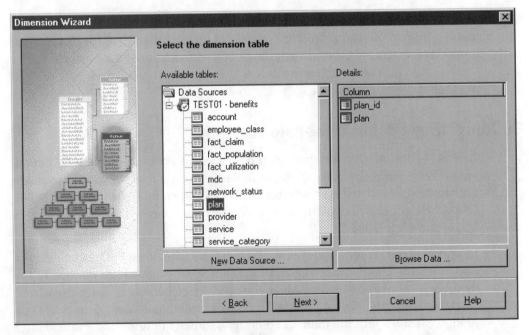

Figure 15.26 Dimension wizard selecting table.

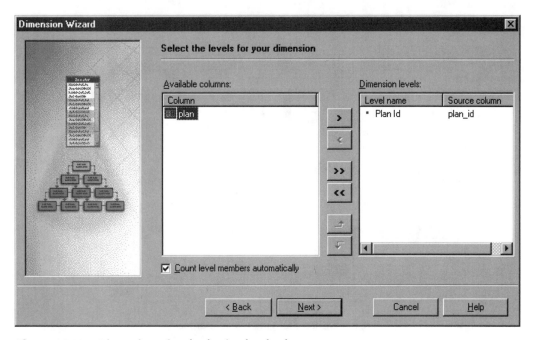

Figure 15.27   Dimension wizard selecting level column.

we can refine our dimension definition. In the editor, change the level name to Plan (Figure 15.29) and the member name column to plan (Figure 15.30).

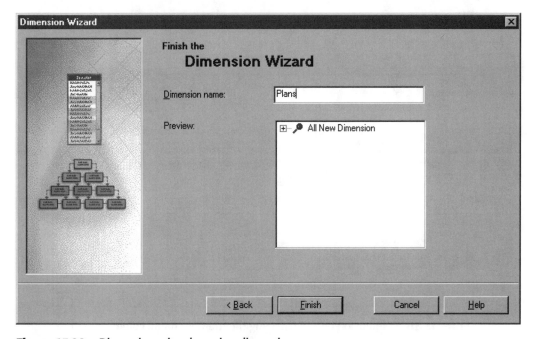

Figure 15.28   Dimension wizard naming dimension.

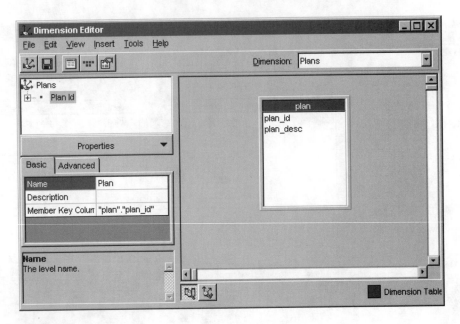

Figure 15.29 Dimension wizard changing a level name.

Repeat these steps for the Provider, Employee Class, MDC, and Network Status dimensions, using the blueprints in Figures 15.8 through 15.11.

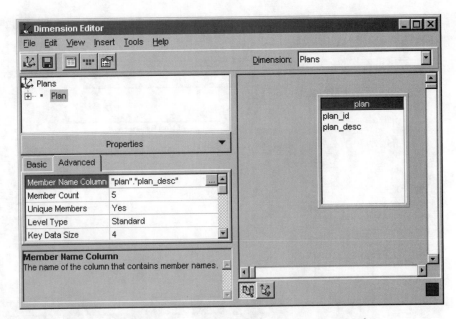

Figure 15.30 Dimension wizard changing the member name column.

Building Multiple-table Dimensions

To build multiple-table dimensions we'll use the wizard again so as to create the Service Class dimension. Start to create a new dimension as you did with the Plans dimension (Figure 15.25) but select "Multiple Dimension Tables" instead of "Single Table." Next, select the dim_svc and dim_svc_category tables as shown in Figure 15.31. After selecting multiple tables, the wizard asks us to verify the assumed table joins. Remember that OLAP Manager guesses joins based only on column name, regardless of any indices or relationships defined in the data source. Verify that the tables are joined by svc_category_id as shown in Figure 15.32. For our levels, select svc_category_id followed by svc_id as shown in Figure 15.33 and then name the dimension "Service Classification."

To finish the dimension, perform the following steps in the cube editor. The properties to be changed can be found on the property tab that is indicated in parentheses. This tab is displayed when the indicated object is selected in the tree pane of the editor:

- Change the name of the "Svc Category Id" level to "Service Category" (Basic).

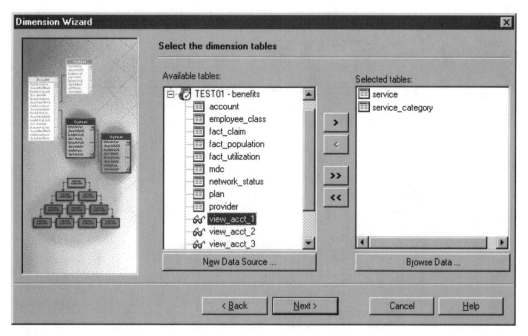

Figure 15.31 Dimension wizard selecting multiple tables.

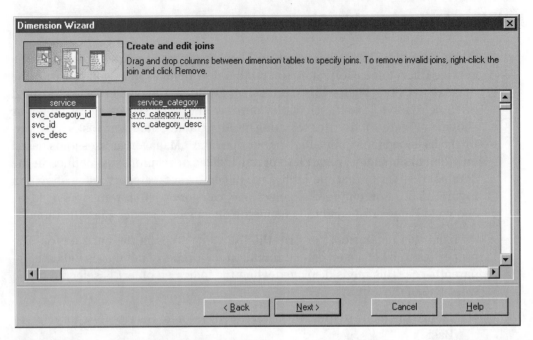

Figure 15.32 Dimension wizard joining tables.

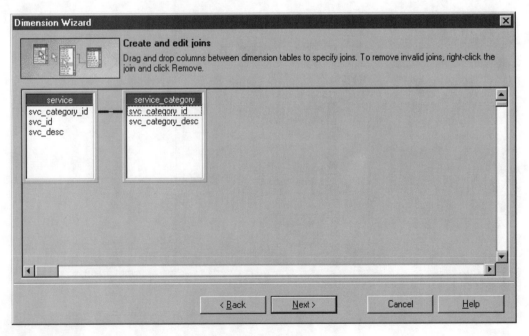

Figure 15.33 Dimension wizard selecting level columns.

- Change the member name column of the "Service Category" level to "svc_category" in the dim_svc_category table (Basic).

- Change the name of the "Svc Id" level to "Service Classification" (Basic).

- Change the member name column of the Service Classification level to "Service" in the dim_svc table (Advanced).

To build our account dimensions, repeat these steps using the information shown in the period dimension blueprint in Figure 15.14.

Building a Time Dimension

As we saw in Chapter 4, the dimension wizard makes it easy to build a time dimension based upon a single date column. To create our period dimension, proceed through the dimension wizard, selecting "Single Table Dimension" and the view_period view we created earlier in the tutorial. Because the view contains a column of the date type, the wizard offers you the opportunity to identify the dimension as a time dimension. Take advantage of this opportunity as shown in Figure 15.34.

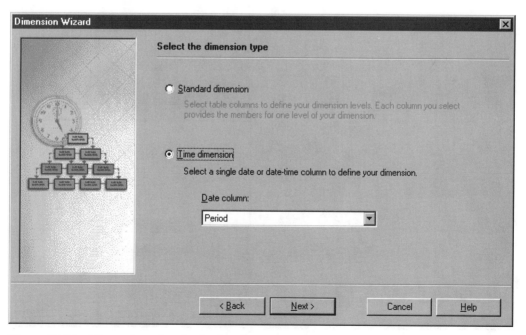

Figure 15.34   Dimension wizard selecting time column.

Next we must identify the levels for our period dimension. Select the year, quarter, and month as shown in Figure 15.35. Because we're not concerned with fiscal years, leave the beginning period as the first of January. Finally, name the dimension "Periods" and save it.

Processing the Dimensions

You can process the dimensions now or let Microsoft OLAP Services process them along with the cube. As a general rule, it's better to process the dimensions after you create them. That way, you can discover any problems before processing the cube. To process all of the dimensions now, right click on the shared dimensions folder in the OLAP Manager console and select "Process All Dimensions."

Create the Base Cubes

We'll build our four cubes using the OLAP Manager cube wizard. As with the dimension wizard, the cube wizard allows us to define our basic cube structure with minimal effort.

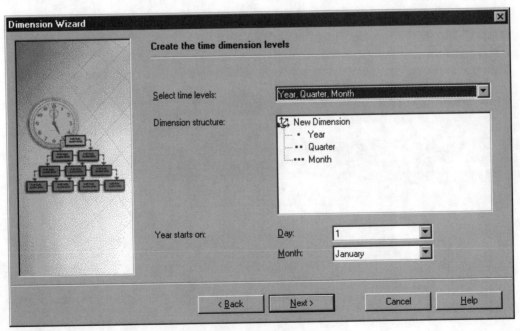

Figure 15.35 Dimension wizard selecting time levels.

The Population Cube

Start the new cube wizard as we described in Chapter 4, and select the fact_population table as the source table, as shown in Figure 15.36. Next select the columns for the measures as shown in Figure 15.37 and then the dimensions as shown in Figure 15.38. Finally, name the cube "Population" as shown in Figure 15.39.

As with the dimension wizard, OLAP Manager brings up the cube editor after the wizard finishes (Figure 15.40). For our population cube, in the cube editor we will need to change little of the fundamental structure created by the wizard. Our measures have clearly understandable names (unlike the default-level names like "plan id" created in our dimension). Because of the column names in our fact and dimension tables OLAP Manager guesses the correct table joins.

Remember, however, that when we are looking at "Members" and "Lives" as measures by themselves in a specific period we want to see the value for the last leaf member in the period as opposed to a total of the values for all periods. As we discussed in the section titled "Analyze Data," we will accomplish this through calculated members. Although users will primarily view our population

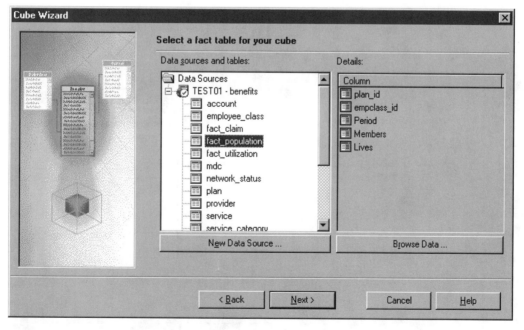

Figure 15.36　Cube wizard selecting fact table.

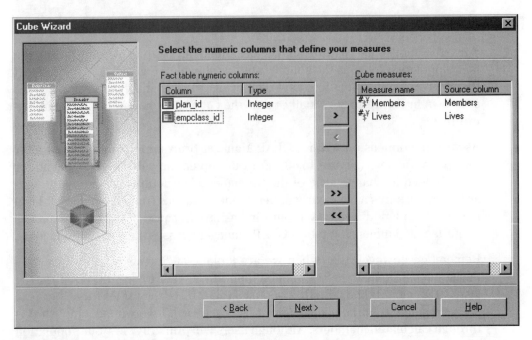

Figure 15.37   Cube wizard selecting fact table measure column.

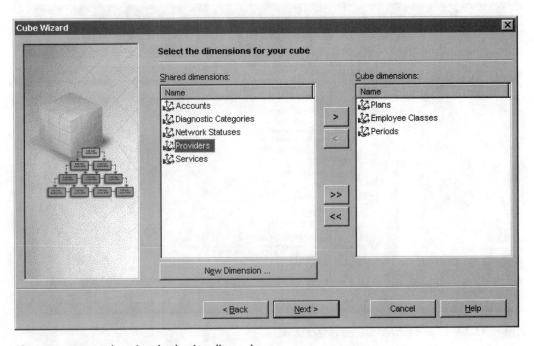

Figure 15.38   Cube wizard selecting dimension.

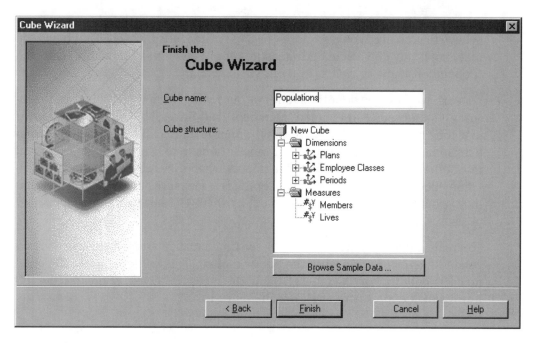

Figure 15.39   Cube wizard naming cube.

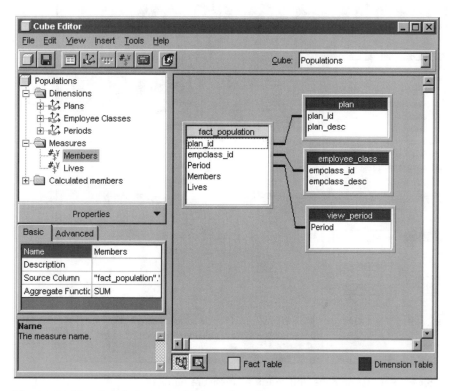

Figure 15.40   Population cube in the cube editor.

data through a virtual cube that combines our other cubes, there's no reason to believe that no one would explore our population cube by itself. That being the case, we'll put our calculated measures for "Lives" and "Members" into the "Population" cube as well as into our virtual cube.

To start, we first consider the names of our measures and our calculated measures. Our measures are named "Members" and "Lives," but since all measures in a cube must have unique names, we either need to call our calculated members something else or change the names of our "real" measures. As users will most often look at the calculated members when they are exploring our population cube, we'll change the names of the real measures to reflect the fact that they are aggregate values over time (Figure 15.41) and name our calculated measures "Members" and "Lives."

To create calculated measures for these time balance amounts, select the calculated member button from the editor toolbar. This will open the calculated member builder. For "Members," name the measure "Lives" and enter the following MDX expression (as shown in Figure 15.42):

```
([Measures].[MembersAgg],ClosingPeriod([Month]))
```

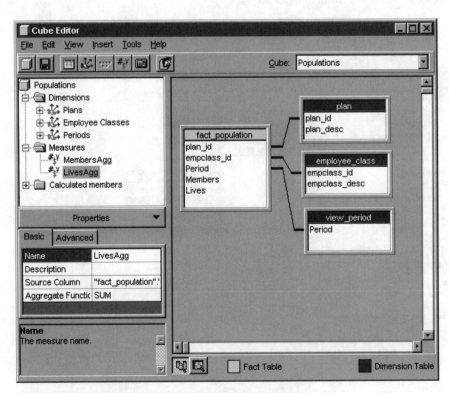

Figure 15.41 Population cube and modified measure names.

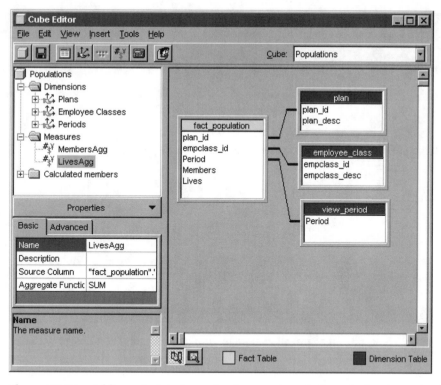

Figure 15.42 Adding calculated member for members in the calculated member builder.

Repeat this for "Lives" (substituting "Lives" for "Members" in the MDX expression).

Finally, we'll want to optimize our cube schema for processing. As we described in Chapter 3, optimizing cube schema involves modifying the member key columns for dimension levels in the cube so they point to the columns in tables that are as close as possible to the fact table. This enables Microsoft OLAP Services to create the most efficient possible SQL for querying the data source when it is processing. You can do this manually by editing the member key column property for each level, or you can let OLAP Manager do it for you. To have OLAP Manager perform this task, select "Optimize Schema" from the editor's "Tools" menu.

Before moving on to our next cube, we should design aggregations and process our population cube. This is an optional step at this point (we can simply save the cube definition and move on to the next cube), but it's generally a good idea to design aggregations and process a cube as soon as you finish creating it. If there are any problems with the cube definition, processing will quickly let you know, and it will be easier to fix any problems with the design when the cre-

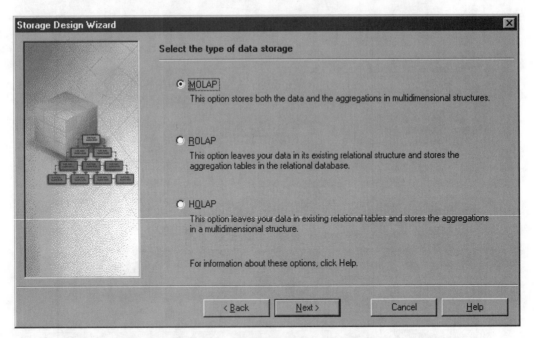

Figure 15.43 Selecting an aggregation storage form in the aggregation design wizard.

ation of the cube is still fresh in your mind. Using the supplied data, this cube will process fairly quickly. If the amount of data would result in lengthy processing time, you would want to base your cube on a view that restricts the total amount of data. If you have the Enterprise version of OLAP Services you have another option. You can edit the primary partition to include a WHERE clause that limits the amount of fact data that would be used to populate the cube. We described this process in Chapter 3.

Because storage is not an important issue in this tutorial, we'll simply walk through the steps for designing aggregations and processing the cube. The choices you make for storage (MOLAP, HOLAP, or ROLAP) are entirely up to you, as are the aggregation performance targets you will use in the analyzer. To design aggregations, save the cube definition by pressing the "Save" button on the toolbar and choose "Design Storage" from the editor's "Tools" menu. Select the storage form you wish to use, as shown in Figure 15.43. Next enter a performance target and click "Start" to have Microsoft OLAP Services design the aggregations (Figure 15.44). Finally, select "Process now" and press "Finish" to process the cube (Figure 15.45).

If you followed the steps we have just outlined, your population cube should process successfully. If it doesn't, check your cube design in the editor to be

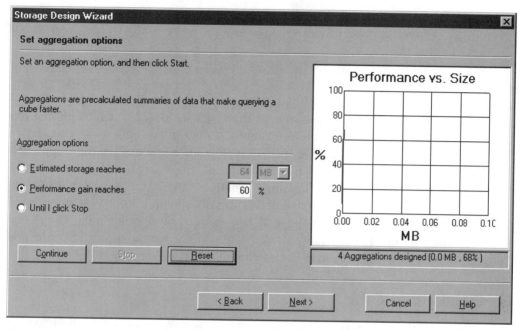

Figure 15.44   Designing aggregations for selected performance targets.

Figure 15.45   Finishing the aggregation design wizard.

sure it matched the specification of our design as shown previously in Figure 15.17. When the cube processes successfully, we're ready to move on to our next cube.

The Utilization Cube

To build the utilization cube, repeat the steps we described for building our population cube by using the information found in the cube blueprint shown previously in Figure 15.18. As with "Lives" and "Members" in the population cube, we do have one calculated member that we can create based on information in the utilization cube: "Average Length of Stay." Add this calculated measure as we described earlier, using the formula shown in the cube blueprint in Figure 15.18. When you are finished, the editor should look similar to the one shown in Figure 15.46. Finally, design aggregations for the utilization cube and process it as we described in the section titled "The Population Cube."

The Claims Paid Cube

Build the Paid Claims cube by following the steps we described for building the population and utilization cube, using the measures and dimensions indicated

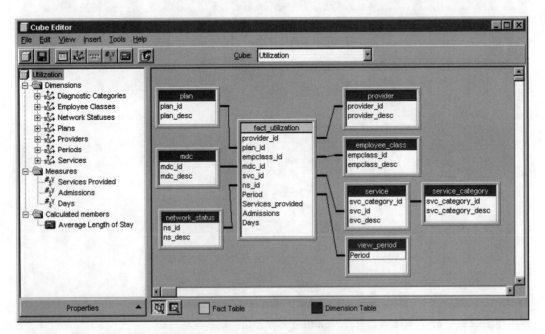

Figure 15.46 Cube editor with completed utilization cube definition.

in our Paid Claims cube blueprint (Figure 15.19). We do have one calculated member to add here. Remember that we enabled Microsoft OLAP Services to properly aggregate measures through addition or subtraction by using the expense multiplier. For our users, however, we should reverse the effect of this multiplication so they see values with their expected signs. To do this, add a calculated member called "Paid" that multiplies "Paid Amount" by the expense multiplier through the following MDX expression:

```
[Measures].[Paid Amount]*[Measures].[Expense Multiplier]
```

The final cube definition in the cube editor should look similar to the one shown in Figure 15.47.

As we did when we built our utilization cube, finish up by designing aggregations for the Paid Claims cube and process it as we described in the section titled "The Population Cube."

The Claims Submitted Cube

We create the Submitted Claims cube in the same way we built the "Paid Claims" cube (don't forget to add a calculated member that backs out the effect of the

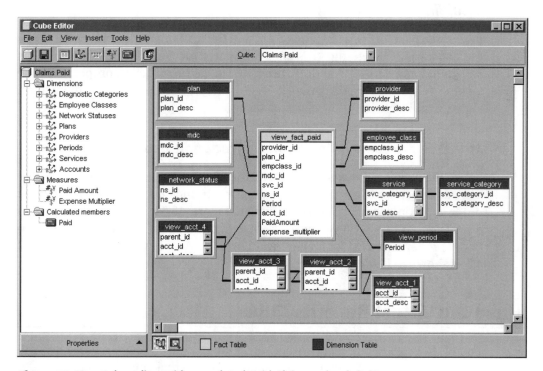

Figure 15.47 Cube editor with completed Paid Claims cube definition.

expense multiplier). Once we are in the editor, however, we have some additional tasks to accomplish to satisfy our design for this cube. In our design, we noted that because submitted claims all enter through the first level of our account dimension, we don't need OLAP Services to create aggregations for lower levels in the dimension. Because OLAP Services offers no other way to restrict aggregations by measure, we designed this cube so we can prevent unwanted aggregations.

We have two choices to prevent OLAP Services from creating unnecessary aggregation in the Submitted Claims cube. We can disable all levels in the account dimension below "Acct Level 1," or we can customize the aggregation usage for the account dimension, turning off aggregations for levels below "Acct Level 1." Both options will achieve identical ends: we will have a cube that contains submitted claims with no aggregations below "Acct Level 1" in the account dimension. Disabling the levels will prevent us from seeing members below "Acct Level 1" when we browse the cube directly. However, because users will primarily view the submitted claims data through a virtual cube, the distinction between disabling levels and disabling aggregation by level is largely irrelevant because all levels in a dimension are visible in a virtual cube, regardless of whether they are disabled in the source cube. Because the tasks for either method are simple and very similar, we'll describe both of them here. Which one you implement is completely up to you.

Disabling Account Dimension Levels

In the tree pane of the cube editor, expand the account dimension so all levels are displayed. Change the "Disabled" property for "Acct Level 2" to "No," as shown in Figure 15.48. You don't need to change the disabled property for the lower levels because OLAP Manager automatically disables a level if any level above it is disabled.

Modifying Account Dimension Aggregation Usage

Select the account dimension in the editor tree pane. On the advanced properties tab, select the "Aggregation Usage" property and choose "Custom" from the property drop-down menu as shown in Figure 15.49. Expand the account dimension so that all levels are displayed, and change the "Enable Aggregations" property to "No" for levels "Acct Level 2," "Acct Level 3," and "Acct Level 4," as shown in Figure 15.50.

Build the Virtual Benefits Cube

Finally, to provide our users with a single interface for our four cubes, we will build a virtual cube. We can create and modify a virtual cube in OLAP Manager

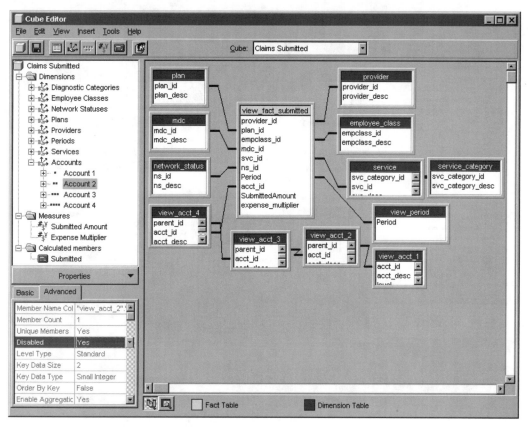

Figure 15.48 Disabling levels in a cube dimension.

using the virtual cube wizard. As we described in Chapter 3, the process is very straightforward. The challenge for our health care benefits application is to add calculated members to our virtual cube. We'll start by creating our virtual cube and then close out this tutorial by showing you how to use DSO to create calculated members in the virtual cube.

Creating the Virtual Cube

Start the virtual cube wizard by right clicking on the virtual cube folder in the OLAP Manager console and selecting "New Virtual Cube . . .". Select our four cubes as shown in Figure 15.51 and then select all of the measures from all of our cubes, as shown in Figure 15.52. Note that our expense multiplier measure will have two names in the selected list: "Expense Multiplier" and "Expense Multiplier 1." So that you can easily identify which multiplier belongs to which cube, change the names to "Paid Multiplier" and "Submitted

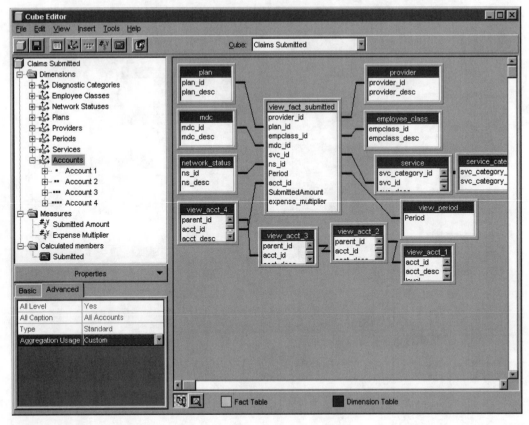

Figure 15.49 Editing aggregation usage for a cube dimension.

Multiplier" by selecting the measure with the mouse and then left clicking once to edit the name.

Next, select all of the dimensions, as shown in Figure 15.53. Finally, name the virtual cube "Benefits" as shown in Figure 15.54. Note that if you leave "Process Now" selected, when you press "Finish" OLAP Manager will process the virtual cube immediately, along with any of our other cubes that have not been processed.

Adding Calculated Members

As we mentioned in Chapter 3, OLAP Manager offers no means for adding calculated members to virtual cubes. At the time this book was being written, Microsoft stated its intention to make available an add-in for the OLAP Manager for this purpose. Hopefully, the add-in will be available from the Microsoft SQL Server Web site by the time you read this. We've also included a simple utility

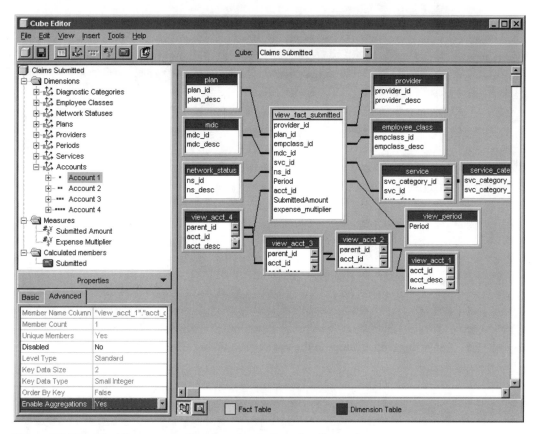

Figure 15.50 Disabling aggregation for a level of a cube dimension.

on the CD-ROM that accompanies this book that enables you to add calculated members to any cube (whether virtual or "real").

Nevertheless, as we'll show you here, the steps for adding calculated members to cubes are fairly simple. Figure 15.55 shows the basic code in Visual Basic (VB). The parameters that are passed to the procedure (all strings) are the following: the machine name of the server Microsoft OLAP Services is running on, the OLAP Services database that contains the cube you wish to add the calculated member to, the name of the cube, a member name for the calculated member, and the MDX formula.

```
Public Sub CreateCalculatedMember(sServer As String, sDB As String, sCube As
String, sMemberName As String, sStatement As String)

  Dim dsoServer As New DSO.Server 'DSO Server object
  Dim dsoDB As DSO.MDStore        'DSO Database object
  Dim dsoCube As DSO.MDStore      'DSO Cube object
```

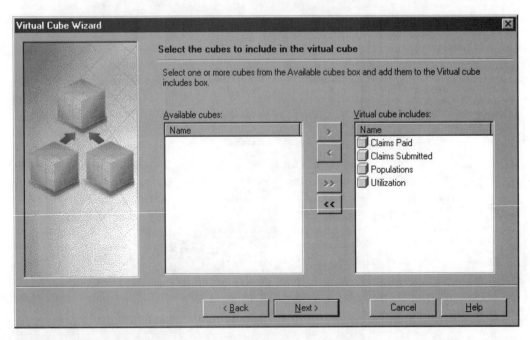

Figure 15.51 Selecting source cubes in the virtual cube wizard.

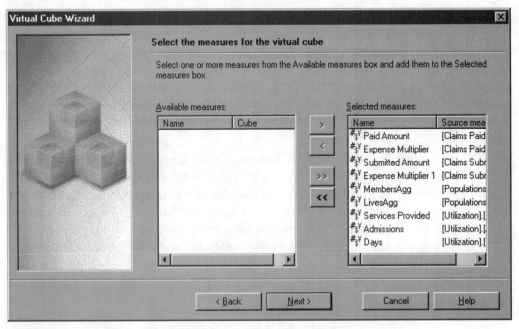

Figure 15.52 Selecting cube measures in the virtual cube wizard.

```
Dim dsoCommand As DSO.Command     'DSO Command object
Dim ctrDB As Integer              'Counters for looping through collections
Dim ctrCube As Integer

'establish a connection with the desired server
dsoServer.Connect sServer

'Step through each database on the server until we find the one we want
For ctrDB = 1 To dsoServer.MDStores.Count
  Set dsoDB = dsoServer.MDStores(ctrDB)
  If dsoDB.Name = sDB Then
    'Step through cubes in the database until we find the one we want
    For ctrCube = 1 To dsoDB.MDStores.Count
      Set dsoCube = dsoDB.MDStores(ctrCube)
    Next ctrCube
  End If
Next ctrDB

'create a command object to hold the MDX
'that creates our calculated member
Set dsoCommand = dsoServer.CreateObject(clsCubeCommand)

'give the command the name we wish to use for our calculated member
dsoCommand.Name = sMemberName

'define the command as a CREATE MEMBER command
dsoCommand.CommandType = cmdCreateMember

'Assign the MDX expression that creates the calculated member
dsoCommand.Statement = sStatement

'Add the command to the cube
dsoCube.Commands.Add dsoCommand

'save our changes to the cube
dsoCube.Update

End Sub
```

As discussed in the documentation for Microsoft OLAP Services, DSO is a collection of COM objects through which we can administer OLAP Services. Once a DSO.Server object is created, we can use it to connect to an instance of OLAP Services by using the server objects connection method and the name of the server ("[server].connect <<server name>>"). The DSO.Server object contains a collection of DSO.Database objects that, in turn, contain a collection of DSO.Cube objects. With a database and cube name we can access the instances of each object we need by stepping through the appropriate collections until we find the ones we want.

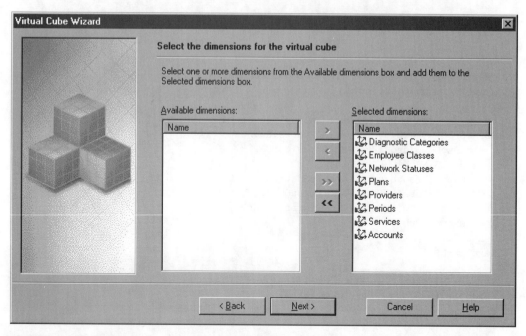

Figure 15.53 Selecting dimensions in the virtual cube wizard.

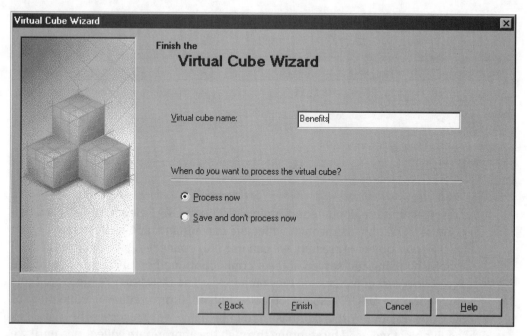

Figure 15.54 Naming a virtual cube in the virtual cube wizard.

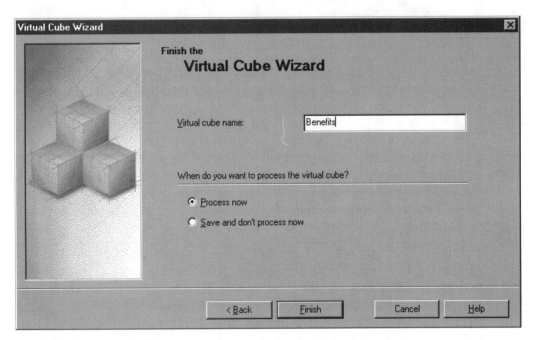

Figure 15.55   Visual Basic code to create a calculated member in a cube.

DSO represents calculated members as command objects of the type cmdCreateMember. To create a calculated member we create a new command object, identify it as a cmdCreateMember command, assign the name for the calculated member, and assign it the MDX that defines that calculated member. To create a calculated member for "Days per 1000 Members" we would call the procedure in Figure 15.55 with the following parameters:

- sServer: "olapserver"
- sDatabase: "Benefits"
- sCube: "Benefits"
- sMemberName: "Days per 1000 Members"
- sStatement:

```
CREATE MEMBER [Benefits].[Measures].[Days per 1000 Members] AS ' [Mea-
sures].[Days]*1000/([Measures].[MemberMonths],[Accounts].[All
Accounts],[Diagnostic Categories].[All Diagnostic Categories],[Network
Status].[All Network Status],[Providers].[All Providers],[Services].[All
Services])', FORMAT_STRING = 'Standard'
```

Summary

In this chapter we built a database in Microsoft OLAP Services that helps benefits managers at Amalgamated Industries understand and manage Amalgamated's healthcare plans. Beyond basic OLAP Services tasks, we learned how to handle an irregular hierarchy in an OLAP Services dimension, how to use MDX in a calculated member to deal with semi-additive measures ("Members" and "Lives"), and how to use multiple cubes to efficiently handle measures with different dimensionality. We even delved into a little DSO programming, creating a VB procedure that adds a calculated member to a virtual cube. In Chapter 16 we'll work on another project that offers us the opportunity to handle some new challenges.

Because the primary point of an OLAP system is the analysis of the data that lives in it, we've provided a few sample MDX queries on the CD-ROM that accompanies this book for you to run against our benefits database. Please read the document titled "benefitsmdx.html" located in the "html\" directory on the CD-ROM for descriptions of the queries. The queries themselves can be found in the document titled "benefits.mdx", which can be opened in the "MDX Sample" application that Microsoft installs with OLAP Services.

CHAPTER 16

Tutorial 2: Grocery Store Frequent Shopper Program

The adoption by supermarkets of scanner checkout technology and frequent shopper programs provides today's supermarket managers with an unparalleled wealth of information about their businesses and their customers. Scanner checkout offers detailed information regarding how much product is moving and when, down to the precise item and minute. This data enables managers to make sound business decisions about such practices as inventory and pricing. Marrying this technology with frequent shopper cards extends supermarkets' knowledge bases with detailed information about real shoppers. Such copious amounts of detailed information, arrangeable by almost limitless dimensions, screams out for OLAP.

In this tutorial we will create a database for analyzing shopping patterns in a small supermarket chain called Whole Foods Emporium (WFE). The database and dimensionality for this tutorial closely resemble the FoodMart sample that Microsoft included with its OLAP Services documentation. However, in this tutorial we'll move beyond the basic tasks involved in building an OLAP Services database to cover more advanced features. In addition to basic OLAP Services tasks, this tutorial you will show you how to do the following:

- Derive dimension metadata from other dimensions (in the section "Identify Dimensions")
- Use count aggregation (in the section "Identify Measures")
- Create distinct count calculations (in the section "Identify Calculations")

- Physically optimize the database for distinct count calculations (in the section "Design Dimensions and Cubes")
- Use HOLAP and MOLAP storage (in the section "Create the Base Cubes")

Before beginning this tutorial you will need to create an SQL Server 7 database using the tables and data found in the Microsoft Access database named grocery.mdb from the CD-ROM that accompanies this book. Instructions for doing this can be found in the "setuprdb.doc" file on the CD-ROM.

Analyze Needs

As we did with the company in the health care tutorial in Chapter 15, we start by first evaluating what Whole Foods Emporium (WFE) is currently doing with its database and what needs to be done. This needs analysis will involve examining the current workflow and the requirements for the desired model.

Current Workflow

WFE only recently adopted a frequent shopper program. Before the program, managers received weekly printouts from the IT department showing sales and store traffic data based on data extracted from the scanner system. Of course, this data contained no information about customers other than basic counts of shopper visits. The new system, however, includes a data warehouse that contains customer, product, and store data. It also includes batch processes for importing transactions from the scanner system on a daily basis.

Desired Model

WFE's managers are very excited about having the ability to see real customer information along with their sales data. However, because these managers have never had access to such data before, they're not exactly sure how they want to see it. They want to start off simply with sales trends by product and store along basic demographic categories. The initial goal is to gather enough information in a usable form so they can track sales activity and, most important, develop marketing activities and merchandizing strategies that could increase store sales. At a minimum, they require the following dimensionality in order to perform useful analysis (we'll actually define our dimensions and try to discover other dimensionality that could prove useful when we analyze our data in the next section:

Customer and geography. Analyzing data by customer by where they live reveals where customers come from. Among other things, this information would allow managers to focus advertising in appropriate markets.

Stores. Analyzing data by store shows where customers shopped. For example, this would enable managers to evaluate the mix of merchandise in a given store to reflect the desires of customers.

Products. Analyzing data by product tells managers what customers purchased. It would also reveal what was not purchased so managers could replace slow-moving merchandise with product that will sell better.

Time. Analyzing data according to the time indicates when purchases were made. For example, managers could see if certain products sold better at certain times of the year and adjust their purchasing accordingly.

To quantify observations based on these dimensions, managers want to see at least the following measures (Note: These are just basic definitions. We'll discuss these measures in more detail when we analyze the source data in the next section):

Sales in dollars. For example, Store A took in $85,000 on Friday.

Customer traffic. For example, 850 purchases were made at Store A on Friday.

Quantity of items purchased. For example, 85 bottles of soda were bought from Store A on Friday.

Counts of products purchased. For example, six different brands of soda were bought from Store A on Friday.

Counts of customers making purchases. For example, 52 different customers purchased soda from Store A on Friday.

Once the basic system is built and managers have had time to explore the frequent shopper data, WFE expects to define more specific questions so it can make further analysis and enhancements down the road.

Analyze Data

The data warehouse that contains our frequent shopper data includes all the information gathered about our shoppers when they signed up for their frequent shopper cards. This includes basic biographical data such as name, address, date of birth, household income, and household size. It also contains detailed data about the products sold in our stores and the transaction information retrieved from checkout scanners. When this data is taken together, we have enough information to tell us who bought what where and when.

Identify Dimensions

The register system provides two data tables: txn_summary and txn_detail. Each record in txn_summary represents a customer checking out at the cash register. In addition to a customer's frequent shopper card number, it contains the store where the purchase was made and a time stamp indicating when the checkout began. Txn_detail contains a record that holds the SKUPC code of each scanned item, along with the unit price and quantity purchased.

The fact data by itself offers us relatively limited dimensionality (Customer, Store, Product, and Time). Although this provides our managers with useful information about store sales activity, it fails to provide the information they want to base their marketing and merchandising decisions on. Managers may learn the shopping habits of specific customers (which can prove useful in developing highly targeted direct mail campaigns), but they know little about the type of people shopping at their store and what products different demographic groups of customers buy. For example, say that government demographic statistics show that the population of 25-to-34-year-olds is growing significantly in the towns surrounding our store. Knowing this, it would be useful to learn the types of products that age group buys so we can stock more of the product (and more of similar products) and advertise these products to attract these new residents. Commercial data services such as MicroVision can provide additional demographic and lifestyle information to help us understand our customers and markets better.

Besides Customers, Stores, Products, and Time, the customer table shows us possibilities for many other dimensions for the type of demographic data we are interested in. For example, each customer record contains the customer's address, gender, date of birth, and a host of other useful demographic identifiers such as household size, marital status, and so on. To make this initial database manageable for the purposes of this tutorial, we'll include only two additional demographic dimensions for our cube based on customer metadata: one containing gender information and one containing age group information. Gender is fairly straightforward. Each customer belongs to one of three genders: Male, Female, and Unknown (not everyone fills out the frequent shopper application completely). For age groups, we can assign customers to the relevant group based upon their date of birth (DOB).

Because our facts are organized by time through a date stamp, we can, and will, use a standard time dimension. First, however, let's consider time in a bit more detail from the perspective of managers at Whole Foods Emporium. In addition to viewing data by month or day, our managers also find it useful to track sales by parts of the day like "morning," "lunch," "afternoon," and so on (we'll use the standard broadcasting/advertising term of "daypart"). Observing that traffic dips during lunchtime, managers may decide to add more prepared foods in the deli and a salad bar to the produce section to increase traffic during that part of the day. Although we can obviously fit such a level within a standard time hierarchy (between day and hours), our managers would find it even more effective to view data *across* other periods. For example, viewing data across other periods would enable our managers to easily notice that lunch traffic rose in January (adding those hot soups made a difference) or that it dipped in July (customers don't seem to be enthusiastic about hot soup in the summer).

In summary, we'll include the dimensions in our frequent shopper database to include the following:

Customers. In this dimension facts are organized by frequent shopper card number. Since demographic information will be organized in separate dimensions, we'll organize customers by their geographic home, with levels for State and City.

Stores. In the "Stores" dimension facts are organized by specific store. WFE stores are organized by geographic location. Because WFE only has one store in any given city (so looking at data by store city provides the same information as looking at store), we'll limit our levels to State and Store.

Products. In this dimension facts are organized by SKUPC. We'll explore the levels and hierarchy for this dimension when we analyze our dimension metadata.

Time. In the "Time" dimension, facts are organized by minute.

Dayparts. This dimension is derived from time as we discussed earlier in this section.

Genders. This dimension is derived from customer information as we discussed.

Age Groups. This dimension is also derived from customer information.

Identify Measures

Our managers analyze business performance according to five primary criteria: sales in dollars, customer traffic, quantity of items purchased, count of products purchased, and count of customers making purchases. The only explicit measures in our database, however, are "amount," "quantity," and "unit_price" in the transaction detail table. The amount column in txn_detail provides us with the very important dollars-spent measure. Quantity, of course, tells us how many units of products we've sold. Unit price isn't very important except at the very leaf level. Indeed, any aggregation of unit price would be meaningless. Knowing the average price per unit sold would be useful above the leaf level, but we'll take care of that when we discuss calculations in the next section.

We can derive overall store traffic (visits or the gross number of customers serviced) from the number of records in the summary table. Each record represents a distinct trip through the checkout lane, or a visit. To obtain a count of visits we can select any column in the transaction summary table and aggregate using the count function. Although the value of the column's data is irrelevant (since we're just taking a count), we'll use the "txn_id" column as the source for our visits measure if just because the value does serve as the identifier for the records we're counting.

The aggregation functions available to us in Microsoft OLAP Services, however, do not permit us to get net figures for the number of products sold or the number of customers serviced (counts of the unique customers or products). To get these amounts we'll need to use some form of MDX calculation within a client query or in a calculated member. We'll cover this when we discuss calculations in the next section. The base measures that are available directly from our fact tables are summarized in the following list (unless otherwise noted, they enter at the leaf level of all dimensions):

Sale. The dollars spent.

Visits. The count of visits to a store. Based on the number of transaction summary records, Visits will enter a cube at the "All level" for products.

Units. The gross number of items purchased.

Identify Calculations

As we mentioned in the previous section, a useful measure for our managers is the average price per unit sold. The value is simply the sale amount divided by the number of units sold:

```
[measures].[sale]/[measures].[Units]
```

As we also mentioned, this evaluates to "unit_price" at the leaf level.

Let's now take a closer look at the issues entailed in obtaining the counts of unique customers or products in a multidimensional structure. Basically, distinct counts are not necessarily additive up a given dimension hierarchy. For example, imagine that WFE has only two departments. The table in Figure 16.1 shows these two departments, the amount spent, and the number of customers who made purchases. In the "Amount Spent" column the data adds up nicely. The data does not add up in the "Customer" column, however. 200 different customers made purchases in the bakery department, and 150 unique customers purchased goods from produce. Within all departments, however, only 300 different customers made a purchase during May. Although some customers made purchases from *only* bakery *or* produce, others made purchases from *both* bakery *and* produce. This being the case—and since we only want to count each customer once for the total regardless of whether they made a purchase in one or both departments—the total will be less than the sum of the purchases from the specific departments.

Department	Amount Spent	Customers who Made Purchase
All Departments	5,000	300
Bakery	3,000	150
Produce	2,000	200

Figure 16.1   Table of sales by department for May.

Our problem is that Microsoft OLAP Services offers no "DISTINCT COUNT" aggregation function. Fortunately, MDX does provide the ability to implement the calculation. At least in terms of execution, it will be quite simple for us to obtain correct distinct count values. As we described in Chapter 7, the MDX function Count(*set [,ExcludeEmpty]*) returns a count of the number of tuples in *set* that have data (using the *ExcludeEmpty* flag) or regardless of data (leaving out the *ExcludeEmpty* flag). Now the issue becomes only a question of defining our *set*.

In determining our set, we need to find the tuples that we want to count. Since we've already begun our example with customer counts, we'll start with that dimension. Although we have yet to define the levels for our Customer dimension (we'll do so later when we build the dimension), we know that the count of customers would be the number of customers at the leaf level that are descendants of the currently selected customer dimension member. To get this set we use the Descendants(*member, Level*) MDX function:

```
Descendants([Customers].CurrentMember,[Customers].[Customer])
```

To obtain a count we can plug this into the count function:

```
Count(Descendants([Customers].CurrentMember,[Customers].[Customer]))
```

At this point, however, we only have the count of existing members, regardless of whether they made a purchase. To filter the count, we can cross-join our set of customers with a measure and use the *ExcludeEmpty* flag so that Count only counts those customers with data for that measure. Since we want a count of customers who made purchases, we'll use the "amount" measure we identified earlier. Remember, however, that we can use any measure in our MDX expression because the value of the measure is irrelevant for counting purposes. Our only concern is whether some value exists.

Putting our member set and measure together we get the following expression:

```
Count(CrossJoin({[Measures].[Cust Trans}, Descendants([Customers].
CurrentMember, [Customers].[Customer])), ExcludeEmpty)
```

For example, with a cell for the age group of 18-to-24-year-olds and the month of September, this expression will return the total number of customers aged 18 to 24 who bought something at any store in September. To create a formula for obtaining a distinct count of products purchased we simply substitute the appropriate product dimension information for our customer dimension information:

```
Count(CrossJoin({[Measures].[Prod Trans]}, Descendants([Products].
CurrentMember, [Products].[Product])), ExcludeEmpty)
```

Continuing with our age group/month cell, this expression will return the number of different products purchased by 18-to-24-year-olds in September.

From our base measures we can derive many other useful statistics such as average amount spent per visit (who spends a lot when they come to Whole Foods Emporium), amount spent per customer (where are my revenues coming from), and the number of items purchased per visit. Since we demonstrated how to create calculated members in detail in the tutorial in Chapter 15, we'll ignore these additional calculations here for the sake of brevity. In summary, we'll use calculated members to obtain the following measures:

Average price per unit. This measure is determined by the formula: Sales/Units.

Customer count. This measure is the count of distinct customers.

Product count. This measure is the count of distinct products.

Identify/Create Dimension Data Source Tables/Views

The data source contains three tables that contain the data we need for our core dimensions—stores, customer, and period (the "period" table contains the data we need for our time dimension)—plus four tables for products. It also contains a city table that contains state information for cities.

The store table contains columns for "store_id", "store_name" and "city_id." Through the city table we can determine the state a given store is in with the "city_id" value. WFE has only one store in any given town, so sales by city would offer us no more information than sales by store. In fact, our stores are named by the city they are located in. WFE also has no intention of building more than one store in any given city over the next few years for fear of cannibalizing sales from existing stores. On the other hand, though WFE is a relatively small chain, with only four stores spread across only two states, it does plan to build more stores in both states. With multiple stores in a state, at some point WFE's management may find it useful to look at statewide sales. Even though we're not using anything from the City table in the dimension, we can still use the store, city, and state directly as a multiple table source for the "Stores" dimension.

Products are organized in a clear snowflake schema. The database has a top level of departments in product_department, followed by subdepartments in product_subdepartment, categories in product_category, and the individual products themselves in product_skupc. All of our facts relate to products through SKUPC.

Customer, gender, and demographic dimension metadata can all be found in the "customer" table. The customer and gender dimensions can be built directly with the Customer table itself. However, as we discussed earlier, we need to do a little work to create a usable source for our age group dimension. A standard grouping for ages in marketing is in ten-year blocks from age 25 to age 65, with additional groupings for under 18, 18 to 24, and 65 and over. Although the WFE warehouse doesn't actually contain a table with such values, for convenience we've already provided a table that contains these groups in the sample database for this tutorial. In the Age Group table, each age group is identified by a simple integer key: 1 for under 18, 2 for 18-to-24, and so on. We could have created this metadata through a view based on ages in our Customer table, but there's no guarantee that we have a customer in each age group. To our marketing people it will be just as important to know that there are no transactions in a given age group as it will be to know the distribution of customers among age groups.

Although we've defined our age groups, we still need a way for Microsoft OLAP Services to recognize the relationship between age groups' facts. Since age group is a property of our customers, we can establish the relationship to our facts through customer metadata. Using the "DOB" column in our Customer table, we can create a simple SQL expression to determine the appropriate age group identifier. Note that this view does not have to be used to define our Cus-

The Sands in the Hourglass

Since WFE naturally has no way of preventing its customers from aging, in reality customers will move between age groups over time. For expedience, however, we choose to ignore this fact in this database. Because our managers will only be analyzing a single year's worth of data at a time, failing to reflect minor changes of a customer's demographic will have negligible impact on the validity of analyses (based on the assumption that people's shopping habits don't generally change dramatically just because of a birthday). Reflecting changes to dimension data over time introduces a myriad of issues in Microsoft OLAP Services, which we covered in greater detail in Chapter 10.

tomer dimension. All that OLAP Services requires is some way to relate dimension metadata to the fact table. The relationship can be direct (such as store_id in the store view to store_id in the "txn_summary"). The relationship can also be by way of the metadata of another dimension (assuming we use the customer table or a view of the Customer table that includes gender_id, we can relate gender_id in the gender view to gender_id in the customer metadata and cust_card in the customer metadata to cust_card in txn_summary). The relationship can also be by way of some other table or view (such as age_group_id in our Age Group table to age_group_id in a view that contains only age_group_id and cust_card, to txn_summary). For the sake of providing an example, we'll go with the third option here and define the relationship through the view shown in Figure 16.2.

The Customer table contains numerous columns that we can use to define levels in our Customer dimension. For example, we could use "State" (from the City table through the shared city_id column), "City," and "Customer" or "Zip Code" and "Customer" or even "Area Code" and "Customer." One of our managers' concerns is to learn where our store customers come from so they can target those locations for advertising (or those locations where we have little penetration but feel we can get more). Therefore, we'll start with a hierarchy of "State," "City," and "Customer." We can build this dimension using only these snowflaked tables.

Our database includes a table called "period" that includes records containing date stamps for every hour in every day for the current year. Our facts, however, are organized with time stamps by minute. Although it may be interesting to

```
CREATE VIEW dbo.view_cust_agegroup
AS
SELECT cust_card,
demo_id = Case
  when DateDiff(year,dob,getdate())<=18 then 1
  when DateDiff(year,dob,getdate()) between 19 and 24 then 2
  when DateDiff(year,dob,getdate()) between 25 and 34 then 3
  when DateDiff(year,dob,getdate()) between 35 and 44 then 4
  when DateDiff(year,dob,getdate()) between 45 and 54 then 5
  when DateDiff(year,dob,getdate()) between 55 and 64 then 6
  else 7
end
FROM customer
```

Figure 16.2 SQL for a view that establishes relationship between age groups and facts through the customer card number.

know that five bagels were purchased at 9:35 AM on June 12, 1998, it's doubtful that our managers would be able to put such knowledge to any practical use. For the purpose of our database, we don't really care about facts detailed to the minute. As we discussed earlier when we identified our dimensions, for the standard Time dimension our managers only want detail down to the day, and for our "Dayparts" dimension managers want to see detail only down to the hour. The period table will work fine for building "Time" and "Dayparts" dimensions with these desired levels. However, we still need a way to establish the relationship between our dimension and the facts.

One option is to expand the period table to include minutes. It would be straightforward to create a script to generate the row values, but the resulting data would occupy a good deal of space in our data source (over half a million additional records for one year). Another option is to use GROUP BY in a view to summarize fact data to the hour. This can be an expensive proposition when we process our cubes and very expensive if we decide to use HOLAP or MOLAP storage. A third option is create a view for our dimension metadata that unions the "sales_time" column in the period table with the time stamp in txn_summary. Such a view would include every hour for our dimensions plus all of the minutes needed to relate our dimensions to our data. The SQL for defining this view is shown in Figure 16.3. Note that we include the SQL expression that generates our daypart keys so we can use this one view for both the "Time" and "Dayparts" dimensions.

Identify/Create Fact Tables/Views

The txn_detail table contains the columns for our Sale and Unit measures while txn_summary contains the data for our "Customers," "Stores," and "Time" dimensions. Because we can only use a single fact table in a cube, we must create a view that joins these two tables. We do need to make one more adjustment, however. The values in the quantity column for our "Unit" measure are either units or weights depending on the product. For the analysis we intend to do with this database, however, managers care only about the count of products sold rather than the weight or volume of products sold. For example, bulk flour is sold by the pound, while prepackaged flour is sold by unit. If I bought 1.8 pounds of bulk flour, I purchased one unit of bulk flour, just as purchasing a bag of prepackaged flour counts as one unit, regardless of whether it were a one-pound or five-pound package. To convert the quantity for products sold by weight we can use the "units" column in the skupc table in a column expression in our view. Figure 16.4 shows the SQL for our sales view.

As we discussed earlier in the chapter, the easiest way to obtain visit counts is to simply define a measure based on any column in the txn_summary table, using the count() function for aggregation.

```
CREATE VIEW dbo.view_dim_period
AS
SELECT DISTINCT txn_summary.sales_time,
  daypart_id =
    case
      when DatePart(hh,txn_summary.sales_time) between 7 And 10
then 1
      when DatePart(hh,txn_summary.sales_time) between 11 And 13
then 2
      when DatePart(hh,txn_summary.sales_time) between 14 And 17
then 3
      when DatePart(hh,txn_summary.sales_time) between 18 and 22
then 4
      else 5
    end,
  daypart_desc =
    case
      when DatePart(hh,txn_summary.sales_time) between 7 And 10
then
        'Morning'
      when DatePart(hh,txn_summary.sales_time) between 11 And 13
then
        'Lunch'
      when DatePart(hh,txn_summary.sales_time) between 14 And 17
then
        'Afternoon'
      when DatePart(hh,txn_summary.sales_time) between 18 and 22
then
        'Evening'
```

Figure 16.3 SQL for time metadata view.

Design Dimensions and Cubes

As in the tutorial in Chapter 15, and for similar reasons, we'll create all of our dimensions as shared dimensions. We know we'll have at least two cubes (Sales and Visits) that will share many of our dimensions, and there's always reason to believe that we'll build another cube down the road that could make use of one or more of the dimensions we create here. Though we accomplished most of our design during our evaluation of dimension data sources, we still have a few details to work out here.

Keeping in mind that a primary goal of OLAP is to make the data being analyzed as straightforward and intuitive as possible, we want to create member names

```
          else 'Closed'
      end
FROM txn_summary

UNION SELECT DISTINCT period.sales_time,
  daypart_id =
    case
      when DatePart(hh,period.sales_time) between 7 And 10 then 1
      when DatePart(hh,period.sales_time) between 11 And 13 then
2
      when DatePart(hh,period.sales_time) between 14 And 17 then
3
      when DatePart(hh,period.sales_time) between 18 and 22 then
4
      else 5
    end,
  daypart_desc =
    case
      when DatePart(hh,period.sales_time) between 7 And 10 then
        'Morning'
      when DatePart(hh,period.sales_time) between 11 And 13 then
        'Lunch'
      when DatePart(hh,period.sales_time) between 14 And 17 then
        'Afternoon'
      when DatePart(hh,period.sales_time) between 18 and 22 then
        'Evening'
      else 'Closed'
    end
  FROM period
```

Figure 16.3   (continued)

for genders instead of using the single-character abbreviations we'll use for our key column. "U," for example, is ambiguous as an abbreviation and may prove confusing to some of those using our cube (it means "Unknown" because, as we mentioned earlier, the customer didn't indicate his or her gender on the frequent shopper card application). The SQL expression for defining the member name column is shown in the dimension blueprint for our Genders dimension in Figure 16.5. Figures 16.6 through 16.11 show all the information required to build all of our remaining dimensions.

When we defined the sources for our facts, we identified at least two cubes, Visits and Sales. For now, we'll stick with these two cubes, knowing they will be

```
CREATE VIEW dbo.view_fact_sales
AS
SELECT
  txn_summary.Txn_id,
  txn_summary.store_id,
  txn_summary.cust_card,
  txn_summary.sales_time,
  txn_detail.skupc,
  units = CASE
    WHEN skupc.unit_id<>0 THEN 1
    ELSE txn_detail.quantity
  END,
  txn_detail.amount
FROM txn_summary INNER JOIN txn_detail ON
  txn_summary.txn_id = txn_detail.txn_id INNER JOIN skupc ON
  txn_detail.skupc = skupc.skupc
```

Figure 16.4   SQL for sales facts.

able to provide all the data we need for the intended use of our database (marketing and merchandizing planning) and turn our attention to storage form. We know that our managers rarely want to see specific customers or products during analysis. Both our Customer and Products dimensions are also fairly large, with roughly 9,000 and 12,000 members, respectively (and both should grow frequently). These facts make our cubes prime candidates for HOLAP or ROLAP storage. There's no reason to duplicate the leaf-level data in Microsoft OLAP Services when our users will wish to access it only rarely, if ever. There's

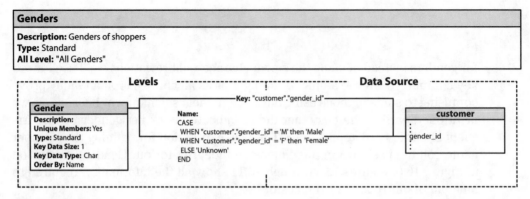

Figure 16.5   Genders dimension blueprint.

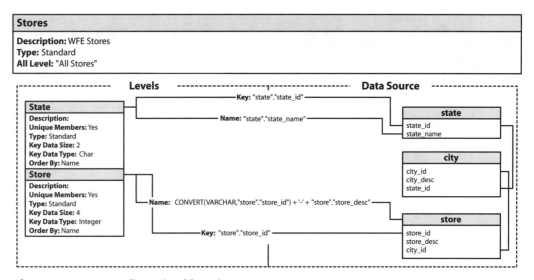

Figure 16.6   Stores dimension blueprint.

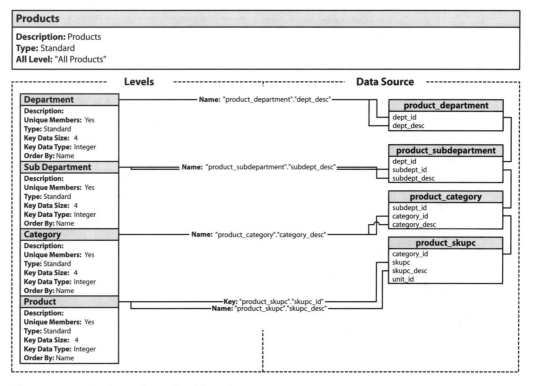

Figure 16.7   Products dimension blueprint.

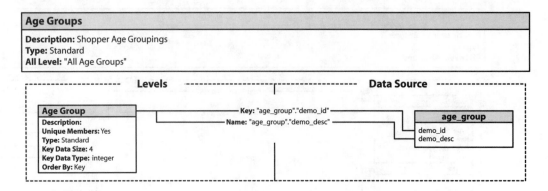

Figure 16.8   Age Groups dimension blueprint.

good reason, however, to keep our aggregations in MOLAP because it will satisfy queries much more quickly than will ROLAP. Thus, we'll start by proposing HOLAP storage for our cubes.

Now, let's turn to our customer and product distinct counts. We know that to get our distinct count of customers we must always retrieve data from the leaf of our Customers dimension. Similarly, when obtaining our distinct product count we must also always retrieve data from the leaf of the Products dimen-

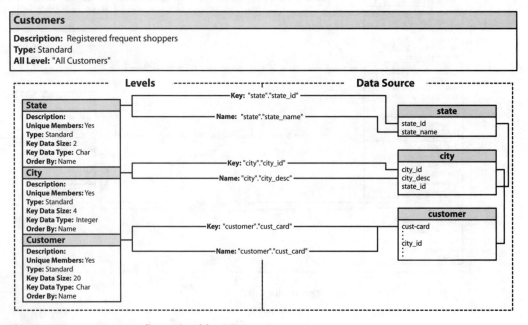

Figure 16.9   Customers dimension blueprint.

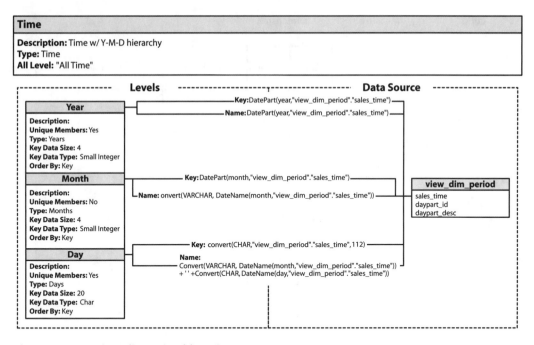

Figure 16.10 Time dimension blueprint.

sion. These facts strongly steer us away from HOLAP. Since we have some data that's ideal for HOLAP and some that's better suited to MOLAP, we should use a second cube.

Putting our distinct count data in its own cubes provides additional benefits. Microsoft OLAP Services will process separate queries to different cubes in

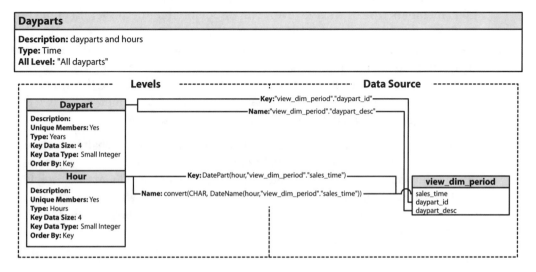

Figure 16.11 Dayparts dimension blueprint.

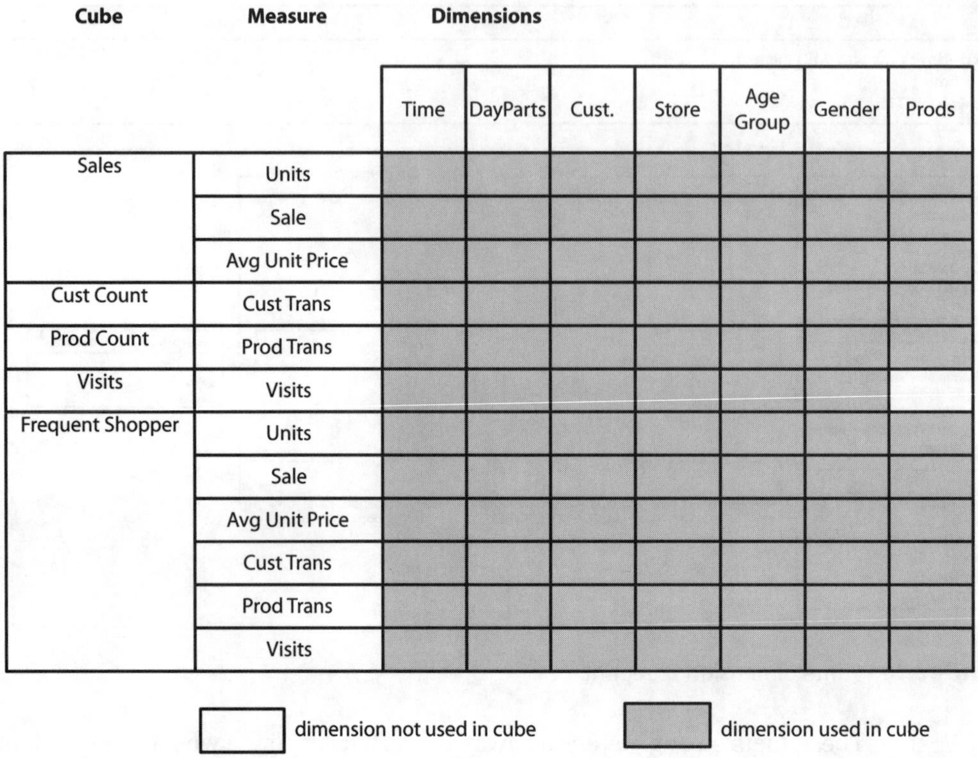

Cube	Measure	Time	DayParts	Cust.	Store	Age Group	Gender	Prods
Sales	Units							
	Sale							
	Avg Unit Price							
Cust Count	Cust Trans							
Prod Count	Prod Trans							
Visits	Visits							
Frequent Shopper	Units							
	Sale							
	Avg Unit Price							
	Cust Trans							
	Prod Trans							
	Visits							

☐ dimension not used in cube   ▨ dimension used in cube

Figure 16.12 MDS schema of cube, dimension, and measure usage.

parallel if it can. We also know that queries involving the aggregation of large levels (a configurable property of the OLAP Services server, with a default of 1,000 members from the same level) will be remoted to the server. Keeping our distinct counts in the same cube as our other measures could mean bogging everything down for simple queries. We can also customize our aggregations for each cube to avoid unnecessary aggregations. Since customer count will always use leaf for customers, we can limit aggregations for the Customer dimension to "Bottom Only." The same is true for Product Count, where we can limit aggregations for the Products dimension to "Leaf Only."

In summary, we will create four cubes in our database: Sales, Visits, Customer Count, and Product Count. As in Chapter 15, to offer our users a single view into all the data we will use a virtual cube that we'll call Frequent Shopper. Figure 16.12 provides a high-level view of the associations between cubes and their dimensions. Diagrams detailing the design of our four cubes can be found in Figures 16.13 through 16.17.

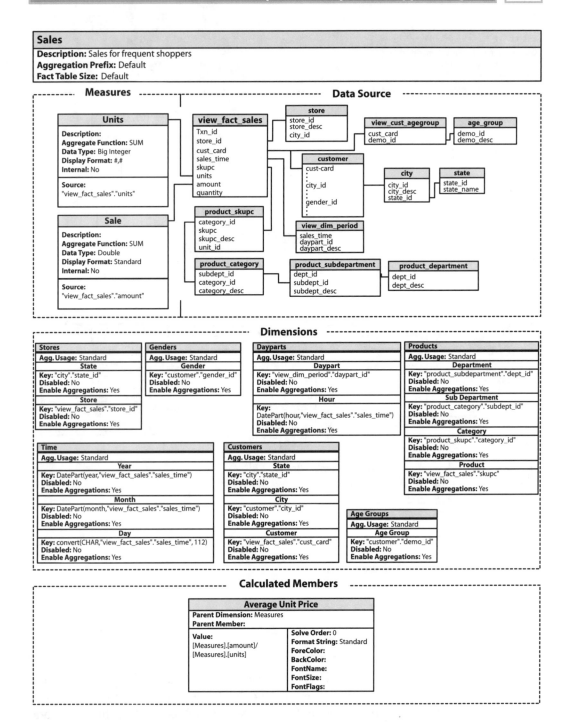

Figure 16.13 Sales cube blueprint.

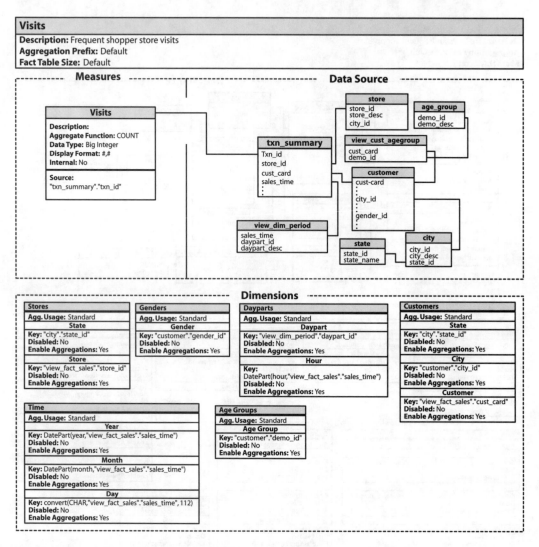

Figure 16.14 Visits cube blueprint.

Create a Database

We'll keep all of our Microsoft OLAP Services objects for this project in a database called "Whole Foods." To create the database, right click on the server in the OLAP Manager tree pane and select "New Database . . .". In the new database dialog, enter the name for the database and a short description, as shown in Figure 16.18.

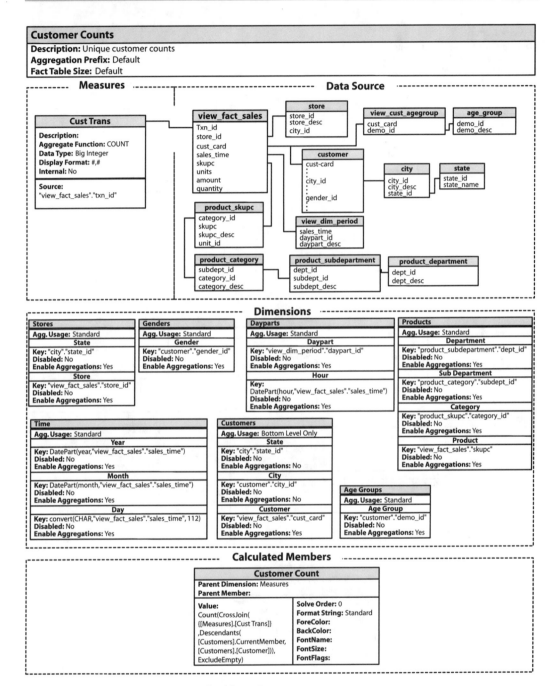

Figure 16.15 Customer Count cube blueprint.

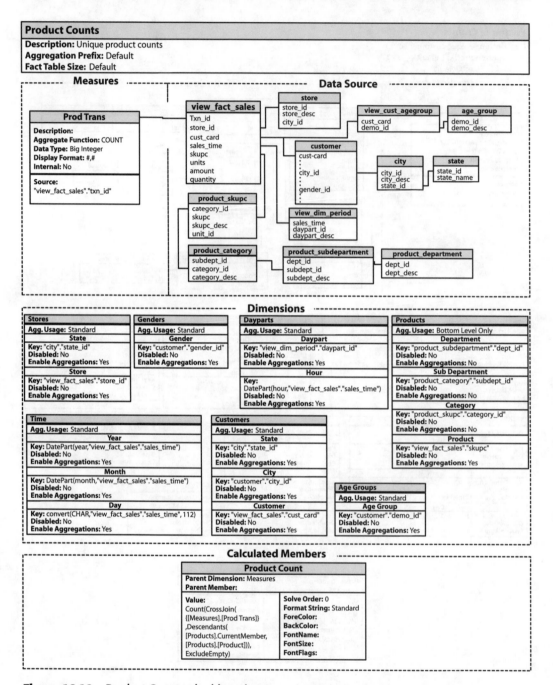

Figure 16.16 Product Count cube blueprint.

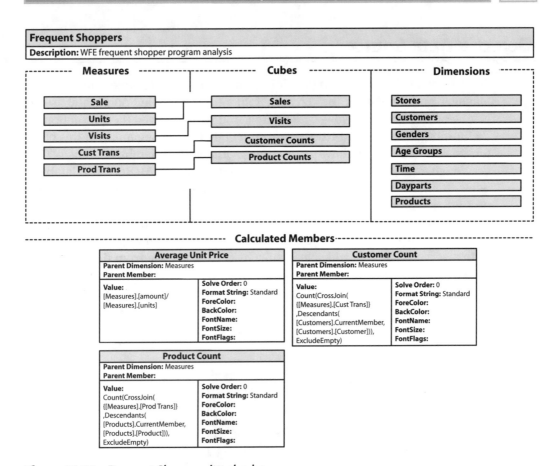

Figure 16.17   Frequent Shopper virtual cube.

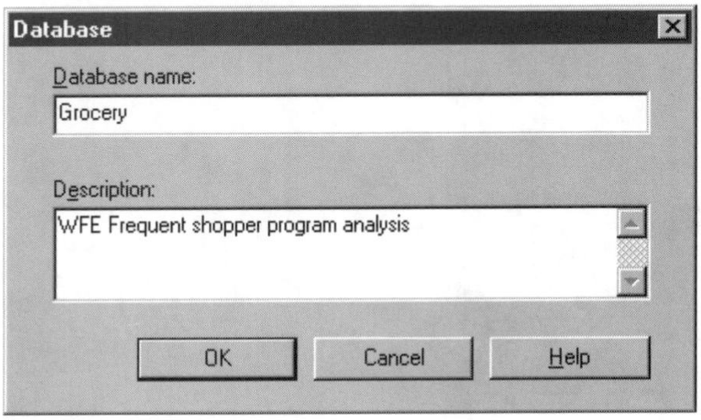

Figure 16.18   Creating a new database in OLAP Manager.

Select a Data Source

To identify the data source, right click on the "Data Sources" folder in the OLAP Manager tree pane under the "Library" folder for the Whole Foods database we just created and select "New Data Source…". If you followed the instructions in "setuprdb.doc" on the CD-ROM as recommended at the beginning of this chapter, you should already have created an SQL Server 7 database named "Grocery" containing the tables and views we need for our OLAP Services database. Select "OLE DB Provider for SQL Server" from the provider tab of the data link properties dialog as shown in Figure 16.19 and click the button labeled "Next >>." On the connection tab of the dialog, select or enter the name of the SQL Server in item 1, enter the appropriate log on information required to connect to that server in item 2, and select the "Grocery" database from the drop-down list in item 3 as shown in Figure 16.20. Click the "Test Connection" button to verify that you can indeed connect to the database and then click "OK" to save the data source.

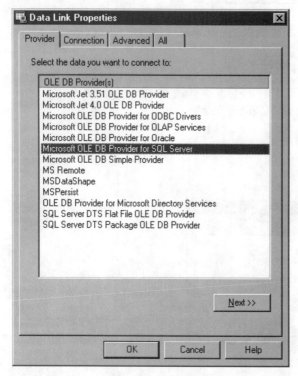

Figure 16.19   Selecting a data source provider.

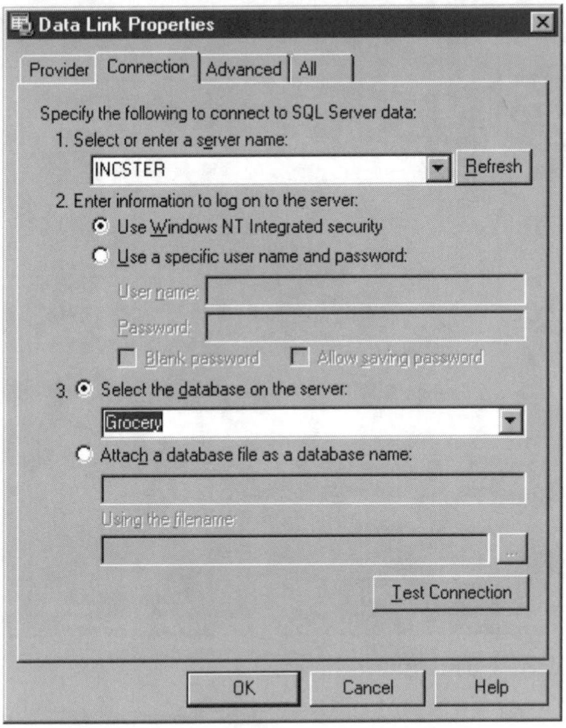

Figure 16.20   Selecting a SQL Server data source.

Build Dimensions

As we did in our tutorial in Chapter 15, we'll start with the dimension wizard and then make any needed adjustments for all of our dimensions through the dimension editor. Using the dimension wizard will allow us to build a basic dimension structure quickly and with little effort. To start to create a dimension using the wizard, right click on the "Shared Dimensions" folder in the OLAP Manager tree pane below the Whole Foods database and select "New Dimension . . .".

Building Single-table Dimensions

In this section we'll walk through the process of building single-table dimensions with Genders. Because a single view contains all of our gender dimension information, select the star schema option as shown in Figure 16.21 and click "Next." Select the customer table from the data source as shown in Figure 16.22

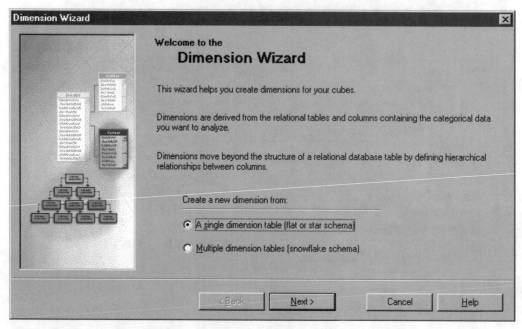

Figure 16.21   Dimension wizard selecting dimension schema.

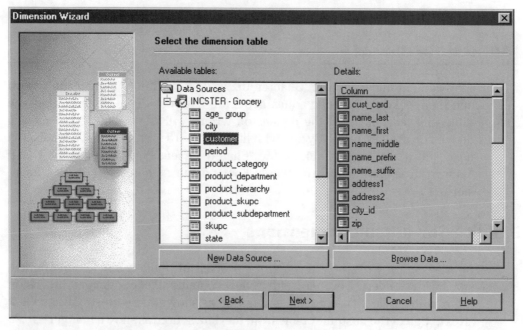

Figure 16.22   Dimension wizard selecting table.

and click "Next." For the Genders dimension we have only one option for defining our single level: "gender_id." When we're finished with the wizard, we'll define the member name column with an SQL expression, in the dimension editor to offer our users more intuitive member names. Right now, select "gender_id" for our single level, as shown in Figure 16.23.

Because our customer table contains columns of the type "datetime," the wizard will next present you with the option to create a time dimension. We'll take advantage of this later when we build our Time dimension in the section "Building the Time Dimension." Right now, just click "Next" to proceed to the step where the wizard asks us to name the dimension. Name the dimension "Genders" as shown in Figure 16.24 and click "Finish." When the wizard finishes, OLAP Manager displays the dimension editor, which is where we can refine our dimension definition. In the dimension editor, change the level name to "Gender" (see Figure 16.25). We also want to use an SQL expression to provide intuitive names for gender members. To do this, in the member name column property enter the SQL expression shown in the blueprint for our Genders dimension (see Figure 16.5), as shown in Figure 16.26.

Repeat these steps for the Age Groups and Dayparts dimensions, using the blueprints shown in Figures 16.8 and 16.11.

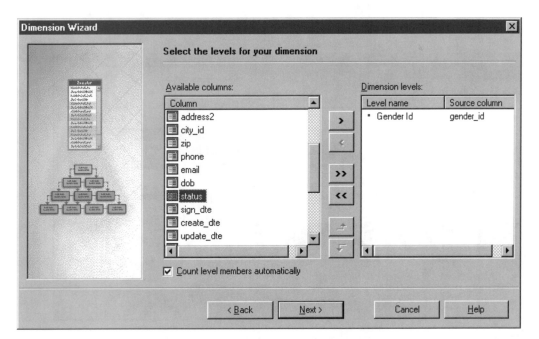

Figure 16.23 Dimension wizard selecting level column.

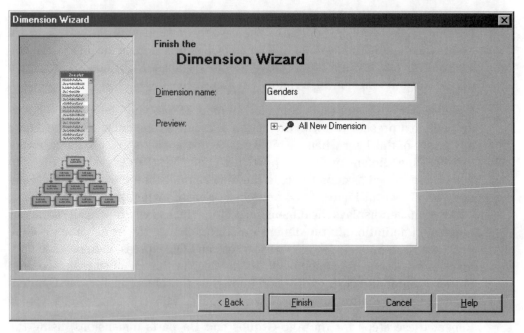

Figure 16.24 Dimension wizard naming dimension.

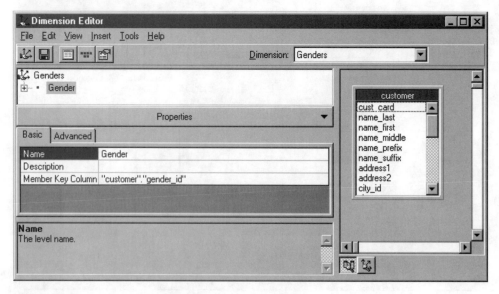

Figure 16.25 Dimension wizard changing a level name.

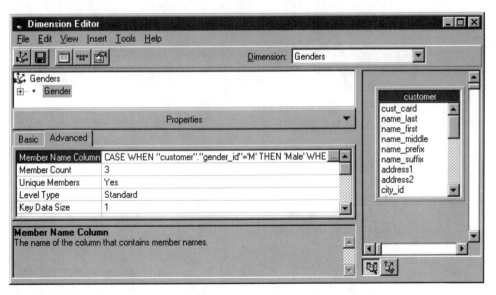

Figure 16.26 Dimension wizard changing the member name column.

Building Multiple-table Dimensions

We'll use the wizard again to create the Stores dimension. Begin creating a new dimension as you did with the Genders dimension (see Figure 16.21), but select "Multiple Dimension Tables" instead of "Single Table." Next, select the City and State tables as shown in Figure 16.27. After you select "Multiple Dimension Tables," the wizard asks you to verify the assumed table joins. Remember that OLAP Manager guesses joins based only on column name, regardless of any indices or relationships defined in the data source. Verify that the store table joins the city table by city_id and that the city table joins the state table by state_id, as shown in Figure 16.28. For our levels, select state_id from the state table followed by store_id from the Store table, as shown in Figure 16.29. Finally, name the dimension "Stores."

To finish the dimension, perform the following steps in the dimension editor. The properties to be changed can be found on the property tab indicated in parentheses. This tab is displayed when the indicated object is selected in the tree pane of the editor:

- Change the name of the "State Id" level to "State" (Basic).

- Change the member name column of the "State" level to "State_name" in the State table (Basic).

- Change the name of the "Store Id" level to "Store" (Basic).

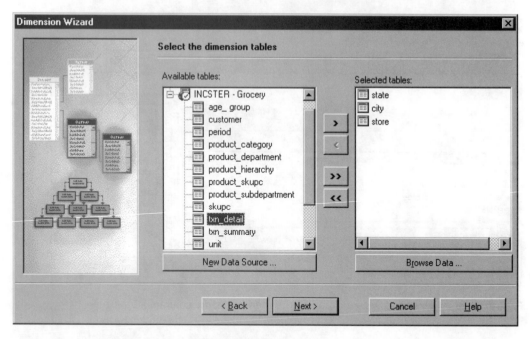

Figure 16.27 Dimension wizard selecting multiple table.

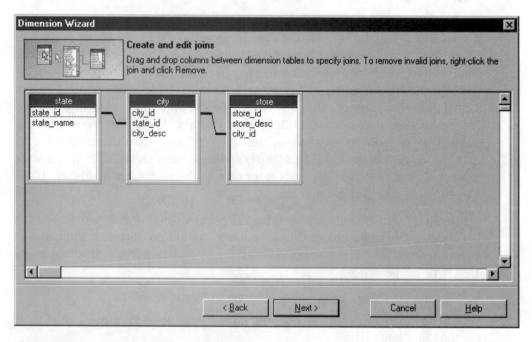

Figure 16.28 Dimension wizard joining tables.

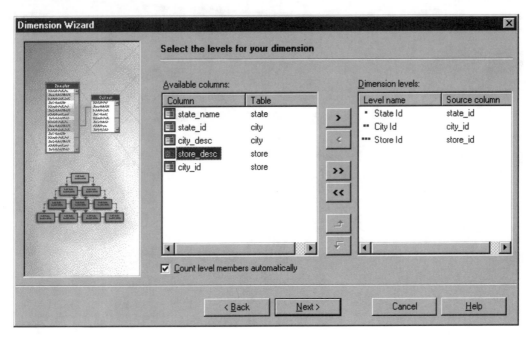

Figure 16.29 Dimension wizard selecting level columns.

- Change the member name column of the "Store" level to "store_desc" in the Store table (Advanced).

To build our Products and Customer dimensions, repeat these steps using the information shown in the dimension blueprints in Figures 16.7 and 16.9.

Building the Time Dimension

As we saw in Chapter 4, the dimension wizard makes it easy to build a Time dimension based upon a single date column. To create our Time dimension, proceed through the dimension wizard, selecting single-table dimension and the view_dim_period view that we created earlier in this tutorial. Because the view contains a column of type "date," the wizard offers you the opportunity to identify the dimension as a Time dimension. Take advantage of this opportunity, as shown in Figure 16.30. Next, we must identify the levels for our Time dimension. Select the "Year, Week, and Day" option as shown in Figure 16.31. Since we're not concerned with fiscal years, leave the beginning period as January 1. Finally, name the dimension "Time" and save it.

As we discussed in Chapter 4, the dimension wizard does a wonderful job of creating a basic time hierarchy using the SQL expressions that are appropriate

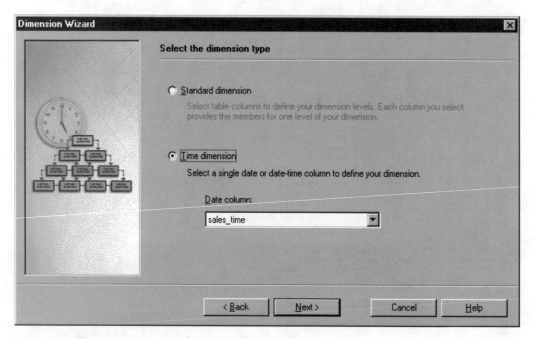

Figure 16.30 Dimension wizard selecting time column.

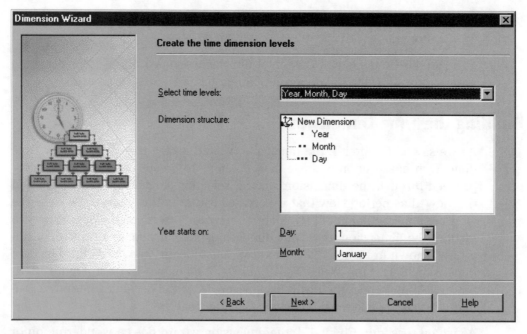

Figure 16.31 Dimension wizard time levels selection.

Day	Sales
1	5,000
2	3,000
3	2,000
4	5,000
5	3,000
⋮	⋮
30	2,000
31	5,000
1	3,000
2	3,000
3	2,000
⋮	⋮

Figure 16.32   Sales by day from cube using a Time dimension with default dimension wizard member name property for day level.

for the selected data source. There is room for improvement, however, and we'll make some of them now. Note that for the "Day" level, the wizard entered the following SQL expression:

```
convert(CHAR, DateName(day, "view_dim_period"."sales_time"))
```

This does indeed return the day of the month. However, in queries that might return the days from several months it will be difficult for users to distinguish which month the days belong to. For example, Figure 16.32 shows the results of a query asking for sales figures for the day-level descendants of the fourth quarter. In this result set, the user has no way to determine which month the two rows labeled "1" belong to. To rectify this, we'll modify the SQL expression for the member name column of the day level to include the month:

```
convert(VARCHAR, DateName(month, "view_dim_period"."sales_time")) + ' '
  + convert(CHAR, DateName(day, "view_dim_period"."sales_time"))
```

Figure 16.33 shows the results of our previous query with our modified member name for day.

Processing the Dimensions

You can process the dimensions now or let Microsoft OLAP Services process them along with the cube. As a general rule, it's better to process the dimensions after you create them. That way, you can discover any problems before processing the cube. To process all of the dimensions now, right click on the

Day	Sales
October 1	5,000
October 2	3,000
October 3	2,000
October 4	5,000
October 5	3,000
⋮	⋮
October 30	2,000
October 31	5,000
November 1	3,000
November 2	3,000
November 3	2,000
⋮	⋮

Figure 16.33 Sales by day from cube using a Time dimension with modified member name property for day level.

"Shared Dimensions" folder in the OLAP Manager console and select "Process All Dimensions."

Create the Base Cubes

We'll build our four cubes using the OLAP Manager cube wizard. As with the dimension wizard, the cube wizard allows us to define our basic cube structure with minimal effort.

The Sales Cube

Start the new cube wizard as we described in Chapter 4, and select the "view_fact_sales" view as the source table, as shown in Figure 16.34. Next select the columns for the measures, as shown in Figure 16.35, and then the dimensions as shown in Figure 16.36. When you move on to the final step in the wizard after selecting dimensions, the wizard will warn you that it can't determine an automatic join between the "age_group" table and the fact table. Remember that we will be relating our age groups through the "view_cust_age-group" view that we created earlier. Because this view is not a part of any existing dimension schema, the wizard does not know to include it in our cube schema so it can't relate "age_group" to our facts. We'll add the view to the cube schema after we've finished with the wizard. In the last step of the wizard, name the cube "Sales," as shown in Figure 16.37.

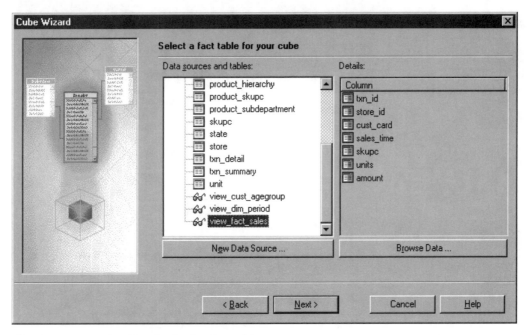

Figure 16.34 Cube wizard selecting fact table.

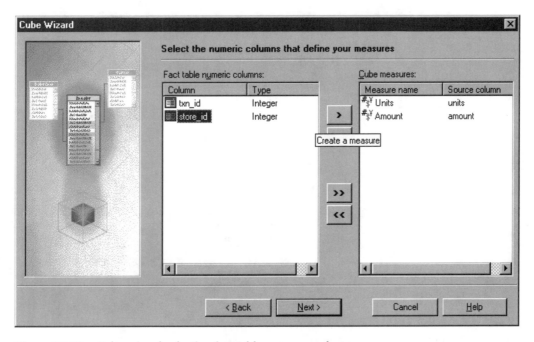

Figure 16.35 Cube wizard selecting fact table measure column.

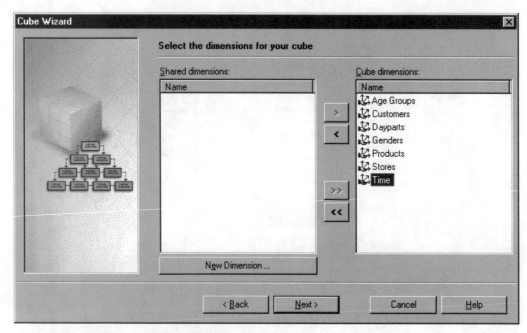

Figure 16.36 Cube wizard selecting dimension.

Figure 16.37 Cube wizard naming cube.

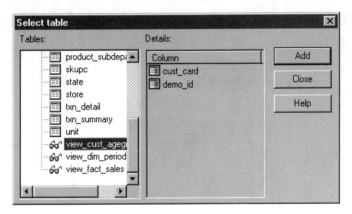

Figure 16.38   Adding a view to the cube schema.

After the cube wizard finishes OLAP Manager brings up the cube editor. At this point, we can add "view_cust_agegroup" to the cube schema so that we can relate the metadata for our Age Groups dimension to the fact table. Do this by selecting "Insert|Tables" from the cube editor menu and selecting "view_cust_agegroup" as shown in Figure 16.38. Note that after adding the view to the cube schema, OLAP Manager joined the view to the fact table through "cust_card." To establish the relationship between "age_group" and our facts, join "age_group" to "view_cust_agegroup" by dragging the "demo_id" from "view_cust_agegroup" and dropping it on "demo_id" in "age_group."

We have one more modification to make to the schema. Note that the City table joins both the Customer and Store tables based upon the "city_id" column. OLAP Manager will not allow us to save the cube with both of these joins and will warn us that there is a loop in the schema (i.e., the facts are joined to Stores, which are joined to City, which are joined to Customer, which in turn is joined to the facts). Remove the join between "Store" and "City" by selecting the join with the mouse and then pressing the "Delete" key on your keyboard. The final schema should resemble the one shown in Figure 16.39.

There is one calculated member that we should add to this cube: "Average Price per Unit." Our managers will usually use the Frequent Shopper virtual cube to analyze data. However, it will be helpful to include in the original cube any calculated members that are applicable to a cube in case anyone browses the cube directly for some reason. To create the calculated member, select the "Calculated Member" button from the editor toolbar to open the calculated member builder. Name the measure "Average Price per Unit" and enter the following MDX expression as shown in Figure 16.40:

```
[Measures].[Sale]/[Measures].[Units]
```

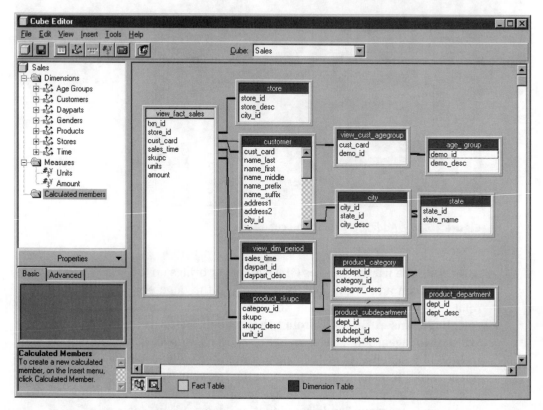

Figure 16.39 Sales cube in the cube editor.

Finally, we'll want to optimize our cube schema for processing. As we described in Chapter 3, optimizing cube schema involves modifying the member key columns for dimension levels in the cube so they point to columns in the tables that are as closely related as possible to the fact table(including the fact table itself). This enables Microsoft OLAP Services to create the most efficient possible SQL for querying the data source when it is processing a partition of a cube by eliminating unnecessary joins. You can do this manually by editing the member key column property for each level, or you can let OLAP Manager do it for you. To have OLAP Manager perform this task, select "Optimize Schema" from the editor's "Tools" menu.

Before moving on to our next cube, we should design aggregations and process our Sales cube. This is an optional step at this point (we can simply save the cube definition and move on to the next cube), but it's generally a good idea to design aggregations and process a cube as soon as you finish creating it. If there are any problems with the cube definition, processing will quickly let you know, and it will be easier to fix those problems with the design when the creation of

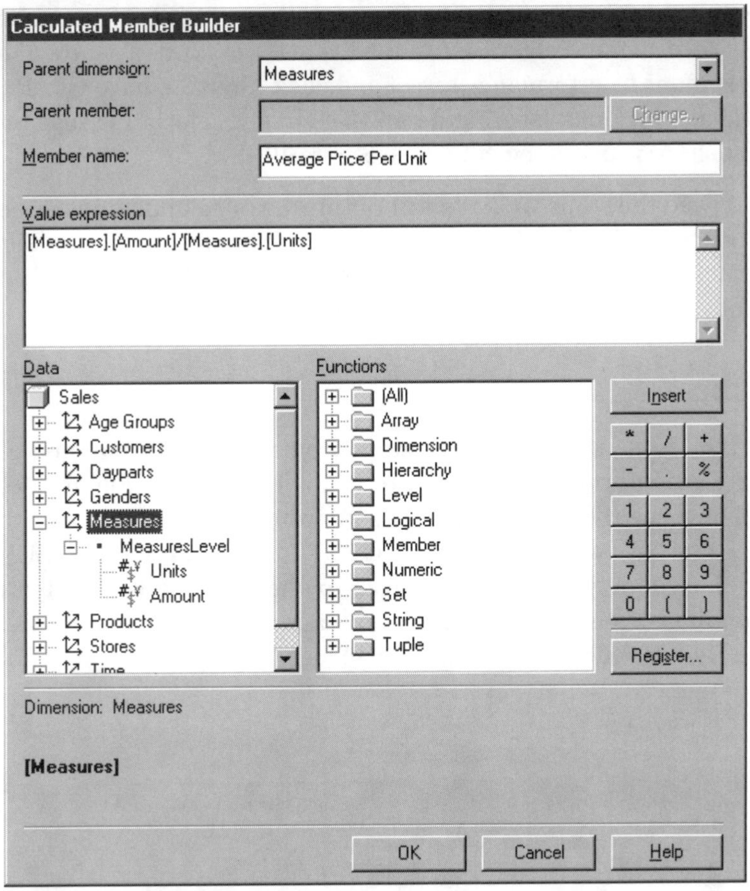

Calculated Member Builder

Parent dimension: `Measures`

Parent member: `[                    ]` Change...

Member name: `Average Price Per Unit`

Value expression

`[Measures].[Amount]/[Measures].[Units]`

Data

- Sales
  - Age Groups
  - Customers
  - Dayparts
  - Genders
  - Measures
    - MeasuresLevel
      - Units
      - Amount
  - Products
  - Stores
  - Time

Functions

- (All)
- Array
- Dimension
- Hierarchy
- Level
- Logical
- Member
- Numeric
- Set
- String
- Tuple

Insert

`*` `/` `+`
`-` `.` `%`
`1` `2` `3`
`4` `5` `6`
`7` `8` `9`
`0` `(` `)`

Register...

Dimension: Measures

[Measures]

OK   Cancel   Help

Figure 16.40 Adding calculated member for Average Price per Unit in the calculated member builder.

the cube is still fresh in your mind. Using the data supplied for this tutorial, this cube will process fairly quickly. If the amount of data would result in lengthy processing time, you would want to base your cube on a view that restricts the total amount of data. If you have the Enterprise version of OLAP Services you have another option. You can edit the primary partition to include a WHERE clause that limits the amount of fact data that would be used to populate the cube, as we described in Chapter 3.

As we pointed out during the cube design process, managers rarely want to explore leaf-level data for customers. To save OLAP storage space we decided to use HOLAP storage for our Sales and Visits cube. The steps for designing and processing cube aggregations are identical regardless of the storage form you choose. To design aggregations for our Sales cube, save the cube definition by pressing the "Save" button on the toolbar and choose "Design Storage" from the editor's "Tools" menu. Select HOLAP as the storage form, as shown in Figure 16.41. Next enter a performance target and click "Start" to have OLAP Services design the aggregations (see Figure 16.42). Finally, select "Process Now" and press "Finish" to process the cube (see Figure 16.43).

If you followed the steps we have just outlined, your Populations cube should process successfully. If it doesn't, check your cube design in the editor to be sure it matched the blueprint shown in Figure 16.13. When the cube processes successfully, we're ready to move on to our next cube.

The Visits Cube

To build the Visits cube, repeat the steps we described for building our Sales cube using the information found in the cube blueprint in Figure 16.14. Note that we'll be using the txn_id column as our only measure, changing the name to "Visits," and aggregating using the COUNT function rather than SUM. When finished, the editor should look similar to the one shown in Figure 16.44. Finally, optimize the schema, design aggregations, and process the Visits cube as we described in the section titled "The Sales Cube."

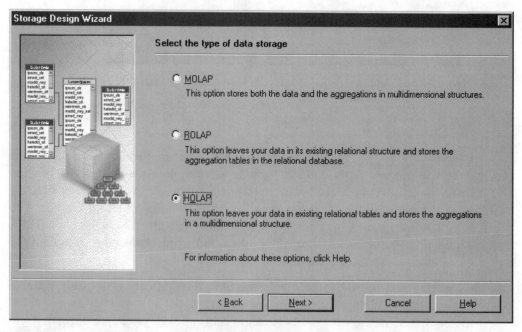

Figure 16.41 Selecting an aggregation storage form in the aggregation design wizard.

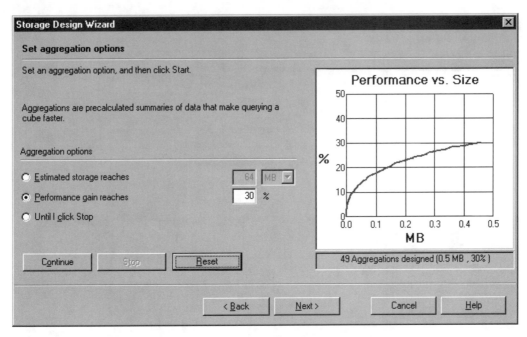

Figure 16.42   Designing aggregations for selected performance targets.

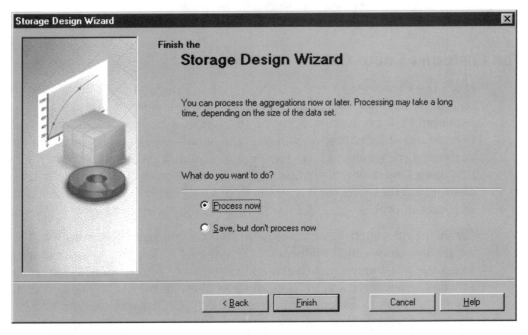

Figure 16.43   Finishing the aggregation design wizard.

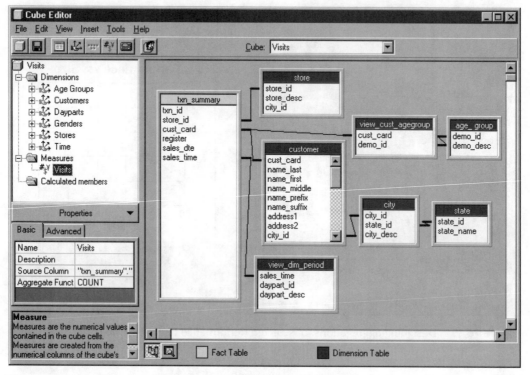

Figure 16.44 Cube editor with completed Visits cube definition.

The Customer Count Cube

Build the Customer Count cube by following the steps we described for building the Visits and Sales cubes, using the measures and dimensions indicated in our blueprint in Figure 16.15. (Since we have used these steps to build our other cubes, we will omit the details here). Obviously, given the purpose of this cube, we do have one calculated member to create here: Customer Count. We also want to restrict Microsoft OLAP Services from creating aggregations for any levels in our Customer dimension other than the bottom level.

Create the calculated member just as you did for the Sales cube, using the MDX expression shown in the blueprint (Figure 16.15). To disable aggregations, select the "Customers" dimension and change the "Aggregation Usage" property on the advanced tab to "Bottom Level Only." Figure 16.45 shows a completed Customer Count cube definition in the OLAP Manager cube editor.

As with our other cubes, finish up by optimizing the schema, designing aggregations, and processing the Customer Count cube, as we described in the sec-

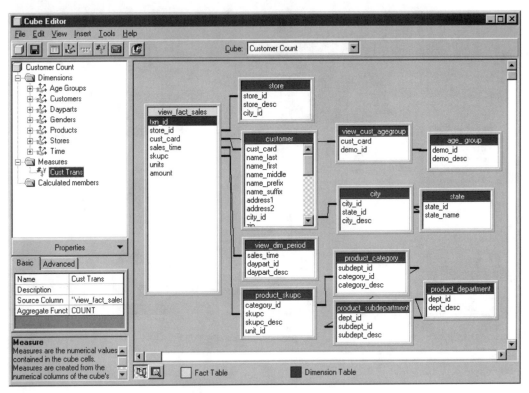

Figure 16.45   Cube editor with completed Customer Count cube definition.

tion titled "The Sales Cube." Remember that all queries that use the "Customer Count" calculated member will require that OLAP Services always access leaf-level data. To optimize query response time we want to use MOLAP storage for our Customer and Product Count cubes instead of HOLAP storage as we used for the Sales cube.

The Product Count Cube

Our Product Count cube is identical to our Customer Count cube, except that our calculated member counts products instead of customers, and we'll restrict aggregations for our Products dimension instead of for the Customer dimension. Create the cube in the same way you created the Customer Count cube, but use the information found in the Product Count cube blueprint in Figure 16.16. Figure 16.46 shows a completed Product Count cube definition in the OLAP Manager cube editor.

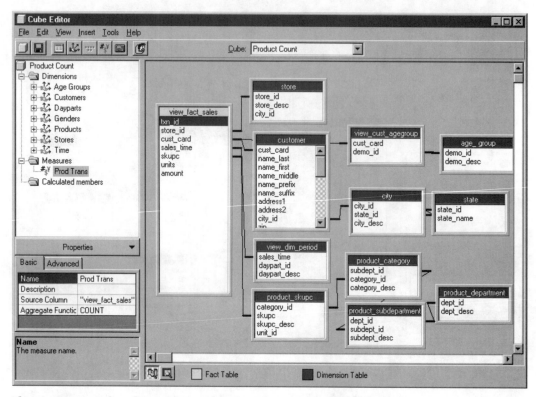

Figure 16.46 Cube editor with completed Product Count cube definition.

Finish up by optimizing the schema, designing aggregations, and processing the Customer Count cube as we described in the section titled "The Sales Cube." Remember, as with the Customer Count cube, we want to use MOLAP storage for the Product Count cube.

Build the Virtual Frequent Shopper Cube

We'll end this tutorial by creating our virtual cube so our users will have a single interface for our four cubes. You create and modify a virtual cube in OLAP Manager by using the virtual cube wizard. As we described in Chapter 3, the process is very straightforward. After you create the virtual cube you will also want to add the calculated members that we created in our base cubes. Again, the OLAP Manager in the first release of Microsoft OLAP Services offers no means for adding calculated members to virtual cubes. To learn how to add calculated members to virtual cubes through DSO, see the tutorial in Chapter 15.

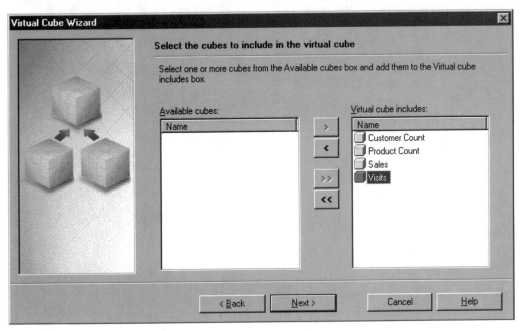

Figure 16.47   Selecting source cubes in the virtual cube wizard.

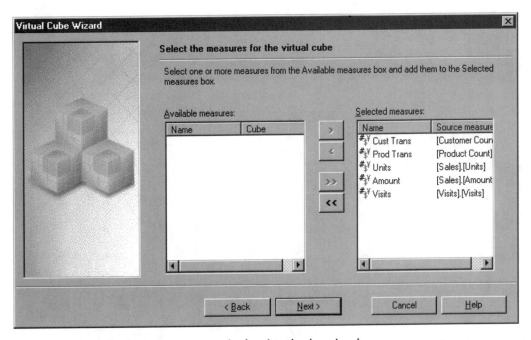

Figure 16.48   Selecting cube measures in the virtual cube wizard.

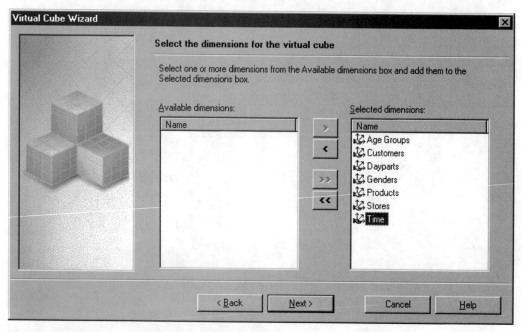

Figure 16.49 Selecting dimensions in the virtual cube wizard.

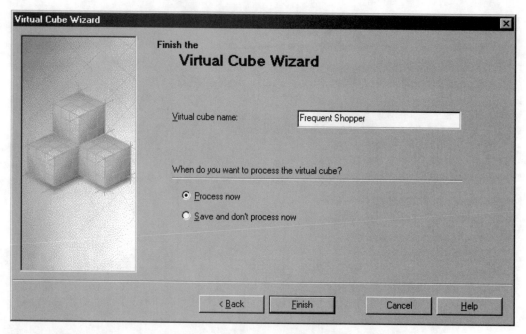

Figure 16.50 Naming a virtual cube in the virtual cube wizard.

Creating the Virtual Cube

Start the virtual cube wizard by right clicking on the "Virtual Cube" folder in the OLAP Manager console and selecting "New Virtual Cube . . .". Select our four cubes as shown in Figure 16.47 and then select all of the measures from all of our cubes, as shown in Figure 16.48. Next, select all of the dimensions as shown in Figure 16.49. Finally, name the virtual cube "Frequent Shopper" as shown in Figure 16.50. Note that if you leave "Process Now" selected, when you press "Finish" OLAP Manager will process the virtual cube immediately, along with any of our other cubes that have not been processed.

Summary

In this chapter we constructed a Microsoft OLAP Services database that helps managers at Whole Foods Emporium analyze the data obtained from their new frequent shopper card program. In addition to stepping through basic OLAP Services tasks, we learned how to perform distinct count calculations and ways to optimize a database for them. We also learned how to enhance analysis by creating multiple dimensions from the data within a single dimension table.

Because the primary point of an OLAP system is to go beyond storing data and actually perform analysis, we've provided a few sample MDX queries on the CD-ROM that accompanies this book for you to run against our benefits database. Please read the document titled "grocerymdx.html" located in the "html\" directory on the CD-ROM for descriptions of the queries. The queries themselves can be found in the document named "grocery.mdx", which can be used in the "MDX Sample" application that Microsoft installs with OLAP Services.

Intrinsic Cell and Member Properties

O LE DB for OLAP gives you the ability to treat the members and cells returned by queries as groups of related properties. This allows multiple related pieces of information to be returned to a client for both members and cells. If you do not request specific cell or member properties in a query, then a default set is returned. This appendix provides a reference to aid you in specifying the properties in MDX queries. (You may also wish to refer to the documentation for OLE DB for OLAP or ADO MD for programmer-level information on how to extract and use the returned property information.)

When you are considering the use of member properties, it is important that you recognize that Microsoft OLAP Services does not make a syntactic distinction between intrinsic member properties and properties that you define (which might otherwise be called "member attributes"). This means that you should avoid creating member properties whose names collide with those of the intrinsic member properties. In the first release of OLAP Services, you do not have the ability to define custom cell properties, so this is not yet a consideration for cell properties.

The main purpose of the cell properties supported in the first release of OLAP Services is to assist in the rendering of cells. Client tools that look for these properties will be able to render results as these properties specify, while other clients will not. If you are interested in creating the functional equivalent of custom cell properties, you can always create additional calculated members that return their values and construct your front-end tool to look for them and interpret them accordingly.

Member Properties

A query specifies the member properties to return for a dimension in the axis specification that contains that dimension. This syntax is covered in Chapter 5. To summarize, the total axis specification will look like the following:

| Without property specification | `{ set specification } on axis` |
| With property specification | `{ set specification } [Dimension] Properties Property [, Property...] on axis` |

To request a specific set of member properties for the dimensions in an axis, you follow the set specification with `Dimension Properties` (or just `Properties`) and then list the unique names of each property. You would separate multiple property names by commas, and after the last property name you will place the `on axis` as usual. For example, a query that requests the store manager name and mailing address on the rows axis would look like this:

```
SELECT
{ [Measures].[Target Inventory] } on columns,
{ [Geography].[Stores].Members }
  DIMENSION PROPERTIES [Geography].[Stores].[Manager],
  [Geography].[Stores].[Mailing Address] on rows
FROM Inventory
```

It is important to recognize that whereas the .Properties() function evaluates its property name on a cell-by-cell basis, each property name that you list here is bound to one and only one dimension level. If you have the same property name at two or more levels in the dimension, then you will want to qualify the name of the property with the unique name of the level (such as [Business Unit].[Store].[Manager] as opposed to [Business Unit].[Division].[Manager]). All of the intrinsic properties are bound on a level-by-level basis.

The intrinsic properties supported for the members of a dimension and of a level are listed in the Table A.1.

Table A.1 Intrinsic Member Properties

PROPERTY NAME	TYPE	MEANING
NAME	DBTYPE_WSTR	Name (not unique name) of the member
ID	DBTYPE_UI4	Internal database ordering number for the member; sorting on this provides hierarchical database ordering
KEY	*	Member key value as defined in the member key column from the dimension table

Because these are member properties and they are returned through the standard OLE DB for OLAP interface, they will all be returned through a column of type Variant. Names are returned as Unicode strings (wide characters), and IDs are returned as 32-bit integers. A member key's type depends on its definition in the dimension.

The intrinsic properties that may be queried for on an axis scope are listed in Table A.2.

By "axis scope" we mean that you cannot ask for these by dimension or level. When you request them, they will be provided for every dimension that appears in the axis. The following query succeeds:

```
SELECT
{ [Measures].[Target Inventory] } on columns,
{ [Geography].[Stores].Members }
  PROPERTIES MEMBER_UNIQUE_NAME on rows
FROM Inventory
```

while the following fails:

```
SELECT
{[Measures].[Target Inventory] on columns,
{ [Geography].[Stores].Members }
  PROPERTIES [Geography].MEMBER_UNIQUE_NAME on rows
FROM Inventory
```

When you specify member properties in a query that is to be returned as an MD data set, the member properties are returned in addition to the default properties: member unique name, caption, and so on. For a query that is to be returned as a "flattened" rowset, if you do not specify any member properties then the (non-unique) names for members in each level of the query result will be returned. If the query does specify member properties for an axis, then only the properties that you request for the axis will be returned. When you request these axis properties in a query that is requested as a rowset, the rowset will contain one MEMBER_UNIQUE_NAME column and/or one MEMBER_CAPTION column per level that contributes a member to the results, as described in Chapter 12. Note that MEMBER_NAME is a synonym for MEMBER_CAPTION.

You can mix requests for dimension- and level-scoped properties in the same query with axis-scoped dimension properties.

Table A.2 Intrinsic Properties at Axis Scope

PROPERTY NAME	TYPE	MEANING
MEMBER_CAPTION	DBTYPE_WSTR	Name (not unique name) of the member
MEMBER_NAME	DBTYPE_WSTR	Name (not unique name) of the member
MEMBER_UNIQUE_NAME	DBTYPE_WSTR	Unique name of the member

Cell Properties

Any cell properties to be returned by a query are specified in the last clause. If the query has a WHERE slicer clause, then the cell properties clause follows it. If the query does not, then the cell properties follow the FROM clause. The syntax of the cell properties clause is as follows:

```
CELL PROPERTIES property-name [, property-name...]
```

The intrinsic properties supported for a cell are listed in Table A.3.

By default, if you do not explicitly request any cell properties in a query, the VALUE and FORMATTED_VALUE properties are returned for each cell. If you request any cell properties in a query, then only those that you request are returned. For example, if you are going to use the result of a query only to format a spreadsheet grid of numbers for display, then you may only want to query for the formatted values. If you are going to use the result of a query only to create a chart from the numerical values, then you may want to only query for the unformatted value. For example, the following query requests the formatted value plus font name, size, flags, and color information:

```
SELECT
{[Measures].[Sales], [Measures].[Peak Inventory]} on rows
{[Time].[Quarter].Members} on columns
FROM [StoreInfo]
CELL PROPERTIES [Formatted_Value], [Font_Name], [Font_Size],
[Font_Flags], [Fore_Color], [Back_Color]
```

No cell properties will be returned for an MDX query that is returned as a "flattened" rowset.

Table A.3 Intrinsic Cell Properties

PROPERTY NAME	TYPE	MEANING
VALUE *		Raw data value for the cell (returned in a Variant)
FORMATTED_VALUE	DBTYPE_WSTR	Formatted string of raw value for displaying
FORMAT_STRING	DBTYPE_WSTR	Format string used to render value into formatted value
FONT_NAME	DBTYPE_WSTR	Name of font to use when rendering cell value
FONT_SIZE DBTYPE_UI2		Font size to render value with
FONT_FLAGS	DBTYPE_I4	Flags for font-rendering effects (e.g., bold, italic, strikethrough)
FORE_COLOR	DBTYPE_UI4	Color value for foreground color
BACK_COLOR	DBTYPE_UI4	Color value for background color

Glossary

aggregate. (v) To compute an aggregated value, for example, a sum over a set of values. (adj) The term for a value that has been computed by aggregating.

aggregation. (v) The process of computing an aggregate value. (n) Microsoft OLAP Services's documentation refers to an *aggregation* as the set of values that result from aggregating lower-level data to a particular level of aggregation.

applicable. Refers to whether or not a value can meaningfully exist at a location.

attribute. In data warehousing literature, the term *attribute* is used for a value that is associated with a member of a single dimension.

axis. A dimension of an MDX query (used to distinguish the query result dimension from a dimension of the cube on which the query was made).

balanced hierarchy. A balanced hierarchy is one in which every leaf member is the same hierarchical distance from the root level as every other leaf member. Contrast with *irregular hierarchy*.

base cube. A base cube is a regular cube that a virtual cube is using.

base measure. A base measure is a measure drawn from a fact table for which aggregated values may be stored. Contrast with *calculated measure*.

calculated measure. A calculated member of the measures dimension. Contrast with *base measure*.

calculated member. A member of an OLAP Services dimension that is defined in terms of a formula.

cell. The smallest specifiable region of a cube, identified by one member from each dimension of the cube. See also *slice*.

cell property. A cell property is information that is associated with a cell. For example, the raw binary value for a cell and the formatted textual representation of that value are separate default properties for each cell that is returned by a query.

child. In a hierarchy, a child member is one hierarchical step further from the root than its parent. Every child has only one parent member. Compare *parent*.

column expression. A column expression is an SQL expression whose result appears to be the same as a column of a table or view but is calculated in a query. For example, in the following query the multiplication is a column expression since it returns a single column of results:

```
SELECT units * price AS SaleAmt
```

content. A measure available at the intersection of all non-measures dimensions. See also *cell*, *location*, and *slice*.

cube. Shorthand for *hypercube*. In Microsoft OLAP Services, *cube* is the name given to the database construct that associates measures and their values in a multidimensional space.

descendant. Within a hierarchy, a given member's descendants include any members found along the path from the member to the leaf-level members.

dimension. A dimension is a collection of members, positions, or units of the same type. Each data point in a multidimensional data set is associated with one member from each of the multiple dimensions. In OLAP Services, the members of a dimension may contain no hierarchy or exactly one hierarchy.

dimension table. In terms of a star schema, a dimension table describes the grouping principles by which related data values may be aggregated. In terms of OLAP Services, a dimension table provides member and hierarchical relationship information for the definition of a dimension.

external function. An external function is a function that is extrinsic to OLAP Services and is loaded from a library. External functions provide a means for extending the calculation ability of OLAP Services. Also known as a user-defined function (UDF).

fact table. A fact table contains data values that are intended to be aggregated by one or more grouping principles. In OLAP Services, a fact table is a table that is used as the source of data for a cube.

hierarchy. A hierarchy is the organization of members into a logical tree structure, wherein every member has at most one parent member and an arbitrary number of child members. See *child* and *parent*.

HOLAP. An acronym for "hybrid OLAP," used to denote some combination of MOLAP and ROLAP characteristics. In OLAP Services, HOLAP is used to refer to a partition in which some aggregate values are stored and accessed through specialized structures and others are stored and accessed in relational database management system (RDBMS) structures. Compare *MOLAP* and *ROLAP*.

hypercube. A multidimensional construct formed from the cross-product of a number of dimensions. See also *cell*.

irregular hierarchy. A hierarchy in which some leaf members are a greater number of hierarchical steps away from the root members than others. See *hierarchy*.

leaf. In a hierarchy, a leaf member is a member that has no children. The leaf level is the collection of all members in the hierarchy that have no children.

level. 1. *Named set of equally weighted members*: For example, in a time dimension, all minutes would usually be placed in one level because they all represent a common interval, while hours would be placed in another level since they all represent another (different) common interval. 2. *Measure of hierarchical distance*: A level can be specified as a collection of members that have some common hierarchical distance, either in terms of hierarchical steps to the root or hierarchical steps to a leaf. In OLAP Services, a level is defined by its distance from the root of a dimension; all members at the root are considered to be in one level, all of their children are considered to be in the next level, and so on.

location. A location is a slice from all dimensions except the measures. See *slice*.

measure. A measure is a unit-bearing data type. Strictly speaking, in OLAP Services *measure* is more synonymous with the term *variable* because it can refer to derived values. OLAP Services represents measures as members of a measures dimension that is associated with each cube.

member. A member is a single element or unit within a dimension.

member key. A member key is the internal identifier OLAP Services uses to identify members and to access related data values in storage.

member key column. A member key column is a table column or column expression that is used to define the member key values for a dimension's level.

member name. A member name is the textual name for a member that is used to identify it in queries and in query results.

member name column. A member name column is a table column or column expression that is used to define the names associated with the members in a dimension's level.

member property. A member property is a data type associated with a single member. It is a synonym for *attribute*.

MDX. An acronym for "MultiDimensional Expressions," MDX is the query and calculation language used by Microsoft OLAP Services.

MOLAP. An acronym for the somewhat redundant term "multidimensional OLAP." It refers to the storage and access of OLAP-related data by means that are more optimized for OLAP activity. In OLAP Services, MOLAP is used to describe a specialized storage form for pre-aggregated data. Compare *HOLAP* and *ROLAP*.

named set. In Microsoft OLAP Services, a named set is a metadata construct that identifies a set of tuples for use in MDX commands and expressions.

parent. In a hierarchy, the term *parent* refers to a member one hierarchical unit closer to the root of the hierarchy than another given member. There is a 1-N relationship between a parent and its children. Compare *child*.

partition. A partition is a physically segregated storage region. In Microsoft OLAP Services, partitions may be calculated and queried separately from each other.

regular cube. A regular cube is a cube whose data is drawn from a fact table and may contain stored aggregates of data in one or more partitions. Contrast with *virtual cube*.

ROLAP. Acronym for "relational OLAP." Refers to the storage and access of OLAP-related data on an RDBMS and through SQL. In OLAP Services, ROLAP is used to describe the storage and accessing of precalculated aggregate data on RDBMS databases.

root. In a hierarchy, a root member is one with no parent. The root level is composed of members that have no parents.

set. In OLAP Services, a set is an ordered and possibly empty collection of tuples. Unlike the classic definition of a set, an OLAP Services set may contain any number of occurrences of the same tuple.

sibling. In a hierarchy, for any given child member a sibling is a member that is a child of the same parent as the given member.

slice. A slice is a region of a hypercube that is defined by restricting some number of dimensions of that hypercube to one member each while leaving the other dimensions fully unrestricted. A cell is equivalent to a slice that is specified by one member from every dimension. A location is a slice defined by a member from every dimension except measures. Compare *cell* and *location*.

slicer. In an MDX query, a slicer is an expression that defines a cube slice that in turn forms the context from which all cell values are drawn.

snowflake schema. A snowflake schema is a relationship of RDBMS tables in which columns from more than one relational table define a single dimension relative to a fact table. See *star schema*.

star schema. An arrangement of tables in a relational database in which a central fact table containing aggregatable values is connected to a set of dimension tables (one dimension table per dimension), which define the grouping relationships by which data from the fact table may be aggregated. See *dimension table* and *fact table*.

tuple. A tuple is analogous to a composite member. A tuple is specified by one member from one or more dimensions. It defines a slice; a tuple containing one member from every dimension of a cube defines a cell.

user-defined function (UDF). See *external function*.

value. The quantity for a single instance of a measure.

virtual cube. A virtual cube is an unmaterialized view of one cube or multiple cubes. In the case of multiple cubes, the cubes are joined together along all common dimensions. Contrast with *base cube* and *regular cube*.

virtual dimension. In Microsoft OLAP Services, a virtual dimension is a construct that behaves syntactically and computationally like a regular dimension but is made up of the values of a member property.

About the CD-ROM

The CD-ROM that accompanies this book contains all the data you need to follow the examples presented in Chapter 4 and the tutorials in Chapters 15 and 16. In addition, we include two simple utilities that should prove useful when you build solutions in Microsoft OLAP Services: Partition Explorer and Calculated Member Editor. The Calculated Member Editor provides you with the ability to create and edit named sets as well as calculated members. Finally, we also include a simple Excel 97 workbook and sample data that demonstrates write-back with Visual Basic for Applications (VBA) and ADO.

The source data for the examples and tutorials is in the form of Access 97 database files. You may use the Access databases as data sources directly or import the data into an SQL Server database. Instructions for importing the data into SQL Server are included in README.TXT files accompanying the Access databases. We also include files containing the Transact-SQL statements you will use to create the views identified in the examples and tutorials. Note that if you use the Access databases directly, you will need to modify the SQL that is used to create views. For example, we use the Transact-SQL "CASE . . . WHEN" statement in column expressions for some dimension views. To create these views in Access you will need to substitute the VBA "IIF()" statement for "CASE . . .WHEN."

Basic documentation for using the Partition Explorer and the Calculated Member Editor can be found alongside the setup files for the applications. For those interested in DSO programming, we also include all of the Visual Basic (VB) project files for these applications. Note that, along with VB, version 6.0 (VB6), to compile and run the projects you will need several OLAP Services DLLs. A list of the required files can be found in the README.TXT file that accompanies the source code.

Finally, the CD-ROM also includes a simple example of how to use the write-back functionality of OLAP Services. The example includes source data, instructions for building the sample cube and enabling write-back in OLAP Services, and an Excel 97 workbook client. All send and retrieve functionality was developed using regular Excel VBA and ADO.

Hardware Requirements

The hardware requirements to use the databases and software contained on the CD-ROM are basically the same as the hardware requirements for OLAP Services. We have only provided executables for Intel-based computer systems. A Windows NT 4.0 (Server or Workstation, service pack 4) system with at least 96MB of RAM and 60MB of hard disk space or more will comfortably run the accompanying software tools along with the tutorials in Access-format files. If you import the database into SQL Server, then we would recommend at least 128MB of RAM for the server machine.

Installing the Software

To install the software tools, follow these simple steps:

1. Start Windows NT on your computer.

2. Place the CD-ROM into your CD-ROM drive.

3. From the Windows Explorer, locate the setup directory for the software that you wish to install. For the Partition Explorer, this will be **X:\Utilities\PartitionExplorer\Setup** (where **X** is the correct letter for your CD-ROM drive). For the Calculated Member Editor, this will be **X:\Utilities\CalcMemberEditor\Setup**.

4. Follow the screen prompts to complete the installation.

To use the sample databases, follow the instructions contained in **X:\Data\DataSource.doc** (where **X** is the correct letter for your CD-ROM drive).

Directory Structure of CD-ROM

To help you locate information on the CD-ROM, we provide its directory structure here. Descriptions of the directory's relevant parts are included in the brackets:

```
readme.txt
Data\
  DataSource.doc [Instructions for setting up tutorial data]
  Chapter4\
    [data files for Chapter 4]
  Chapter15\
    [data files for Chapter 15]
  Chapter16\
    [data files for Chapter 16]
Utilities\
  PartitionExplorer\
    partitionexplorer.doc [how to use the Partition Explorer]
    Setup\
      [setup files for installation of Partition Explorer]
    Source\
      [VB6 project files for Partition Explorer]
  CalcMemberEditor\
    Calcedit.doc [how to use Calculated Member Editor]
    Setup\
      [setup files for installation of Calculated Member Editor]
    Source\
      [VB6 project files for Calculated Member Editor]
  ExcelWriteBack\
    [documentation, data, and Excel workbook demonstrating write-back]
```

User Assistance and Information

The software that accompanies this book is being provided as is without warranty or support of any kind. Should you require basic installation assistance, or if your media is defective, please call our product support number at (212) 850-6194 weekdays between 9 AM and 4 PM Eastern Standard Time. Or we can be reached via e-mail at: wprtusw@wiley.com.

To place additional orders of this book/CD-ROM set, or to request information about other Wiley products, please call (800) 879-4539 or log on at www.wiley.com/compbooks.

To use this CD-ROM, your system must meet the following requirements:

Platform/Processor/Operating System. Windows NT 4.0 (Server or Workstation), Service Pack 4 or higher. To use the enclosed software components, you will either need an Intel x86 compatible processor, or Visual Basic 6.0 to recompile the executable code for your CPU.

RAM. We recommend at least 96 MB of RAM. If you have enough RAM to run Microsoft OLAP Services, you have enough RAM to run the enclosed programs. If you run Microsoft SQL Server and OLAP Services on the same machine, we recommend at least 128 MB of RAM on that machine.

Hard Drive Space. We recommend that you have at least 60 MB of free disk space prior to installing the accompanying software and databases.

Peripherals. You will need a CD-ROM drive, and your video card and monitor should be set to resolution of at least 800 x 600.